THE VINTAGE BOOK OF
OFFICE LIFE

Jeremy Lewis worked in publishing for much of his
life after leaving Trinity College, Dublin, in 1965,
and was a director of Chatto & Windus for ten
years. He was the Deputy Editor of the *London
Magazine* from 1991 to 1994, and is now the
Commissioning Editor of the *Oldie*. He has written
two volumes of autobiography, *Playing for Time*
and *Kindred Spirits*, and his authorised biography
of Cyril Connolly was published by Jonathan Cape
in 1997. The Secretary of the R.S. Surtees Society
and a Fellow of the Royal Society of Literature, he
is married with two daughters, and lives near
Richmond Park.

ALSO BY JEREMY LEWIS

Playing for Time
Kindred Spirits
Cyril Connolly: A Life

THE VINTAGE BOOK OF OFFICE LIFE

or
Love Among the Filing Cabinets

EDITED, WITH AN INTRODUCTION, BY
Jeremy Lewis

VINTAGE

Published by Vintage 1998

2 4 6 8 10 9 7 5 3 1

Introduction and Selection copyright © Jeremy Lewis 1992

First published in Great Britain as
The Chatto Book of Office Life by
Chatto & Windus 1992

Vintage
Random House, 20 Vauxhall Bridge Road,
London SW1V 2SA

Random House Australia (Pty) Limited
20 Alfred Street, Milsons Point, Sydney
New South Wales 2061, Australia

Random House New Zealand Limited
18 Poland Road, Glenfield,
Auckland 10, New Zealand

Random House South Africa (Pty) Limited
Endulini, 5A Jubilee Road, Parktown 2193,
South Africa

Random House UK Limited Reg. No. 954009

A CIP catalogue record for this book
is available from the British Library

ISBN 0 09 927655 0

Papers used by Random House UK Ltd are natural,
recyclable products made from wood grown in sustain-
able forests. The manufacturing processes conform to the
environmental regulations of the country of origin

Printed and bound in Great Britain by
The Guernsey Press Co. Ltd., Guernsey, Channel Islands

Contents

	Preface	1
	Introduction	3
1	The Interview	13
2	Getting to Work	35
3	Settling In	61
4	The Look of the Place	79
5	Ritual, Gossip and the Social Whirl	93
6	Clerks and Clerking	113
7	The Secretarial Life	129
8	The Boss	147
9	Getting Down to Work	171
10	Office Politics	191
11	A Fearful Business	215
12	Tedium Vitae	221
13	Bucking the System	235
14	Escaping the Office, and Eating Lunch	253
15	Getting Away from it All	265
16	Home and the Office	275
17	Office Parties	285
18	Love Among the Filing Cabinets	301
19	Odds and Sods	323
20	Getting the Sack	339
21	The End of the Road	361
	Acknowledgements	387
	Index of Authors	391

Preface

All this has its origins in a piece I wrote about offices in *Fair of Speech*, a collection of essays about euphemisms edited by D. J. Enright and published in 1985 by OUP. Exploring the dainty circumlocutions with which we sugar the pill of life between nine and five – 'He's a bit tied up at the moment' meaning 'He's incoherent with drink, and there's no way he can come to the phone', or 'I'm afraid we're going to have to let you go' meaning 'You're fired!' – I described in some detail the forceful and often alarming figure of the human dynamo. These dynamos, though sometimes hard to live with, are what keep most offices from sinking into a terminal torpor, and can usually be recognised by the cries of rage emanating from their quarters and the smoke seeping out from under the door. My particular dynamo was based, to a large extent, on Carmen Callil, with supporting contributions from other eminent publishers with whom I'd worked, including André Deutsch and Norah Smallwood, her predecessor as managing director of Chatto & Windus; and when, much to my alarm, she read my piece ('Darling it *is* all about me, isn't it?'), far from resenting my ungentlemanly behaviour, she made me promise that, if ever I did a book on office life, I would give it to her to publish.

Since – unlike Carmen – I have a mind like a sieve and remember almost nothing of what I read, I have had to rely, even more than most anthologists, on other people's tips and recommendations. I'd like to thank the following for deluging me with suggestions, not all of which – alas – I've been able to use, if only for reasons of space: Michael Ballantyne, Anthony Baring, Mark Bell, Jonathan Burnham, John Carey, Jenny Chapman, Shirley Chew, Margaret Clarke, I. F. Clarke, Richard Cobb, Jilly Cooper, Marian Covington, Katherine Duncan-Jones, Digby Durrant, Janice Elliott, David Ellis, D. J. Enright, the late Roy Fuller, Victoria Glendinning, Robert Gray, J. C. Hall, Duff Hart-Davis, Selina Hastings, Christopher Hawtree, James Douglas Henry, Mary Hocking, Harry Hoff (William Cooper), Richard Hoggart, Miles Huddleston, Roger Hudson, David Hughes, Mick Imlah, Howard Jacobson, Alan Judd, Roy Kerridge, David Kynaston, Alastair Langlands, Jane Langlands, Emma Lawson, Cat Ledger, Hermione Lee, Hattie Lewis, Jemima Lewis, Gail Lynch, Norman Mackenzie, John Mellors, William Mitchell, Janet Montefiore, Grace Opumingi, Frances Partridge, Isabel Quigly, Kate Rae, David Roberts,

Alan Ross, Rosalin Sadler, Alison Samuel, Deborah Singmaster, Rowena Skellton-Wallace, Carol Smith, Charles Sprawson, Gillian Tindall, Jane Turner, Jenny Uglow, Richard Usborne (who kindly provided a limerick, never previously published), Peter Vansittart, Anthony Weale, A. N. Wilson and Ian Whitcomb. I owe most to my wife Petra, a veteran of office life and an authority on the subject, and on much else.

Introduction

In a halfway rational world, I suppose, offices and office life would be something of an endangered species, exciting a similar start of surprise as an old-fashioned corner shop or a uniformed nanny pushing a penny-farthing pram. Most office workers, after all, claim to resent their way of life, rolling their eyes heavenwards at the mention of the boss's name, groaning and slapping their foreheads at the thought of that meeting on Monday morning, and dreaming of giving it all up in a sudden bid for freedom; modern technology should, in theory, make it easier to work at home, flashing faxes to and fro and attending meetings via a cordless telephone in the garden, while the cat picks its way between the print-outs and the baby beams in the sun; given the strains of urban life, the horrors of commuter trains and inner-city rents, surely the office as most of us know it should soon become a thing of the past – to the relief of all concerned, except for a few power-crazed obsessives and workaholics, whose lives (or so the rest of us like to persuade ourselves, when feeling particularly harried or inadequate) are so starved of ordinary pleasures that only work can afford them any satisfaction?

And yet, far from withering away, the office seems to be flourishing as never before. Bureaucrats and administrators abound, far outnumbering those useful souls – nurses or salesmen or publisher's editors – whose toils they supervise; men and women who, fifty years ago, might have worked on the factory floor now find themselves, in Peter de Vries's words, 'pleasantly detained in the everlasting grind of moving paper from one place to another', while the clerks of yesteryear describe themselves, grandiloquently, as 'executives' or 'managers' or 'information processors'. Far from simplifying matters, modern technology – faxes and computers and photocopying machines – merely adds to the tidal waves of bumph to be read and discussed and shuffled about, and necessitates more meetings and more memos and more staff to decide what to do about it. Blue collars have long ago been abandoned for white, while the rise of the working wife and mother has seen the proliferation of the female equivalent of the Man in the Gray Flannel Suit.

Nor is that the end of the story: for the fearful truth is that, however much office workers may rant and rage, office life is, for most of us, a matter of love as well as of hate. Even the dullest of offices has an intrinsic fascination for those who work there, both in terms of the work itself and, even more importantly, in social terms: for, like a rock pool or the underside of a stone, the office teems with unsuspected life. Sinclair Lewis – among the shrewdest and most sympathetic of all writers on office life, matched only by Dickens, Trollope, P. G. Wodehouse and Roy Fuller – remarked on the similarities between an office and a village: not surprisingly, given the amount of time we spend in these curious places, the friendships and the gossip and the intrigues and even the passions of office life may well loom larger than those of domestic life. Office life – like life in general – is often tedious and frightening and baffling, conducive to ulcers and nervous sweat and terrible sleepless nights, filled with dread of what the morning will bring or a miserable awareness of life seeping away, almost unremarked. We dream of escape, of shaking off the yoke, yet even at the weekend or on holiday, away from it all and dreading its resumption, part of us longs to know what's going on back at the office, while a chance encounter with a fellow-practitioner will usually provoke an excited flurry of shop talk (aptly described by Sinclair Lewis as 'the purest and most rapturous form of conversation'). As for the ultimate dream of retirement – so longed for and yet, by its very nature, so dreadful – it's no surprise to learn that, deprived of routine, status and companionship all at once, so many office workers peg out within months of receiving their retirement clock or inscribed silver goblet; and what more melancholy sight is there than some former leader of men, shorn now of all his grandeur, his views no longer sought, lugubriously pushing a supermarket trolley full of cat food, or eagerly applying to do the books at his local golf club or church bazaar?

However congenial or entertaining its social side may be, office life is, in the last resort, about survival and making ends meet and earning an honest (or dishonest) crust: and since even the most diffident among us must struggle, however ineffectually, to keep afloat, while more aggressive spirits are obsessed by a craving for power and wealth, it's only to be expected that offices should be intensely political places. The personalities and the machinations of tyrants, time-servers, stooges, loyal lieutenants, heirs apparent and old retainers have an impact on and a fascination for those who work there far greater than those of ordinary politicians. Beneath the apparently tedious, bland surface of office life, with its euphemisms and its formal ways and its elaborate circumlocutions, every known emotion and motivation seethes and bubbles – ambition, greed, ruthlessness, duplicity, cowardice, treachery, lust, kindliness, tolerance, forgiveness, affection and even love. That so few modern novelists have the experience or the sympathy to write about the ways in which most of their fellow men and women spend their waking hours may help to explain why the fate of the novel has become a matter of some indifference: but office life in general, and commerce in particular, has long been subject to the snobbery of left and right, disdained by dons and university English departments and viewed with glum suspicion by old-fashioned men of the left.

2

Once involved in an office, each of us learns – to a greater or lesser extent – to play the parts expected of us. We adopt slightly – sometimes greatly – different personae to those we wear at home: most of us have a touch of the Wemmicks, our faces hardening and growing anxious as we approach our place of work, and softening and relaxing as we head back home again. We learn to simulate (yet not entirely simulate, for our concerns may well become genuine and addictive, and the play a real-life drama) excitement and disappointment, rage and delight, enthusiasm and contempt. Yet even here we are torn: part of us knows perfectly well that we are going through the motions, feigning concern about the monthly sales figures or fury at a competitor stealing a march or frenzied glee at securing a favourable contract, and that the passions of office life are transient and as volatile and as phoney as those we see on stage; and yet because office life is, in the last resort, based on fear – fear of the boss, fear of the sack, fear of poverty and hunger – part of us is in deadly earnest, and fighting for our life.

That said, office life almost always involves a certain suspension of disbelief, if only to oil the wheels: we have to pretend it all matters a very great deal, in much the same way as a games player has to pretend, and momentarily believe, that hoofing a sodden lump of leather from one end of a field to another, or lashing out at a ball with a stick, is more important than anything else in the world – which may well be why taking team games seriously is probably a better preparation for institutional or working life than some of us, baffled by the absurdity of it all, could ever have dreamed. Those awkward spirits who, through a combination of timidity and scepticism, find it hard to suspend their disbelief (or their ineptitude) on the games field and flinch away from manifestations of the team spirit may have difficulties in flinging themselves fully into office life, but remain uneasily perched on the touchline, observers and commentators rather than whole-hearted participants. All too easily bored, idle, disruptive or disaffected, such figures tend to be passengers, drifting along on the backs of others and eschewing all responsibility, while enlivening the proceedings with their sardonic disenchantment. Yet even the most loyal and serious-minded players may find themselves wavering at times. 'Did

[5]

one then never grow up?' wonders the desk-bound narrator of Roy Fuller's *The Father's Comedy*: 'Was one never completely guarded by one's personality and beliefs? Even at fifty there were moments when he must pretend to a greater seriousness than he really owned: when a knock on his office door could make his heart jump and his hands hastily conceal a pocket mirror, or a slip of paper on which he had been repeatedly signing his name.'

And just as the members of a cricket or a soccer team, once off the field, seem altogether less heroic and less glamorous, so too the members of our tiny hierarchies – so compelling to those within, so meaningless to those without – dwindle and change once away from their place of work. The stout, hen-pecked man in the house next door, busily cleaning his car or tending his cabbage patch, may well, come Monday morning, metamorphose into the Himmler of the local building society, while the boisterous wag in the pub is a dutiful, timid clerk once seated behind his desk: that the mighty at work may mean nothing at home or in the street offers a kind of consolation to those who tremble at their approach, yet since they usually excite admiration and even affection as well as alarm, it's hard not to sympathise with, while at the same time relishing, Mr Pooter's sense of outrage when Mr Perkupp's hallowed name means nothing whatsoever at the Lord Mayor's Ball.

3

Readers anxious to learn about the history of the office – when carbon paper or dictating machines were invented, or the rise of the female 'typewriter', decently segregated from her masculine colleagues for fear of inflammation – will find little to sustain them in these pages; nor is there much here for those eager, thrusting middle managers who want to be told how to succeed in the office, where to place one's desk in order to obtain a psychological advantage over the enemy and how best to produce, and interpret the curious, constipated language of the office memo and the progress report. What interests me are the reactions of articulate but pleasingly run-of-the-mill nine-to-fivers to the demands and the rewards, the pleasures and the pains, of everyday office life, written in such a way as to reflect sentiments and emotions familiar to anyone who has spent any time in such places. I am more interested in form than in content, in the way battles are fought rather than in the course of any particular battle, and I find the views of the foot-soldier – doubling up, perhaps, as a novelist or a poet or an autobiographer – more revelatory and illuminating than those of the general: which may help to explain why, perhaps wrongly, I failed to consult or quote from the memoirs of retired industrialists or businessmen. I decided, too, to exclude all those books, often of a self-help nature, which describe management techniques or power in the office: from a literary point of view this proved a great relief, but it did mean excluding C. Northcote Parkinson, the wittiest and shrewdest of commentators on office and institutional life – though I consoled myself with the hope that the Law itself, and such familiars as the Abominable No-man, were so well known as to need no repetition.

Some final hedging of bets, since anthologists are invariably, and rightly, berated for their omissions. Since I had no intention of providing a history of the office, I have – to my relief – made no effort to include mediaeval clerks or the denizens of eighteenth-century coffee houses; and I decided, for no better reasons than shortage of space combined with native ignorance, to restrict myself to writers who had written in English, fearing that nineteenth-century French and Russians, and twentieth-century Middle Europeans, might well sweep all before them. I have arranged my material thematically and chronologically, taking an office worker through from his or her first interview and the first day in the job to the sack or the sad oblivion of retirement, by way of such hazards as the boss, the office lunch, the office party and love among the filing cabinets; and if the same cast of characters recurs again and again throughout this seems both right and proper, for – as every office worker knows – repetition and familiarity are of the essence of office life.

Actuarial Romance

Most of us see some romances in life. In my capacity as Chief Manager of a Life Assurance Office, I think I have within the last thirty years seen more romances than the generality of men, however unpromising the opportunity may, at first, seem.

From 'Hunted Down' in *The Uncommercial Traveller* by Charles Dickens, 1860

The Office as Prison

No-one ever seriously believes that they will be in an office *all their working lives*. For forty-five years. Secretly they believe something will rescue them – a football pool, arson. 'I'm sorry, sir. Yes, completely burnt to the ground. As you see sir, just a gaping hole. Not a hope of it starting up again I'm afraid. All the files gone, the records – the whole Board consumed in the flames too, I'm afraid. But I understand they were well insured, very well insured. Compensation should amount to three-quarters full salary for the rest of each employee's lifetime. Yes – quite sure, sir. Oh thank you, sir. Good morning, sir.'

Or think of those moments when, quite unexpectedly, you have to leave your office in the middle of the morning. Is it not incredible how violent the feeling of relief is, how fierce, how wild, how irresponsible you feel? You bounce on to buses and into taxis, you could sing or shout, the streets seem filled with massed bands of girls (or young men) all as happy and cheerful and released as you.

Nor of course is it only – or even mostly – the lower echelons of The Office who react like this. Four years ago a survey was made among two thousand directors of British companies. Over 75% said that their main ambition was to retire, and over 65% said that they felt their time at work was wasted. Most of these felt they would be better employed playing golf.

From *The Office* by Jonathan Gathorne-Hardy, 1970

Lacrimae Rerum

It was five-thirty and the corridors were choked with the homeward rush of clerks. There was a smell of plastic raincoats, face powder, cigarette smoke. Witt edged his way to the lifts against the stream, his exhaustion making him preternaturally aware of every face, every tone of voice. He saw once again how his weakness turned his life into art and felt a sudden warm affection and pity for this mass of humanity, seeing vaguely but surely how he could find the words to depict the rush through the grey evening to the separate worlds of love, habit, and pain.

From *Image of a Society* by Roy Fuller, 1956

Peter Goole

While when we turn to Peter, he
The cause of this catastrophe,
There fell upon him such a fate
As makes me shudder to relate.
Just in its fifth and final year,
His University Career
Was blasted by the new and dread
Necessity of earning bread.
He was compelled to join a firm
Of Brokers – in the summer term!
And even now, at twenty-five,
He has to *WORK* to keep alive!
Yes! All day long from 10 till 4!
For half the year or even more;
With but an hour or two to spend
At luncheon with a city friend.

From 'Peter Goole, Who Ruined His Father and Mother by Extravagance' in
New Cautionary Verses by Hilaire Belloc, 1930

Hustling

As he approached the office he walked faster and faster, muttering, 'Guess better hustle.' All about him the city was hustling, for hustling's sake. Men in motors were hustling to pass one another in the hustling traffic. Men were hustling to catch trains, with another train a minute behind, and to leap from the trains, to gallop across the pavement, to hurl themselves into buildings, into hustling express elevators. Men in dairy lunches were hustling to gulp down the food which cooks had hustled to fry. Men in barber shops were snapping, 'Jus' shave me once over. Gotta hustle.' Men were feverishly getting rid of visitors in offices adorned with the signs, 'This Is My Busy Day' and 'The Lord Created the World in Six Days – You Can Spiel All You Got to Say in Six Minutes.' Men who had made five thousand, the year before last, and ten thousand last year, were urging on nerve-yelping bodies and parched brains so that they might make twenty thousand this year; and the men who had broken down immediately after making their twenty thousand dollars were hustling to catch trains, to hustle through the vacations which the hustling doctors had ordered.

Among them Babbitt hustled back to his office, to sit down with nothing much to do except see that the staff looked as though they were hustling.

From *Babbitt* by Sinclair Lewis, 1922

Does One Never Grow Up?

His appointment with the Chairman was for three o'clock. Coming into his office after lunch he could not bring himself to start any work. He opened the file of the matter on which he was to see the Chairman, but the few points at issue were simple and instantly familiar. Nor had he any need to rehearse his attitude to the Chairman, the tactics he had planned. He confirmed that his fingernails were clean, that his pen and pencil were in his waistcoat pocket, that no jellies lurked in the corners of his eyes. He closed the file, rose, and walked to the window – conscious in that moment of the dichotomy between the dignity of his body and the essential youthfulness, not to say immaturity, of his thoughts, of his whole approach to the forthcoming interview. Did one then never grow up? Was one never completely guarded by one's personality and habits? Even at fifty there were moments when he must pretend to a greater seriousness than he really owned; when a knock on his office door could make his heart jump and his hands hastily conceal a pocket mirror, or a slip of paper on which he had been repeatedly signing his name.

From *The Father's Comedy* by Roy Fuller, 1961

A Lamb's Eye View

From ten to eleven
Eat breakfast for seven.
From eleven to noon
Think I've come too soon.
From noon till one
Think what's to be done.
From one to two
Find nothing to do.
From two to three
Think it will be
A very great bore
To stay till four.

Charles Lamb

Busy and of Doubtful Temper

He enjoyed being sick in February; he was delighted by their consternation that he, the rock, should give way.

He had eaten a questionable clam. For two days he was languorous and petted and esteemed. He was allowed to snarl 'Oh, let me alone!' without reprisals. He lay on the sleeping-porch and watched the winter sun slide along the taut curtains, turning their ruddy khaki to pale blood red. The shadow of the draw-rope was dense black, in an enticing ripple on the canvas. He found pleasure in the curve of it, sighed as the fading light blurred it. He was conscious of life, and a little sad. With no Vergil Gunches before whom to set his face in resolute optimism, he beheld, and half admitted that he beheld, his way of life as incredibly mechanical. Mechanical business – a brisk selling of badly built houses. Mechanical religion – a dry, hard church, shut off from the real life of the streets, inhumanly respectable as a top-hat. Mechanical golf and dinner-parties and bridge and conversation. Save with Paul Riesling, mechanical friendships – back-slapping and jocular, never daring to essay the test of quietness.

[11]

He turned uneasily in bed.

He saw the years, the brilliant winter days and all the long sweet afternoons which were meant for summery meadows, lost in such brittle pretentiousness. He thought of telephoning about leases, of cajoling men he hated, of making business calls and waiting in dirty anterooms – hat on knee, yawning at fly-specked calendars, being polite to office-boys.

'I don't hardly want to go back to work,' he prayed. 'I'd like to – I don't know.'

But he was back next day, busy and of doubtful temper.

From *Babbitt* by Sinclair Lewis, 1922

One

THE INTERVIEW

Every office job will begin, as it must, with some kind of interview. Humble applicants will be treated to the more conventional type of interview, involving the grave perusal of CVs, the taking up of references and the disconcerting exchange of glances over the top of half-moon spectacles; those who are much sought after and in a position to dictate their own terms will be tactfully 'sounded out' over drinks or a heavy lunch. Most of us, it goes without saying, never get beyond the conventional variety. Job interviews are widely, if mistakenly, thought to be nerve-racking in the extreme, on a par with a trip to the dentist: some hardy souls, however, make a point of attending as many interviews as they can, so as to keep in trim. Unless enviably blasé or indifferent, the interviewee will appear at least ten minutes early, looking far shinier than would normally be the case, with hair freshly washed, shoes gleaming and egg stains carefully sponged away. Perched, bird-like, on the edge of a chair, he or she is understandably anxious to impress – displaying an unexpected enthusiasm for turnover figures, looking suitably stern when occasion demands, baring the teeth in a wolfish grin at the mention of rival concerns, springing sharply up and down to greet new interrogators or receive a welcome mug of coffee, and exuding an uneasy blend of sycophancy, charm, boastfulness, diffidence, bafflement and brightness. Interviews for first jobs are especially painful for both parties. The interviewee – fresh from school or university – has neither working experience nor practical knowledge to fall back on, while academic qualifications, however impressive, may well count for less than a month or two on the road or in a warehouse. The interviewer, bereft of those conversational lubricants provided by gossip or shop-talk, is reduced to asking unanswerable questions like 'Why do you want to go into insurance?' or 'What makes you think you're cut out to be a publisher?' or 'Why do you want to work here in particular?' Honest answers – 'Because I can't think of anything else to do' or 'I suppose it's all I'm fit for' or 'Because I can't get in anywhere else' – are disallowed, though both parties are well aware that the truth lies thereabouts, unless the interviewee is one of those precocious individuals who has known since the cradle where his or her destiny lay. Instead the newcomer, who invariably knows next to nothing about the company or the work it does, flounders about in search of persuasive answers, feigning – like the Man in the Gray Flannel Suit – a desperate and long-standing interest in matters hitherto unconsidered or unknown. Subsequent interviews tend to be less daunting and less demanding for all concerned: the interviewee may be utterly unsuitable, but at least he will have something to say for himself, while the interviewer – in between sneaking a glance at his watch and wondering what's for lunch – may learn something of life in a rival firm.

The Man in the Gray Flannel Suit Starts Out

The next morning, Tom put on his best suit, a freshly cleaned and pressed grey flannel. On his way to work he stopped in Grand Central Station to buy a clean white handkerchief and to have his shoes shined. During his luncheon hour he set out to visit the United Broadcasting Corporation. As he walked across Rockefeller Plaza, he thought wryly of the days when he and Betsy had assured each other that money didn't matter. They had told each other that when they were married, before the war, and during the war they had repeated it in long letters. 'The important thing is to find a kind of work you really like, and something that is useful,' Betsy had written him. 'The money doesn't matter.'

The hell with that, he thought. The real trouble is that up to now we've been kidding ourselves. We might as well admit that what we want is a big house and a new car and trips to Florida in the winter, and plenty of life insurance. When you come right down to it, a man with three children has no damn right to say that money doesn't matter.

There were eighteen elevators in the lobby of the United Broadcasting building. They were all brass coloured and looked as though they were made of money. The receptionist in the personnel office was a breathtakingly beautiful girl with money-coloured hair – a sort of copper gold. 'Yes?' she said.

'I want to apply for a position in the public-relations department.'

'If you will sit down in the reception room, I'll arrange an interview for you,' she said.

The company had a policy of giving all job applicants an interview. Every year about twenty thousand people, most of them wildly unqualified, applied for jobs there, and it was considered poor public relations to turn them away too abruptly. Beyond the receptionist's desk was a huge waiting room. A rich wine-red carpet was on the floor, and there were dozens of heavy leather armchairs filled with people nervously smoking cigarettes. On the walls were enormous coloured photographs of the company's leading radio and television stars. They were all youthful, handsome, and unutterably rich-appearing as they smiled down benignly on the job applicants. Tom picked a chair directly beneath a picture of a big-bosomed blonde. He had to wait only about twenty minutes before the receptionist told him that a Mr Everett would see him.

Mr Everett's office was a cubicle with walls of opaque glass brick, only about three times as big as a priest's confessional. Everett himself was a man about Tom's age and was also dressed in a gray flannel suit. The uniform of the day, Tom thought. Somebody must have put out an order.

'I understand that you are interested in a position in the public-relations department,' Everett said.

'I just want to explore the situation,' Tom replied. 'I already have a good position with the Schanenhauser Foundation, but I'm considering a change.'

It took Everett only about a minute to size Tom up as a 'possibility.' He gave him a long printed form to fill out and told him he'd hear from the United Broadcasting Corporation in a few days. Tom spent almost an hour filling out all the pages of the form, which, among other things, required a list of the childhood diseases he had had and the names of countries he had visited. When he had finished, he gave it to the girl with the hair of copper gold and rang for one of the golden elevators to take him down.

Five days later Tom got a letter from Everett saying an interview had been arranged for him with Mr Gordon Walker in Room 3672 the following Monday at 11:00 a.m. In the letter Walker was given no title. Tom didn't know whether he were going to have another routine interview, or whether he were actually being considered for a position. He wondered whether he should tell Dick Haver, the director of the Schanenhauser Foundation, that he was looking for another job. The danger of not telling him was that the broadcasting company might call him for references any time, and Dick wouldn't be pleased to find that Tom was applying for another job behind his back. It was important to keep Dick's good will, because the broadcasting company's decision might depend on the recommendation Dick gave him. In any one of a thousand ways, Dick could damn him, without Tom's ever learning about it. All Dick would have to do when the broadcasting company telephoned him would be to say, 'Tom Rath? Well, I don't know. I don't think I'd want to go on record one way or the other on Mr Rath. He's a nice person, you understand, an awfully nice person. I'd be perfectly willing to say that!'

On the other hand, it would be embarrassing to tell Dick he was seeking another job and then be unable to find one. Tom decided to delay seeing Dick until after he had had his next interview.

Walker's outer office was impressive. As soon as Tom saw it, he knew he was being seriously considered for a job, and maybe a pretty good one. Walker had two secretaries, one chosen for looks, apparently, and one for utility. A pale-yellow carpet lay on the floor, and there was a yellow leather armchair for callers. Walker himself was closeted in an inner office which was separated from the rest of the room by a partition of opaque glass brick.

The utilitarian secretary told Tom to wait. It was extremely quiet. Neither of the two girls was typing, and although each had two telephones on her desk and an interoffice communication box, there was no ringing or buzzing. Both the secretaries sat reading typewritten sheets in black notebooks. After Tom had waited about half an hour, the pretty secretary, with no audible or visible cue, suddenly looked up brightly and said, 'Mr Walker will see you now. Just open the door and go in.'

Tom opened the door and saw a fat pale man sitting in a high-backed upholstered chair behind a kidney-shaped desk with nothing on it but a blotter and pen. He was in his shirt sleeves, and he weighed about two hundred and fifty pounds. His face was as white as a marshmallow. He didn't stand up when Tom came in, but he smiled. It was a surprisingly warm, spontaneous smile, as though he had unexpectedly recognized an old friend. 'Thomas Rath?' he said. 'Sit down! Make yourself comfortable! Take off your coat!'

Tom thanked him and, although it wasn't particularly warm, took off his coat. There wasn't any place to put it, so, sitting down in the comfortable chair in front of Walker's desk, he laid the coat awkwardly across his lap.

'I've read the application forms you filled out, and it seems to me you might be qualified for a new position we may have opening up here,' Walker said. 'There are just a few questions I want to ask you.' He was still smiling. Suddenly he touched a button on the arm of his chair and the back of the chair dropped, allowing him to recline, as though he were in an airplane seat. Tom could see only his face across the top of the desk.

'You will excuse me,' Walker said, still smiling. 'The doctor says I must get plenty of rest, and this is the way I do it.'

Tom couldn't think of anything more appropriate to say than 'It looks comfortable . . .'

'Why do you want to work for the United Broadcasting Corporation?' Walker asked abruptly.

'It's a good company . . .' Tom began hesitantly, and was suddenly impatient at the need for hypocrisy. The sole reason he wanted to work for United Broadcasting was that he thought he might be able to make a lot of money there fast, but he felt he couldn't say that. It was sometimes considered fashionable for the employees of foundations to say that they were in it for the money, but people were supposed to work at advertising agencies and broadcasting companies for spiritual reasons.

'I believe,' Tom said, 'that television is developing into the greatest medium for mass education and entertainment. It has always fascinated me, and I would like to work with it . . .'

'What kind of salary do you have in mind?' Walker asked. Tom hadn't expected the question that soon. Walker was still smiling.

'The salary isn't the primary consideration with me,' Tom said, trying desperately to come up with stock answers to stock questions. 'I'm mainly interested in finding something useful and worthwhile to do. I have personal responsibilities, however, and I would hope that something could be worked out to enable me to meet them . . .'

'Of course,' Walker said, beaming more cheerily than ever. 'I understand you applied for a position in the public-relations department. Why did you choose that?'

Because I heard there was an opening, Tom wanted to say, but quickly thought better of it and substituted a halting avowal of life-long interest in public relations. 'I think my experience in working with *people* at the Schanenhauser Foundation would be helpful,' he concluded lamely . . .

From *The Man in the Gray Flannel Suit* by Sloan Wilson, 1956

'I like dull work'

Our first stop was Wonderland. There was a job in the clerical department of Sears. The man there had a long disapproving nose, and he held his hands stiffly curled in the middle of his desk. He mainly looked at his hands. He said he would call me, but I knew he wouldn't.

On the way back to the parking lot, we passed a pet store. There were only hamsters, fish and exhausted yellow birds. We stopped and looked at slivers of fish swarming in their tank of thick green water. I had come to this pet store when I was ten years old. The mall had just opened up and we had all come out to walk through it. My sister, Donna, had wanted to go into the pet store. It was very warm and damp in the store, and smelled like fur and hamster. When we walked out, it seemed cold. I said I was cold and Donna took off her white leatherette jacket and put it around my shoulders, letting one hand sit on my left shoulder for a minute. She had never touched me like that before and she hasn't since.

The next place was a tax information office in a slab of building with green trim. They gave me an intelligence test that was mostly spelling and 'What's wrong with this sentence?' The woman came out of her office holding my test and smiling. 'You scored higher than anyone else I've interviewed,' she said. 'You're really overqualified for this job. There's no challenge. You'd be bored to death.'

'I want to be bored,' I said.

She laughed. 'Oh, I don't think that's true.'

We had a nice talk about what people want out of their jobs and then I left.

'Well, I hope you weren't surprised that you had the highest score,' said my mother.

We went to the French bakery on Eight-Mile Road and got cookies called elephant ears. We ate them out of a bag as we drove. I felt so comfortable, I could have driven around in the car all day.

Then we went to a lawyer's office on Telegraph Road. It was a receding building made of orange brick. There were no other houses or stores around it, just a parking lot and some taut fir trees that looked like they had been brushed. My mother waited for me in the car. She smiled, took out a cross-word puzzle and focused her eyes on it, the smile still gripping her face.

The lawyer was a short man with dark, shiny eyes and dense immobile shoulders. He took my hand with an indifferent aggressive snatch. It felt like he could have put his hand through my rib cage, grabbed my heart, squeezed it a little to see how it felt, then let go. 'Come into my office,' he said.

We sat down and he fixed his eyes on me. 'It's not much of a job,' he said. 'I have a paralegal who does research and legwork, and the proof-reading gets done at an agency. All I need is a presentable typist who can get to work on time and answer the phone.'

'I can do that,' I said.

'It's very dull work,' he said.

'I like dull work.'

He stared at me, his eyes becoming hooded in thought. 'There's some-thing about you,' he said. 'You're closed up, you're tight. You're like a wall.'

'I know.'

My answer surprised him and his eyes lost their hoods. He tilted his head back and looked at me, his shiny eyes bared again. 'Do you ever loosen up?'

The corners of my mouth jerked, smilelike. 'I don't know.' My palms sweated.

His secretary, who was leaving, called me the next day and said that he wanted to hire me. Her voice was serene, flat and utterly devoid of inflection.

[19]

'That typing course really paid off,' said my father. 'You made a good investment.' He wandered in and out of the dining room in pleased agitation, holding his glass of beer. 'A law office could be a fascinating place.' He arched his chin and scratched his throat.

From *Bad Behavior* by Mary Gaitskill, 1988

An Opening in Leather

Why the leather trade? Father had met a man who belonged to the Chamber of Commerce and who had said he knew a firm of Leather Factors that had an opening for an office boy. Begin (he said), at the bottom of the ladder, like Henry Ford. I shall not forget that spiritless January morning when Father took me to a place in the Bermondsey district of London. The one pleasant but intimidating thing was that for the first time I sat with Father in a corner seat of a First Class compartment of the train on the old South Eastern and Chatham railway. I was wearing a new suit, a stiff collar that choked me, a bowler hat which bit hard into my forehead and kept slipping over my ears. I felt sick. There were two or three city gentlemen in the compartment, smoking pipes; my father presented me with a copy of the *Christian Science Sentinel* and told me to read it while he closed his eyes and prayed for me. I disliked being seen with this paper. He prayed as far as Hither Green – I opened my eyes for a glance at a house which had been torn in half by a bomb in the autumn raids – and then he leaned across to me and, not as quietly as I would have liked, for the city gentlemen were staring at us, he reminded me of the story of the infant Samuel. Father was becoming emotional. To me the situation was once more like the sacrifice of Isaac.

'When he heard the voice of God calling, Samuel answered "Speak Lord, thy servant heareth". When the manager sends for you, I want you to remember that. Say to yourself "Speak Lord . . ." as Samuel did and go at once. It's just an idea. You will find it helpful. I always do that when I go to see the Buyer at Harrods.'

I had thought of myself as growing up fast at school. Now, under my bowler hat, I felt I was sinking back into infancy. At London Bridge, where we got out, a yellow fog was coating the rain as we went down the long flights of sour stone stairs into the malodorous yet lively air peculiar to the river of Bermondsey. We passed the long road tunnels under the railway tracks, tunnels which are used as vaults and warehouses convenient to the Pool of London. There was always fog hanging like sour breath in these tunnels. There was a daylight gloom in this district of London. One breathed the heavy, drugging, beer smell of hops and there was another smell of boots and dog dung: this came from the leather which had been steeped a month in puer or dog dung before the process of tanning. There was also – I seemed to be haunted by it at the critical moments of my childhood – the stinging smell of vinegar from a pickle factory; and smoke blew down from an emery mill. Weston Street was a street of leather and hide merchants, leather dressers and fell-mongers. Out of each brass-plated doorway came either that oppressive odour of new boots; or, from the occasional little slum houses, the sharp stink of London poverty. It was impossible to talk for the noise of dray horses striking the cobbles.

We arrived at a large old-fashioned building and walked into a big office where the clerks sat on high stools at tilted desks. The green-shaded lamps were lit. A hard bell struck over an inner door. 'Speak Lord', I instantly murmured – and a smart office boy who had given a wisp of vaseline to his forelock took us to the office of the head of the firm.

This ancient gentleman was like God himself – Grandfather and all Victorians would have recognised him. He was a tall, massive, hump-shouldered man in his late seventies, with a waving mat of long thick white hair which had a yellow streak in it, and a white beard. He had pale-blue eyes, very sharp, a wily smile and an alert but quavering voice. He was the complete City gentleman of the old school. My father and he were courtly with each other; the old man was soon on to the slump of the 1870's when his uncle had sent him to Vienna for the firm and where (he slyly said) he had got the better of a competitor because of his knowledge of German. He said he was glad to hear I was a church-goer, for he himself held a Bible class every Sunday; and his secretary, an old woman like my grandmother, taught in Sunday School too. He mentioned his eleven children, four of the sons being in the business. My father said I was good at French. The old gentleman suddenly snapped at me:

'Assez pour tirer d'affaires?'

I was bowled out and could not speak. The old gentleman grinned kindly. We were interrupted by a sugary, languid tinkle on the old-fashioned telephone that stood in the middle of his large desk. It was really two desks joined; it had spawned some odd side-tables and was covered with papers, letters and periodicals. I watched the bent knees of the old man rise, then his back heave up, then the hump elongate itself and finally a long arm with a powerful and shaking hand on it stretched across the wide desk and reached the telephone. The quavering voice changed now to a virile, barking note, the mild blue eyes became avid, the teeth looked the teeth of a lynx. His talk was brisk and commanding:

[21]

when it was over he sank back in his chair and gazed at us as if he had never seen us before and, panting a little, said:

'The *Arabic* has docked with 4,000 bales'.

His knees went up and down under his desk feeling for a concealed bell, and the office boy came pelting in.

From *A Cab at the Door* by V. S. Pritchett, 1968

Secure Above All

'One thing we can offer, Miss Broadbent, is security.' And here he sat back in his chair, smiling like Joe Stalin. 'Most of them can't, you know, in our line of business. But we study our costs, we operate on a generous profit margin, we advertise our products, and we create the demand.' He leaned forward. 'And that's the only way these days, I can assure you!'

It flashed through Jane's mind: he was a salesman himself. He was selling her the job.

'Yes, security! We have a first-class pension plan, and excellent prospects. It's a very large organization, Miss Broadbent. There are plans for my future. And as my secretary, these would naturally include you.' He paused for effect.

'You'd be a director's secretary before long!'

Jane nodded, and looked at him encouragingly.

'D'you think you could manage that, eh? D'you think you could cope?'

'Yes. I'm sure I could.'

He was about to offer her the job, when an invisible fly appeared, buzzing round his nose. He was by nature more suspicious than Julius Caesar. If the God of Rome had been less trusting, Brutus and Co could never have ganged up on him. It would have been off to the lions with them at the first hint of conspiracy.

'You're not thinking of getting *married*, are you?'

'Hardly. Or I wouldn't be changing my job, would I?'

I'd be back in the luxury of the oil company, Jane thought, with them all collecting for my electric toaster, and a booze-up at the pub on my last night.

'Ah! That's all right then.' And he offered her the job, at ten shillings a week less than his starting price.

'But the advert said £9 a week.'

He stroked that long nose, and looked at her sharply once or twice. Injured innocence, Jane sat now. Her lowly station had its advantages, down in the visitors' chair.

[22]

'Ten shillings' rise after the first three months. If satisfactory, that is.'

'No.'

It wasn't a fly. It had become a wasp. It made the air about him hum. He drew a piece of paper towards him, and did some rapid calculations. As if it made any difference.

'Oh, have it your own way. Ten shillings after two months!'

Jane sat up until her nose nearly touched the rim of his desk. Like a five-year-old in the market-place, buying a toffee apple on the cheap.

'The advert said £9. *Now.*'

He threw up his hands in the air. He was a dealer in second-hand clothes, who parks his 3-litre a couple of streets away from the stall. 'How can I make a living?' that gesture said. 'My wife and kids will starve!'

'I give in!' His smile was like a wrung-out lemon. 'Ten shillings rise at the end of the first month. If satisfactory, that is.'

Jane stood up and looked down at him. She held out her frail woman's hand.

'Yes. I accept.'

From *The Underlings* by Barbara Benson, 1977

The Rep's Life

'So you want a job? What can you do?'

Again the inspiration. No use, with a bloke like this, cracking up your own merits. Stick to the truth. I said: 'Nothing, sir. But I want a job as a travelling salesman.'

'Salesman? Hm. Not sure that I've got anything for you at present. Let's see.'

He pursed his lips up. For a moment, half a minute perhaps, he was thinking quite deeply. It was curious. Even at the time I realized that it was curious. This important old bloke, who was probably worth at least half a million, was actually taking thought on my behalf. I'd deflected him from his path and wasted at least three minutes of his time, all because of a chance remark I'd happened to make years earlier. I'd stuck in his memory and therefore he was willing to take the tiny bit of trouble that was needed to find me a job. I dare say the same day he gave twenty clerks the sack. Finally he said:

'How'd you like to go into an insurance firm? Always fairly safe, you know. People have got to have insurance, same as they've got to eat.'

Of course I jumped at the idea of going into an insurance firm. Sir Joseph was 'interested' in the Flying Salamander. God knows how many companies he was 'interested' in. One of the underlings wafted himself forward with a scribbling-pad, and there and then, with the gold stylo out of his waistcoat pocket, Sir Joseph scribbled me a note to some higher-up in the Flying Salamander. Then I thanked him, and he marched on, and I sneaked off in the other direction, and we never saw one another again.

From *Coming Up For Air* by George Orwell, 1939

Lupin's New Life

NOVEMBER 3. Good news at last. Mr Perkupp has got an appointment for Lupin, and he is to go and see about it on Monday. Oh, how my mind is relieved! I went to Lupin's room to take the good news to him, but he was in bed, very seedy, so I resolved to keep it over till the evening . . .

MARCH 21. Today I shall conclude my diary, for it is one of the happiest days of my life. My great dream of the last few weeks – in fact, of many years – has been realized. This morning came a letter from Mr Perkupp, asking me to take Lupin down to the office with me. I went to Lupin's room; poor fellow, he seemed very pale, and said he had a bad headache. He had come back yesterday from Gravesend, where he spent part of the day in a small boat on the water, having been mad enough to neglect to take his overcoat with him. I showed him Mr Perkupp's letter, and he got up as quickly as possible. I begged of him not to put on his fast-coloured clothes and ties, but to dress in something black or quiet-looking.

Carrie was all of a tremble when she read the letter, and all she could keep on saying was: 'Oh, I *do* hope it will be all right.' For myself, I could scarcely eat any breakfast. Lupin came down dressed quietly, and looking a perfect gentleman, except that his face was rather yellow. Carrie, by way of encouragement, said: 'You do look nice, Lupin.' Lupin replied: 'Yes, it's a good make-up, isn't it? A regular-downright-respectable-funereal-first-class-City-firm-junior-clerk.' He laughed rather ironically . . .

It seemed hours before we reached the office. Mr Perkupp sent for Lupin, who was with him nearly an hour. He returned, as I thought, crestfallen in appearance. I said: 'Well, Lupin, how about Mr Perkupp?' Lupin commenced his song: 'What's the matter with Perkupp? He's all right!' I felt instinctively my boy was engaged. I went to Mr Perkupp, but I could not speak. He said: 'Well, Mr Pooter, what is it?' I must have looked a fool, for all I could say was: 'Mr Perkupp, you are a good man.' He looked at me for a moment, and said: 'No, Mr Pooter, you are the good man; and we'll see if we cannot get your son to follow such an excellent example.' I said: 'Mr Perkupp, may I go home? I cannot work any more today.'

My good master shook my hand warmly as he nodded his head. It was as much as I could do to prevent myself from crying in the 'bus; in fact, I should have done so, had my thoughts not been interrupted by Lupin, who was having a quarrel with a fat man in the 'bus, whom he accused of taking up too much room.

In the evening Carrie sent round for dear old friend Cummings and his wife, and also to Gowing. We all sat round the fire, and in a bottle of 'Jackson Frères', which Sarah fetched from the grocer's, drank Lupin's health. I lay awake for hours, thinking of the future. My boy in the same office as myself – we can go down together by the 'bus, come home together, and who knows but in the course of time he may take great interest in our little home. That he may help me to put a nail in here or a nail in there, or help his dear mother to hang a picture. In the summer he may help us in our little garden with the flowers, and assist us to paint the stands and pots. (By-the-by, I must get in some more enamel paint.) All this I thought over and over again, and a thousand happy thoughts beside. I heard the clock strike four, and soon after fell asleep, only to dream of three happy people—Lupin, dear Carrie, and myself.

From *The Diary of a Nobody* by George and Weedon Grossmith, 1892

Bumph as a Way of Life

'. . . We go very much by the book here, as you may have gathered. You've no rooted objection to bumph as a way of life?'

Gryce contrived an amused but vigorous twitch of the head to convey at once a blind acceptance of the rules of the game and a rueful bewilderment at their complexity.

'*Very much used to it* by now.'

'Let's see what you've told us about yourself. Born so-and-so so-and-so, educated blah blah blah, married very good, previous employment all present and correct, and for the last three years until quite recently you've been with Comform.'

'I have indeed.'

On its journey to Albion House his questionnaire had been folded in three, so that although straightened out again it did not quite lie flush, and Gryce was able to glimpse the papers underneath. Beneath what looked like an inter-office slip giving details of the vacancy under discussion, there was a closely-typed letter on a Comform billhead. So they'd taken up references. What most of the other documents were Gryce could not surmise, but he was sure he recognised the distinctive pale-brown quarto sheet jutting marginally out at the bottom of the pile. It was from the Cardinal Building Society, a billet he'd left nine years ago. Going very much by the book was one thing, but this was thoroughness gone mad in his view.

'Glowing references, you'll be relieved to hear,' said Lucas, observing that Gryce was trying to read his file upside down. 'Comform was rather a departure for you, I gather?'

Gryce didn't know what to make of this. One office was much like another in his experience.

'I mean,' Lucas pursued, 'you seem mainly to have worked for what I suppose one would call institutions – Docks and Inland Waterways, insurance, building societies, cetera. No manufacturing process involved. I see under armed forces, details of any service in, you've put Clerk/GD in the RAF Records Office. You weren't brought into contact with aircraft in any way.'

'That's true enough. Fact, I didn't set eyes on a plane in all my two years. Except flying overhead, of course.'

'What I'm getting at is that Comform is the only appointment you've had where there's been so to speak an end product. I'm saying it was rather a departure.'

'I get your drift now. Yes and no, if the truth be known. You see the actual factory was, still is if it comes to that, down in the West Country. My end of it was very much offices and showrooms. I never saw anything actually being made.'

That, on instant playback, seemed a pretty negative reply to have given. But it appeared to be the one Lucas wanted.

'Then you've no particular objection to being merely a link in the chain – even if you can't see how the chain connects with the various cogs and wheels?'

Gryce sensed this time that Lucas was definitely asking a leading question, albeit an excessively fanciful one. An answer in the order of 'Oh good heavens, no!' seemed to be called for. He plumped for this line, but decided to embellish it a little.

'Oh good heavens, no! I've always found that whatever job I'm doing is in itself an end product. That is, you do what's required of you to the best of your ability, and someone else picks up his own process from there.'

Lucas appeared well satisfied. Gryce was glad, on balance, that he had not over-egged the pudding by adding, 'No man can ask for more.'

'I'm pleased you said that. It's really just the attitude we're looking for as regards this particular vacancy. It's an in-house post as you know, Stationery Supplies, serving all the other departments in the building, and a certain type of personality might feel cut off from the mainstream. Far from the madding crowd.'

'Oh good heavens, no!' The job was his. It was in the bag.

From *Office Life* by Keith Waterhouse, 1978

Internal Navigation

Exactly at ten in the morning he walked into the lobby of his future workshop [the Internal Navigation Office], and found no one yet there but two aged seedy messengers. He was shown into a waiting-room, and there he remained for a couple of hours, during which every clerk in the establishment came to have a look at him. At last he was ushered into the Secretary's room.

'Ah!' said the Secretary, 'your name is Tudor, isn't it?'

Charley confessed to the fact.

'Yes,' said the Secretary, 'I have heard about you from Sir Gilbert de Salop.' Now Sir Gilbert de Salop was the great family friend of this branch of the Tudors. But Charley, finding that no remark suggested itself to him at this moment concerning Sir Gilbert, merely said, 'Yes, sir.'

'And you wish to serve the Queen?' said the Secretary.

Charley, not quite knowing whether this was a joke or not, said that he did.

'Quite right – it is a very fair ambition,' continued the great official functionary – 'quite right – but, mind you, Mr Tudor, if you come to us you must come to work. I hope you like hard work; you should do so, if you intend to remain with us.'

Charley said that he thought he did rather like hard work. Hereupon a senior clerk standing by, though a man not given to much laughter, smiled slightly, probably in pity at the unceasing labour to which the youth was about to devote himself.

'The Internal Navigation requires great steadiness, good natural abilities, considerable education, and – and – and no end of application. Come, Mr Tudor, let us see what you can do.' And so saying, Mr Oldeschole, the Secretary, motioned him to sit down at an office table opposite to himself.

[27]

Charley did as he was bid, and took from the hands of his future master an old, much-worn quill pen, with which the great man had been signing minutes.

'Now,' said the great man, 'just copy the few first sentences of that leading article – either one will do,' and he pushed over to him a huge newspaper.

To tell the truth, Charley did not know what a leading article was, and so he sat abashed, staring at the paper.

'Why don't you write?' asked the Secretary.

'Where shall I begin, sir?' stammered poor Charley, looking piteously into the examiner's face.

'God bless my soul! there; either of those leading articles,' and leaning over the table, the Secretary pointed to a particular spot.

Hereupon Charley began his task in a large, ugly, round hand, neither that of a man nor of a boy, and set himself to copy the contents of the paper. 'The name of Pacifico stinks in the nostril of the British public. It is well known to all the world how sincerely we admire the versatility of Lord Palmerston's genius; how cordially we simpathize with his patriotic energies. But the admiration which even a Palmerston inspires must have a bound, and our simpathy may be called on too far. When we find ourselves asked to pay–.' By this time Charley had half covered the half-sheet of foolscap which had been put before him, and here at the word 'pay' he unfortunately suffered a large blot of ink to fall on the paper.

'That won't do, Mr Tudor, that won't do – come, let us look,' and stretching over again, the Secretary took up the copy.

'Oh dear! oh dear! this is very bad; versatility with an "i!" – sympathy with an "i!" sympathize with an "i!" Why, Mr Tudor, you must be very fond of "i's" down in Shropshire.'

Charley looked sheepish, but of course said nothing.

'And I never saw a viler hand in my life. Oh dear, oh dear, I must send you back to Sir Gilbert. Look here, Snape, this will never do – never do for the Internal Navigation, will it?'

Snape, the attendant senior clerk, said, as indeed he could not help saying, that the writing was very bad.

'I never saw worse in my life,' said the Secretary. 'And now, Mr Tudor, what do you know of arithmetic?'

Charley said that he thought he knew arithmetic pretty well; – 'at least some of it,' he modestly added.

'Some of it!' said the Secretary, slightly laughing. 'Well, I'll tell you what – this won't do at all;' and he took the unfortunate manuscript between his thumb and forefinger. 'You had better go home and endeavour to write something a little better than this. Mind, if it is not very much better it won't do. And look here; take care that you do it yourself. If you bring me the writing of any one else, I shall be sure to detect you. I have not any more time now; as to arithmetic, we'll examine you in "some of it" to-morrow.'

So Charley, with a faint heart, went back to his cousin's lodgings and waited till the two friends had arrived from the Weights and Measures. The men there made a point of staying up to five o'clock, as is the case with all model officials, and it was therefore late before he could get himself properly set to work. But when they did arrive, preparations for calligraphy were made on a great scale; a volume of Gibbon was taken down, new quill pens, large and small, and steel pens by various makers were procured; cream-laid paper was provided, and ruled lines were put beneath it. And when this was done, Charley was especially cautioned to copy the spelling as well as the wording.

He worked thus for an hour before dinner, and then for three hours in the evening, and produced a very legible copy of half a chapter of the 'Decline and Fall.'

'I didn't think they examined at all at the Navigation,' said Norman.

'Well, I believe it's quite a new thing,' said Alaric Tudor. 'The school-master must be abroad with a vengeance, if he has got as far as that.'

And then they carefully examined Charley's work, crossed his t's, dotted his i's, saw that his spelling was right, and went to bed.

Again, punctually at ten o'clock, Charley presented himself at the Internal Navigation; and again saw the two seedy old messengers warming themselves at the lobby fire. On this occasion he was kept three hours in the waiting-room, and some of the younger clerks ventured to come and speak to him. At length Mr Snape appeared, and desired the acolyte to follow him. Charley, supposing that he was again going to the awful Secretary, did so with a palpitating heart. But he was led in another direction into a large room, carrying his manuscript neatly rolled in his hand. Here Mr Snape introduced him to five other occupants of the chamber; he, Mr Snape himself, having a separate desk there, being, in official parlance, the head of the room. Charley was told to take a seat at a desk, and did so, still thinking that the dread hour of his examination was soon to come. His examination, however, was begun and over. No one ever asked for his calligraphic manuscript, and as to his arithmetic, it may be presumed that his assurance that he knew 'some of it', was deemed to be adequate evidence of sufficient capacity. And in this manner, Charley Tudor became one of the Infernal Navvies.

From *The Three Clerks* by Anthony Trollope, 1858

The Luck of the Irish

... Now, in his prime, he considered himself: a fine big fellow with a soldierly straightness to him, his red hair thick as ever and a fine moustache to boot. And another thing. He believed that clothes made the man and the man he had made of himself was a Dublin squire. Sports clothes took years off him, he thought, and he always bought the very best of stuff. As he rode downtown on the bus that morning there wasn't a soul in Montreal who would say there goes a man who's out of work. Not on your earthly. Not even when he went through the doorway of the Unemployment Insurance Commission and marched right up to *Executive & Professional*, which seemed the right place for him.

'Fill it out at the table over there, Mr Coffey,' said the counter clerk. Nice young fellow, no hint of condescension in his tone, very helpful and natural as though this sort of thing happened to everyone. Still, pen in hand, *write in block letters or type*, Coffey was faced once again with the misleading facts of a life. In block letters, he began:

Born May 14, 1917, Dublin, Ireland.

Education Plunkett School, Dublin. National University of Ireland, University College, Dublin.

Specify degrees, honours, other accomplishments (He had not finished his B.A., but never mind.) Bachelor of Arts. (Pass.) 1940.

List former positions, giving dates, names of employers, etc. (Flute! Here we go.) Irish Army 1940–45. Commissioned 2nd Lieut, 1940. 1st Lieut, 1942. Assistant to Press Officer, General Headquarters. Kylemore Distilleries, Dublin, 1946–48, Special Assistant to Managing Director. 1949–53, Assistant in Advertising Department. Coomb-Na-Baun Knitwear, Cork, 1953–1955, Special Assistant.

Cootehill Distilleries, Dublin. ⎫
Coomb-Na-Baun Knitwear, Dublin. ⎬ August, 1955–December, 1955,
Dromore Tweeds, Carrick-on- ⎪ Special Representative for
  Shannon. ⎭ Canada.

List Present Position His position as of this morning, January 2, 1956, was null and bloody void, wasn't it? So he put a line through that one. Then read it all over, absentmindedly brushing the ends of his moustache with the pen. He signed with a large, much-practised signature.

The wooden plaque in front of the young man who looked over his application bore the name *J. Donnelly*. And naturally J. Donnelly, like all Irish Canadians, noticed Coffey's brogue and came out with a couple of introductory jokes about the Ould Sod. But the jokes weren't half as painful as what came after them.

'I see you have your B.A., Mr Coffey. Have you ever considered teaching as a profession? We're very short of teachers here in Canada.'

'Holy smoke,' said Coffey, giving J. Donnelly an honest grin. 'That was years ago. Sure, I've forgotten every stitch.'

'I see,' J. Donnelly said. 'But I'm not quite clear why you've put down for a public relations job? Apart from your – ah – army experience, that is?'

'Well now,' Coffey explained. 'My work over here as Canadian representative for those three firms you see there, why that was all promotion. Public relations, you might call it.'

'I see ... But, frankly, Mr Coffey, I'm afraid that experience would hardly qualify you for a public relations position. I mean, a senior one.'

There was a silence. Coffey fiddled with the little brush dingus in his hat. 'Well now, look here,' he began. 'I'll put my cards on the table, Mr Donnelly. These firms that sent me out here wanted me to come back to Ireland when they gave up the North American market. But I said no. And the reason I said no is because I thought Canada was the land of opportunity. Now, because of that, because I want to stay, no matter what, well, perhaps I'll have to accept a more junior position here than what I was used to at home. Now, supposing you make me an offer, as the girl said to the sailor?'

But J. Donnelly offered only a polite smile.

'Or – or perhaps if there's nothing in public relations, you might have some clerical job going?'

'Clerical, Mr Coffey?'

'Right.'

'Clerical isn't handled in this department, sir. This is for executives. Clerical is one floor down.'

'Oh.'

'And at the moment, sir, ordinary clerical help is hard to place. However, if you want me to transfer you?'

'No, don't bother,' Coffey said. 'There's nothing in public relations, is there?'

J. Donnelly stood up. 'Well, if you'll just wait, I'll check our files. Excuse me.'

He went out. After a few minutes a typewriter began to clacket in the outer office. Coffey shuffled his little green hat and deerskin gauntlets until J. Donnelly returned. 'You might be in luck, Mr Coffey,' he said. 'There's a job just come in this morning for assistant editor on the house organ of a large nickel company. Not your line exactly, but you might try it?'

What could Coffey say? He was no hand at writing. Still, needs must and he had written a few army releases in his day. He accepted the slip of paper and thanked the man.

'I'll phone them and tell them you'll be on deck at eleven,' J. Donnelly said. 'Strike while the iron's hot, eh? And here's another possibility, if the editor job doesn't work out.' He handed over a second slip of paper. 'Now, if nothing comes of either of those,' he said, 'come back here and I'll transfer you to clerical, okay?'

Coffey put the second slip in his doeskin weskit and thanked the man again.

'Good luck,' J. Donnelly said. 'The luck of the Irish, eh, Mr Coffey?'

... At two-thirty Mona Prentiss, receptionist, went into the office of Georges Paul-Emile Beauchemin, public relations director of Canada Nickel, and handed him Coffey's application form. Yes, the man was outside and had been waiting since this morning. Would Mr Beauchemin care to see him?

Mr Beauchemin had time to kill. He had just finished buying someone a very good lunch in exchange for two hockey tickets. In half an hour, at the mid-week meeting, he planned to hand the tickets over to Mr Mansard. Mr Mansard was a vice-president and a hockey fan. So Mr Beauchemin was in a good mood. He said to show the guy in.

Miss Prentiss came back up the corridor. 'Will you follow me please, sir?' And Coffey followed, suddenly wishing he'd worn his blue suit although it was shiny in the seat, watching her seat – melon buttocks rubbing under grey flannel skirt, court heels tic-tac, cashmere sweater, blonde curls. A pleasant rear view, yes, but he did not enjoy it. Sick apprehension filled him because, well, what were his qualifications for *this* job? What indeed?

'This is Mr Coffey, sir,' she said, shutting the door on them. And hooray! The face that fits. Because, by some miracle, Coffey had met Mr Beauchemin, had met him last November at a party in the Press Club where the Coffeys had been Gerry Grosvenor's guests.

'Hello there,' Coffey said, jovially advancing with his large hand outstretched, the ends of his moustache lifting in a smile. And Beauchemin took the proffered hand, his mind running back, trying to place this guy. He could not recall him at all. A limey type and, like most limey types, sort of queer. Look at this one with his tiny green hat, short bulky car coat and suede boots. A man that age should know better than to dress like a college boy, Beauchemin thought. He looked at Coffey's red face

and large military moustache. Georges Paul-Emile Beauchemin had not
served. That moustache did not win him. Oh no.

'I don't suppose you remember me?' Coffey said. 'Ginger Coffey. Was
with Cootehill Distilleries here. Met you at a Press Club do once with
Gerry Grosvenor, the cartoonist.'

'Oh yes, eh?' Beauchemin said vaguely. 'Old Gerry, eh? You're – ah –
you're Irish, eh?'

'Yes,' Coffey said.

'Good old Paddy's day, eh?'

'Yes.'

'Lots of Irish out here, you know. Last year I took my little girl out to
see the Paddy's day parade on Sherbrooke Street. Lot of fun, eh?'

'Yes, isn't it?' Coffey said.

'So you're not with – ah –' Beauchemin glanced at the application form
– 'Not with Distillery any more?'

'Well no. We had a change of top brass at home and they wanted me
to come back. But I like it here, we were more or less settled, kiddy in
school and so on. Hard changing schools in mid-term, so I decided to
chance my luck and stay on.'

'Sure,' Beauchemin said. 'Cigarette?' Perhaps this guy had been sent
by someone from upstairs. It was wise to check. 'How did you know we
were looking for an editorial assistant, eh?'

Coffey looked at his little green hat. 'Well, it was the – ah – the
unemployment commission people. They mentioned it.'

Reassured (for if it had been a brass recommendation he would have
had to send a memo) Beauchemin leaned back, openly picked up the
application form. A nobody. Seventeen from fifty-six is thirty-nine. Let
him out on age.

'Well, that's too bad,' he said. 'Because – what did you say your first
name was again?'

'Ginger. Had it since I was a boy. Red hair, you see.'

'Well, Gin-ger, I'm afraid this job's not for you. We want a junior.'

'Oh?'

'Yes, some kid who's maybe worked a couple of years on a suburban
weekly, someone we can train, bring along, promote him if he works
out.'

'I see,' Coffey said. He sat for a moment, eyeing his hat. Fool! Stupid
blundering fool! Why didn't you wait to see if he remembered you? He
doesn't know you from a hole in the wall, coming in with your hand out!
Oh God! Get up, say thank you and go away.

But he could not. In his mind, a ship's siren blew, all visitors ashore.
He and Veronica and Paulie, tears in their eyes, stood on the steerage

[33]

deck waving good-bye to this promised land. This was no time for pride. Try? Ask?

'Well,' Coffey said. 'As a matter of fact, my experience has all been on the other side of the water. I imagine it's quite different here. Maybe – maybe I'd need to start lower on the scale? Learn the ropes as I go along?'

Beauchemin looked at the man's ruddy face, the embarrassed eyes. Worked for a distillery, did he? Maybe they let him go because he was too sold on the product? 'Frankly Gin-ger,' he said. 'You wouldn't fit into the pension plan. You know it's a union-management deal. The older a man comes in, the more expensive for the others in the plan. You know how these things work.'

'But I wouldn't mind if you left me out of the pension plan.'

'Sorry.'

'But – but we New Canadians,' Coffey began. 'I mean, we can't all be boys of twenty, can we? We have to start somewhere? – I mean,' he said, dropping his eyes to his hat once more. 'I'll put it to you straight. I'd appreciate it if you'd make an exception?'

'Sorry,' Beauchemin said. He stood up. 'I tell you what, Gin-ger. You leave your name and address with Mona, outside. If we think of anything we'll get in touch with you, okay? But don't pass up any other offers, meantime. All right? Glad to have met you again. Give my regards to Gerry, will you? And good luck.'

Beauchemin shook hands and watched Coffey put on his silly little hat. Saw him walk to the door, then turn, and raise his right hand in a quick jerky movement of farewell, a kind of joke salute. A vet, Beauchemin thought. I was right. They do okay, free hospitals, pensions, mortgages, educations; the hell with those guys. 'Be seeing you,' he said. 'And shut the door, will you?'

From *The Luck of Ginger Coffey* by Brian Moore, 1960

Two

GETTING TO WORK

Once our newcomer has been offered a job, he or she will find themselves – like millions of others – caught up in the wearisome routine of getting to work: a topic that – along with schools, holidays, pets and mortgages – provides the deskbound classes with conversational fodder for half a lifetime. Familiar ingredients include alarm clocks that fail to go off, cutting oneself while shaving, putting on clothes that prove either too hot or too cold, battling onto a crowded bus or train, sitting in a traffic jam and drumming one's fingers on the steering-wheel and, invariably, being late for a crucial meeting, so incurring the wrath of one's boss and pitying or disapproving looks from better organised and smug-looking colleagues. Late arrivals may well try to improve their morale by riffling through the contents of their briefcases while the underground sits in a tunnel: in addition to an apple, some sandwiches, a pocket calculator and a paperback novel, these will usually include a wodge of documents and office memos which the office worker snatched from his desk the night before on the pretence of reading them at home, knowing perfectly well that they would return to the office in exactly the same state as they left it.

For most office-workers Monday remains the blackest day of the week, casting its melancholy shadow over the domestic jollities of Sunday afternoon, while every Friday has a lightness of spirit and an end-of-term feeling to it: in this, as in so much else, office life – as P. G. Wodehouse long ago observed – has more than a touch of school about it. Nor, despite soaring inner city rents and rates, journeys of up to two hours either way and the feasibility of working at home via modern high technology, does the lemming-like procession show many signs of abating. As we approach the office a certain heaviness of spirit overcomes us on even the brightest day: a cloud of anxiety and dread about matters left undone from the day before, howlers perpetrated and impending rows or reprimands. The joshing, over-bright rituals of greeting and arrival ease the passage from one world to another: once installed behind one's desk, with the post waiting to be read and colleagues sticking their heads round the door like so many grinning glove puppets, the worries that loomed so large at three o'clock in the morning, causing much sweating and tossing about the bed, almost always assume more manageable proportions and a less alarming cast of feature.

Babbitt Goes to Work

There was nothing of the giant in the aspect of the man who was beginning to awaken in the sleeping-porch of a Dutch Colonial house in that residential district of Zenith known as Floral Heights.

His name was George F. Babbitt. He was forty-six years old now, in April, 1920, and he made nothing in particular, neither butter nor shoes nor poetry, but he was nimble in the calling of selling houses for more than people could afford to pay.

His large head was pink, his brown hair thin and dry. His face was babyish in slumber, despite his wrinkles and the red spectacle-dents on the slopes of his nose. He was not fat but he was exceedingly well fed; his cheeks were pads, and the unroughened hand which lay helpless upon the khaki-coloured blanket was slightly puffy. He seemed prosperous, extremely married and unromantic; and altogether unromantic appeared this sleeping-porch, which looked on one sizable elm, two respectable grass-plots, a cement drive, and a corrugated iron garage. Yet Babbitt was again dreaming of the fairy child, a dream more romantic than scarlet pagodas by a silver sea.

For years the fairy child had come to him. When others saw but Georgie Babbitt, she discerned gallant youth. She waited for him, in the darkness beyond mysterious groves. When at last he could slip away from the crowded house he darted to her. His wife, his clamouring friends, sought to follow, but he escaped, the girl fleet beside him, and they crouched together on a shadowy hillside. She was so slim, so white, so eager! She cried that he was gay and valiant, that she would wait for him, that they would sail –

Rumble and bang of the milk-truck.

Babbitt moaned, turned over, struggled back toward his dream. He could see only her face now, beyond misty waters. The furnace-man slammed the basement door. A dog barked in the next yard. As Babbitt sank blissfully into a dim warm tide, the paper-carrier went by whistling, and the rolled-up *Advocate* thumped the front door. Babbitt was roused, his stomach constricted with alarm. As he relaxed, he was pierced by the familiar and irritating rattle of someone cranking a Ford: snap-ah-ah, snap-ah-ah, snap-ah-ah. Himself a pious motorist, Babbitt cranked with the unseen driver, with him waited through taut hours for the roar of the starting engine, with him agonized as the roar ceased and again began the infernal patient snap-ah-ah – a round, flat sound, a shivering cold-morning sound, a sound infuriating and inescapable. Not till the rising voice of the motor told him that the Ford was moving was he released from the panting tension. He glanced once at his favourite tree, elm twigs against the gold patina of sky, and fumbled for sleep as for a drug. He who had been a boy very credulous of life was no longer greatly interested in the possible and improbable adventures of each new day.

He escaped from reality till the alarm-clock rang, at seven-twenty . . .

Myra Babbitt – Mrs George F. Babbitt – was definitely mature. She had creases from the corners of her mouth to the bottom of her chin, and her plump neck bagged. But the thing that marked her as having passed the line was that she no longer had reticences before her husband, and no longer worried about not having reticences. She was in a petticoat now, and corsets which bulged, and unaware of being seen in bulgy corsets. She had become so dully habituated to married life that in her full matronliness she was as sexless as an anæmic nun. She was a good woman, a kind woman, a diligent woman, but no one, save perhaps, Tinka, her ten-year-old, was at all interested in her or entirely aware that she was alive.

After a rather thorough discussion of all the domestic and social aspects of towels she apologized to Babbitt for his having an alcoholic headache; and he recovered enough to endure the search for a B.V.D. undershirt which had, he pointed out, malevolently been concealed among his clean pyjamas.

He was fairly amiable in the conference on the brown suit.

'What do you think, Myra?' He pawed at the clothes hunched on a chair in their bedroom, while she moved about mysteriously adjusting and patting her petticoat and, to his jaundiced eye, never seeming to get on with her dressing. 'How about it? Shall I wear the brown suit another day?'

'Well, it looks awfully nice on you.'

'I know, but gosh, it needs pressing.'

'That's so. Perhaps it does.'

'It certainly could stand being pressed, all right.'

'Yes, perhaps it wouldn't hurt it to be pressed.'

'But, gee, the coat doesn't need pressing. No sense in having the whole darn suit pressed, when the coat doesn't need it.'

'That's so.'

'But the pants certainly need it, all right. Look at them – look at those wrinkles – the pants certainly do need pressing.'

'That's so. Oh, Georgie, why couldn't you wear the brown coat with the blue trousers we were wondering what we'd do with them?'

'Good Lord! Did you ever in all my life know me to wear the coat of one suit and the pants of another? What do you think I am? A busted bookkeeper?'

'Well, why don't you put on the dark grey suit to-day, and step in at the tailor and leave the brown trousers?'

'Well, they certainly need – Now where the devil is that grey suit? Oh, yes, here we are.'

He was able to get through the other crises of dressing with comparative resoluteness and calm.

His first adornment was the sleeveless dimity B.V.D. undershirt, in which he resembled a small boy humourlessly wearing a cheesecloth tabard at a civic pageant. He never put on B.V.D.'s without thanking the God of Progress that he didn't wear tight, long, old-fashioned undergarments, like his father-in-law and partner, Henry Thompson. His second embellishment was combing back his hair. It gave him a tremendous forehead, arching up two inches beyond the former hair-line. But most wonder-working of all was the donning of his spectacles.

There is character in spectacles – the pretentious tortoiseshell, the meek pince-nez of the school-teacher, the twisted silver-framed glasses of the old villager. Babbitt's spectacles had huge, circular, frameless lenses of the very best glass; the ear-pieces were thin bars of gold. In them he was the modern business man; one who gave orders to clerks and drove a car and played occasional golf and was scholarly in regard to Salesmanship. His head suddenly appeared not babyish but weighty, and you noted his heavy, blunt nose, his straight mouth and thick, long upper lip, his chin over-fleshy but strong; with respect you beheld him put on the rest of his uniform as a Solid Citizen.

From *Babbitt* by Sinclair Lewis, 1922

Wemmick Changes Gear

Wemmick was up early in the morning, and I am afraid I heard him cleaning my boots. After that, he fell to gardening, and I saw him from my gothic window pretending to employ the Aged, and nodding at him in a most devoted manner. Our breakfast was as good as the supper, and at half-past eight precisely we started for Little Britain. By degrees, Wemmick got dryer and harder as we went along, and his mouth tightened into a post-office again. At last, when we got to his place of business and he pulled out his key from his coat-collar, he looked as unconscious of his Walworth property as if the Castle and the drawbridge and the

arbour and the lake and the fountain and the Aged, had all been blown
into space together by the last discharge of the Stinger.

From *Great Expectations* by Charles Dickens, 1861

Office Vows

From the conservative dark
Into the ethical life
The dense commuters come
Repeating their morning vow
'I *will* be true to the wife,
I'll concentrate more on my work' . . .

From 'September 1, 1939' in *Another Time* by W. H. Auden, 1940

The Dozing Commuter

On that train, the 17.27 from Charing Cross, sat Ralph Gawber, an
accountant. His thin face and his obvious fatigue gave him a look of
kindliness, and he rode the train with tolerance, responding to the jump
of the carriage with a gentle nod. In his heavy suit, in the harsh August
heat, he had the undusted sanctity of a clergyman who has spent the day
preaching without result in a stubborn slum. He held *The Times* in one
hand, folded flat in a rectangle to make a surface for the crossword, and
with the ballpoint pen in his other hand he might have been studying a
clue. But the crossword was completely inked in. Mr Gawber was asleep.
He had the elderly commuter's habit of being able to sleep without shifting
position; sleep took him and embalmed him lightly like a touch of sadness
he would soon shake off. He was dreaming of having tea with the Queen
in a sunny room in Buckingham Palace. Jammed in the corner, the standing passengers' coats brushing his head, the lunchbox of the shirtless man
next to him nudging his thigh, he dreamed. Around him, travellers slapped
and shook their evening papers, but Mr Gawber slept on. The Queen
suddenly smiled and leaned forward and plucked open the front of her
dress. Her full breasts tumbled out and Mr Gawber put his head between
them and sobbed with shame and relief. They were so cool; and he felt
her nipples against his ears.

He had caught the morning train dressed warmly for the chilly summer
fog which blanketed Catford and gave him a secure feeling of privacy

among the bulky lighted cars half-lost in vapour. The fog cheered him with forgetfulness, slowly and unaccountably, allowing him amnesia. But the sun had burst into his compartment at London Bridge, dramatically lighting the Peek Frean biscuit factory and releasing a powerful odour of shortbread. At once, he loathed his suit. The boats on the river were indistinguishable in the broad dazzle, and by the time Mr Gawber had walked the quarter mile to Kingsway he was perspiring. It seemed to him, in travelling this short distance from his home in South London, as if he had left a far-off place, where the weather was different, and had to cross a frontier to work.

From *The Family Arsenal* by Paul Theroux, 1976

Twenty-five Minutes Later

... strap-hangers of both sexes swayed in clusters over her, and along the whole length of the car, and both the platforms were too densely populated. She could not read; nobody could read. As the train roared and shook through Down Street station, she jumped up to fight her way through straphangers towards the platform, in readiness to descend at Dover Street. On these early trains carrying serious people, if you sat quiet until the train came to your station you would assuredly be swept on to the next station. These trains taught you to meet the future half-way.

As it happened the train stopped about a hundred yards short of Dover Street, and would not move on. Seconds and minutes passed, and the stoppage became undeniably a breakdown. The tunnels under the earth from Dover Street back to Hammersmith were full of stopped trains a few hundred yards apart, and every train was full of serious people who positively had to be at a certain place at a certain time. Lilian's mood changed; the mood of the car changed, and of the train and of all the trains. No one knew anything; no one could do anything; the trains were each a prison. The railway company by its officials maintained a masterly silence as to the origin of the vast inconvenience and calamity. Rumours were born by spontaneous generation. A man within Lilian's hearing, hitherto one of God's quite minor achievements, was suddenly gifted with divination and announced that the electricians at the power station in Lots Road had gone on strike without notice and every electric train in London had been paralysed. Half an hour elapsed. The prisoners, made desperate by the prospect of the fate which attended them, spoke of revolution and homicide, well aware that they were just as capable of these things as a flock of sheep. Then, as inexplicably as it had stopped, the train started.

Two minutes later Lilian, with some scores of other girls, was running madly through Dover Street in vain pursuit of time lost and vanished. Not a soul had guessed the cause of the disaster, which, according to the evening papers, was due to an old, unhappy man who had wandered unobserved into the tunnel from Dover Street station with the ambition to discover for himself what the next world was like. This ambition had been gratified.

As Lilian, in a state of nervous exhaustion, flew on tired wings up the office stairs she of course had to compose herself into a semblance of bright, virginal freshness for the day's work, conformably with the employer's theory that until he reaches the office the employee has done and suffered nothing whatever. And Miss Grig was crossing the ante-room at the moment of Lilian's entry.

'You're twenty-five minutes late, Miss Share,' said Miss Grig coldly. She looked very ill.

'So sorry, Miss Grig,' Lilian answered with unprotesting humility, and offered no explanation.

Useless to explain! Useless to assert innocence and victimization! Excuses founded on the vagaries of trains were unacceptable in that office, as in thousands of offices. Employers refused to take the least interest in trains or other means of conveyance. One of the girls in the room called 'the large room' had once told Lilian that, living at Ilford, she would leave home on foggy mornings at six o'clock in order to be sure of a prompt arrival in Clifford Street at nine o'clock, thus allowing three hours for little more than a dozen miles. But only in the book of doomsday was this detail entered to her credit. Miss Grig, even if she had heard of it – which she had not – would have dismissed it as of no importance. Yet Miss Grig was a just woman.

'Come into my room, Miss Share, will you, please?' said Miss Grig.

Lilian, apprehending she knew not what, thought to herself bitterly that lateness for a delicious shopping appointment or a heavenly appointment to lunch at the Savoy or to motor up the river – affairs of true importance – would have been laughed off as negligible, whereas lateness at this filthy office was equivalent to embezzlement. And she resolved anew, and with the most terrible determination, to escape at no matter what risks from the servitude and the famine of sentiment in which she existed.

From *Lilian* by Arnold Bennett, 1922

The Commuters' Guilty Secret

The eight forty-six was five minutes late. There was a girl aged about twenty in the compartment. She wore a mini-skirt and had slightly fat thighs. No-one looked at her thighs yet all the men saw them out of the corner of their eyes. They shared the guilty secret of the girl's thighs, and Reggie knew that at Waterloo Station they would let her leave the compartment first, they would look furtively at the depression left in the upholstery by her recently-departed bottom, and then they would follow her down the platform.

He folded his paper into quarters to give his pencil some support, puckered his brow in a passable imitation of thought, and filled in the whole crossword in three and a half minutes.

He didn't actually solve the clues in that time, of course. In the spaces of the crossword he wrote: 'My name is Reginald Iolanthe Perrin. My mother couldn't appear in our local Gilbert and Sullivan Society production of *Iolanthe*, because I was on the way, so they named me after it instead. I'm glad it wasn't *The Pirates of Penzance*.'

He put the paper away in his briefcase, and said to the compartment, 'Very easy today.'

They arrived at Waterloo Station eleven minutes late. The loudspeaker announcement blamed 'reaction to rolling stock shortages at Nine Elms'. The slightly fat girl left the compartment first. The upholstery had made little red lines on the back of her thighs.

From *The Death of Reginald Perrin* by David Nobbs, 1975

The Hazards of the Tube

One day on the tube going to work I recognized the face of a man straphanging a few yards away. He had been a Brigade Signals Officer in 5th Indian ('Flaming Arsehole') Division. I pushed nearer to him and said loudly, 'I can't remember your name but I do remember your Arsehole.' He wasn't pleased by that remark and the bystanders' reaction to it, and our conversation was perfunctory.

From *Memoirs of an Advertising Man* by John Mellors, 1976

There was one factor with which Mr Copley, in his anticipatory triumph, had failed to reckon; namely, that to obtain the full effect and splendour of his *coup de théâtre* it was necessary for him to get to the office before Mr Tallboy. In his day-dream, he had taken this for granted – naturally so, since he was a punctual man at all times, and Mr Tallboy was apt to be more punctual in departing than in arriving. Mr Copley's idea was that, after making a stately report to Mr Armstrong at 9 o'clock, in the course of which Mr Tallboy would be called in and admonished, he should then take the repentant Group-manager privately to one side, read him a little lecture on orderliness and thought for others, and hand him over his fifty pounds with a paternal caution. Meanwhile, Mr Armstrong would mention the Nutrax incident to the other directors, who would congratulate themselves on having so reliable, experienced, and devoted a servant. The words sang themselves into a little slogan in Mr Copley's head: 'You can Count on Copley in a Crisis.'

But things did not turn out that way. To begin with, Mr Copley's late arrival on the Thursday night plunged him into a domestic storm which lasted into the night and still muttered with thunderous reverberations on the following morning.

'I suppose,' said Mrs Copley, acidly, 'that while you were telephoning to all these people, it was too much trouble to think of your *wife*. I don't count at all, naturally. It's nothing to *you* that I should be left imagining all kinds of things. Well, don't blame *me* if the chicken is roasted to a chip and the potatoes are sodden, and you get indigestion.'

The chicken *was* roasted to a chip; the potatoes *were* sodden; and, in consequence, Mr Copley did get a violent indigestion, to which his wife was obliged to minister with soda-mint and bismuth and hot-water bottles, voicing her opinion of him at every application. Not until six o'clock in the morning did he fall into a heavy and unrefreshing slumber, from which he was aroused at a quarter to eight by hearing Mrs Copley say:

'If you are going to the office to-day, Frederick, you had better get up. If you are *not* going, you may as well say so, and I will send a message. I have called you three times, and your breakfast is getting cold.'

Mr Copley, with a bilious headache over his right eye and a nasty taste in his mouth, would gladly have authorised her to send the message – gladly have turned over upon his pillow and buried his woes in sleep, but the recollection of the Nutrax half-double and the fifty pounds rushed over him in a flood and swept him groaning from between the sheets.

Seen in the morning light, to the accompaniment of black spots dancing before his eyes, the prospect of his triumph had lost much of its glamour. Still, he could not let it go with a mere explanation by telephone. He must be on the spot. He shaved hastily, with a shaking hand and cut himself. The flow of blood would not be staunched. It invaded his shirt. He snatched the garment off, and called to his wife for a clean one. Mrs Copley supplied it – not without reprimand. It seemed that the putting on of a clean shirt on a Friday morning upset the entire economy of the household. At ten minutes past eight, he came down to a breakfast he could not eat, his cheek ludicrously embellished with a tuft of cotton-wool and his ears ringing with migraine and conjugal rebuke.

It was impossible, now, to catch the 8.15. Sourly, he caught the 8.25.

At a quarter to nine, the 8.25 was hung up for twenty minutes outside King's Cross on account of an accident to a goods train.

At 9.30, Mr Copley crawled drearily into Pym's, wishing he had never been born.

As he entered the office from the lift, the reception-clerk greeted him with a message that Mr Armstrong would like to see him at once. Mr Copley, savagely signing his name far away below the red line which divided the punctual from the dilatory, nodded, and then wished he had not, as a pang of agony shot through his aching head. He mounted the stair and encountered Miss Parton, who said brightly:

'Oh, *here* you are, Mr Copley! We thought you were lost. Mr Armstrong would like to see you.'

'I'm just going,' said Mr Copley, savagely. He went to his room and took off his coat, wondering whether a phenacetin would cure his headache or merely make him sick. Ginger Joe knocked at the door.

'If you please, sir, Mr Armstrong says, could you spare him a moment.'

'All right, all right,' said Mr Copley. He tottered out into the passage, and nearly fell into the arms of Mr Ingleby.

'Hullo!' said the latter, 'you're wanted, Copley! We were just sending out the town-crier. You'd better nip along to Armstrong pronto. Tallboy's out for your blood.'

'Ar'rh!' said Mr Copley.

He shouldered Mr Ingleby aside and went on his way, only to encounter Mr Bredon, lurking at the door of his own room, armed with an imbecile grin and a jew's harp.

'See the conquering hero comes,' cried Mr Bredon, following up this remark with a blast upon his instrument.

'Jackanapes!' said Mr Copley. Whereupon, to his horror, Mr Bredon executed three handsome cart-wheels before him down the passage, finishing up accurately before Mr Armstrong's door, and just out of Mr Armstrong's line of sight.

Mr Copley knocked upon the glass panel, through which he could see Mr Armstrong, seated at his desk, Mr Tallboy, upright and indignant, and Mr Hankin standing, with his usual air of mild hesitation, on the far side of the room. Mr Armstrong looked up and beckoned Mr Copley in.

'Ah!' said Mr Armstrong, 'here's the man we want. Rather late this morning, aren't you, Mr Copley?'

Mr Copley explained that there had been an accident on the line.

'Something must be done about these accidents on the line,' said Mr Armstrong. 'Whenever Pym's staff travels, the trains break down. I shall have to write to the Superintendent of the line. Ha, ha!'

Mr Copley realised that Mr Armstrong was in one of his frivolous and tiresome moods. He said nothing.

From *Murder Must Advertise* by Dorothy L. Sayers, 1933

Clock-watching with Leonard Woolf

The routine was regular on five days of the week. I would arrive between 9 and 9.15 am from the rooms I had taken in Heathcote Street just behind Mecklenburgh Square, a ten-minute walk through the picturesque disused burial ground of St George-The-Martyr. Leonard had a passion for exact punctuality, and may well have been watching my arrival from an upper window, stop-watch in hand; but as I am by nature a punctual person I was more likely to be at the Press a few minutes early rather than a few seconds late. There is a story told about one of my predecessors, that according to Leonard's time-piece he had arrived two minutes late one morning. He denied it, pointing to his own wristwatch which indicated precise punctuality. They argued hotly for some time, until Leonard called a taxi and drove with the hapless young man to check by Big Ben. A rare occasion on which Leonard's conviction that he always knew best got the better of his parsimony.

From *Thrown to the Woolfs* by John Lehmann, 1978

A Character for Irregularity

... during this period of my life it was my duty to be present every morning at the office punctually at 10 am. I think I commenced my quarrels with the authorities there by having in my possession a watch which was always ten minutes late. I know that I very soon achieved a character for irregularity, and came to be regarded as a black sheep by men around me who were not themselves, I think, very good public servants. From time to time rumours reached me that if I did not take care I should be dismissed; especially one rumour in my early days, through my dearly beloved friend Mrs Clayton Freeling, – who, as I write this, is still living, and who, with tears in her eyes, besought me to think of my mother. That was during the life of Sir Francis Freeling, who died, – still in harness, – a little more than twelve months after I joined the office. And yet the old man showed me signs of almost affectionate kindness, writing to me with his own hand more than once from his death-bed.

Sir Francis Freeling was followed at the Post Office by Colonel Maberly, who certainly was not my friend. I do not know that I deserved to find a friend in my new master, but I think that a man with better judgement would not have formed so low an opinion of me as he did. Years have gone by, and I can write now, and almost feel, without anger; but I can remember well the keenness of my anguish when I was treated as though I were unfit for any useful work. I did struggle – not to do the work, for there was nothing which was not easy without any struggling – but to show that I was willing to do it. My bad character nevertheless stuck to me, and was not to be got rid of by any efforts within my power. I do admit that I was irregular. It was not considered to be much in my favour that I could write letters – which was mainly the work of our office – rapidly, correctly, and to the purpose. The man who came at ten, and who was always still at his desk at half-past four, was preferred before me, though when at his desk he might be less efficient. Such preference was no doubt proper; but, with a little encouragement, I also would have been punctual. I got credit for nothing, and was reckless.

From the *Autobiography* of Anthony Trollope, 1883

That Young Monkey Pitt

APRIL 10 ... It is disgraceful how late some of the young clerks are at arriving. I told three of them that if Mr Perkupp, the principal, heard of it, they might be discharged.

Pitt, a monkey of seventeen, who has only been with us six weeks, told me 'to keep my hair on!' I informed him I had had the honour of being in the firm twenty years, to which he insolently replied that I 'looked it'. I gave him an indignant look, and said: 'I demand from you some respect, sir.' He replied: 'All right, go on demanding.' I would not argue with him any further. You cannot argue with people like that.

APRIL 11 ... I was half-an-hour late at the office, a thing that has never happened to me before. There has recently been much irregularity in the attendance of the clerks, and Mr Perkupp, our principal, unfortunately chose this very morning to pounce down upon us early. Someone had given the tip to the others. The result was that I was the only one late of the lot. Buckling, one of the senior clerks, was a brick, and I was saved by his intervention. As I passed by Pitt's desk, I heard him remark to his neighbour; 'How disgracefully late some of the head clerks arrive!' This was, of course, meant for me. I treated the observation with silence, simply giving him a look, which unfortunately had the effect of making both of the clerks laugh. Thought afterwards it would have been more dignified if I had pretended not to have heard him at all.

APRIL 28. At the office, the new and very young clerk Pitt, who was very impudent to me a week or so ago, was late again. I told him it would be my duty to inform Mr Perkupp, the principal. To my surprise, Pitt apologized most humbly and in a most gentlemanly fashion. I was unfeignedly pleased to notice this improvement in his manner towards me, and told him I would look over his unpunctuality. Passing down the room an hour later, I received a hard smack in the face from a rolled-up ball of hard foolscap. I turned round sharply, but all the clerks were apparently riveted to their work. I am not a rich man, but I would give half-a-sovereign to know whether that was thrown by accident or design.

From *The Diary of a Nobody* by George and Weedon Grossmith, 1892

'Say I'm visiting the South London reps'

We dissolve through to the sleeping face of Ritson. We are in bed with him, a hot, stuffy, steamy, untidy double bed. His thick face is sweaty. His large mouth is open, the lips cracked and rimmed black with the night before's red wine.

He stirs and mutters, feeling in the bed behind him.

— RITSON (muttering, eyes still shut): Where are you?

Realising that whoever it was has got up, he rolls heavily on to his back and looks blearily at his watch.

— RITSON: Christ!

He gets out of bed. He is naked, with a strong, thick body, rather hairy. He is forty-five. He walks over to the basin, scratching his scrotum, yawning, etc. He runs the cold tap into a glass, puts in two Alka-Seltzer, and then puts his head close to the tap and splashes his face.

He comes back and sits on the bed, listening absently to the fizzing in the glass before putting it on the table beside him. He picks up the telephone, dials, waits. Drinks half the Alka-Seltzer.

— RITSON: Geoffrey Ritson, B Sales Manager please. (Pause.) Martin? It's Geoffrey, anything happening? (Pause.) Good Lord, at *eleven*? Look, could you phone his secretary. Say I'm visiting the South London Reps and won't be in till after lunch, could you? I *will* be in actually, when I can pull myself together, probably in half an hour. Hold the fort till then, old cock . . .

From *The Office* by Jonathan Gathorne-Hardy, 1970

A Person under the Train

The three others looked up as Marcia entered the room.

'Late, aren't you?' Norman snapped.

As if it had anything to do with him, Letty thought. 'There's been some delay on the Underground this morning,' she said.

'Oh, yes,' Norman agreed. 'Did you see that on the blackboard at Holborn station? Trains were delayed "due to a person under the train at Hammersmith", it said. A "person" – is that what you have to say now?'

'Poor soul,' said Edwin. 'One does wonder sometimes how these tragedies occur.'

From *Quartet in Autumn* by Barbara Pym, 1977

'Good morning, fellow proles'

Into the lobby, your chest constricting in anticipation, your throat getting dry. You used to feel this way walking into school Monday mornings. The dread of not having finished your homework – and where were you going to sit at lunch? It didn't help being the new kid every year. The stale disinfectant smell of the corridors and the hard faces of teachers. Your boss, Clara Tillinghast, somewhat resembles a fourth-grade tyrant, one of those ageless disciplinarians who believes that little boys are evil and little girls frivolous, that an idle mind is the devil's playground and that learning is the pounding of facts, like so many nails, into the knotty oak of recalcitrant heads. Ms Clara Tillinghast, aka Clingfast, aka The Clinger, runs the Department of Factual Verification like a spelling class, and lately you have not accumulated many gold stars. You are hanging on by the skin of your chipped teeth. If the Clinger had her way you would have been expelled long ago, but the magazine has a tradition of never acknowledging its mistakes. The folk history of the place has it that no one has ever been fired: not the narcoleptic theater critic who confused two different off-Broadway premieres and ran a review that combined elements of a southern family saga and a farce about Vietnam; not the award-winning plagiarist who cribbed a five-thousand-word piece direct from a twenty-year-old issue of *Punch* and signed her name to it. It's a lot like the Ivy League, from which its staff is mostly drawn, or like a cold, impenetrable New England family which keeps even the black sheep suffocating within the fold. You, however, are a minor cousin at best; if there were a branch of the family business in a distant, malarial colony, you would have been shipped off long ago, *sans* quinine. Your transgressions are numerous. You can't call them specifically to mind, but Clingfast has the list in one of her file cabinets. She takes it out from time to time and reads you excerpts. Clara has a mind like a steel mousetrap and a heart like a twelve-minute egg.

Lucio, the elevator operator, says good morning. He was born in Sicily and has been doing this for seventeen years. With a week's training he could probably take over your job and then you could ride the elevator up and down all day long. You're at the twenty-ninth floor in no time. Say so long to Lucio, hello to Sally, the receptionist, perhaps the only staffer with a low-rent accent. She's from one of the outer boroughs, comes in via bridge or tunnel. Generally people here speak as if they were weaned on Twining's English Breakfast Tea. Tillinghast picked up her broad vowels and karate-chop consonants at Vassar. She's very sensitive about coming from Nevada. The writers, of course, are another story – foreigners and other unclubbables among them – but they come and go from their thirtieth-floor cubbyholes at strange hours. They pass manuscripts under the doors at night, and duck into empty offices if they spot you coming at them down the hallway. One mystery man up there – the Ghost – has been working on an article for seven years.

The editorial offices cover two floors. Sales and advertising are several floors below, the division emphasizing the strict independence of art and commerce in the institution. They wear suits on twenty-five, speak a different language and have carpeting on the floors, lithographs on the walls. You are not supposed to talk to them. Up here, the air is too rarefied to support broadloom, the style a down-at-the-heels hauteur. A shoeshine or an overly insistent trouser press is suspect, quite possibly Italian. The layout suggests a condo for high-rise gophers: the private offices are rodent-sized, the halls just wide enough for two-way pedestrianism.

You navigate the linoleum to the Department of Factual Verification. Directly across the hall is Clara's office, the door of which is almost always open so that all who come and go from the kingdom of facts must pass her scrutiny. She is torn between her desire for privacy, with all the honors, privileges, et cetera, appertaining to her post, and her desire to keep a sharp eye on her domain.

The door is wide open this morning and you can do nothing but make the sign of the cross and walk past. You sneak a glance over your shoulder as you enter the department and see that she's not at her desk. Your colleagues are all in place, except for Phoebe Hubbard, who is in Woods Hole researching a three-part piece on lobster-ranching.

'Good morning, fellow proles,' you say, slipping into your seat. The Department of Factual Verification is the largest room in the magazine. If chess teams had locker rooms they might look like this. There are six desks – one reserved for visiting writers – and thousands of reference books on the walls. Gray linoleum desktops, brown linoleum floors. An absolute hierarchy is reflected in the desk assignments, with the desk farthest from Clara's office and closest to the windows reserved for the senior verificationist, and so on down to your own desk against the bookshelves next to the door – but in general the department is a clubhouse of democratic fellowship. The fanatic loyalty to the magazine which rules elsewhere is compromised here by a sense of departmental loyalty: us against them. If an error slips into the magazine, it is one of you, and not the writer, who will be crucified. Not fired, but scolded, perhaps even demoted to the messenger room or the typing pool.

Rittenhouse, who has served notice to falsehoods and commended facts for over fourteen years, nods and says good morning. He looks worried. You assume that Clingfast has been looking for you, that the notion of last straws has been aired.

'Has the Clinger been around yet,' you ask. He nods and blushes down to his bow tie. Rittenhouse enjoys a touch of irreverence but can't help feeling guilty about it.

'She's rather perturbed,' he says. 'At least it seemed so to me,' he adds, demonstrating the scruples of his profession.

From *Bright Lights, Big City* by Jay McInerney, 1984

Punching In

None of the other machines was so tyrannical as the time-clock. Una admitted to herself that she didn't see how it was possible to get so many employees together promptly without it, and she was duly edified by the fact that the big chiefs punched it, too ... But she noticed that after punching it promptly at nine, in an unctuous manner which said to all beholders, 'You see that even I subject myself to this delightful humility,' Mr S. Herbert Ross frequently sneaked out and had breakfast ...

From *The Job* by Sinclair Lewis, 1917

'Make us a cup of coffee, will you?'

Vic hoots impatiently at the barrier; the security man's face appears at the window and flashes an ingratiating smile. Vic nods grimly back. Bugger was probably reading a newspaper. His predecessor had been fired at Vic's insistence just before Christmas when, returning unexpectedly to the factory at night, he found the man watching a portable TV instead of the video monitors he was paid to watch. It looks as though this one is not much of an improvement. Perhaps they should employ another security firm. Vic makes a mental note to raise the matter with George Prendergast, his Personnel Director.

The barrier is raised and he drives to his personal parking space next to the front entrance of the office block. He checks the statistics of his journey on the digital dashboard display. Distance covered: 9.8 miles. Journey time: 25 mins. 14 secs. Average for the morning rush-hour. Petrol consumption: 17.26 m.p.g. Not bad – would have been better if he hadn't put the Toyota in its place.

Vic pushes through the swing doors to the reception lobby, a reasonably impressive space, its walls lined with light oak panelling installed in a more prosperous era. The furniture is looking a bit shabby, though. The clock on the wall, an irritating type with no numbers on its face, suggests that the time is just before half-past eight. Doreen and Lesley, the two telephonist-receptionists, are taking off their coats behind the counter. They smile and simper, patting their hair and smoothing their skirts.

'Morning, Mr Wilcox.'

'Morning. Think we could do with some new chairs in here?'

'Oh yes, Mr Wilcox, these are ever so hard.'

'I didn't mean *your* chairs, I mean for visitors.'

'Oh . . .' They don't know quite how to react. He is still Mr New Broom, slightly feared. As he pushes through the swing doors and walks down the corridor towards his office, he can hear them spluttering with stifled laughter.

'Good morning, Vic.' His secretary, Shirley, smirks from behind her desk, self-righteous at being at her post before the boss, even though she is at this moment inspecting her face in a compact mirror. She is a mature woman with piled hair of an improbable yellow hue, and a voluptuous bosom on which her reading glasses, retained round her neck by a chain, rest as upon a shelf. Vic inherited her from his predecessor, who had evidently cultivated an informal working relationship. It was not with any encouragement from himself that she began to address him as Vic, but he was obliged to concede the point. She had worked for Pringle's for years, and Vic was heavily dependent on her know-how while he eased himself into the job.

'Morning, Shirley. Make us a cup of coffee, will you?' Vic's working day is lubricated by endless cups of instant coffee. He hangs up his camelhair coat in the anteroom that connects his office with Shirley's and passes into the former. He shrugs off the jacket of his suit and drapes it over the back of a chair. He sits down at his desk and opens his diary.

From *Nice Work* by David Lodge, 1988

Babbitt Clocks In

Epochal as starting the car was the drama of parking it before he entered his office. As he turned from Oberlin Avenue round the corner into Third Street, N.E., he peered ahead for a space in the line of parked cars. He angrily just missed a space as a rival driver slid into it. Ahead, another car was leaving the curb, and Babbitt slowed up, holding out his hand to the cars pressing on him from behind, agitatedly motioning an old woman to go ahead, avoiding a truck which bore down on him from one side. With front wheels scraping the wrought-steel fender of the car in front, he stopped, feverishly cramped his steering-wheel, slid back into the vacant space and, with eighteen inches of room, manœuvred to bring the car level with the curb. It was a virile adventure masterfully executed. With satisfaction he locked a thief-proof steel wedge on the front wheel, and crossed the street to his real-estate office on the ground floor of the Reeves Building.

The Reeves Building was as fireproof as a rock and as efficient as a typewriter; fourteen stories of yellow pressed brick, with clean, upright, unornamented lines. It was filled with the offices of lawyers, doctors, agents for machinery, for emery wheels, for wire fencing, for mining-stock. Their gold signs shone on the windows. The entrance was too modern to be flamboyant with pillars; it was quiet, shrewd, neat. Along the Third Street side were a Western Union Telegraph Office, the Blue Delft Sweet Shop, Shotwell's Stationery Shop, and the Babbitt-Thompson Realty Company.

Babbitt could have entered his office from the street, as customers did, but it made him feel an insider to go through the corridor of the building and enter by the back door. Thus he was greeted by the villagers.

The little unknown people who inhabited the Reeves Building corridors – elevator-runners, starter, engineers, superintendent, and the doubtful-looking lame man who conducted the news and cigar stand – were in no way city-dwellers. They were rustics, living in a constricted valley, interested only in one another and in The Building. Their Main Street was the entrance hall, with its stone floor, severe marble ceiling, and the inner windows of the shops. The liveliest place on the street was the Reeves Building Barber Shop, but this was also Babbitt's one embarrassment. Himself, he patronized the glittering Pompeian Barber Shop in the Hotel Thornleigh, and every time he passed the Reeves shop – ten times a day, a hundred times – he felt untrue to his own village.

Now, as one of the squirearchy, greeted with honourable salutations by the villagers, he marched into his office, and peace and dignity were upon him, and the morning's dissonances all unheard.

They were heard again, immediately.

Stanley Graff, the outside salesman, was talking on the telephone with tragic lack of that firm manner which disciplines clients: 'Say, uh, I think I got just the house that would suit you – the Percival House, in Linton ... Oh, you've seen it. Well, how'd it strike you? ... Huh? ... Oh,' irresolutely, 'oh, I see.'

As Babbitt marched into his private room, a coop with semi-partition of oak and frosted glass, at the back of the office, he reflected how hard it was to find employees who had his own faith that he was going to make sales.

There were nine members of the staff, besides Babbitt and his partner and father-in-law, Henry Thompson, who rarely came to the office. The nine were Stanley Graff, the outside salesman – a youngish man given to cigarettes and the playing of pool; old Mat Penniman, general utility man, collector of rents and salesman of insurance – broken, silent, grey; a

[54]

mystery, reputed to have been a 'crack' real-estate man with a firm of his own in haughty Brooklyn; Chester Kirby Laylock, resident salesman out at the Glen Oriole acreage development – an enthusiastic person with a silky moustache and much family; Miss Theresa McGoun, the swift and rather pretty stenographer; Miss Wilberta Bannigan, the thick, slow, laborious accountant and file-clerk; and four freelance part-time commission salesmen.

As he looked from his own cage into the main room Babbitt mourned, 'McGoun's a good stenog., smart's a whip, but Stan Graff and all those bums –' The zest of the spring morning was smothered in the stale office air . . .

From *Babbitt* by Sinclair Lewis, 1922

The Place Where She Spends Her Life

The packers in the basement and the back of the ground floor were hard at it, with the Light Programme twice life-size. The girl on the switchboard had finished her salmon-pink jersey and was doing the ribbing on something acid mauve with a lurex thread. The smell of new books – like very distant daffodils – plus central heating and a whiff of Californian Poppy, were always in the tiny ground-floor hall. She said good morning, and started the long climb up. The first floor was the Accounts Department – a seething mystery with which she had nothing to do excepting when Miss Heaver, who had been with the house for twenty-eight years, came round with a donation list for a leaving present for somebody. On the next floor – the last with nice ceilings and unspoiled chimney-pieces – were her uncle, his partners, and their secretaries. Up again to what must once have been a bedroom floor, now housing Production, Art Department and Publicity, all jealous of one another's rooms. And finally – and really it was quite a haul – up to Editorial at the top of the house – three small rooms for them of which one was hers, and one smaller, a kind of box room in which once a week the travellers held their smoke-ridden and unexpectedly hilarious conferences: for what on earth book travellers found to laugh at week after week she simply couldn't think. But like the packers, they were always cheerful, at least when she saw or heard of them.

Her room faced south on to the street and there was a parapet where pigeons sometimes sat and ate the dull pieces of bath buns. It was very small, permanently dirty, and either stuffy or freezing, depending upon the window, but as she had apparently no creative ability (her efforts in other directions besides painting had made this agonizingly plain), this was the place where – apart from her bed – she spent most of her life.

From *After Julius* by Elizabeth Jane Howard, 1965

'Have a hotsy-totsy weekend?'

When Russell arrived at the office on Monday, Perry was there before him, busy on the telephone. It crossed his mind that Perry's early appearance might have something to do with the important matter that had been mentioned Friday night; but soon he heard phrases like 'Well, how much if we take it by the week?' and 'Yes, the ad made all that clear.'

He sat in his swivel chair, lit a cigarette, and sampled the pile of mail on his desk. As usual, it consisted mostly of publicity releases. He sometimes wondered whether anyone but other publicity people read publicity releases. The whole process was somehow absurd, if not faintly indecent – a sort of inbreeding.

Rose Pagano, their secretary, came back from the washroom. She was chunky and girdled, homely but extremely pleasant. Russell liked her very much. It was like having a clumsy, affectionate dog around the house.

'Oh, good morning, Russell,' she said. She always sounded breathless.

'Morning, Rose.' This interchange of names was his caste mark. There were three grades of male employees at Tappan Publications: those men without secretaries; those men with secretaries who addressed them by their first names; and the highest group, whose secretaries addressed them as 'Mister' and were addressed as 'Miss'. Russell was at present in the middle group.

'Boss-man is in early,' said Russell with a nod at Perry, still on the phone. With his entrance into the office, he put on the office's manner of speaking, the way a bookkeeper puts on an alpaca jacket. 'What gives?'

'I don't know, he didn't tell me,' said Rose.

Their office was on the thirty-third floor of the Peerless Building on the east side of Broadway in the Forties. They were on the south-west corner of the floor and had windows on two sides of their fairly large room. This was a bonus Russell never mentioned and never forgot. On mornings when it felt like a particularly long haul to the office, one of the consolations was the thought that he would soon be up there in the air. He particularly liked it when it rained.

He swung his chair around and put his legs under the desk, settling into place. It was like drawing on armour. He felt snug and secure. At his post.

Perry finished and hung up. 'Hiya, poopsie,' he called. 'Have a hotsy-totsy week-end?'

From *The Philanderer* by Stanley Kauffmann, 1953

'How are we this morning, Joan?'

The head office of Sunshine Desserts was a shapeless, five-storey block on the South Bank, between the railway line and the river. The concrete was badly stained by grime and rain. The clock above the main entrance had been stuck at three forty-six since 1967, and every thirty seconds throughout the night a neon sign flashed its red message 'Sunshin Des erts' across the river.

As Reggie walked towards the glass doors, a cold shiver ran through him. In the foyer there were drooping rubber plants and frayed black leather seats. He gave the bored receptionist a smile.

The lift was out of order again, and he walked up three flights of stairs to his office. He slipped and almost fell on the second floor landing. He always had been clumsy. At school they had called him 'Goofy' when they weren't calling him 'Coconut Matting'.

He walked across the threadbare green carpet of the open-plan third floor office, past the secretaries seated at their desks.

His office had windows on two sides, affording a wide vista over blackened warehouses and railway arches. Along the other two walls were green filing cabinets. A board had been pegged to the partition beside the door, and it was covered with notices, holiday postcards, and a calendar supplied gratis by a Chinese Restaurant in Weybridge.

He summoned Joan Greengross, his loyal secretary. She had a slender body and a big bust, and the knobbles of her knees went white when she crossed her legs. She had worked for him for eight years – and he had never kissed her. Each summer she sent him a postcard from Shanklin (I.O.W.). Each summer he sent her a postcard from Pembrokeshire.

'How are we this morning, Joan?' he said.

'Fine.'

'Good. That's a nice dress. Is it new?'

'I've had it three years.'

'Oh.'

He rearranged some papers on his desk nervously.

'Right,' he said. Joan's pencil was poised over her pad. 'Right.'

He looked out over the grimy sun-drenched street. He couldn't bring himself to begin. He hadn't the energy to launch himself into it.

'To G. F. Maynard, Randalls Farm, Nether Somerby,' he began at last, thinking of another farm, of golden harvests, of his youth ...

From *The Death of Reginald Perrin* by David Nobbs, 1975

A Solemn Hush

Mr Dombey's offices were in a court where there was an old-established stall of choice fruit at the corner: where perambulating merchants, of both sexes, offered for sale at any time between the hours of ten and five, slippers, pocket-books, sponges, dogs' collars, and Windsor soap, and sometimes a pointer or an oil-painting.

The pointer always came that way, with a view to the Stock Exchange, where a sporting taste (originating generally in bets of new hats) is much in vogue. The other commodities were addressed to the general public; but they were never offered by the vendors to Mr Dombey. When he appeared, the dealers in those wares fell off respectfully. The principal slipper and dogs' collar man – who considered himself a public character, and whose portrait was screwed on to an artist's door in Cheapside – threw up his forefinger to the brim of his hat as Mr Dombey went by. The ticket-porter, if he were not absent on a job, always ran officiously before to open Mr Dombey's office door as wide as possible, and hold it open, with his hat off, while he entered.

The clerks within were not a whit behind-hand in their demonstrations of respect. A solemn hush prevailed, as Mr Dombey passed through the outer office. The wit of the Counting-House became in a moment as mute as the row of leathern fire-buckets hanging up behind him. Such vapid and flat daylight as filtered through the ground-glass windows and skylights, leaving a black sediment upon the panes, showed the books and papers, and the figures bending over them, enveloped in a studious gloom, and as much abstracted in appearance, from the world without, as if they were assembled at the bottom of the sea; while a mouldy little strong room in the obscure perspective, where a shady lamp was always burning, might have represented the cavern of some ocean-monster, looking on with a red eye at these mysteries of the deep.

When Perch the messenger, whose place was on a little bracket, like a timepiece, saw Mr Dombey come in – or rather when he felt that he was coming, for he had usually an instinctive sense of his approach – he hurried into Mr Dombey's room, stirred the fire, quarried fresh coals from the bowels of the coal-box, hung the newspaper to air upon the fender, put the chair ready, and the screen in its place, and was round upon his heel on the instant of Mr Dombey's entrance, to take his great-coat and hat, and hang them up. Then Perch took the newspaper, and gave it a turn or two in his hands before the fire, and laid it, deferentially, at Mr Dombey's elbow. And so little objection had Perch to doing deferential in the last degree, that if he might have laid himself at Mr Dombey's feet, or might have called him by some such title as used to be bestowed upon the Caliph Haroun Alraschid, he would have been all the better pleased.

As this honour would have been an innovation and an experiment, Perch was fain to content himself by expressing as well as he could, in his manner, You are the light of my Eyes. You are the Breath of my Soul. You are the commander of the Faithful Perch! With this imperfect happiness to cheer him, he would shut the door softly, walk away on tiptoe, and leave his great chief to be stared at, through a dome-shaped window in the leads, by ugly chimney-pots and backs of houses, and especially by the bold window of a hair-cutting saloon on a first floor, where a waxen effigy, bald as a Mussulman in the morning, and covered after eleven o'clock in the day, with luxuriant hair and whiskers in the latest Christian fashion, showed him the wrong side of its head for ever.

From *Dombey and Son* by Charles Dickens, 1848

The Arrival of President Dodsworth

The General Offices of the Revelation Motor Company were in an immense glass and marble building on Constitution Avenue, North, above Court House Square, opposite the flashing new skyscraper of the Plymouth National Bank. The entrance to the floor given to executive offices was like the lobby of a pretentious hotel – waiting-room in brocade and tapestry and Grand Rapids renaissance; then something like an acre of little tables with typists and typists and typists, very busy, and clerks and clerks and clerks, with rattling papers; and a row of private offices resembling furniture showrooms, distinguished by enormous desks in imitation of refectory tables, covered with enormous sheets of plate glass, and fanatically kept free of papers and all jolly disorder.

The arrival of President Dodsworth was like that of a General Commanding. 'Good morning!' rumbled the uniformed doorman, a retired sergeant. '*Good morning!*' chirped the girl at the inquiry desk, a charming girl whose gentleman-friend was said to be uncommonly high up in the fur business. 'Good morning!' indicated the typists and clerks, their heads bowing like leaves agitated by a flitting breeze as he strode by them. '*Good* morning!' caroled Sam's private stenographer as he entered his own office. 'GOOD MORNING!' shouted his secretary, an offensively high-pressure young slave-driver. And even the red-headed Jewish office boy, as he took Sam's coat and hung it up so that it would not dry, condescended 'Mornin', boss.'

Yet today all this obsequiousness, normally not unpleasant to the Great Man, annoyed him; all this activity, this proof that ever so many people were sending out ever so many letters about things presumably of importance, seemed to him an irritating fussiness. What did it matter whether he had another hundred thousand dollars to leave to Brent? What did it matter whether John B. Johnson of Jonesburg did or did not take the local Revelation agency? Why were all these hundreds of young people willing to be turned into machines for the purposes of rattling papers and bowing to the president?

The Great Man approached his desk, put on his eye-glasses, and graciously received a stock-report, as one accomplishing empires.

But the Great Man was thinking:

'They make me tired – poor devils! Come on, Fran! Let's go! Let's drift way round to China!'

From *Dodsworth* by Sinclair Lewis, 1929

Three
SETTLING IN

The first day in a new job has much in common with the first day in a new school: the new bug is shown to a desk and where to hang his or her coat, and lavatories, fire escapes and coffee-making equipment are pointed out and instantly forgotten; after which he or she is ushered from room to room and introduced to a small army of absolute strangers, all of them smiling and holding out their hands as they rise from behind their desks, make awkward, jocular sounds of welcome (some even going so far, perhaps, as to produce old chestnuts like 'Welcome to the mad-house') before subsiding with a sigh of relief as the newcomer, quite dazed by all he has seen, is shunted on to the next contender. Apart from a few angry or suspicious spirits who appear to resent all newcomers, finding them threatening, presumptuous or disruptive – still more so if they have, through no fault of their own, replaced a popular and probably hard-done-by member of staff – most of the old lags go out of their way to make the new arrival feel at home: showing them the ropes, raiding the stationery cupboard, explaining how to work the photocopier and the fax machine, initiating them into office politics and gossip, warning them whom to beware of and who is an easy touch, and making a point of including them in lunch-hour forays to the pub or the canteen. During these first few days most new arrivals, unless horribly brash and self-confident, appear endearingly diffident and baffled: not so diffident and baffled as to seem half-witted or incompetent, but sufficiently so as to ensure the sympathy and support of those around them, whether bosses, peers or underlings. Even within a similar or compatible line of business, much will seem alien and unfamiliar; and for some time the new arrival, unless involved in a purely functional job like copy-typing, will find that he or she has little or nothing to do, and fills in the long hours moving a few modest sheets of paper about the desk, reading and re-reading the telephone list or the fire regulations, starting guiltily whenever the telephone rings or a head pops round the door ('How are you getting on? Do say if there's anything you need!'), and springing eagerly forward at the faintest intimation of useful employment. Newcomers tend to be treated kindly at meetings, and their opinions politely sought, particularly if they have recently arrived from a rival concern: failures to understand are laughingly explained away, as are normally unforgivable confusions and short-circuitings of rank and hierarchy. But the honeymoon period of suspended animation can only last so long. Friendships are made, and enmities incurred; a certain level of knowledge and expertise is (rightly or wrongly) taken for granted, and the benefit of the doubt no longer automatically given; he comes to be treated like anybody else. The new arrival is new no longer; he has become an integral part of office life.

Mike's First Day

The City received Mike with the same aloofness with which the more western portion of London had welcomed him on the previous day. Nobody seemed to look at him. He was permitted to alight at St Paul's and make his way up Queen Victoria Street without any demonstration. He followed the human stream till he reached the Mansion House, and eventually found himself at the massive building of the New Asiatic Bank, Limited.

The difficulty now was to know how to make an effective entrance. There was the bank, and here was he. How had he better set about breaking it to the authorities that he had positively arrived and was ready to start earning his four pound ten *per mensem*? Inside, the bank seemed to be in a state of some confusion. Men were moving about in an apparently irresolute manner. Nobody seemed actually to be working. As a matter of fact, the business of a bank does not start very early in the morning. Mike had arrived before things had really begun to move. As he stood near the doorway, one or two panting figures rushed up the steps, and flung themselves at a large book which stood on the counter near the door. Mike was to come to know this book well. In it, if you were an *employé* of the New Asiatic Bank, you had to inscribe your name every morning. It was removed at ten sharp to the accountant's room, and if you reached the bank a certain number of times in the year too late to sign, bang went your bonus.

After a while things began to settle down. The stir and confusion gradually ceased. All down the length of the bank, figures could be seen, seated on stools and writing hieroglyphics in large letters. A benevolent-looking man, with spectacles and a straggling grey beard, crossed the gangway close to where Mike was standing. Mike put the thing to him, as man to man.

'Could you tell me,' he said, 'what I'm supposed to do? I've just joined the bank.' The benevolent man stopped, and looked at him with a pair of mild blue eyes. 'I think, perhaps, that your best plan would be to see the manager,' he said. 'Yes, I should certainly do that. He will tell you what work you have to do. If you will permit me, I will show you the way.'

'It's awfully good of you,' said Mike. He felt very grateful. After his experience of London, it was a pleasant change to find someone who really seemed to care what happened to him. His heart warmed to the benevolent man.

'It feels strange to you, perhaps, at first, Mr –'

'Jackson.'

'Mr Jackson. My name is Waller. I have been in the City some time, but I can still recall my first day. But one shakes down. One shakes down quite quickly. Here is the manager's room. If you go in, he will tell you what to do.'

'Thanks awfully,' said Mike.

'Not at all.' He ambled off on the quest which Mike had interrupted, turning, as he went, to bestow a mild smile of encouragement on the new arrival. There was something about Mr Waller which reminded Mike pleasantly of the White Knight in 'Alice through the Looking-glass.'

Mike knocked at the managerial door, and went in.

Two men were sitting at the table. The one facing the door was writing when Mike went in. He continued to write all the time he was in the room. Conversation between other people in his presence had apparently no interest for him, nor was it able to disturb him in any way.

The other man was talking into a telephone. Mike waited till he had finished. Then he coughed. The man turned round. Mike had thought, as he looked at his back and heard his voice, that something about his appearance or his way of speaking was familiar. He was right. The man in the chair was Mr Bickersdyke, the cross-screen pedestrian.

These reunions are very awkward. Mike was frankly unequal to the situation. Psmith, in his place, would have opened the conversation, and relaxed the tension with some remark on the weather or the state of the crops. Mike merely stood wrapped in silence, as in a garment.

That the recognition was mutual was evident from Mr Bickersdyke's look. But apart from this, he gave no sign of having already had the pleasure of making Mike's acquaintance. He merely stared at him as if he were a blot on the arrangement of the furniture and said, 'Well?'

The most difficult parts to play in real life as well as on the stage are those in which no 'business' is arranged for the performer. It was all very well for Mr Bickersdyke. He had been 'discovered sitting'. But Mike had had to enter, and he wished now that there was something he could do instead of merely standing and speaking.

'I've come,' was the best speech he could think of. It was not a good speech. It was too sinister. He felt that even as he said it. It was the sort of thing Mephistopheles would have said to Faust by way of opening conversation. And he was not sure, either, whether he ought not to have added, 'Sir.'

Apparently such subtleties of address were not necessary, for Mr Bickersdyke did not start up and shout, 'This language to me!' or anything of that kind. He merely said, 'Oh! And who are you?'

'Jackson,' said Mike. It was irritating, this assumption on Mr Bickersdyke's part that they had never met before.

'Jackson? Ah, yes. You have joined the staff?'

Mike rather liked this way of putting it. It lent a certain dignity to the proceedings, making him feel like some important person for whose services there had been strenuous competition. He seemed to see the bank's directors being reassured by the chairman. ('I am happy to say, gentlemen, that our profits for the past year are £3,000,006-2-2½ – (cheers) – and' – impressively – 'that we have finally succeeded in inducing Mr Mike Jackson – (sensation) – to – er – in fact, to join the staff! (Frantic cheers, in which the chairman joined.')

'Yes,' he said.

Mr Bickersdyke pressed a bell on the table beside him, and picking up a pen, began to write. Of Mike he took no further notice, leaving that toy of Fate standing stranded in the middle of the room.

From *Psmith in the City* by P. G. Wodehouse, 1910

Starting Out at the Hogarth Press

MY FIRST DAY

I arrived much too early this morning and had a long wait before Mrs Cartwright and Miss Belcher arrived to open the Press. They both wore overalls: Miss Belcher a flowered one and Ma Cartwright a plain beige one which has a long way to go round her as she is very stout. She has a shock of white hair, pink cheeks and pebble-type glasses through which she blinks nervously. She nearly fell down the area steps when she arrived – she runs everywhere on very high heels and appears to be very efficient, typing at a terrific speed.

Leonard Woolf obviously does not think her at all efficient. In fact he was bloody awful to her in front of Miss Belcher and myself because she tried to cover up some trivial mistake. When he's annoyed, his voice goes up into a sort of exasperated wail, especially when he's saying words like 'Why???' and 'Absurd!!!' which he drags out to show how unreasonable something is. He does have a special way of talking which I think comes of the care he takes to say exactly what he means. It's a kind of drawl . . .

It's been an unlucky day. I've made a bad start. This morning LW gave me a letter to type returning a rejected MS to an author. I must say the letter was short and none too sweet. LW thinks people can either write or they can't and if they can't it's not worthwhile wasting time over them. The letter was just two lines: 'Dear Sir, We regret we are unable to accept the enclosed MS. Yours faithfully,'. It took me about an hour to type it out under Miss Belcher's scornful eye. I put it into LW's tray and when he came down after lunch he glanced at it and then handed it back to me, pointing with a trembling finger at the word 'except' which I had written instead of 'accept'.

Perhaps I ought to go to Pitman and take a course in typing. I am feeling very despondent and there are so many things in this job that I will have to do which I am very bad at and never likely to get better at.

From *A Boy at the Hogarth Press* by Richard Kennedy, 1972

Getting the Hang of Things

A secretary in a tight pink sweater told Tom that Ogden couldn't see him for another hour, but that he had asked her to show him to the office he was to occupy. Tom thanked her and followed her down the hall. The passageway ran out of carpet by the time they got to his door, but Tom was surprised at the size of his quarters. He had a room about fifteen feet square entirely to himself, and there was a small alcove where a pert brown-haired secretary sat at a small desk copying letters. 'Mr Rath, this is Miss Lawrence,' the girl in the pink sweater said. 'She will be your secretary.'

'It's nice to meet you,' Miss Lawrence said. She stood up, and smiled.

Tom's desk was fancily shaped, much like the one behind which Walker had given him his first interview, but he had an ordinary swivel chair instead of a reclining one. He sat down in it. There were two telephones on the desk, an interoffice communication box, and a small panel with three red buttons on it. Experimentally he pushed one of the buttons. Almost immediately, the door to his office opened and a distinguished and statuesque blonde girl in a dark-green blouse and expensive-looking tweed skirt came in. 'You buzzed, sir?' she asked in a rather upstage Boston accent.

'Who are you?'

'I'm the office girl. I deliver the interoffice mail. Did you buzz for me?'

'By mistake,' Tom said. 'Thank you very much.'

She left, and he sat examining the other buttons with interest. Maybe the second one's for a redhead and the third one's for a brunette, he thought. After a moment of hesitation, he pushed the second one. This time Miss Lawrence came in. 'Yes?' she asked.

'What's the third button for?'

'Nothing,' she said, grinning. 'It's for men who have two secretaries. Do you know how to use the interoffice communication system?'

He said no, and she showed him. She also explained the telephone system and brought from her desk a stack of papers for him to sign which placed him officially on the pay roll and insured him against almost everything in the world but getting fired. Just as he finished signing them, his interoffice communication box uttered some ominous crackling sounds, like a radio in a thunderstorm. He flicked a switch on it, and Ogden's voice suddenly shouted at him so loudly that he jumped, 'Are you there, Rath?'

Tom turned the volume down to make Ogden more polite. 'Just got here,' he said.

'Come up and see me in half an hour,' Ogden almost whispered. There were more noises like static.

'I'll be there,' Tom said.

From *The Man in the Gray Flannel Suit* by Sloan Wilson, 1956

'I'm to ask for Mr Riddle'

'It's Mr Riddle,' said a girl of about her own age seated at a desk behind a wooden barrier marked *Enquiries*, having heard her name and business. 'Upstairs.' She turned back to her papers.

'I'm to ask for Mr Riddle, do you mean?'

'Mr Riddle. That's right.'

'Where do I find him?'

'Mr Riddle.' The girl showed signs of impatience. 'Up the stairs.'

Nell was feeling impatient herself. She ran up a flight of dusty stone steps, glancing at closed doors as she went. She met no-one. There was a distant sound of typewriters and a sharpish smell like celluloid or Aunt Peggy's nail varnish. The windows were unexpectedly clean, revealing the clear blue spring sky. Then she saw a door marked with the pregnant name. She opened it rather quickly and went in.

'Here, here, we're very full of energy this morning, aren't we?' cried a fat man perched on the edge of a desk. 'When she's been here six months she won't run up the stairs like that, what's the betting, George?'

A pair of watery eyes looked across at Nell. Their owner was sitting at the desk. The room was small and rather dark and stiflingly, startlingly hot. A small gas fire, looking as if at any moment it might burst into flames, so red and quivering was it, hissed madly in the black fireplace. There was a strong and triumphant smell of cigarette smoke: very, very old: this morning's – for both gentlemen were smoking, although the seated one was doing so with less abandon than the perched one – and even future, for it was possible to deduce that the room would never, as far as human thought could reach, smell of anything else.

'Good morning, Miss Sely,' said the elderly one, conveying reproof. 'You are a few minutes late but we'll excuse that as it's the first morning. I am Mr Riddle and you will be working for me. This is Mr Belwood, our Chief Accountant.' (Mr Belwood made a mock-obsequious inclination of his head and brandished his cigarette.) 'The Ladies Cloakroom is on the next landing. Now if you will kindly hang your coat and hat behind the door, we will get to work. That is your desk, in the corner near the window. I suppose, like all young people, you like fresh air.'

From *Here Be Dragons* by Stella Gibbons, 1956

'Welcome to the Madhouse'

'Mr Graph-paper, Mr Seeds, Miss Divorce, Mrs Rashman, Mr Ad Dah, Mr Beastly, Mr Charles Penney, Mr New Penny, Mr Hakim.'

Catching one name in three, Clement Gryce shook hands with such of his new colleagues as were near enough to touch, and nodded to those who were out of reach behind their desks.

Most of them said a word or two: 'How d'y'do.' 'Glad to have you aboard.' 'Welcome to the madhouse.' They seemed a nice enough lot taken all round, though Gryce put question marks over the heads of two of them, Beastly and Graph-paper, who could very easily have shaken hands if they'd bothered to stand up and lean forward a bit. Graph-paper, he already knew from his interview with Copeland who had mentioned a Mr Grant-hyphen-something or other, was Copeland's deputy. Beastly looked as if he might be next in the chain of command.

'Not forgetting Thelma who looks after us all.' Copeland, who put Gryce in mind of the actor Mervyn Johns, waved an arm towards the dumpy office girl, a recent school-leaver by the look of her. She bore a passing resemblance to the girl who had played Judy Garland's room-mate in an old film recently repeated on television. Gryce gave her a brief smile and permitted his glance, as it swivelled back to Copeland, to take a short detour via the other two females present.

Mrs Rashman must have been about fifty, or ten years older than himself. That didn't necessarily rule her out. Some of these homely-looking ones really knew how to let their hair down once they'd watered the pot plants and left the office for the day, so it was rumoured. But the younger one – thirtyish? thirty-fiveish? – was probably the likelier of the two, so long as her real name proved to be something less provocative than Miss Divorce. That was definitely the once-over she had given him when the commissionaire had shown him in. She reminded Gryce of a well-known news reader. Gryce watched TV a lot and nearly everyone he met reminded him of some celebrity or character actor, though he could not always put a name to the face.

'Now, where are we going to park you?' Copeland went on. 'As I think I told you, the whole department is to be reorganised quite soon so I'd rather not move in a new desk just yet. Who's on holiday?' he asked the man he had introduced as Mr Seeds. 'Isn't Fart still away?'

'I believe till next Monday.'

'Let us consult the holy writ.' Taking Gryce's arm, Copeland steered him across to the staff notice-board . . .

'Do you prefer coffee-flavoured dishwater or tea-flavoured dishwater?'

The familiar office joke made Gryce feel quite at home. 'Coffee-flavoured, I usually have.' He smiled again at the overweight junior who, with a good deal of clattering, was extracting a number of beakers from a filing cabinet and arranging them in a wire tray.

'Don't worry, we're not offending Thelma,' said Seeds. 'She doesn't brew it herself, it's all untouched by 'uman 'ands.'

'Ah, an infernal machine.'

'The wonders of modern technology. If you press the button marked tea it pours forth a liquid resembling coffee . . .'

'. . . whereas the button marked coffee produces a frothy substance that could be mistaken for tea, yes,' completed Gryce. Thelma was now clomping flat-footedly from desk to desk with her tray of beakers. This was obviously a morning routine: she collected the money for the vending machine, at the same time jotting down individual requirements on a scrap of cardboard – three coffees, one tea and one 7-Up so far, Gryce noted as Thelma reached his desk – and then did the rounds again dispensing the completed orders. It seemed inefficient: two journeys instead of one. In Gryce's last billet, the office girl had kept a little book and they had settled up weekly; but he could quite see that given the need to feed the vending machine with tenpenny pieces, Thelma would have to find a daily supply of coins.

Raising his right buttock slightly he felt among the coins in his pocket for the milled edge of a tenpenny piece, but Seeds had beaten him to it. 'My treat, as you're a new boy.' He mustn't forget to reciprocate in the afternoon tea break. When he had a desk of his own, after the departmental reorganisation that Copeland had spoken about, he could see this becoming a little daily custom, always supposing that he was still sitting next to Seeds or in his near vicinity. Seeds would stand him coffee in the mornings and he would stand Seeds tea, or whatever he preferred, in the afternoons. Since all drinks seemed to cost the same, Gryce had no objection to arrangements of this kind. They were what made the wheels go round, in his opinion . . .

'I was saying,' Gryce went on. 'Curious about these desks. I was telling our friend here, for my sins I served three years before the mast at Comform.'

'Comform,' repeated Beazley. He had a barking voice. He sounded as if he were accustomed to giving orders, or would like to become so accustomed.

'I was just noticing, all the desks here are Comform. So I suspect are the chairs.'

'They should make you feel quite at home.'

'*Sha!*' That was how Gryce laughed. 'Can't get away from the place, eh?' He was glad they had found a little joke to share. It broke the ice. Certainly it meant that Beazley could not be as unfriendly as he looked. Perhaps he was shy with strangers, as gruff people sometimes were. Encouraged, Gryce continued quickly before Beazley could turn back to his work:

'The curious thing is, I don't *think* British Albion had a contract with Comform. In fact I'd swear to it. Bear in mind, I *was* in furniture sales for three years.'

'Probably before your time,' said Beazley.

'Probably. This particular desk has certainly seen better days.'

He wondered if he'd perhaps gone too far there. Criticising the office furniture on your first day was not really on. He rehearsed an apologetic rider, he could say there was a good few years' life in the old desks yet: but Beazley, with a curious glance at him, had already turned back to his revolving card-index. Copeland was still talking to Seeds but Gryce was pretty sure he must have overheard the remark about Vaart's desk having seen better days. Again he felt embarrassed.

He rose with the object of crossing to the windows and looking out to see if there were any likely restaurants or sandwich bars he had missed on an earlier recce of the district – he would have to establish pretty soon what his colleagues usually did about lunch. But his path took him past Hakim's desk and Hakim seemed to think he was looking for the lavatory.

'Yes! The geography!' Hakim didn't have the sing-song accent you would have expected, he must have been in the country a long time, perhaps even born here. 'Down the central aisle; all the way through Traffic Control, then turn right and the door is staring you in the face.'

'Thank you. Thank you.' Gryce found he was not only repeating himself effusively but also executing an unnatural wriggling bow, to show Mr Hakim that he had no colour prejudice of any kind whatsoever. Hakim had risen and had extended his right arm slightly. Gryce thought he meant to shake hands again and so he put out his own hand, just as Hakim retracted his. Hakim smiled, showing white teeth, and produced his hand again; but by now Gryce had deflected his own gesture to make it look as if he was adjusting the strap of his wrist-watch. The performance continued with variations: it finished with the two men grazing knuckles rather than actually shaking hands.

'Whoops,' said Hakim, unexpectedly.

'Sha!'

Gryce backed away nodding vigorously, as if to indicate that he and Hakim had just had a stimulating exchange which they must take up again. 'Would you like me to show you the way?' asked Hakim.

'No, that's more than kind of you, I'll find it. Through Traffic Control, then right?'

'And it's straight ahead.'

'Many thanks indeed.'

From *Office Life* by Keith Waterhouse, 1978

'Warn him not to use the directors' lav'

'And by the way,' said Mr Hankin, arresting Miss Rossiter as she rose to go, 'there is a new copy-writer coming in to-day.'

'Oh, yes, Mr Hankin?'

'His name is Bredon. I can't tell you much about him; Mr Pym engaged him himself; but you will see that he is looked after.'

'Yes, Mr Hankin.'

'He will have Mr Dean's room.'

'Yes, Mr Hankin.'

'I should think Mr Ingleby could take him in hand and show him what to do. You might send Mr Ingleby along if he can spare me a moment.'

'Yes, Mr Hankin.'

'That's all. And, oh, yes! Ask Mr Smayle to let me have the Dairyfields guard-book.'

'Yes, Mr Hankin.'

Miss Rossiter tucked her note-book under her arm, closed the glass-panelled door noiselessly after her and tripped smartly down the corridor. Peeping through another glass-panelled door, she observed Mr Ingleby seated on a revolving chair with his feet on the cold radiator, and talking with great animation to a young woman in green, perched on the corner of the writing-table.

'Excuse me,' said Miss Rossiter, with perfunctory civility, 'but Mr Hankin says can you spare him a moment, Mr Ingleby?'

'If it's Tom-Boy Toffee,' replied Mr Ingleby defensively, 'it's being typed. Here! you'd better take these two bits along and make it so. That will lend an air of verisimilitude to an otherwise –'

'It isn't Tom-Boy. It's a new copy-writer.'

'What, already?' exclaimed the young woman. 'Before those shoes were old! Why, they only buried little Dean on Friday.'

'Part of the modern system of push and go,' said Mr Ingleby. 'All very distressing in an old-fashioned, gentlemanly firm. Suppose I've got to put this blighter through his paces. Why am I always left with the baby?'

'Oh, rot!' said the young woman, 'you've only got to warn him not to use the directors' lav., and not to tumble down the iron staircase.'

'You are the most callous woman, Miss Meteyard. Well, as long as they don't put the fellow in with me –'

'It's all right, Mr Ingleby. He's having Mr Dean's room.'

'Oh! What's he like?'

'Mr Hankin said he didn't know, Mr Pym took him on.'

'Oh, gosh! friend of the management,' Mr Ingleby groaned.

'Then I think I've seen him,' said Miss Meteyard. 'Tow-coloured, super-cilious-looking blighter. I ran into him coming out of Pymmie's room yesterday. Horn-rims. Cross between Ralph Lynn and Bertie Wooster.'

'Death, where is thy sting? Well, I suppose I'd better push off and see about it.'

Mr Ingleby lowered his feet from the radiator, prised up his slow length from the revolving chair, and prowled unhappily away.

'Oh, well, it makes a little excitement,' said Miss Meteyard.

From *Murder Must Advertise* by Dorothy L. Sayers, 1933

Rumblings of Nervous Diarrhœa

... In the April of 1909 I was instructed to report to an office called the Land Registry, of which I had never heard. It was in Lincoln's Inn Fields, and at once I thought of the scenes in Dickens's *Bleak House* and the death of the solicitor Mr Tulkinghorn. I pictured the Land Registry as an establishment similar to that of the sinister lawyer, where I should be employed as a junior at a high desk in a little ante-room.

On the morning of the 21st of April, I set out with deep misgiving, worried about Mother being left alone all day, and afraid of the unknown before me. I entered Herne Hill station, and as I walked through the subway to the up-platform, a spasm of dismay shook me. I saw myself imprisoned for life in a job in which I was likely to have no aptitude and no interest. My heart was still sullen with the mood of renunciation of my drawing and painting: for I had savagely resolved that I would never touch pencil or brush again.

I have kept that perverse resolution; but the obstinacy could not then destroy, and never has since, the abounding joy in life, moment by moment, that has made me so rich.

I saw a Dover boat-train glide through the station, and again a spasm of despair shook me, as I thought of the monotonous future in the Civil Service, with no opportunity for exploring the wonders of the world; no freedom, no solitude. I resolved that as soon as I reached Mr Tulkinghorn's office I would demand to be allowed to bring my little dog with me; a fox-terrier of dubious lineage given us by a woman who had clung to Mother for some years, since meeting her at one of the gatherings of Post Office cronies. This quiet, kind soul lived in a public-house at Penge, over the hill southwards, and came regularly during Mother's last illness, with offerings of eggs, jellies, and other sick-room fare.

To my dismay, I found the Land Registry anything but a Dickensian lawyer's office. It was a red-brick, modern institution, standing at the corner of Lincoln's Inn Fields, just outside the great gateway into Lincoln's Inn proper. I have not yet discovered how I found my way to it, for I knew nothing about London, other than the two suburbs where I had spent my sixteen years.

The idea of taking my dog, Roger, with me vanished abruptly as I inquired of the commissionaire in the entrance hall where I was to report. By that time I was ready to ask him as to my own identity, for in strange places and circumstances I have always found that I dissolve like a lump of sugar in a cup of tea, unaware of what sweetness I may be adding to the situation.

In a dreamlike condition, with distant rumblings of nervous diarrhœa, I was carried to the first floor and deposited in a vast room filled with bound volumes of property titles – the registry; and there, under the direction of a pale little man with a cripple's face and curved spine, I was seated in a bay window overlooking the Gothic gateway of the Inn, my table surrounded by card-index cabinets, which it would be my duty to keep up to date, hour by hour, as the documents of land and house property registration flowed through the department.

From *Over the Bridge* by Richard Church, 1955

An Auctioneer's Qualifications

The time had now come for me to be articled to my uncle and to go into his office.

I was a lanky youth of seventeen. I had an astonishing store of knowledge about a number of things which were scarcely relevant to a commercial career. I could read the New Testament in Greek and recite much of the Georgics from memory. I knew the names of most wild flowers, could recognise most butterflies and moths and tell you their life-histories, knew the birds' songs, their nests, and eggs, and had read the whole of Geikie's *Geology*. I could sometimes catch fish when wise old anglers couldn't; could shoot, ride a horse, sail a boat. I had read without discrimination every novel, play, or biography I could lay hands on, and I swallowed poetry with the voracity of a sea-lion swallowing fish. My method (which makes me shudder to think of it now) was to obtain from the Public Library the collected works of some poet, Tennyson or Browning or Longfellow, and read the whole lot, slap through, from page one to the end. In this fashion I had read the whole of *The Dynasts* when I was sixteen.

With these qualifications I set out to become an auctioneer.

From *Portrait of Elmbury* by John Moore, 1945

'Stuck for life in a bog hole'

Within the week I was sitting at a desk – or a table, as I learned to call it – just up the street from my uncle John. There were perhaps thirty others in the room, which was painted orphanage-green. Its cheerlessness was too absolute to have been accidental; despair seemed to have been knowingly mixed in with the paint and ingrained in the dark wooden floor tiles. There was not even a wall calendar as a sign that humans had passed that way; the only small unruliness came from a torn screen on which were pinned a dozen holiday postcards. At the other side of the screen was a woman who, more than any other at that time, was to influence my life. Her name was Kay Kelly. She was our typist and, on my first day, caught sight of the misery on my face, mimicked it most cruelly and within ten minutes had become my friend of ten years. Being myself only eighteen, I took her to be all of forty (she was thirty-two). She was slim; her hair was brown and bobbed. The screen was her way of cutting herself off, not only from draughts, but from the sight of the Staff Officer, Mr Drumm. Once, when she came over to my table for a chat, he arose from his chair and said pointedly: 'Good morning, Miss Kelly.'

She gave him a summer meadow of a smile. 'Good morning, Mr Drumm.'

His nostrils flared, and what had been underlined was now italicised as well. 'I said *good morning*, Miss Kelly.'

It took her a moment to realise that she was being ordered back to her typewriter. She laughed aloud: an unforced bubble of amusement that caused his Adam's apple to jolt to attention. It was as if she had committed the unimaginable *lèse-majesté* of telling him that he was a caution and needed only a clown's red nose to bring the house down. She swished across the room, still laughing.

'What are you going to do with yourself?' she asked me on that first day, her eyes wide. 'And ah, God, no, don't say you're going to be like that crowd of jack-asses, stuck for life in a bog hole.'

She nodded towards the other clerks, most of them middle-aged, who, so as not to wear out their blue serge, had donned the jackets, now ragged and spilling their innards, that they had worn on their first day, perhaps before the 1916 Rising. I did not hesitate, but told her what no one save myself knew. She did not even blink.

'A writer?' she said in a whisper. 'Aren't you great?'

From *Out After Dark* by Hugh Leonard, 1989

Dick Swiveller Enters upon his Duties

'I suppose,' said the dwarf, turning briskly to his legal friend, 'that Mr Swiveller enters upon his duties at once? It's Monday morning.'

'At once, if you please, sir, by all means,' returned Brass.

'Miss Sally will teach him law, the delightful study of the law,' said Quilp; 'she'll be his guide, his friend, his companion, his Blackstone, his Coke upon Littleton, his Young Lawyer's Best Companion.'

'He is exceedingly eloquent,' said Brass, like a man abstracted, and looking at the roofs of the opposite houses, with his hands in his pockets; 'he has an extraordinary flow of language. Beautiful, really.'

'With Miss Sally,' Quilp went on, 'and the beautiful fictions of the law, his days will pass like minutes. Those charming creations of the poet, John Doe and Richard Roe, when they first dawn upon him, will open a new world for the enlargement of his mind and the improvement of his heart.'

'Oh, beautiful, beautiful! Beau-ti-ful indeed!' cried Brass. 'It's a treat to hear him!'

'Where will Mr Swiveller sit?' said Quilp, looking round.

'Why, we'll buy another stool, sir,' returned Brass. 'We hadn't any thoughts of having a gentleman with us, sir, until you were kind enough to suggest it, and our accommodation's not extensive. We'll look about for a second-hand stool, sir. In the meantime, if Mr Swiveller will take my seat, and try his hand at a fair copy of this ejectment, as I shall be out pretty well all the morning –' . . .

From *The Old Curiosity Shop* by Charles Dickens, 1841

A Hair on His Nose

John Reid, the burra sahib, was a large, forthright Aberdonian bachelor with penetrating blue eyes and a big nose. 'Welcome to Amritsar,' he said as he shook me warmly by the hand.

He had a questing, humorous personality, and I took to him instantly. He was eager to hear the latest gossip from Head Office in London, and as we talked I noticed that a long black hair had come to rest on his nose. Instinctively I leant across his desk. 'Excuse me, sir,' I said, 'but there's a hair on your nose.'

At the same moment as I seized the hair I realised to my consternation that it was growing. Instinct prompted me again. I plucked it out by the root. We stared at one another. 'I've always wanted to do that,' said John Reid, and laughed.

I joined in, though my heart was pounding. I could not believe what I had done within five minutes of meeting my new boss in his own office . . .

From *A Life to Remember* by William McQuilty, 1991

Taking Formal Possession

. . . Mr Swiveller shook off his despondency and assumed the cheerful ease of an irresponsible clerk.

As a means towards his composure and self-possession, he entered into a more minute examination of the office than he had yet had time to make; looked into the wig-box, the books, and ink-bottle; untied and inspected all the papers; carved a few devices on the table with the sharp blade of Mr Brass's penknife; and wrote his name on the inside of the wooden coal-scuttle. Having, as it were, taken formal possession of his clerkship in virtue of these proceedings, he opened the window and leaned negligently out of it until a beer-boy happened to pass, whom he commanded to set down his tray and to serve him with a pint of mild porter, which he drank upon the spot and promptly paid for, with the view of breaking ground for a system of future credit and opening a correspondence tending thereto, without loss of time. Then, three or four little boys dropped in, on legal errands from three or four attorneys of the Brass grade: whom Mr Swiveller received and dismissed with about as professional a manner, and as correct and comprehensive an understanding of their business, as would have been shown by a clown in a pantomime under similar circumstances. These things done and over, he got upon his stool again and tried his hand at drawing caricatures of Miss Brass with a pen and ink, whistling very cheerfully all the time.

From *The Old Curiosity Shop* by Charles Dickens, 1841

Four

THE LOOK OF
THE PLACE

Probably because most writers are more familiar with newspapers and old-fashioned publishing houses than with City solicitors or merchant bankers, and have grown up on a diet of Dickens, those offices that find their way into print tend to be dingy, decrepit places with dirty windows and scuffed carpets, in which every available surface is covered with cracked coffee cups and tottering mounds of bumph. The Dickensian office, often situated in what was once a private house, has a long and honourable pedigree: whether it will survive the open-plan and the 'paper-free' office, only time can tell. Certainly the look and the sounds of the office have changed beyond recognition since the days when John Moore or Anthony Powell first went to work. Even in publishing houses, self-contained and shabbily elegant rooms in which exhausted editors could snooze or recover from lunch or make endless private telephone calls have been replaced by an open or glassed-off corner of a desk-filled room the size of a football pitch; the clatter and chime of the typewriter has been replaced by the scuttle of the VDU, with its frigid winking eye, while the letter is being elbowed out by the fax; long-serving wooden desks, the drawers of which were replete with a familiar compost of rubber bands, paper-clips, toffees, bits of string, tins of shoe polish, apple cores and – beneath all this – unanswered or embarassing letters, have been chopped up and replaced with formica 'work stations'. All this makes for a diligent, hygienic and all too visible place of work, in which scheming and sloth and indiscretion – the spice in the suet of office life – are harder to come by than in the more private, more human world of the Dickensian office, and may have to be practised off-stage, to the detriment of office life in social if not in functional terms. Be that as it may, many of the props of office life are as familiar today as they were in the days of the Anglo-Bengalee Disinterested Loan and Life Assurance Company: the gleaming reception area, the shiny name-plate, the grave commissionaire, the immaculate receptionist – and, it may be, the rather less immaculate working conditions behind the shining facade.

A Large Brass Plate

The Anglo-Bengalee Disinterested Loan and Life Assurance Company started into existence one morning, not an Infant Institution, but a Grown-up Company running along at a great pace, and doing business right and left: with a 'branch' in a first floor over a tailor's at the West-end of the town, and main offices in a new street in the City, comprising the upper part of a spacious house resplendent in stucco and plate-glass, with wire blinds in all the windows, and 'Anglo-Bengalee' worked into the pattern of every one of them. On the door-post was painted again in large letters, 'Offices of the Anglo-Bengalee Disinterested Loan and Life Assurance Company,' and on the door was a large brass plate with the same inscription: always kept very bright, as courting inquiry; staring the City out of countenance after office hours on working days, and all day long on Sundays; and looking bolder than the Bank. Within, the offices were newly plastered, newly painted, newly papered, newly countered, newly floor-clothed, newly tabled, newly chaired, newly fitted up in every way, with goods that were substantial and expensive, and designed (like the company) to last. Business! Look at the green ledgers with red backs, like strong cricket-balls beaten flat; the court-guides, directories, day-books, almanacks, letter-boxes, weighing-machines for letters, rows of fire-buckets for dashing out a conflagration in its first spark, and saving the immense wealth in notes and bonds belonging to the company; look at the iron safes, the clock, the office seal – in its capacious self, security for anything. Solidity! Look at the massive blocks of marble in the chimney-pieces, and the gorgeous parapet on the top of the house! Publicity! Why, Anglo-Bengalee Disinterested Loan and Life Assurance Company is painted on the very coal-scuttles. It is repeated at every turn until the eyes are dazzled with it, and the head is giddy. It is engraved upon the top of all the letter paper, and it makes a scroll-work round the seal, and it shines out of the porter's buttons, and it is repeated twenty times in every circular and public notice wherein one David Crimple, Esquire, Secretary and resident Director, takes the liberty of inviting your attention to the accompanying statement of the advantages offered by the Anglo-Bengalee Disinterested Loan and Life Assurance Company: and fully proves to you that any connexion on your part with that establishment must result in a perpetual Christmas Box and constantly increasing Bonus to yourself, and that nobody can run any risk by the transaction except the office, which, in its great liberality, is pretty sure to lose. And this, David Crimple, Esquire, submits to you (and the odds are heavy you believe him), is the best guarantee that can reasonably be suggested by the Board of Management for its permanence and stability.

This gentleman's name, by the way, had been originally Crimp; but as the word was susceptible of an awkward construction and might be misrepresented, he had altered it to Crimple.

Lest with all these proofs and confirmations, any man should be suspicious of the Anglo-Bengalee Disinterested Loan and Life Assurance Company; should doubt in tiger, cab, or person, Tigg Montague, Esquire, (of Pall Mall and Bengal), or any other name in the imaginative List of Directors; there was a porter on the premises – a wonderful creature, in a vast red waistcoat and a short-tailed pepper-and-salt coat – who carried more conviction to the minds of sceptics than the whole establishment without him. No confidences existed between him and the Directorship; nobody knew where he had served last; no character or explanation had been given or required. No questions had been asked on either side. This mysterious being, relying solely on his figure, had applied for the situation, and had been instantly engaged on his own terms. They were high; but he knew, doubtless, that no man could carry such an extent of waistcoat as himself, and felt the full value of his capacity to such an institution. When he sat upon a seat erected for him in a corner of the office, with his glazed hat hanging on a peg over his head, it was impossible to doubt the respectability of the concern. It went on doubling itself with every square inch of his red waistcoat until, like the problem of the nails in the horse's shoes, the total became enormous. People had been known to apply to effect an insurance on their lives for a thousand pounds, and looking at him, to beg, before the form of proposal was filled up, that it might be made two. And yet he was not a giant. His coat was rather small than otherwise. The whole charm was in his waistcoat. Respectability, competence, property in Bengal or anywhere else, responsibility to any amount on the part of the company that employed him, were all expressed in that one garment.

Rival offices had endeavoured to lure him away; Lombard Street itself had beckoned to him; rich companies had whispered 'Be a Beadle!' but he still continued faithful to the Anglo-Bengalee. Whether he was a deep rogue, or a stately simpleton, it was impossible to make out, but he appeared to believe in the Anglo-Bengalee. He was grave with imaginary cares of office; and having nothing whatever to do, and something less to take care of, would look as if the pressure of his numerous duties, and a sense of the treasure in the company's strong-room, made him a solemn and a thoughtful man.

As the cabriolet drove up to the door, this officer appeared bareheaded on the pavement, crying aloud 'Room for the chairman, room for the chairman, if you please!' much to the admiration of the bystanders, who, it is needless to say, had their attention directed to the Anglo-Bengalee Company thenceforth, by that means. Mr Tigg leaped gracefully out, followed by the Managing Director (who was by this time very distant and respectful), and ascended the stairs, still preceded by the porter: who cried as he went, 'By your leave there! by your leave! The Chairman of the Board, Gentle-MEN!' In like manner, but in a still more stentorian voice, he ushered the chairman through the public office, where some humble clients were transacting business, into an awful chamber, labelled Board-room: the door of which sanctuary immediately closed, and screened the great capitalist from vulgar eyes.

The board-room had a Turkey carpet in it, a sideboard, a portrait of Tigg Montague, Esquire, as chairman; a very imposing chair of office, garnished with an ivory hammer and a little hand-bell; and a long-table, set out at intervals with sheets of blotting-paper, foolscap, clean pens, and ink-stands. The chairman having taken his seat with great solemnity, the secretary supported him on his right hand, and the porter stood bolt upright behind them, forming a warm background of waistcoat. This was the board; everything else being a light-hearted little fiction.

From *Martin Chuzzlewit* by Charles Dickens, 1844

The Lair of Newby Senior

My father's office was on the first floor. It was at the back of the house overlooking what had been the garden until Mr Lane in an orgy of expansion had had it built over to provide more space for the business. It was a tall, narrow, rather gloomy chamber like a drawing by Phiz in *A Christmas Carol*. Originally it had probably been a dressing-room; leading off it was a powder closet to which one descended by a pair of steps. In the window seat there was a concealed wash basin made of lead, with brass taps that had been polished by so many generations of charwomen that they bore only a vestigial resemblance to taps at all.

In one corner was what my father described as 'my portable desk'. It was really a mahogany chest with brass-bound corners which could be opened out into a sloping desk. It was portable in the sense that it had probably been made originally to be carried on some African's noddle on safari. In it he kept old fixture cards which showed the breadth of his sporting interests before he took up rowing: Rugby football, cross-country running, boxing, swimming, wrestling and, of course, weight-lifting.

[83]

There were three pictures on the walls. One, a photograph of Lord Roberts of Kandahar, 'Bobs' as my father called him, wearing a funny hat without a brim and looking angry on the rifle ranges at Bisley; the second a coloured reproduction of a rococo interior with a riot of cardinals at table 'Drinking the Health of the Chef in Moët et Chandon'; and the third, framed instructions for 'The Prevention of Fire in Private Residences', with an injunction under the heading GAS, 'In the event of a leak send for the gas fitter and watch him carefully as he will sometimes seek for an escape with a light – and may find it at the risk of blowing up the building and all it contains!'

There was little room to move in my father's room, except to the window with its wash basin and to the roll-topped desk at which my father sat, for the whole floor was piled deep with newspapers. He kept every copy of the *Observer* and the *Morning Post* as they were published. In the cellars below they were piled high in the transepts, going back with their prophecies of doom and their sudden fits of optimism that were invariably wrong to a period infinitely remote, before 1914. What hedged him in here in his office were the editions of the last five years or so. 'I remember reading something about it,' he used to say when confronted with some topic that interested him and in the succeeding weeks he could be found, bent double, grunting as he untied the careful knot with which he had secured a bundle twenty years before, in search of the quotation in question. To my knowledge he never succeeded in finding what he was looking for, but at any rate he always found something else of interest that tended to deflect him from his original course.

From *Something Wholesale* by Eric Newby, 1962

An Auctioneer's Office . . .

The office stood in the High Street, quite close to Tudor House; by squinting sideways you could still see Double Alley out of its big plate-glass window.

It needed a coat of paint outside and a thoroughly good clean-up inside. It was shabby with the shabbiness of enormous respectability. A coat of paint might have suggested that it needed (like a tart) to advertise its presence. Such a notion would have been abhorrent to my uncle. As for cleaning it within, there were documents and shelves of books on which the dust had lain since 1750. In the course of a spring-clean papers would be disturbed, books no doubt would be mislaid, it would be difficult to find things afterwards. That notion was abhorrent to my uncle also.

If the place was drab and dusty, then the very drabness and dustiness were earnests of its integrity. Cheapjacks and bucket-shops, no doubt, had to look smart; we could afford to be shabby, as a gentleman can afford to wear shabby clothes.

Although the building was large, with plenty of rooms to spare on the first and second floors, everybody who worked there crowded together on the ground floor. This was either because nobody had ever been able to face the task of clearing the junk from the upstairs rooms or because none of the partners would move up there for fear of being left out of whatever was going on. Instead my uncle and his two partners sat together in a very small office so full of maps and papers that if a fat farmer should visit them there was literally no room to turn round.

A slightly bigger office – the one with the plate-glass window – accommodated the articled clerks, who perched like monkeys on high stools at a long polished desk. In a corner of this room, hidden away and surrounded by a sort of barricade, as if we were ashamed of them (as indeed so old-fashioned a firm might be), reposed our only typewriter and an astonishingly pretty typist.

The walls of this office – and indeed of every room in the building – were lined with books: books in red morocco bindings, several thousand of them, which contained the 'Particulars of Sale' of every property that had passed through the firm's hands – almost every dwelling-house, in fact, every farm, smallholding, shop, pub, orchard, and meadow within six miles of Elmbury. From these dreary-looking books, if you shook off the dust and opened them at random, sometimes there would leap out at you names that were pieces of poetry: the ancient country names of wood and field; names like Poppies' Parlour, Salley Furlong, Coneygree, Hungry Harbour, Merry-come-Sorrow.

There were other books, rows of great ledgers, which contained a record of all the firm's transactions since its foundation in 1750. If somebody could have translated the contents of those books into terms of flesh-and-blood – of human prosperity and human catastrophe – he would have been able to read the complete social history of a county during a period of one and a half centuries. Indeed, he would have found, within the stout leather covers of those books, a microcosm of English life and history . . .

From *Portrait of Elmbury* by John Moore, 1945

... and that of a Private Eye

I had an office in the Cahuenga Building, sixth floor, two small rooms at the back. One I left open for a patient client to sit in, if I had a patient client. There was a buzzer on the door which I could switch on and off from my private thinking parlour.

I looked into the reception-room. It was empty of everything but the smell of dust. I threw up another window, unlocked the communicating door and went into the room beyond. Three hard chairs and a swivel chair, a flat desk with a glass top, five green filing-cases, three of them full of nothing, a calendar and a framed licence bond on the wall, a phone, a washbowl in a stained wood cupboard, a hat-rack, a carpet that was just something on the floor, and two open windows with net curtains that puckered in and out like the lips of a toothless old man sleeping.

The same stuff I had had last year, and the year before that. Not beautiful, not gay, but better than a tent on the beach.

From *The High Window* by Raymond Chandler, 1943

Judkins & Judkins

The offices of Judkins & Judkins were in one of the Bloomsbury squares. The rooms were spacious, with good mouldings and first-rate door-knobs of the period. Hugh's room was the smaller half of what had been designed originally as the drawing-room. It was divided from Bernard's sphere of influence by folding-doors which were kept for ever bolted. The effect of this was that if anyone spoke louder than a conversational murmur they could be overheard on the farther side of the partition. Hugh used to complain about this often; but it gave him an opportunity for seeing that Bernard arranged nothing behind his back. On the whole he preferred the risk of Bernard getting wind of his own plans to foregoing the advantage of hearing what his brother spoke in any angry or excited moment. Bernard spent most of the day dozing or conning the weekly papers, so that the gain was almost always to Hugh, who had too constant a stream of visitors for Bernard to keep track of them even if he had felt inclined to do so.

From *What's Become of Waring?* by Anthony Powell, 1939

More of the Same

Their office, a room with fine cornices overlooking a courtyard, had once been someone's back dining-room and was divided by folding doors from the premises of an archaeological society where almost complete silence reigned. Peter and Emmeline each had roll-top desks of their own, hers by the window, his under the green glare of a lamp he hardly ever turned off. Their secretary occupied a deal table half into the fireplace; she had wedged the legs with blotting-paper but when her violence became excessive they would both look up and wince. There were maps stuck over with flags (to denote the position of clients), their own posters, three shelves of files, a small safe of which only the secretary could remember the combination, a hat-rack, a cupboard for tea-cups and sherry. Two swivel chairs were provided for clients, who could thus face either Peter or Emmeline...

From *To the North* by Elizabeth Bowen, 1932

Peter Simple's Dwelling Place

The years passed in my tiny office on the third floor; for four days a week, week after week, allowing for the six weeks' annual holiday and rare absences through illness, I sat at the same desk while Claudie sat at the same desk opposite me. Behind me was the door which led to the fire-escape, marked 'Fire Escape' in large red letters. It had a complicated locking system which in the case of fire might have caused trouble; the door was as difficult to close as it was to open, and sometimes in windy weather it would swing wide, leaving my back exposed to the elements and my papers blowing around the room. Our desks often tended, through the vibration of Claudie's vigorous typing, to move together, causing my own desk to vibrate with increasing force until I invariably said, in the muttering tone she imitated so well, 'I think we've got a bit of osmosis'. Apart from the desks with their trays and blotters, there was little furniture. There were two small tables, one holding a file of the *Telegraph*, the other a file of *The Times*. There was a dull green filing-cabinet with four drawers. One contained very little except the remains of Miss Thompson's filing system with its neat, pink cards, virtually abandoned when she left in 1957, a mouldering monument of efficiency which I kept for superstitious reasons; it was of no practical use whatever. Claudie's own filing system was simple: she put almost all correspondence into the waste-paper basket as soon as she had answered it, retaining in a green folder, for a few weeks only, such letters which she thought interesting or important, then putting most of these into the waste-paper basket in turn. In our early days I used sometimes to complain about this system; but after a time I became reconciled to it. After all, in its rough and ready way it did prevent the room from filling up entirely with waste-paper.

The two middle drawers of the filing cabinet were largely empty except for my 'personal files' and details of publications; the lowest and largest drawer contained a pair of Claudie's shoes, a carton of cigarettes and one or two other personal possessions such as unwanted Christmas presents of talcum powder or children's books. It also contained a bottle of vodka with only a teaspoonful of liquid in it, together with a small cheap drinking-glass, relics of some forgotten party. As with the column in general and everything that concerned it, there was a strong feeling of immemorial custom about this filing cabinet and its contents. If Claudie ever felt any inclination to clear it out, and I doubt if she did, she never acted upon it. We understood each other.

From *The Dubious Codicil* by Michael Wharton, 1990

The Chatter of Machines

Quiet bell-sounds punctured the rubbery office air as typing and duplicating machines chattered to and fro: and underneath and away, like the pounding of engine-room pistons, a muffled thumping of deep motor traffic blotted up any edges of silence. A light smell arose from paper, ribbon-ink, pencils, lubricating oil and from the extraordinary metal presence, like the slow thick taste of tin on the tongue, of the filing cabinets.

From *The Last Hours of Sandra Lee* by William Sansom, 1961

The Morning Noise

The morning noise of the office took over. I remember it now in these sweet waking hours of the night that I still treasure so much, here far away from the scene of my life in those days, far away in time.

The morning clattered on, with the sound of Ivy's typewriter and Cathy the book-keeper's muttering, the sound of all our shoes on the bare boards of the office floor and the rattle of cups as one of us made the tea. There was also the usual visit of Patrick's wife, Mabel, who that morning had found someone other than me to make a scene about, and whose noise-creating was indirect, consisting of the efforts of the others to reason her out of her fit. The outside telephone shrilled and the intercom buzzed. Ivy responded superciliously.

'Mr York is in a meeting. May I take a message?' – 'Mr Ullswater is out of London for a few days. Who is calling? Can you spell that name, please?' (Ivy's 'n's sounded 'd' so that 'name' sounded like 'dame') – 'Mrs Hawkins is in a meeting. Oh, I don't know when she'll be free, would you like to try again?' – 'I'm afraid that Mrs Hawkins . . .'

From *A Far Cry from Kensington* by Muriel Spark, 1989

Familiar Noises

The noises were all familiar ones to him: the low background hum of the air conditioning, the fast rhythmic clattering of typewriters being used by properly trained girls and the sporadic pecking of machines being handled by men or novices, the murmur of private conversations and the louder voices of those who were talking business – 'Have you finished with the book of words, Amanda light of my heart?' Clerks who were crossing the central aisle to the filing cabinets or back again felt obliged as they did so to sing snatches of dated songs. The male ones, that was: the women did not sing, but they added to the medley by sliding back the drawers of the filing cabinets with unnecessary force, as women in Gryce's experience always did. (One or two of them, though, were quite presentable – something to bear in mind if there was nothing doing with Miss Divorce.)

From *Office Life* by Keith Waterhouse, 1978

An Old-fashioned Publishing House

The premises at 3 Henrietta Street to which young writers were to be lured were not outwardly inviting. The front door, kept open during the day, gave on to a shabby uncarpeted passage with a staircase at the end. On the left was another door inscribed with the name of the firm; possibly followed by the word ENQUIRIES, though I am not sure about that. If so, the hope was not one to build on. Within stood simply the trade-counter (where booksellers' representatives collected copies from publishers' stock), no focus beyond that barrier existing to which an enquiry might specifically be directed; nor, for that matter, was any one individual responsible for answering the telephone.

Three or four breezy young men, invoice clerks, would be engaged in caustic conversation among themselves at their long high desk on the far side of the room, and their attention had to be caught. That was not always easy. Out of sight to the right lay the (one-man) packing-department, from which a Dickensian ancient kept up a fusillade of cockney banter with the invoice clerks, with whom he was perpetually at war.

In theory all arrivals at Duckworth's came to this bar of judgment: authors; visiting American publishers; literary agents; book-jacket designers; travellers in printing, binding, papermaking; sellers of advertising space; not least, the steady flow of the mentally deranged, whose routine was – no doubt still is – to call regularly on publishers. If clients had to wait, there was nowhere for them to sit. Later a kind of hutch was constructed between counter, wall, and window, furnished with a couple of hard chairs. Writers familiar with the severities of ground-floor conditions would not bother to be announced on the house-telephone (a concession to modernity), but come straight up to the room of whomever they wanted to see.

On the first floor, a small room at the top of the stairs was occupied by Balston. Cramped, austere, there was just room for two visitors. Balston's room overlooked Henrietta Street, where it approached the southwest corner of Covent Garden. The considerably larger room next door, with a small view of the market, was shared by Gerald Duckworth, and, when on duty, Milsted. Their roll-top desks were set back to back, so that each had a window from which to watch what was happening outside, but they were hidden from each other by a towering wall of dust-covered books, accumulated on the space between since the foundation of the firm. More books and manuscripts, usually a newspaper or two, littered the floor round Gerald Duckworth's seat, beside which, for the use of a potential caller, stood an armchair in the last stages of decomposition. Dust was everywhere, disorder infinite.

Order was only a little more apparent in the room behind this one (its outlook onto the backs of houses), occupied by Lewis and myself. Lewis's roll-top desk faced the door, but he could not see who entered without craning round a stack similar to that set between the two partners; in this case, recently published books, proofs of books, 'dummies' of books, estimates, invoices, letters currently to be considered; everything else that could find no other place to rest than the top of the desk.

Further into the room stood my own smaller (non-roll-top) desk, beside it another crumbling armchair, unearthed from some cubby-hole, after energetic efforts on my part, and installed – not without all opposition – for visitors. Formerly authors had been required to stand in the presence of their publisher's staff.

This room was lined from floor to ceiling with the dust-wrapped file-copies of the firm's output since the beginning; a record not too scrupulously kept over the years. Beyond the office in which Lewis and I sat was a tiny closet, where a succession of secretary-typists lived out their usually disgruntled being.

Some aspirants to the publishing profession are, at the opening of their career, charged to enact a season in the packing-department. I have always regretted no such obligation was imposed on me, since everyone whose life is concerned with books is likely to spend a good deal of time tying up parcels of them, an art I have never properly mastered. Professional instruction would have been invaluable.

As it was I began my novitiate writing invoices (for which I showed little talent), sitting on one of those high office stools that must have been in the mind of William Johnson Cory, when, in the *Eton Boating Song*, he wrote of weather that tempted their abandonment. I would indite invoices in the morning; in the afternoon ascend to the first-floor, there to learn about seeing books through the press; composing ads; reading manuscripts; dealing with authors and agents; all the things that make up a publisher's day.

From *Messengers of Day* by Anthony Powell, 1978

The Old and the New

When I walked into Room 6 of the New Corridor of the *Manchester Guardian* in Cross Street on a January morning in 1957, to start work as virtual, though not titular, women's page editor, it was as quiet as a chapel on a weekday; not a soul within shouting distance. There was, typically, no one to welcome me, yet, also typically, a silent welcome had been organized. On my desk there was a new blotting pad, a portable typewriter, a paste pot and a beautiful pair of long scissors. When in March, 1969, I took my place on the *Guardian* floor of Thomson House, Gray's Inn Road, London, I squeezed into a small desk interlocking with a dozen or so others, with hardly two feet of space between each. Typewriters clacked fore and aft, telephones were seldom silent, everyone became involved in everyone's conversations. The noise, the lack of space, natural light and air, and above all, of privacy, appalled me. Yet after a year I knew I had no wish to go back to my splendid isolation. I, like the *Guardian*, had been dragged protesting into a new era.

From *Forgetting's No Excuse* by Mary Stott, 1989

Five

RITUAL, GOSSIP AND
THE SOCIAL WHIRL

New arrivals soon discover that offices – like schools or regiments or religious institutions – are complicated, hierarchical institutions in which ritual, ceremony and the dread team spirit have important parts to play, in which grizzled or balding equivalents of school prefects mutter about 'pulling one's weight' and much store is set on such symbols of status as parking spaces, carpets, china tea as opposed to Typhoo and porcelain to drain it from as opposed to a paper cup; and that is often the social aspect of office life, rather than the work itself, that makes it tolerable and even, at times, exciting and enjoyable. Though glad to be shot of the Hong Kong and Shanghai Bank after his two-year stint at a desk, P. G. Wodehouse realised this better than anyone else, and no one has written about it with greater sympathy and affection. Not only do routine and ritual make the humdrum palatable: they also make more feasible that suspension of disbelief without which it is hard to survive, let alone flourish. Some of us, on the other hand – whether through timidity or scepticism, or a solitary disposition – may find the whole business oppressive, claustrophobic and frequently absurd: those who flout or ignore the rules may find themselves spurned or left behind – as I found to my cost when, as an over-rational advertising trainee, I tried to read Dickens under my desk rather than join in games of office cricket. And the sense of team spirit, of having a face that fits, may spill over into one's private life, as Martyn Goff's homosexual youngest director discovered when his boss tried to pressurise him into marriage for the good of his career. At a more benign, everyday level, familiar jokes and customs, and the addictive, illicit delights of gossip and scandal oil the wheels and contribute to the sense of the office as a village, the misdeeds and improprieties of whose inhabitants may loom far larger in our lives than those we leave at home: only the most austere and dedicated among us will avert the gaze when a colleague, carefully closing the door behind him, tiptoes towards us, eyes bulging with excitement, one finger raised to his lips, with the news ('For God's sake don't pass it on') that X is having an affair with Y and has been spotted with her in the stationery cupboard, or that A is about to be given the sack. Many office workers are congenitally indiscreet, blurting out secrets over a pint in the pub and heedlessly ignoring injunctions to silence: news of impending scandals or sackings may slip out via the managing director's secretary, a note on a desk read upside-down, mutterings in the lavatories or under-employed telephonists filling in the long hours listening in to the powers – that – be as they go about their business. All this makes for a vivid if sometimes nerve-racking social life: and, like Sinclair Lewis's Mr Wrenn – who gives up his job in a mood of restless defiance to see something of the world beyond – those of us who find ourselves on the outside looking in may miss it, in some ways, more than we thought.

Mike Grows Fond of the Bank

. . . Mike, as day succeeded day, began to grow accustomed to the life of the bank, and to find that it had its pleasant side after all. Whenever a number of people are working at the same thing, even though that thing is not perhaps what they would have chosen as an object in life, if left to themselves, there is bound to exist an atmosphere of good-fellowship; something akin to, though a hundred times weaker than, the public school spirit. Such a community lacks the main motive of the public school spirit, which is pride in the school and its achievements. Nobody can be proud of the achievements of a bank. When the business of arranging a new Japanese loan was given to the New Asiatic Bank, its employees did not stand on stools, and cheer. On the contrary, they thought of the extra work it would involve; and they cursed a good deal, though there was no denying that it was a big thing for the bank – not unlike winning the Ashburton would be to a school. There is a cold impersonality about a bank. A school is a living thing.

Setting aside this important difference, there was a good deal of the public school about the New Asiatic Bank. The heads of departments were not quite so autocratic as masters, and one was treated more on a grown-up scale, as man to man; but, nevertheless, there remained a distinct flavour of a school republic. Most of the men in the bank, with the exception of certain hard-headed Scotch youths drafted in from other establishments in the City, were old public school men. Mike found two Old Wrykinians in the first week. Neither was well known to him. They had left in his second year in the team. But it was pleasant to have them about, and to feel that they had been educated at the right place.

As far as Mike's personal comfort went, the presence of these two Wrykinians was very much for the good. Both of them knew all about his cricket, and they spread the news. The New Asiatic Bank, like most London banks, was keen on sport, and happened to possess a cricket team which could make a good game with most of the second-rank clubs. The disappearance to the East of two of the best bats of the previous season caused Mike's advent to be hailed with a good deal of enthusiasm. Mike was a county man. He had only played once for his county, it was true, but that did not matter. He had passed the barrier which separates the second-class bat from the first-class, and the bank welcomed him with awe. County men did not come their way every day.

Mike did not like being in the bank, considered in the light of a career. But he bore no grudge against the inmates of the bank, such as he had borne against the inmates of Sedleigh. He had looked on the latter as bound up with the school, and, consequently, enemies. His fellow workers in the bank he regarded as companions in misfortune. They were all in the same boat together. There were men from Tonbridge, Dulwich, Bedford, St Paul's, and a dozen other schools. One or two of them he knew by repute from the pages of Wisden. Bannister, his cheerful predecessor in the Postage Department, was the Bannister, he recollected now, who had played for Geddington against Wrykyn in his second year in the Wrykyn team. Munroe, the big man in the Fixed Deposits, he remembered as leader of the Ripton pack. Every day brought fresh discoveries of this sort, and each made Mike more reconciled to his lot. They were a pleasant set of fellows in the New Asiatic Bank, and but for the dreary outlook which the future held – for Mike, unlike most of his fellow workers, was not attracted by the idea of a life in the East – he would have been very fairly content.

The hostility of Mr Bickersdyke was a slight drawback. Psmith had developed a habit of taking Mike with him to the club of an evening; and this did not do anything towards wiping out of the manager's mind the recollection of his former passage of arms with the Old Wrykinian. The glass remaining Set Fair as far as Mr Rossiter's approval was concerned, Mike was enabled to keep off the managerial carpet to a great extent; but twice, when he posted letters without going through the preliminary formality of stamping them, Mr Bickersdyke had opportunities of which he availed himself. But for these incidents life was fairly enjoyable. Owing to Psmith's benevolent efforts, the Postage Department became quite a happy family, and ex-occupants of the postage desk, Bannister especially, were amazed at the change that had come over Mr Rossiter. He no longer darted from his lair like a pouncing panther. To report his subordinates to the manager seemed now to be a lost art with him. The sight of Psmith and Mr Rossiter proceeding high and disposedly to a mutual lunch became quite common, and ceased to excite remark.

'By kindness,' said Psmith to Mike, after one of these expeditions. 'By tact and kindness. That is how it is done. I do not despair of training Comrade Rossiter one of these days to jump through paper hoops.'

So that, altogether, Mike's life in the bank had become very fairly pleasant . . .

By this time Mike had grown so used to his work that he could tell to within five minutes when a rush would come; and he was able to spend a good deal of his time reading a surreptitious novel behind a pile of ledgers, or down in the tea-room. The New Asiatic Bank supplied tea to its employees. In quality it was bad, and the bread-and-butter associated with it was worse. But it had the merit of giving one an excuse for being away from one's desk . . .

Life in a bank is at its pleasantest in the winter. When all the world outside is dark and damp and cold, the light and warmth of the place are comforting. There is a pleasant air of solidity about the interior of a bank. The green shaded lamps look cosy. And, the outside world offering so few attractions, the worker, perched on his stool, feels that he is not so badly off after all. It is when the days are long and the sun beats hot on the pavement, and everything shouts to him how splendid it is out in the country, that he begins to grow restless.

Mike, except for a fortnight at the beginning of his career in the New Asiatic Bank, had not had to stand the test of sunshine. At present, the weather being cold and dismal, he was almost entirely contented. Now that he had got into the swing of his work, the days passed very quickly; and with his life after office-hours he had no fault to find at all.

His life was very regular. He would arrive in the morning just in time to sign his name in the attendance-book before it was removed to the accountant's room. That was at ten o'clock. From ten to eleven he would potter. There was nothing going on at that time in his department, and Mr Waller seemed to take it for granted that he should stroll off to the Postage Department and talk to Psmith, who had generally some fresh grievance against the ring-wearing Bristow to air. From eleven to half past twelve he would put in a little gentle work. Lunch, unless there was a rush of business or Mr Waller happened to suffer from a spasm of conscientiousness, could be spun out from half past twelve to two. More work from two till half past three. From half past three till half past four tea in the tea-room, with a novel. And from half past four till five either a little more work or more pottering, according to whether there was any work to do or not. It was by no means an unpleasant mode of spending a late January day.

From *Psmith in the City* by P. G. Wodehouse, 1910

The Muse of Romance

There is plenty of romance in business. Fine, large, meaningless, general terms like romance and business can always be related. They take the place of thinking, and are highly useful to optimists and lecturers.

But in the world of business there is a bewildered new Muse of Romance, who is clad not in silvery tissue of dreams, but in a neat blue suit that won't grow too shiny under the sleeves.

Adventure now, with Una, in the world of business; of offices and jobs and tired, ordinary people who know such reality of romance as your masquerading earl, your shoddy Broadway actress, or your rosily amorous dairymaid could never imagine. The youths of poetry and of the modern motor-car fiction make a long diversion of love; while the sleezy-coated office-man who surprises a look of humanness in the weary eyes of the office-woman, knows that he must compress all the wonder of madness into five minutes, because the Chief is prowling about, glancing meaningly at the little signs that declare, 'Your time is your employer's money; don't steal it.'

A world is this whose noblest vista is composed of desks and type-writers, filing-cases and insurance calendars, telephones, and the bald heads of men who believe dreams to be idiotic. Here, no galleon breasts the sky-line; no explorer in evening clothes makes love to an heiress. Here ride no rollicking cowboys, nor heroes of the great European war. It is a world whose crises you cannot comprehend unless you have learned that the difference between a 2-A pencil and a 2-B pencil is at least equal to the contrast between London and Tibet; unless you understand why a normally self-controlled young woman may have a week of tragic discomfort because she is using a billing-machine instead of her ordinary correspondence typewriter. The shifting of the water-cooler from the front office to the packing-room may be an epochal event to a copyist who apparently has no human existence beyond bending over a clacking typewriter, who seems to have no home, no family, no loves; in whom all pride and wonder of life and all transforming drama seem to be satisfied by the possession of a new V-necked blouse. The moving of the water-cooler may mean that she must now pass the sentinel office-manager; that therefore she no longer dares break the incredible monotony by expeditions to get glasses of water. As a consequence she gives up the office and marries unhappily.

A vast, competent, largely useless cosmos of offices. It spends much energy in causing advertisements of beer and chewing-gum and union suits and pot-cleansers to spread over the whole landscape. It marches out ponderous battalions to sell a brass pin. It evokes shoes that are uncomfortable, hideous, and perishable, and touchingly hopes that all women will aid the cause of good business by wearing them. It turns noble valleys into fields for pickles. It compels men whom it has never seen to toil in distant factories and produce useless wares, which are never actually brought into the office, but which it nevertheless sells to the heathen in the Solomon Islands in exchange for commodities whose very names it does not know; and in order to perform this miracle of transmutation it keeps stenographers so busy that they change from dewy girls into tight-lipped spinsters before they discover life.

The reason for it all, nobody who is actually engaged in it can tell you, except the bosses, who believe that these sacred rites of composing dull letters and solemnly filing them away are observed in order that they may buy the large automobiles in which they do not have time to take the air. Efficiency of production they have learned; efficiency of life they still consider an effeminate hobby.

An unreasonable world, sacrificing bird-song and tranquil dusk and high golden noons to selling junk – yet it rules us. And life lives there. The office is filled with thrills of love and distrust and ambition. Each alley between desks quivers with secret romance as ceaselessly as a battle-trench, or a lane in Normandy.

From *The Job* by Sinclair Lewis, 1917

Settling In

The settling-in period was always enjoyable for Gryce. It was what he most looked forward to when changing billets.

He acquired his own beaker, a Silver Jubilee remnant which young Thelma found for him in a nearby Oxfam shop. He learned that as well as the paper towels and hot-air machine in the men's room, there was a further option in the way of personal hand towels which were changed each Wednesday. He would wait until he had his own desk before signing for a personal hand towel.

He got to know something about his colleagues and their little foibles. Grant-Peignton picked his nose with his little finger. Seeds jingled change. Beazley, Mrs Rashman and Pam took saccharine in their coffee. Ardagh often brushed back the lock of hair that, together with his small moustache, made him look like Hitler.

The work of the department, it came as no surprise to Gryce, could easily have been done by four people or two at a push. Most of it seemed to fall, and none too heavily, on the shoulders of Seeds, Beazley and Grant-Peignton, with Copeland supervising. The others, apart from an hour or so's chores which they spread out over the day, were left pretty well to their own devices.

They wrote letters and filled in crosswords. After lunch each day a small group composed of Pam, Ardagh and the Penney twins did the *Evening Standard* word game on a competitive basis, the loser to buy the next day's paper. The Penney twins were also the departmental representatives of the seventh floor football pools syndicate, another example of over-manning if you wanted Gryce's opinion, since the operation for the entire floor could easily have been handled by one person. The Penney twins collected the football pool money on Tuesday mornings. They took Gryce aside and explained that while it would not be fair on the others to ask him to join the syndicate in the middle of the season, an invitation would certainly be extended to him at the appropriate time. Gryce quite understood this.

From *Office Life* by Keith Waterhouse, 1978

Failing to Play the Game

On the day of my elevation the personnel officer led me along a brightly-lit corridor on the second floor, and into the small cluster of rooms that formed the production department. As he flung open the teak door I was reassured – but not entirely surprised – by the familiar spectacle of Robert's bowling arm in action: only this time, instead of bowling an imaginary ball, he sent a knot of office paper flashing down the room towards a purple-featured man in his forties, with tight, well-oiled curls, a bright red bow tie and the bunched and weaving stance of a boxer, who was standing in front of an olive-coloured wastepaper basket with a ruler in his hand with which he lashed out at the paper ball, sending it spinning over the head of the fielder, a grizzled, elderly man with a tattoo on his right forearm. As I quickly discovered, cricket played an important part in the life of the production department; but at the sight of a newcomer they courteously broke off the game – scribbling the score on a pad of paper for future reference – and the man with the purple face hurried forward to explain what the work involved, and what was expected of me . . .

Although advertising men are eager to be thought of as tireless human dynamos, fizzing with ideas as they pace up and down the office waving their hands in the air, or burning the midnight oil, black coffee to hand and collar buttons undone, while the rest of the world settles down to a TV dinner, life in our department at least was torpid to a degree. Much of the morning in particular was given over to playing office cricket; and although the pitch ran right in front of my desk, so that the ball often landed in my In Tray or flew angrily over my head like a great white wasp, I invariably waived my turn at the wicket and sat instead behind my desk with a stuffed expression on my face, trying to look as though I were enjoying myself while wishing that they would let us have some peace and quiet so that I could concentrate on the book that lay open on my lap.

After a while I abandoned the pretence of being an appreciative spectator, wearing the kind of clip-on smile appropriate to a member of the royal family while watching a display of tribal dancing – and I would have had to be sports-mad to the point of lunacy to find the spectacle of Robert bowling a piece of crumpled memo paper at a middle-aged man with a ruler *that* compelling – and, bringing my book up on to the desk, settled down for a long and total immersion in *Nicholas Nickleby*. As I read greedily on about the doings of Lord Frederick Verisopht and Sir Mulberry Hawk, the thwack of ruler on paper ball and the eager cries of the cricketers faded into an agreeable background drone: this, I felt – swinging one leg over the arm of my chair – is what office life is all about. Hardly had I reached this point before the book was suddenly torn from my hand: my boss with the purple nose, risking life and limb as he strode across the pitch in the face of one of Robert's demon balls, stood glowering angrily down at me. This was not, he informed me – his voice atremble with indignation – a public library; if he found me reading again in office hours he would have no alternative but to – Overcome with emotion, he turned sharply about, seized the ruler from the warhorse, and subjected Robert's bowling to the most terrible punishment. How on earth was I to fill in the long hours? Should I carve my name on the desk instead, or write out the plots of Dickens's novels on the clean white sheet of blotting paper with which each desk was so thoughtfully provided?

From *Playing for Time* by Jeremy Lewis, 1987

The Importance of Routine

I was on the platform at Victoria last year, catching by chance a Commuter train. For some reason the train was, apparently, a different colour from usual, it was also made of aluminium. The Commuters didn't like it. They shifted and muttered together like old buffaloes at a water hole sensing something wrong. They refused to believe the porters that it was all right, and eventually a special announcement had to be made over the loudspeaker confirming, as it were, that their train was their train . . .

And the routes one takes to work or other regularly visited places. These are not necessarily the quickest or shortest, but we take them because we have always taken them. Not to take one of the usual routes causes considerable anxiety. I have often turned abruptly round in mid new route and scurried thankfully back to old route. If London were a jungle, our routes would be where they'd set traps for us – successfully.

All these habits – because that is what the repeated exercise of our jungle lore becomes – are of course useful. The point of habit is to remove from the area of decision as many more (or less) important functions as possible. If we clean our teeth at the same time every morning and evening we don't have to waste time wondering whether we have cleaned them or not, whether we should clean them, how often, and with what. Habit is an automatic pilot freeing the mind for anything else it cares to do.

But there is more to it than this. It is often actually pleasurable carrying out a habit – or can be. The worn paths enjoy being followed, as though nature, realising the importance of habit, had made its exercise rewarding. Because the maths master has made his joke about the eternal triangle two thousand times doesn't mean he won't make it with just as much pleasure the two thousand and first time.

It is this fact, that repetition can bring pleasure, which introduces a soothing element into office events. Since they are enjoyable just because they are repeated, the office worker can, contrary to, or as well as, what I said earlier, have a sense of rhythm. Not just the reappearance of the Christmas party, the annual accounts, the turning on of the central heating – to take some major rhythms. But minute rhythms like the slow breathing of the In Tray, emptying and filling, filling and emptying; every Tuesday a new towel in the Gentlemen's from Rent-a-Towel; the twice-weekly arrival of more stationery; the morning ritual of asking your secretary who's rung, and for her, the ritual of telling you.

From *The Office* by Jonathan Gathorne-Hardy, 1970

Reminders of Solidity

All around him were such reminders of solidity, continuity and flow. There were the Christmas decorations of the Tomlinsons, each year more tarnished. In the office Miss Menzies, his assistant (over whom he was 'head librarian': the department now had no librarian proper), had exactly eighteen 'business' outfits, a variety and number that had at first stupefied him, unused though he was to noticing women's clothes, but a number which in the end had formed part of the soothing pattern of his existence. Individual outfits faded and were replaced, but the number remained constant, one outfit for each day of the week until three weeks had passed and the cycle began again. In time he had grown to recognize the days of the week from these outfits. Their passing away, their conversion into rough clothes (impossible, though, to imagine Miss Menzies in rough clothes, and uncorseted), their disintegration, as he imagined, into dusters, were like the shedding of the leaves of his tree; her new garments were like the leaves of spring.

From *Mr Stone and the Knights Companion* by V. S. Naipaul, 1963

Techniques of Deception

I am very good with these techniques of deception, although I am not always able anymore to deceive myself (if I were, I would not know that, would I? Ha, ha). In fact, I am continually astonished by people in the company who do fall victim to their own (our own) propaganda. There are so many now who actually believe that what we do is really important. This happens not only to salesmen, who repeat their various sales pitches aloud so often that they acquire the logic and authority of a mumbo-jumbo creed, but to the shrewd, capable executives in top management, who have access to all data and ought to know better. It happens to people on my own level and lower. It happens to just about everybody in the company who graduated from a good business school with honors: these are uniformly the most competent and conscientious people in the company, and also the most gullible and naïve. Every time we launch a new advertising campaign, for example, people inside the company are the first ones to be taken in by it. Every time we introduce a new product, or an old product with a different cover, color, and name that we present as new, people inside the company are the first to rush to buy it – even when it's no good.

When salesmen and company spokesmen begin believing their own arguments, the result is not always bad, for they develop an outlook of loyalty, zeal, and conviction that is often remarkably persuasive in itself. It produces that kind of dedication and fanaticism that makes good citizens and good employees. When it happens to a person in my own department, however, the result can be disastrous, for he begins relying too heavily on what he now thinks is the truth and loses his talent for devising good lies. He is no longer convincing. It's exactly what happened to Holloway, the man in my own department who broke down (and is probably going to break down again soon).

'But it's true, don't you see?' he would argue softly to the salesmen, the secretaries, and even to me, with a knowing and indulgent smile, as though what he was saying ought to have been as obvious to everyone as it was to him. 'We *are* the best.' (The point he missed is that it didn't matter whether it was true or not; what mattered was what people *thought* was true.)

He is beginning to smile and argue that way again and to spend more time talking to us than we want to spend listening to him. My own wish when he is buttonholing me or bending the ear of someone else in my department is that he would hurry up and have his nervous breakdown already, if he is going to have one anyway, and get it – and himself – out of the way. He is the only one who talks to Martha, our typist who is going crazy, and she is the only one who listens to him without restlessness and irritation. She listens to him with great intensity because she is paying no attention to him at all.

Everyone grew impatient with him. And he lost his power to understand (as he is losing this power again) why the salesmen, who would come to him for solid proof to support their exaggerations and misrepresentations, turned skeptical, began to avoid him, and refused to depend on him any longer or even take him to lunch. He actually expected them to get by with only the 'truth.'

It's a wise person, I guess, who knows he's dumb, and an honest person who knows he's a liar. And it's a dumb person, I guess, who's convinced he is wise, I conclude to myself (wisely), as we wise grown-ups here at the company go gliding in and out all day long, scaring each other at our desks and cubicles and water coolers and trying to evade the people who frighten us. We come to work, have lunch, and go home. We goose-step in and goose-step out, change our partners and wander all about, sashay around for a pat on the head, and promenade home till we all drop dead. Really, I ask myself every now and then, depending on how well or poorly things are going with Green at the office or at home with my wife, or with my retarded son, or with my other son, or my daughter, or the colored maid, or the nurse for my retarded son, is this *all* there is for me to do? Is this really the *most* I can get from the few years left in this one life of mine?

And the answer I get, of course, is always . . . *Yes!*

From *Something Happened* by Joseph Heller, 1974

A Dependence on Repeated Jokes

The premises were opened at 7.30 in the morning by an old clerk called Haylett who wobbled in fast, lame and gouty, but always wearing a flower in his buttonhole. He was one of those gardeners of *The Waste Land*. He was satiny pink, fat and very bald and went about singing bits of music-hall songs or making up words. He then went over to the warehouse and let the workmen into the warehouse. One of these, a young, feeble-minded man, cross-eyed and strong, would lumber down to the safes and carry up a load of heavy ledgers which he set out on the various desks. Dust flew out of them. His name was Paul – he, like one of the carmen, who was known as Ninety, because it was the number of the house where he lived – had no surname. Paul lived with his mother and was very religious. When he had put down his ledgers, Paul would advance upon Mr Haylett and say his usual morning greeting in a toneless voice and unsmiling:

'Well, my venereal friend'.

To this the gay old Mr Haylett replied:

'Good morrow, good morrow, good morrow'. And add one of his made-up words: 'Hyjorico', and shake with laughter. Paul, who wore a heavy leather apron, lowered his head and looked murder at Mr Haylett, and went off on his bandy legs, waving his clenched fists dangerously.

At eight we office boys arrived and often saw this scene. The other boy whose name was Les Daulton had to teach me my job. He was a weak-voiced, fair creature, as simple as Paul and also famous for his comic mis-pronunciations. Offices – like my mother's shop in Kentish Town of the earlier generation – depend for their life on repeated jokes. Goods were often collected from Thameside quays: Daulton always called them 'Kways' and the clerks concentrated on getting him to say it. Daulton gave a simple smile. He knew he was a success. Once we had arrived Mr Haylett went to the W.C. in the basement where he sat smoking his first cigar and reading the paper...

From *A Cab at the Door* by V. S. Pritchett, 1968

Hard at Work

Miss Meteyard scrambled down leggily and followed Miss Rossiter to the typists' room.

This was a small, inconvenient cubicle, crowded at the moment to bursting-point. A plump girl in glasses, with head tilted back and brows twisted to keep the smoke of a cigarette out of her eyes, was rattling off the names of Derby runners on her type-writer, assisted by a bosom-friend who dictated the list from the columns of the *Morning Star*. A languid youth in shirt-sleeves was cutting the names of sweep-subscribers from a typed sheet, and twisting the papers into secretive little screws. A thin, eager young man, squatting on an upturned waste-paper basket, was turning over the flimsies in Miss Rossiter's tray and making sarcastic comments upon the copy to a bulky, dark youth in spectacles, immersed in a novel by P. G. Wodehouse and filching biscuits from a large tin. Draped against the door-posts and blocking the entrance to all comers, a girl and another young man, who seemed to be visitors from another department, were smoking gaspers and discusssing lawn-tennis.

From *Murder Must Advertise* by Dorothy L. Sayers, 1933

A Love of Small Things

—PETER: . . . For one thing, there's all the gossip. You've heard about the fuss Bee's making over her desk, I daresay. Apparently Betty Piggott has been having an affair with Leslie Elliott for *five years*. I suppose you'd call that trivial. But triviality depends on your point of view. I find it quite absorbing.

And then it's so dramatic. Do you remember when that little man with a beard scrambled onto a water tank or cupboard or wherever it was in the Ladies loo on the fifth floor? I thought I'd die of excitement. I will tell you one thing. I don't really *like* too much real life any more. I'm quite ready to admit it. In the office you get little dramas, little friendships, little loves and hates. With one or two additions which we won't go into, my entire emotional life is satisfied here.

—LAWRENCE: Yes, but this is a very small part of office life, isn't it?

—PETER: What do you mean small? It *is* office life. In fact for a great many people it is *life*. What seems to you small may be satisfying really deep needs.

For instance I am very easily bored. Bat squeaks of boredom go through me the whole time. In an office I can always leave, move on to some other subject, get away.

Another thing, I have to have an almost continuous flow of conversation. It doesn't really matter how superficial. Here everyone has the same terms of reference. That's extremely important. I can go into any office on four floors and they'll be electrified that you're leaving. The office is the only place where I feel liberated. It's the only place, for example – the only time in my life – where I can effortlessly transcend class barriers.

—LAWRENCE (barely suppressing impatience): But, Peter – the *work*. I enjoy a bit of gossip as much as the next man. But the appalling triviality of the work; the monotony of it, the undemandingness of it. You might as well spend the rest of your life ... I don't know ... piling up pins or something. Balancing tiddlywinks in heaps.

—PETER: Well, let's be practical, dear. If we didn't work in an office, what would we do? Oddly enough, I have rather a lot of energy, inherited from my mother. I'm not creative. I can't write. I certainly couldn't be a labourer. Doctor? Barrister? Politician? I can't see myself being any of those. Willy-nilly, it's an office for me I fear.

You say it's undemanding – but that's the whole point. It's the defects of British business that makes it such a delightful life. I can't *understand* those cries for efficiency and so on. They appal me. We're still in the Pastoral Age of business, a business Arcadia, which these people are trying to destroy. I hope they fail. Every day I do my best to ensure that they will. If I had my way the emphasis would be quite the other way round: Business *In*efficiency Exhibitions, Cost *In*effectiveness courses ...

—LAWRENCE: But the endless competition, the struggling to get approval, the degrading sucking up. The stupid battles to get one's way. The ruthlessness.

PETER: Not in Specifications, ducky. And who's ruthless in Packaging and Design? No-one's been sacked for fifteen years. In America perhaps. Not here. It was even better before the war I don't doubt, but it's still Arcadia. In any case, even in America, competitiveness is human nature. You can't blame offices. No – I thought it was triviality you were complaining about.

—LAWRENCE: Well, it is. I meant it. I know it's a relief that people don't push us too hard, perhaps it's not so ruthless. But honestly, Peter, you can't deny it's trivial, footling, year after year the same footling, bloody boring, pointless little things. You're not being serious?

—PETER: I'm perfectly serious, dear. The trouble with you is you can't see things in human terms. You see things in the abstract. It's rather chilling.

Look, take me. I suffer from mild morning depression, you know. How would I get out of it without the office?

I want you to try and imagine it from my point of view. Imagine what I'm like. I get fearfully worried if my mother moves my toothbrush. I always come to work by the same route – well, occasionally a change, accompanied by instant anxiety.

So what happens? I arrive and find a little pile of familiar, easy, what you'd call trivial work. The pleasure of settling down to it! I begin to feel calm. I forget myself. It's like tapestry; time passes, the mind is active or drifts, distant sounds of – you know – the tinkle of the tea trolley, the ping of a typewriter bell.

It's like Vivaldi. It's an initial subjective reaction. If you like it, every variation is fascinating, however small. You know what I mean – there are tiny nuances within the repetition. Take leaden afternoons like this, when the rain is falling on bored buildings, so many bored buildings. Today there's a feeling of *universal* boredom, a great *brotherhood* of boredom. I find it very warming.

And don't you love autumn? I come by exactly the same route of course, but London seems to me to have changed. It feels like a huge public school or university. There's a smell of ink in the air.

It's a love of small things. I can remember my tables at my prep school when I got into the Senior Common Room. Did you have the same? One was allowed to make a little niche for oneself – two or three tables and some wall, with oneself in the middle. All one's possessions spread about. I can remember the layout of it all now.

And it's the same with work, a letter comes. I answer it. He raises a query. I answer it and raise one myself. Finally, all is settled and we thank each other. Or there are some details about screws; a question of patent infringement. I have to re-read the laws on patents and copyright, redefine it to myself for the five hundredth time, look up what Tankard and Baggott have to say. I *never* tire of Tankard and Baggott. There's always some subtlety one's missed or forgotten. I keep their book on my desk. You may have noticed it on the left next to the paper clip tin. I read it. Outside it's raining. In a minute I shall go and find out exactly *what* Cyril can have needed all those bags for. Do you see what I mean?

It's really a question of the small canvas. People who do *petit-point* and who get absorbed in thousands of small stitches. Or *trompe l'œil*. I think in a way it may be for people who want to stay in the nursery. Certainly I've found myself thinking of the office as I ride towards it as a large squat nanny, waiting comfortably there to gently fuss me with all the details of her tiny, cosy world.

In essence it's a question of temperament, don't you agree? A question of artistic temperament. You – of *course*, I'd never realised before – there's something swashbuckling about you, Van Gogh. You've never been tamed. Whereas me – I'm a miniaturist, a Tailor of Gloucester.

From *The Office* by Jonathan Gathorne-Hardy, 1970

How to Become a Contented Executive

'Have you ever thought about settling down, Bissel?'

'I've thought about it.'

'And?'

'I don't seem to have met the right person.'

The Chairman appeared to review the answer, weighing it in the balance and emphasising his reply by switching off his smile for the first time. 'When you're twenty-six, Bissel, you hope to fall in love. At your age that nonsense should have worn off. You marry a suitable companion who'll help you in your career; you need that help right now if you're going farther, don't you?' Leonard contented himself with an uneasy nod. 'I've just come back from the States where I've seen figures. The married executive is the contented executive and the contented executive works the hardest. Right?' Leonard nodded again. 'You're one of the cleverest young men we've had for a long time, so I don't need to labour such an obvious point.' The smile was turned on again. 'I hope you'll translate those nods of agreement into positive action very shortly.' He stood up as a sign of dismissal. 'Of course, I'll be the first to congratulate you.'

Leonard stood. Would anyone outside the firm (except his father) ever believe that such a conversation had taken place? What was he expected to answer? He mumbled 'Thank you' and left the room at a further nod from the Chairman. Miss Reeves' pert face wore the same smile as when he had entered. He wondered whether she was party to the matter of the interview: great men had a habit of over-confiding in their secretaries.

From *The Youngest Director* by Martyn Goff, 1961

Defining Acquaintanceship

Bob and I had never had one of those less-than-a-minute chats that are sufficient to define acquaintanceship in large companies, yet we knew who the other was, just by having seen the other's name on the distribution lists of memos and on the doors of our offices; a sense of discomfort, or near guilt, was associated with our never having gotten around to performing the minimal social task of introducing ourselves, a discomfort which increased every time we ran into each other. There are always residual people in an office who occupy that category of the not-introduced-to-yet, the not-joked-about-the-weather-with: the residue gets smaller and smaller, and Bob was one of the very last. His face was so familiar that his ongoing status as stranger was really an embarrassment – and just then, the certainty that Bob and I were gradually going to be brought closer and closer to each other, on his down and my up escalator rides, destined to intersect at about the midpoint of our progress, twenty feet in the air in the middle of a huge vaultlike lobby of red marble, where we would have to make eye contact and nod and murmur, or stonily stare into space, or pretend to inspect whatever belongings could plausibly need inspection on an escalator ride, wrenching past that second of forced proximity as if the other person did not exist, and thereby twisting the simple fact that we had never exchanged pleasantries onto an even higher plane of awkwardness, filled me with desperate aversion. I solved the problem by freezing in mid-stride, the instant I caught sight of him (just before I had actually stepped onto the escalator), pointing in the air with an index finger, as if I had just thought of something important that I had forgotten to do, and walking off quickly in another direction

From *The Mezzanine* by Nicholson Baker, 1988

A Life of Sorts

When they left the office, where did they go? How did they live? How did women like the Twocurrys come to be in Athens at all? Alan said they had been the daughters of an artist, a romantic widower, who had saved up to bring himself and his little girls to Greece. They had found two rooms in the Plaka and the father, while alive, made a living by drawing Athenian scenes which he sold to tourists. That had been way back in the '80s and the sisters still lived on in the Plaka rooms. Before the war Miss Gladys had worked at the Archaeological School piecing together broken pots. She had taken Miss Mabel with her every day and, said Alan, 'the Head, not knowing what on earth to do with her, shut Mabel up with a typewriter. Weeks later, mysterious sounds were heard through the door ... thump-thump-thump. *She had taught herself to type.* When the war started, the Archaeological School closed down and the

Twocurrys were thrown upon the world. I seized them as they fell. And now,' Alan gave his painful grin, 'you know their whole history.'

'So the office is all their life.'

'I doubt whether they have any other.'

Harriet doubted whether she herself had any other. But it was a life of sorts.

From *Friends and Heroes* by Olivia Manning, 1965

Six

CLERKS AND CLERKING

Downtrodden, underpaid, perky and even raffish when young yet becoming dimmer and shabbier as the years go by, the office clerk has long been emblematic of the Chaplinesque 'little man' who endures much yet somehow survives it all. Nowadays, of course, clerks are no longer described as such, and many of them will anyway be women: yet the great majority of office workers – order processors and computer experts and, no doubt, whole armies of 'supervisors' and 'managers' and even 'executives' – are clerks by another name, and it's more than likely that our new arrival will become, and remain a member of, this vast, anonymous cohort. The Dick Swivellers of our age, they can be spotted in any City pub at lunch time, clad in ill-fitting dark suits, baying and joshing at the bar, casting furtive glances at their watches and at a clutch of their female colleagues huddled round a table in the corner, emitting deafening barks of laughter as the office wag strikes again, trading views on rugger or exotic holidays; or, grown older and greyer now, with thinning hair and tell-tale lines, plodding stolidly home in the evening, clutching a briefcase, an evening paper and – spurred, perhaps, by a sudden spasm of guilt or affection – a bunch of flowers for the lady wife. No doubt some of the cheeky, disrespectful clerks employed by Dodson and Fogg ended their days as loyal Old Retainers of the Tim Linkinwater variety, their eyes grown dim from years of peering at ledgers – or, these days, computer print-outs and flickering VDUs.

Not all clerks, it goes without saying, are figures of pathos, though this is how the literary world loves to see them: if knowledge is power, then the long-serving or ambitious clerk may well use his insights to rise to the top of the tree himself or even – as in some recent financial scandals – to blackmail or betray his former employers.

Poor, Harmless Creatures

... He was a tall, thin, pale person, in a black coat, scanty grey trousers, little pinched-up gaiters, and brown beaver gloves. He had an umbrella in his hand – not for use, for the day was fine – but, evidently, because he always carried one to the office in the morning. He walked up and down before the little patch of grass [in St James's Park] on which the chairs are placed for hire, not as if he were doing it for pleasure or recreation, but as if it were a matter of compulsion, just as he would walk to the office every morning from the back settlements of Islington. It was Monday; he had escaped for four-and-twenty hours from the thraldom of the desk; and was walking here for exercise and amusement – perhaps for the first time in his life. We were inclined to think he had never had a holiday before, and that he did not know what to do with himself. Children were playing on the grass; groups of people were loitering about, chatting and laughing; but the man walked steadily up and down, unheeding and unheeded, his spare pale face looking as if it were incapable of bearing the expression of curiosity or interest.

There was something in the man's manner and appearance which told us, we fancied, his whole life, or rather his whole day, for a man of this sort has no variety of days. We thought we almost saw the dingy little back office into which he walks every morning, hanging his hat on the same peg, and placing his legs beneath the same desk: first, taking off that black coat which lasts the year through, and putting on the one which did duty last year, and which he keeps in his desk to save the other. There he sits till five o'clock, working on, all day, as regularly as the dial over the mantel-piece, whose loud ticking is as monotonous as his whole existence: only raising his head when some one enters the counting-house, or when, in the midst of some difficult calculation, he looks up to the ceiling as if there were inspiration in the dusty skylight with a green knot in the centre of every pane of glass. About five, or half-past, he slowly dismounts from his accustomed stool, and again changing his coat, proceeds to his usual dining-place, somewhere near Bucklersbury. The waiter recites the bill of fare in a rather confidential manner – for he is a regular customer – and after inquiring 'What's in the best cut?' and 'What was up last?' he orders a small plate of roast beef, with greens, and half-a-pint of porter. He has a small plate to-day, because greens are a penny more than potatoes, and he had 'two breads' yesterday, with the additional enormity of 'a cheese' the day before. This important point settled, he hangs up his hat – he took it off the moment he sat down – and bespeaks the paper after the next gentleman. If he can get it while he is at dinner, he eats with much greater zest; balancing it against the water-bottle, and eating a bit of beef, and reading a line or two, alternately. Exactly at five minutes before the hour is up, he produces a shilling, pays the reckoning, carefully deposits the change in his waistcoat-pocket (first deducting a penny for the waiter), and returns to the office, from which, if it is not foreign post night, he again sallies forth in about half an hour. He then walks home, at his usual pace, to his little back room at Islington, where he has his tea; perhaps solacing himself during the meal with the conversation of his landlady's little boy, whom he occasionally rewards with a penny, for solving problems in simple addition. Sometimes, there is a letter or two to take up to his employer's, in Russell Square; and then, the wealthy man of business, hearing his voice, calls out from the dining-parlour, – 'Come in, Mr Smith:' and Mr Smith, putting his hat at the feet of one of the hall chairs, walks timidly in, and being condescendingly desired to sit down, carefully tucks his legs under his chair, and sits at a considerable distance from the table while he drinks the glass of sherry which is poured out for him by the eldest boy, and after drinking which, he backs and slides out of the room, in a state of nervous agitation from which he does not perfectly recover, until he finds himself once more in the Islington Road. Poor, harmless creatures such men are; contented but not happy; broken-spirited and humbled, they may feel no pain, but they never know pleasure.

From *Sketches by Boz* by Charles Dickens, 1837

'Our Mr Wrenn'

He stands out in the correspondence of the Souvenir and Art Novelty Company as 'Our Mr Wrenn,' who would be writing you directly and explaining everything most satisfactorily. At thirty-four Mr Wrenn was the sales-entry clerk of the Souvenir Company. He was always bending over bills and columns of figures at a desk behind the stock-room. He was a meek little bachelor – a person of inconspicuous blue ready-made suits, and a small unsuccessful moustache.

From *Our Mr Wrenn* by Sinclair Lewis, 1914

Signs of Revolt

Caesar's double-bed is warm
As an unimportant clerk
Writes *I DO NOT LIKE MY WORK*
On a pink official form.

From 'The Fall of Rome' in *Nones* by W. H. Auden, 1952

A Hideous Fate

I have always hated office-work, and business of every kind; yet I could never see an opening in any other direction. I have been all my life a clerk – like so many thousands of other men. Nowadays, if I happen to be in the City when all the clerks are coming away from business, I feel an inexpressible pity for them. I feel I should like to find two or three of the hardest driven, and just divide my superfluous income between them. A clerk's life – a life of the office without any hope of rising – that is a hideous fate!

From *The Odd Women* by George Gissing, 1893

Lost in a Crowd

This was Turgis, the clerk, who might be described as Stanley's senior or Mr Smeeth's junior. He was in his early twenties, a thinnish, awkward young man, with a rather long neck, poor shoulders, and large, clumsy hands and feet. You would not say he was ugly, but on the other hand you would probably admit, after reflection, that it would have been better for him if he had been actually uglier. As it was, he was just unprepossessing. You would not have noticed him in a crowd – and a great deal of his time was spent in a crowd – but if your attention had been called to him, you would have given him one glance and then decided that that was enough. He was obviously neither sick nor starved, yet something about his appearance, a total lack of colour and bloom, a slight pastiness and spottiness, the faint grey film that seemed to cover and subdue him, suggested that all the food he ate was wrong, all the rooms he sat in, beds he slept in, and clothes he wore, were wrong, and that he lived in a world without sun and clean rain and wandering sweet air. His features were not good nor yet too bad. He had rather full brown eyes that might have been called pretty if they had been set in a girl's face; a fairly large nose that should have been masterful but somehow was not; a small, still babyish mouth, usually open, and revealing several big and irregular teeth; and a drooping rather than retreating chin. His blue serge suit bulged and bagged and sagged and shone, and had obviously done all these things five days after it had left the multiple cheap tailors' shop, in the window of which a companion suit, clothing the wax model of a light-weight champion, still maliciously challenged Turgis with its smooth surface and sharp creases every time he sneaked past it. His soft collar was crumpled, his tie a little frayed, and there was a pulpy look about his shoes. Any sensible woman could have compelled him to improve his appearance almost beyond recognition within a week, and it was quite clear that no sensible woman took any interest in him.

From *Angel Pavement* by J. B. Priestley, 1930

Folie de Grandeur

'... the firm in which I'm a sort of a – of a managing partner ...'

Dick Swiveller in *The Old Curiosity Shop* by Charles Dickens, 1841

The Clerk at His Best

The man whom I found myself facing was a well-built, fresh-complexioned young fellow with a frank, honest face and a slight, crisp, yellow moustache. He wore a very shiny top hat and a neat suit of sober black, which made him look what he was – a smart young City man, of the class who have been labelled Cockneys, but who give us out crack Volunteer regiments, and who turn out more fine athletes and sportsmen than any other body of men in these islands.

From 'The Stockbroker's Clerk' in *The Memoirs of Sherlock Holmes* by Sir Arthur Conan Doyle, 1893

'Like a mole I journey in the dark'

I couldn't touch a stop and turn a screw;
    And set the blooming world a-work for me,
Like such as cut their teeth – I hope, like you –
    On the handle of a skeleton gold key;
I cut mine on a leek, which I eat it every week;
    I'm a clerk at thirty bob as you can see.

But I don't allow it's luck and all a toss;
    There's no such thing as being starred and crossed;
It's just the power of some to be a boss,
    And the bally power of others to be bossed
I face the music, sir; you bet I ain't a cur;
    Strike me lucky if I don't believe I'm lost!

For like a mole I journey in the dark,
    A-travelling along the underground
From my Pillar'd Halls and broad Suburbean Park,
    To come the daily dull official round;
And home again at night with my pipe all alight,
    A-scheming how to count ten bob a pound . . .

From 'Thirty Bob a Week' in *Ballads and Songs* by John Davidson, 1894

Hell on Earth

He drifted into indefinite mercantile clerkships, an existence possibly preferable to that of the fourth circle of Inferno.

From *A Life's Morning* by George Gissing, 1888

Dodson and Fogg

The clerks' office of Messrs Dodson and Fogg was a dark, mouldy, earthy-smelling room, with a high wainscotted partition to screen the clerks from the vulgar gaze: a couple of old wooden chairs: a very loud-ticking clock: an almanack, an umbrella-stand, a row of hat-pegs, and a few shelves, on which were deposited several ticketed bundles of dirty papers, some old deal boxes with paper labels, and sundry decayed stone ink bottles of various shapes and sizes. There was a glass door leading into the passage which formed the entrance to the court, and on the outer side of this glass door, Mr Pickwick, closely followed by Sam Weller, presented himself on the Friday morning succeeding the occurrence, of which a faithful narration is given in the last chapter.

'Come in, can't you!' cried a voice from behind the partition, in reply to Mr Pickwick's gentle tap at the door. And Mr Pickwick and Sam entered accordingly.

'Mr Dodson or Mr Fogg at home, sir?' inquired Mr Pickwick, gently, advancing, hat in hand, towards the partition.

'Mr Dodson ain't at home, and Mr Fogg's particularly engaged,' replied the voice; and at the same time the head to which the voice belonged, with a pen behind its ear, looked over the partition, and at Mr Pickwick.

It was a ragged head, the sandy hair of which, scrupulously parted on one side, and flattened down with pomatum, was twisted into little semi-circular tails round a flat face ornamented with a pair of small eyes, and garnished with a very dirty shirt collar, and a rusty black stock.

'Mr Dodson ain't at home, and Mr Fogg's particularly engaged,' said the man to whom the head belonged.

'When will Mr Dodson be back, sir?' inquired Mr Pickwick.

'Can't say.'

'Will it be long before Mr Fogg is disengaged, sir?'

'Don't know.'

Here the man proceeded to mend his pen with great deliberation, while another clerk, who was mixing a Seidlitz powder, under cover of the lid of his desk, laughed approvingly.

'I think I'll wait,' said Mr Pickwick. There was no reply; so Mr Pickwick sat down unbidden, and listened to the loud ticking of the clock and the murmured conversation of the clerks . . .

From *The Pickwick Papers* by Charles Dickens, 1837

Trollope and the Ink Bottle

As it was, the conduct of some of us was very bad. There was a comfortable sitting-room upstairs, devoted to the use of some one of our number who in turn was required to remain on the place all night. Hither one or two of us would adjourn after lunch, and play *écarté* for an hour or two. I do not know whether such ways are possible now in our public offices.

And here we used to have suppers and card-parties at night – great symposiums, with much smoking of tobacco; for in one part of the building there lived a whole bevy of clerks. These were gentlemen whose duty it then was to make up and receive the foreign mails. I do not remember that they worked later or earlier than the other sorting-clerks; but there was supposed to be something special in foreign letters, which required that the men who handled them should have minds undistracted by the outer world. Their salaries, too, were higher than those of their more homely brethren; and they paid nothing for their lodgings. Consequently there was a somewhat fast set in those apartments, given to cards and to tobacco, who drank spirits and water in preference to tea. I was not one of them, but was a good deal with them.

I do not know that I should interest my readers by saying much of my Post Office experiences in those days. I was always on the eve of being dismissed, and yet was always striving to show how good a public servant I could become, if only a chance were given me. But the chances went the wrong way. On one occasion, in the performance of my duty, I had put a private letter containing bank-notes on the Secretary's table, – which letter I had duly opened, as it was not marked private. The letter was seen by the Colonel, but had not been moved by him when he left his room. On his return it was gone. In the meantime I had returned to the room, again in the performance of some duty. When the letter was missed I was sent for, and there I found the Colonel much moved about his letter, and a certain chief clerk, who, with a long face, was making suggestions as to the probable fate of the money. 'The letter has been taken,' said the Colonel, turning to me angrily, 'and, by G –! there has been nobody in the room but you and I.' As he spoke, he thundered his fist down upon the table. 'Then,' said I, 'by G –! you have taken it.' And I also thundered my fist down; – but, accidentally, not upon the table. There was there a standing movable desk, at which, I presume, it was the Colonel's habit to write, and on this movable desk was a large bottle full of ink. My fist unfortunately came on the desk, and the ink at once flew up, covering the Colonel's face and shirt-front. Then it was a sight to see that senior clerk, as he seized a quire of blotting-paper, and rushed to the aid of his superior officer, striving to mop up the ink; and a sight also to see the Colonel, in his agony, hit right out through the blotting-paper at that senior clerk's unoffending stomach. At that moment there came in the Colonel's private secretary, with the letter and the money, and I was desired to go back to my own room. This was an incident not much in my favour, though I do not know that it did me special harm.

From the *Autobiography* of Anthony Trollope, 1883

. . . The outer door had been opened, and feet were being wiped. That meant that Mr Smeeth had arrived, and Mr Smeeth liked to find Stanley busy during these first few minutes. So Stanley broke off, and dashed at a bit of work he had saved for this moment.

'*Good*-morning, everybody,' said Mr Smeeth, putting down his hat and his folded newspaper, and then rubbing his hands. 'It's getting a bit nippy in the mornings now, isn't it? Real autumn weather' . . .

You could tell at once by the way in which Mr Smeeth entered the office that his attitude towards Twigg and Dersingham was quite different from that of his young colleagues. They came because they had to come; even if they rushed in, there was still a faint air of reluctance about them; and there was something in their demeanour that suggested they knew quite well that they were shedding a part of themselves, and that the most valuable part, leaving it behind, somewhere near the street door, where it would wait for them to pick it up again when the day's work was done. In short, Messrs Twigg and Dersingham had merely hired their services. But Mr Smeeth obviously thought of himself as a real factor of the entity known as Twigg and Dersingham: he was their Mr Smeeth. When he entered the office, he did not dwindle, he grew; he was more himself than he was in the street outside. Thus, he had a gratitude, a zest, an eagerness, that could not be found in the others, resenting as they did at heart the temporary loss of their larger and brighter selves. They merely came to earn their money, more or less. Mr Smeeth came to work.

His appearance was deceptive. He looked what he ought to have been, in the opinion of a few thousand hasty and foolish observers of this life, and what he was not – a grey drudge. They could easily see him as a drab ageing fellow for ever toiling away at figures of no importance, as a creature of the little foggy City street, of crusted ink-pots and dusty ledgers and day books, as a typical troglodyte of this dingy and absurd civilisation. Angel Pavement and its kind, too hot and airless in summer, too raw in winter, too wet in spring, and too smoky and foggy in autumn, assisted by long hours of artificial light, by hasty breakfasts and illusory lunches, by walks in boots made of sodden cardboard and rides in germ-haunted buses, by fuss all day and worry at night, had blanched the whole man, had thinned his hair and turned it grey, wrinkled his forehead and the space at each side of his short grey moustache, put eyeglasses at one end of his nose and slightly sharpened and reddened the other end, and given him a prominent Adam's apple, drooping shoulders and a narrow chest, pains in his joints, a perpetual slight cough, and a hay-fevered look at least one week out of every ten. Nevertheless, he was not a grey drudge. He did not toil on hopelessly. On the contrary, his days at the office were filled with important and exciting events, all the more important and exciting because they were there in the light, for just beyond them, all round them, was the darkness in which lurked the one great fear, the fear that he might take part no longer in these events, that he might lose his job. Once he stopped being Twigg and Dersingham's cashier, what was he? He avoided the question by day, but sometimes at night, when he could not sleep, it came to him with all its force and dreadfully illuminated the darkness with little pictures of shabby and broken men, trudging round from office to office, haunting the Labour Exchanges and the newspaper rooms of Free Libraries, and gradually sinking into the workhouse and the gutter.

This fear only threw into brighter relief his present position. He had spent years making neat little columns of figures, entering up ledgers and then balancing them, but this was not drudgery to him. He was a man of figures. He could handle them with astonishing dexterity and certainty. In their small but perfected world, he moved with complete confidence and enjoyed himself. If you only took time and trouble enough, the figures would always work out and balance up, unlike life, which you could not possibly manipulate so that it would work out and balance up. Moreover, he loved the importance, the dignity, of his position. Thirty-five years had passed since he was an office boy, like Stanley, but a trifle smaller and younger; he was a boy from a poor home; and in those days a clerkship in the City still meant something, cashiers and chief clerks still wore silk hats, and to occupy a safe stool and receive your hundred and fifty a year was to have arrived. Mr Smeeth was now a cashier himself and he was still enjoying his arrival. Somewhere at the back of his mind, that little office boy still lived, to mark the wonder of it. Going round to the bank, where he was known and respected and told it was a fine day or a wet day, was part of the routine of his work, but even now it was something more than that, something to be tasted by the mind and relished. The 'Good-morning, Mr Smeeth,' of the bank cashiers at the counter still gave him a secret little thrill. And, unless the day had gone very badly indeed, he never concluded it, locking the ledger, the cash book, and the japanned box for petty cash, away in the safe and then filling and lighting his pipe, without being warmed by a feeling that he, Herbert Norman Smeeth, once a mere urchin, then office boy and junior clerk to Willoughby, Tyce and Bragg, then a clerk with the Imperial Trading Co., then for two War years a lance-corporal in the orderly room of the depot of the Middlesex Regiment, and now Twigg and Dersingham's cashier for the last ten years, had triumphantly arrived. It was, when you came to think of it – as he had once boldly ventured to point out to a friendly fellow boarder at Channel View, Eastbourne (they had stayed up rather late, after their wives had gone upstairs, to split a bottle of beer and exchange confidences) – quite a romance, in its way. And the fear that grew in the dark and came closer to the edge of it to whisper to him, that fear did not make it any less of a romance.

Mr Smeeth now unlocked the safe, took out his books and the petty cashbox, looked over the correspondence and attended to that part meant for him, made a note that Brown and Gorstein, and North-Western and Trades Furnishing Co., and Nickman and Sons had not fulfilled their promises and sent cheques, dealt with the two small cheques that some other people had sent, gave Miss Matfield three letters to type, asked Turgis to telephone to Briggs Brothers and the London and North-Eastern Railway, delighted Stanley by giving him a message to take out, and, in short, plunged into the day's work and set Twigg and Dersingham in motion, even though Twigg had been quiet and unstirring for years in Streatham Cemetery, and the present Mr Dersingham was only in motion yet on the District Railway, on his way to the office.

Stanley disappeared, as usual, like a shell from a gun, before Mr Smeeth could possibly change his mind; Miss Matfield contemptuously rattled off her letters (the little *ping* of the typewriter bell sounding like a repeated ironical exclamation); Turgis talked down the telephone rather gloomily; and Mr Smeeth made the neatest little figures, sometimes in pencil, sometimes in ink, and opened more and more books on his high desk. And for ten minutes or so, no word was spoken that had not immediate reference to the affairs of the office.

From *Angel Pavement* by J. B. Priestley, 1930

The Loyal Old Retainer

It was a sight to behold Tim Linkinwater slowly bring out a massive ledger and day book, and, after turning them over and over, and affectionately dusting their backs and sides, open the leaves here and there, and cast his eyes, half-mournfully, half-proudly, upon the fair and unblotted entries.

'Four-and-forty year, next May!' said Tim. 'Many new ledgers since then. Four-and-forty year!'

Tim closed the book again.

'Come, come,' said Nicholas, 'I am all impatience to begin.'

Tim Linkinwater shook his head with an air of mild reproof. Mr Nickleby was not sufficiently impressed with the deep and awful nature of his undertaking. Suppose there should be any mistake – any scratching out! –

Young men are adventurous. It is extraordinary what they will rush upon, sometimes. Without even taking the precaution of sitting himself down upon his stool, but standing leisurely at the desk, and with a smile upon his face – actually a smile – there was no mistake about it; Mr Linkinwater often mentioned it afterwards – Nicholas dipped his pen into the inkstand before him, and plunged into the books of Cheeryble Brothers!

Tim Linkinwater turned pale, and, tilting up his stool on the two legs nearest Nicholas, looked over his shoulder in breathless anxiety. Brother Charles and brother Ned entered the counting-house together; but Tim Linkinwater, without looking round, impatiently waved his hand as a caution that profound silence must be observed, and followed the nib of the inexperienced pen with strained and eager eyes.

The brothers looked on with smiling faces, but Tim Linkinwater smiled not, nor moved for some minutes. At length, he drew a long slow breath, and, still maintaining his position on the tilted stool, glanced at brother Charles, secretly pointed with the feather of his pen towards Nicholas, and nodded his head in a grave and resolute manner, plainly signifying 'He'll do.'

Brother Charles nodded again, and exchanged a laughing look with brother Ned; but, just then, Nicholas stopped to refer to some other page, and Tim Linkinwater, unable to contain his satisfaction any longer, descended from his stool, and caught him rapturously by the hand.

'He has done it!' said Tim, looking round at his employers and shaking his head triumphantly. 'His capital B's and D's are exactly like mine; he dots all his small i's and crosses every t as he writes it. There an't such a young man as this in all London,' said Tim, clapping Nicholas on the back; 'not one. Don't tell me! The City can't produce his equal. I challenge the City to do it!'

With this casting down of his gauntlet, Tim Linkinwater struck the desk such a blow with his clenched fist, that the old blackbird tumbled off his perch with the start it gave him, and actually uttered a feeble croak, in the extremity of his astonishment.

'Well said, Tim, well said, Tim Linkinwater!' cried brother Charles, scarcely less pleased than Tim himself, and clapping his hands gently as he spoke. 'I knew our young friend would take great pains, and I was quite certain he would succeed in no time. Didn't I say so, brother Ned?'

'You did, my dear brother; certainly, my dear brother, you said so, and you were quite right,' replied Ned. 'Quite right. Tim Linkinwater is excited, but he is justly excited, properly excited. Tim is a fine fellow. Tim Linkinwater, sir – you're a fine fellow.'

'Here's a pleasant thing to think of!' said Tim, wholly regardless of this address to himself, and raising his spectacles from the ledger to the brothers. 'Here's a pleasant thing. Do you suppose I haven't often thought what would become of these books when I was gone? Do you suppose I haven't often thought that things might go on irregular and untidy here, after I was taken away? But now,' said Tim, extending his forefinger towards Nicholas, 'now, when I've shown him a little more, I'm satisfied. The business will go on, when I'm dead, as well as it did when I was alive – just the same – and I shall have the satisfaction of knowing that there never were such books – never were such books! No, nor never will be such books – as the books of Cheeryble Brothers.'

Having thus expressed his sentiments, Mr Linkinwater gave vent to a short laugh, indicative of defiance to the cities of London and Westminster, and, turning again to his desk, quietly carried seventy-six from the last column he had added up, and went on with his work.

From *Nicholas Nickleby* by Charles Dickens, 1839

Gilding the Lily

According to Tomlinson, Mr Stone had 'gone into industry'. And it was also Tomlinson who designated Mr Stone as 'head librarian'. 'Richard Stone,' he would say. 'An old college friend. Head librarian with Excal.' The 'with' was tactful; it concealed the unimportant department of the company Mr Stone worked for. The title appealed to Mr Stone and he began using it in his official correspondence, fearfully at first, and then, encountering no opposition from the company or the department (which was in fact delighted, for the words lent a dignity to their operations), with conviction.

From *Mr Stone and the Knights Companion* by V. S. Naipaul, 1963

A Dragon of Honesty

Mr Fidus Neverbend was an absolute dragon of honesty. His integrity was of such an all-pervading nature, that he bristled with it as a porcupine does with its quills. He had theories and axioms as to a man's conduct, and the conduct especially of a man in the Queen's Civil Service, up to which no man but himself could live. Consequently no one but himself appeared to himself to be true and just in all his dealings.

A quarter of an hour spent over a newspaper was in his eyes a downright robbery. If he saw a man so employed, he would divide out the total of salary into hourly portions, and tell him to a fraction of how much he was defrauding the public. If he ate a biscuit in the middle of the day, he did so with his eyes firmly fixed on some document, and he had never been known to be absent from his office after ten or before four.

From *The Three Clerks* by Anthony Trollope, 1858

'The City'

Business men with awkward hips
And dirty jokes upon their lips,
And large behinds and jingling chains,
And riddled teeth and riddling brains,
And plump white fingers made to curl
Round some anaemic city girl,
And so lend colour to the lives
And old suspicions of their wives.

Young men who wear on office stools
The ties of minor public schools,
Each learning how to be a sinner
And tell 'a good one' after dinner,
And so discover it is rather
Fun to go one more than father.
But father, son and clerk join up
To talk about the Football Cup.

From *Mount Zion* by John Betjeman, 1932

Seven

THE SECRETARIAL
LIFE

Just as most male office workers were traditionally clerks, so – until recently – their female equivalents were almost exclusively employed as secretaries (or 'typewriters', as they were known in Gissing's day, when they were carefully segregated from their masculine colleagues). Things have changed a bit over the past twenty years or so, though not as much as many would like: a few male secretaries are employed in the more dashing or arty professions, while female managers and executives are making their presence felt. Even so, it's still hard for a girl – whatever her qualifications or degrees – to get a foot in the door in (say) publishing unless she has also done a secretarial course: a *sine qua non* for her is merely a desirable bonus in her male equivalent. Not surprisingly, then, those secretaries who find their way into print are invariably female, or that frustration and inequality should – for the ambitious at least – be inherent to the secretarial lot. The cartoon-strip relationship between the boss (male) and his secretary (female) is crudely sexual, but in real life – unless both parties prove instantly incompatible – it may well be a subtler affair, combining intimacy, admiration (perhaps), exasperation, affection and a good deal of knowledge, both private and professional. And although the humdrum copy typist occupies a lowly position in the office hierarchy, the boss's private secretary may well be in a position of far greater knowledge and influence than formal ranking might suggest. Not only do they type out confidential memos, but their bosses may confide in them and even ask their advice: like those astute switchboard operators who, by listening in to confidential conversations, know more about the politics of an office than some of its directors, they know in advance what the rest of us are longing to hear. Not surprisingly, then, influential secretaries are sometimes treated with a certain deference and sycophancy. Such heady delights, however, are reserved for the few: more familiar ingredients include disentangling hideous syntax, making coffee, fending off irate phone calls ('He'll call you back' or 'He's in a meeting' meaning 'He refuses to talk to you' or 'He's still out at lunch'), grousing about some new villainy or incompetence on the part of the powers-that-be and clipping a brave smile to the face when asked to type a contract or ten letters at a quarter to five ('I know it's a lot to ask, but would you mind awfully . . . ?'). Love and sex are, of course, additional hazards or delights: if I have lingered too long over J. B. Priestley's Cockney sparrow it is only because – like Penelope Fitzgerald's Annie Aslam or Christina Stead's puzzleheaded girl – she is the kind of old-fashioned secretary with whom any reasonable colleague would fall instantly in love.

'Business Girls'

From the geyser ventilators
    Autumn winds are blowing down
On a thousand business women
    Having baths in Camden Town.

Waste pipes chuckle into runnels,
    Steam's escaping here and there,
Morning trains through Camden cutting
    Shake the Crescent and the Square.

Early nip of changeful autumn,
    Dahlias glimpsed through garden doors,
At the back precarious bathrooms
    Jutting out from upper floors,

And behind their frail partitions
    Business women lie and soak,
Seeing through the draughty skylight
    Flying clouds and railway smoke.

Rest you there, poor unbelov'd ones,
    Lap your loneliness in heat.
All too soon the tiny breakfast,
    Trolley-bus and windy street!

From *A Few Late Chrysanthemums* by John Betjeman, 1954

An Old-fashioned View

'Get rid of the girl, right away, without 'esitation. They never should have started girls in the City. The place has never been right since. Powderin' noses! Cups o' tea! You don't know where y'are.'

From *Angel Pavement* by J. B. Priestley, 1930

Equal Opportunities

Soon after her arrival Valda had drawn attention to herself. Her little Mr Leadbetter, the administrative officer, had come out of his hutch, ears up, holding a button, and asked if she would sew it on. This, he estimated, would not take a minute. Valda politely consented. And, laying aside her papers, brought from a desk drawer a housewifely pouch of needles and coloured threads. With Mr Leadbetter's jacket aswoon in her lap, she narrowed her own eye to the needle's and was soon stitching. Leadbetter stood to watch her. His shirt was striped and blue, his trousers came to his armpits, depending from canvas braces, also striped, that had long ago been made to last. It was pleasant to doff his armour and watch the handsome Valda at her humble and womanly task. When she had done, when she had wound the thread and broken it off, he was grateful.

'Thank you, Valda. I am not handy with such things. And would jab myself to pieces.' It was important to show appreciation.

To this, Valda replied, echoing his own benevolent thoughts: 'These are small things to do for one another.'

The following week Valda came into his office, where he was reading over a penultimate draft, and asked him to change her typewriter ribbon.

Mr Leadbetter stared.

She said, 'I am not handy with machines.'

He was baffled and displeased. 'Have you never needed a new ribbon before? Were you not trained to do these things?'

'It will not take a minute.'

'You had better get one of the girls to show you.' It was incomprehensible.

'They will dirty their hands.' She said, 'It is a small thing to do.'

Now he understood. He went out and got one of the other girls – the real girls – in a rage. 'Miss Fenchurch needs help with her machine.' It was the first time he had not called her Valda, but respect was accorded only from pique. The second girl looked with ingratiating timidity at him, and with terror at Valda, and at once bent to the machine as if over a cradle.

When the time came, Mr Leadbetter wrote in Valda's file that she tended to be aggressive over trifles. 'Tended' was official code for going the whole hog . . .

From *The Transit of Venus* by Shirley Hazzard, 1980

'Type it again'

The first day of the third week, the lawyer came out of his office, stiffer than usual, his eyes lit up in a peculiar, stalking way. He was carrying one of my letters. He put it on my desk, right in front of me. 'Look at it,' he said. I did.

'Do you see that?'

'What?' I asked.

'This letter has three typing errors in it, one of which is, I think, a spelling error.'

'I'm sorry.'

'This isn't the first time, either. There have been others that I let go because it was your first few weeks. But this can't go on. Do you know what this makes me look like to the people who receive these letters?'

I looked at him, mortified. There had been a catastrophe hidden in the folds of my contentment for two weeks and he hadn't even told me. It seemed unfair, although when I thought about it I could understand his reluctance, maybe even embarrassment, to draw my attention to something so stupidly unpleasant.

'Type it again.'

I did, but I was so badly shaken that I made even more mistakes. 'You are wasting my time,' he said, and handed it to me once again. I typed it correctly the third time, but he sulked in his office for the rest of the day.

This kind of thing kept occurring all week. Each time, the lawyer's irritation and disbelief mounted. In addition, I sensed something else growing in him, an intimate tendril creeping from one of his darker areas, nursed on the feeling that he had discovered something about me.

I was very depressed about the situation. When I went home in the evening I couldn't take a nap. I lay there looking at the gray weather poodle and fantasised about having a conversation with the lawyer that would clear up everything, explain to him that I was really trying to do my best. He seemed to think that I was making the mistakes on purpose.

At the end of the week he began complaining about the way I answered the phone. 'You're like a machine,' he said. 'You sound like you're in the Twilight Zone. You don't think when you respond to people.'

When he asked me to come into his office at the end of the day, I thought he was going to fire me. The idea was a relief, but a numbing one. I sat down and he fixed me with a look that was speculative but benign, for him. He leaned back in his chair in a comfortable way, one hand dangling sideways from his wrist. To my surprise, he began talking to me about my problems, as he saw them.

'I sense that you are a very nice but complex person, with wild mood swings that you keep hidden. You just shut up the house and act like there's nobody home.'

'That's true,' I said. 'I do that.'

'Well, why? Why don't you open up a little bit? It would probably help your typing.'

It was really not any of his business, I thought.

'You should try to talk more. I know I'm your employer and we have a prescribed relationship, but you should feel free to discuss your problems with me.'

The idea of discussing my problems with him was preposterous. 'It's hard to think of having that kind of discussion with you,' I said. I hesitated. 'You have a strong personality and . . . when I encounter a personality like that, I tend to step back because I don't know how to deal with it.'

He was clearly pleased with this response, but he said, 'You shouldn't be so shy.'

When I thought about this conversation later, it seemed, on the one hand, that this lawyer was just an asshole. On the other, his comments were weirdly moving, and had the effect of making me feel horribly sensitive. No one had ever made such personal comments to me before.

The next day I made another mistake. The intimacy of the previous day seemed to make the mistake even more repulsive to him because he got madder than usual. I wanted him to fire me. I would have suggested it, but I was struck silent. I sat and stared at the letter while he yelled. 'What's wrong with you!'

'I'm sorry,' I said.

He stood quietly for a moment. Then he said, 'Come into my office. And bring that letter.'

I followed him into his office.

'Put that letter on my desk,' he said.

I did.

'Now bend over so that you are looking directly at it. Put your elbows on the desk and your face very close to the letter.'

Shaken and puzzled, I did what he said.

'Now read the letter to yourself. Keep reading it over and over again.'

I read: 'Dear Mr Garvy: I am very grateful to you for referring . . .' He began spanking me as I said 'referring.' The funny thing was, I wasn't even surprised. I actually kept reading the letter, although my understanding of it was not very clear. I began crying on it, which blurred the ink. The word 'humiliation' came into my mind with such force that it effectively blocked out all other words. Further, I felt that the concept it stood for had actually been a major force in my life for quite a while.

He spanked me for about ten minutes, I think. I read the letter only about five times, partly because it rapidly became too wet to be legible. When he stopped he said, 'Now straighten up and go type it again.'

I went to my desk. He closed the office door behind him. I sat down, blew my nose and wiped my face. I stared into space for several minutes, every now and then dwelling on the tingling sensation in my buttocks. I typed the letter again and took it into his office. He didn't look up as I put it on his desk.

From *Bad Behavior* by Mary Gaitskill, 1988

'Don't you do shorthand?'

Clutching her parcels, Penny charged through the front door, skilfully avoided a workman on a ladder, but cannoned straight into the Sales Manager coming out of the Board Room with an important client. Gibbering apologies, she raced upstairs, tiptoed past the Personnel Officer's room, and eased herself stealthily into her office.

Miss Piggott, the Managing Director's senior secretary, looked at her watch in disapproval. 'It's nane minutes past three,' she said in her ultra refined voice. 'Don't you think you're sailin' a bit close to the wind?'

'Oh gosh, Miss Piggott, I'm sorry,' said Penny, who was the Managing Director's junior secretary, 'but I saw this divine dress and then I found these shoes to match in a sale, and then in the same sale, I saw these garden scissors. I thought you might like them.'

Miss Piggott's disapproving face softened. 'That was very thoughtful of you, Penny. How much do Ay owe you?'

'Nothing, it's a present.' Penny kicked off her shoes, and collapsed into a chair, scattering parcels among the debris on her desk. 'I brought some éclairs, three in fact, in case *he* –' she pointed contemptuously at the door leading off their office – 'gets back in time.'

'He's back,' said Miss Piggott. 'He's been ringing you since two o'clock.'

Penny went pale. 'Mr McInnes is back already? My goodness, is he in a foul mood?'

'A've known him more accommodatin',' said Miss Piggott with a sniff.

'Oh dear,' sighed Penny, tugging a comb through her dark red curls, 'I do wish darling Mr Fraser was still here. Everything was so much nicer then' . . .

Jake McInnes was a powerfully built man in his late twenties, with thick, dark hair, deep-set eyes the colour of mahogany, and a very square jaw. With that nasty smile playing round his mouth, he looks more like a Sicilian bandit than an American businessman, thought Penny.

They glared at each other across the vast desk.

'It's twenty minutes after three. I thought your lunch break ran from twelve-thirty to one-thirty,' he said.

'I'm sorry,' mumbled Penny, 'but I saw this perfectly marvellous dress, and then . . .'

'I don't want any excuses,' he snapped. 'I've told Miss Payne to dock two hours pay from your salary this week.' He picked up her folder. 'You must have been busy while I was away, these letters are beautifully typed.'

'Oh good,' said Penny, beaming at him.

'It's a pity,' he continued softly, 'that they bear absolutely no relation to what I dictated.'

Penny flinched as though he'd struck her.

'Don't you do shorthand?' he asked.

'Not a lot,' admitted Penny, 'but my longhand's terribly fast, so I can get the gist of things. Mr Fraser never complained,' she added defiantly.

'That doesn't surprise me,' said Jake McInnes.

For the next half-hour he went through each letter like an examination paper, until every shred of her self-confidence was ripped to pieces. Then he tore the letters up and dropped them into the wastepaper basket.

Scarlet in the face, Penny got to her feet.

'And another thing,' he added, 'next time you make reservations at a hotel, book single rooms. I don't like arriving in the middle of the night to find I'm expected to share a double bed with Mr Atwater' . . .

From 'The Square Peg' in *Lisa and Co* by Jilly Cooper, 1981

'The Boss is Thinking'

His secretary has a habit of scrumpling the top copies
like sheets of a bed she's slept in. Take
those office beauties further
back
and they're reading
'Bunty And The Boo-Boos'.
Before that they're little screaming things
crawling across the carpet, blue-eyed, in nappies.

Good ones, he thinks, are as rare as seven-toed tabbies;
and the Office Manager tells him: put
just ten girls in an unheated
room
and they're making
warmth like a one-bar fire; yes,
even the inefficient ones are assets too,
smiling and carrying into meetings the teas and coffees.

They like people, they're not sensitive to hierarchies,
they're a kind of undisciplined army. Give
them the lover or father
touch
and they're licking
the saucers and purring, on, on,
into the unpaid overtime and the cut lunch.
Boy friends at night with the Greek wine and the moussakas.

From *The Gavin Ewart Show* by Gavin Ewart, 1971

The Tools of the Trade

The commercial college had trained her to work with a number of people,
as she was now to do in the office; but in the seriousness and savage
continuity of its toil, the office was very different. There was no stopping;
she couldn't shirk in a day or two, as she had done at the commercial
college. It was not so much that she was afraid of losing her job as that
she came to see herself as part of a chain. The others, beyond, were
waiting for her; she mustn't hold them up. That was her first impression
of the office system, that and the insignificance of herself in the presence
of the office-hierarchy – manager above manager and the Mysterious
Owner beyond all. She was alone; once she transgressed they would
crush her. They had no personal interest in her, nine of them, except her
classmate, Miss Moynihan, who smiled at her and went out to lunch with
her.

They two did not dare to sit over parcels of lunch with the curious
other girls. Before fifteen-cent lunches of baked apples, greasy Napoleons,
and cups of coffee, at a cheap restaurant, Miss Moynihan and she talked
about the office-manager, the editors, the strain of copying all day, and
they united in lyric hatred of the lieutenant of the girls, a satiric young

woman who was a wonderful hater. Una had regarded Miss Moynihan as thick and stupid, but not when she had thought of falling in love with Charlie Martindale at a dance at Panama, not in her most fervid hours of comforting her mother, had she been so closely in sympathy with any human being as she was with Miss Moynihan when they went over and over the problems of office politics, office favourites, office rules, office customs.

The customs were simple: Certain hours for arrival, for lunch, for leaving; women's retiring-room embarrassingly discovered to be on the right behind the big safe; water-cooler in the centre of the stenographers' room. But the office prejudices, the taboos, could not be guessed. They offered you every possible chance of 'queering yourself.' Miss Moynihan, on her very first day, discovered, perspiringly, that you must never mention the *Gazette's* rival, the *Internal Combustion News*. The *Gazette's* attitude was that the *News* did not exist – except when the *Gazette* wanted the plate of an advertisement which the *News* was to forward. You mustn't chew gum in the office; you were to ask favours of the lieutenant, not of the office-manager; and you mustn't be friendly with Mr Bush of the circulation department nor with Miss Caldwell, the filing-clerk. Why they were taboo Una never knew; it was an office convention; they seemed pleasant and proper people enough.

She was initiated into the science of office supplies. In the commercial college the authorities had provided stenographers' notebooks and pencils, and the representatives of typewriter companies had given lectures on cleaning and oiling typewriters, putting in new ribbons, adjusting tension-wheels. But Una had not realized how many tools she had to know –

Desks, filing-cabinets, mimeographs, adding-machines, card indexes, desk calendars, telephone-extensions, adjustable desk-lights. Wire correspondence-baskets, erasers, carbon paper, type-brushes, dust-rags, waste-paper-baskets. Pencils, hard and soft, black and blue and red. Pens, nibs, backing-sheets, notebooks, paper-clips. Gum, paste, stationery: the half-dozen sorts of envelopes and letter-heads.

Tools were these, as important in her trade as the masthead and black flag, the cutlasses and crimson sashes, the gold doubloons and damsels fair of pirate fiction; or the cheese and cream, old horses and slumberous lanes of rustic comedy. As important, and perhaps to be deemed as romantic some day; witness the rhapsodic advertisements of filing-cabinets that are built like battle-ships; of carbon-paper that is magic-inked and satin-smooth.

Not as priest or soldier or judge does youth seek honour to-day, but as a man of offices. The business subaltern, charming and gallant as the

jungle-gallopers of Kipling, drills files, not of troops, but of correspondence. The artist plays the keys, not of pianos, but of typewriters. Desks,
not decks; courts of office-buildings, not of palaces – these are the stuff
of our latter-day drama. Not through wolf-haunted forest nor purple
cañons, but through tiled passages and elevators move our heroes of
to-day.

And our heroine is important not because she is an Amazon or a
Ramona, but because she is representative of some millions of women in
business, and because, in a vague but undiscouraged way, she keeps on
inquiring what women in business can do to make human their existence
of loveless routine.

From *The Job* by Sinclair Lewis, 1917

Sir Phoebus

I think of the easy rhyme I thought of the other day, sitting opposite dark
faced smiling Sir Phoebus, at that moment at loss for a phrase succinctly
to discourage but not offend the too-protestant old school-friend would-be
author:

Astarte, Gave a Party, In Cromarty, Everyone was Rather Hearty.

Quite suddenly you see, quite simply, there you are, there. I laugh. Sir
Phoebus lifts an inquiring eyebrow. I tell him I have made a poem. I say
it to him. He laughs: 'Oh to hell with the old school pal,' he says, 'finish
him off for me.'

Finishing off Old Etonians; writing to boring relations; writing
speeches, writing writing writing; seeing government officials 'about land
tenure in the Argentine', about 'mining rights in Alaska', about shipment
of religious statue home to France – a gesture (generous too the thing
cost him 100 guineas), on Sir Phoebus's part 'to make his soul'; paying
servants, doing accounts, coding and decoding, walking dogs, writing
charitable publicity for firm's pet charity (103 different appeals to the
season); reading manuscripts. Signing my letters: Private Secretary – on
one never to be forgotten and glorious occasion receiving a reply from
the Minister of Guess What's secretary addressed to me: Dear Private
Secretary, and signed Private Secretary; deep baying to deep, private
secretaries on the line. 'The Minister hopes . . .' 'Would you be so kind as
to inform the Minister?' 'Sir Phoebus hopes . . .' Ministerial and baronetly
hopes, reliant upon private secretariat. Signing my letters: Charity
Publicity. Signing my letters: Reader, for Editorial Manager. Signing
my letters: Phoebus Ullwater *tout court*, without the hedging chivvying

invaliant p.p. Phoebus Ullwater, in slanting ruffling swashbuckling forgery. Forgery.

I love Sir Phoebus, at this moment, I love him with a deep and grateful love. He is the only man with whom I have consistently (I think, perhaps he does not) behaved myself, as an efficient worker, as a willing donkey, as a happy equable creature, blandly and happily performing its duties; an *animula, vagula, blandula* of the office. So grateful to him that for him at least I can be no tearing devil sobbing and fighting. I look at him with a smiling, happy, guiltless face. I look at him across the desk. I laugh, there are always so many things to laugh about, and so much work to do.

From *Novel on Yellow Paper* by Stevie Smith, 1936

Poppy Sellers

. . . The staff of Twigg and Dersingham had been enlarged at the beginning of this week by the appointment of a second typist. Miss Poppy Sellers had arrived.

The girls who earn their keep by going to offices and working typewriters may be divided into three classes. There are those who, like Miss Matfield, are the daughters of professional gentlemen and so condescend to the office and the typewriter, who work beneath them just as girls once married beneath them. There are those who take it all simply and calmly, because they are in the office tradition, as Mr Smeeth's daughter would have been. Then there are those who rise to the office and the typewriter, who may not make any more money than their sisters and cousins who work in factories and cheap shops – they may easily make considerably less money – but nevertheless are able to cut superior and ladylike figures in their respective family circles because they have succeeded in becoming typists. Poppy belonged to this third class. Her father worked on the Underground, and he and his family of four occupied half a house not far from Eel Brook Common, Fulham, that south-western wilderness of vanishing mortar and bricks that are coming down in the world. This was not Poppy's first job, for she was twenty and had been steadily improving herself in the commercial world since she was fifteen, but it was easily her most important one. She had been chosen out of a large number of applicants, had been started at two pounds and ten shillings a week, and had been told confidentially by Mr Smeeth, who seemed to her a terrifying figure, that she had good prospects if she would only learn and work hard. This Poppy fully intended to do, for – as her testimonials were compelled to admit – she was a very industrious and conscientious girl. She was not sufficiently plain to escape entirely the attentions of the youths who hung about the entrance to the Red Hall Cinema in Walham Green (and Poppy frequently visited the Red Hall with her friend, Dora Black, for she liked entertainment), but nobody yet had said that she was pretty. She was small and slight, had dark hair and brown eyes, and she aimed, rather timidly, at a Japanese or Javanese or general Oriental effect, wearing a fringe and all that, but only succeeded in looking vaguely dingy and untidy. Whenever she despairingly made a special effort, plying hard the lipstick, being lavish with the Oriental-effect face-powder, and raising and keeping her eyebrows so high that it hurt, people asked her if she wasn't feeling very well. This failure to achieve the exotic beauty that was – as both she and Dora Black believed – 'her type,' tended to keep poor Poppy slightly depressed and out of love with herself. During her first few days at Twigg and Dersingham's, she was like a mouse. She was overawed by the newness and importance of everything, and she saw that it would be impossible for her to make a friend of the large, superior, infinitely knowledgeable, tremendously condescending Miss Matfield. But, like a mouse, she kept her eyes open, missing nothing, with her busy little Cockney mind fastening on every crumb of information and gossip. After three days, Miss Dora Black, of Basuto Road, Fulham, knew more, though at second-hand, about the office staff of Twigg and Dersingham than Mr Dersingham himself had learned in three years.

He was interrupted by a touch on his arm, and he looked round to find the new typist at his elbow, looking up at him with her biggish brown eyes. She had a lot of powder on one side of her nose, and none at all, just shiny skin, on the other side. No good.

'Please,' said Miss Sellers in her chirpy little Cockney voice, 'please, have you written to the Anglo-What's-It Shipping?'

'No, I haven't,' he replied.

She merely stared.

'I haven't written to the Anglo-What's-It Shipping,' he continued severely, 'because I've never heard of the Anglo-What's-It Shipping. Don't know them – see?'

'Oo, I'm sorry,' though she did not sound very sorry. 'Have I said something wrong? I can't remember all these names yet. Give me a chance. You know who I mean, don't you? It is Anglo-something, isn't it?'

'If it's the Anglo-Baltic Shipping Co. you're talking about,' said Turgis with dignity, 'then I have written to them. Wrote yesterday, 's'matter of fact. But to the Anglo-Baltic, mind you. There's no what's-it about it.'

The girl looked at him for a moment. 'Oo,' she cried softly, 'squashed!' And then she promptly walked away.

Turgis glanced after her with distaste. 'Getting cheeky now,' he told himself. 'That's the latest – getting cheeky. And just because she can't make up to me. All right, Miss Dirty Fringe, you'll have to be told off soon, you will. Try it again, that's all, just try it again.' And he was filled with a righteous indignation, pointing out to himself that these girls didn't know their place in an office, wouldn't get on with their work properly, and were always trying their little tricks on men who wanted to do their job with no nonsense about it.

From *Angel Pavement* by J. B. Priestley, 1930

Deeply Morbid

Deeply morbid deeply morbid was the girl who typed the letters
Always out of office hours running with her social betters
But when daylight and the darkness of the office closed about her
Not for this ah not for this her office colleagues came to doubt her
It was that look within her eye
Why did it always seem to say goodbye?

Joan her name was and at lunchtime
Solitary solitary
She would go and watch the pictures
In the National Gallery
All alone all alone
This time with no friend beside her
She would go and watch the pictures
All alone.

Will she leave her office colleagues
Will she leave her evening pleasures
Toil within a friendly bureau
Running later in her leisure?
All alone all alone
Before the pictures she seems turned to stone.

Close upon the Turner pictures
Closer than a thought may go
Hangs her eye and all the colours

Leap into a special glow
All for her, all alone
All for her, all for Joan...

From 'Deeply Morbid' in *Harold's Leap* by Stevie Smith, 1950

Shielding the Boss

From Mr Truax himself she learned new ways of delicately getting rid of people. He did not merely rise to indicate that an interview was over, but also arranged a system of counterfeit telephone-calls, with Una calling up from the outside office, and Mr Truax answering, 'Yes, I'll be through now in just a moment,' as a hint for the visitor. He even practised such play-acting as putting on his hat and coat and rushing out to greet an important but unwelcome caller with, 'Oh, I'm so sorry I'm just going out – late f' important engagement – given m' secretary full instructions, and I know she'll take care of you jus' as well as I could personally,' and returning to his private office by a rear door.

From *The Job* by Sinclair Lewis, 1917

Unhappy Miss Tripp

Their secretary, recently down from Lady Margaret Hall, who worked for ten shillings a week and the experience, made more mistakes than usual in her typing and looked gloomily over the wire blind at the sky. There had been several personal calls for her lately: Emmeline said perhaps she had better go home. Peter complained she made more noise than was possible with her typewriter; her touch must be unsympathetic. She had hands like mattresses; also, he did not approve of pin-money girls.

'But we can't afford one who isn't,' said Emmeline, sketching a new poster on the back of an envelope.

'I'd pay nearly ten shillings *not* to have her.'

'She may marry,' said Emmeline hopefully.

'I don't see how she can, poor thing.' Hunching his shoulders as though in a high cold wind he added: 'She doesn't like us.'

'I think she likes the experience.'

'Then she ought to pay *us* ten shillings a week.'

'We might sack her,' said Emmeline, 'that would all be an experience.'

'I don't see how we can.'

It always came back to this. Neither liked to suggest that the other should learn to type . . .

'Miss Tripp,' she said, 'I think I will dictate.'

The stenographer – unaware, naturally, that the call was to Emmeline's faculties – looked up willingly. Bored, she had been patching up her mistakes with a purple pencil. The mistakes were many, but machine-like efficiency is not, she had been given to understand, compatible with high intelligence. Though discouraged by Peter and Emmeline, she took their dictation in shorthand, which involved heavy breathing, took rather longer than long-hand, and was at times impossible to re-read correctly. She looked up smiling, as though at an invitation to dance: Emmeline should have been warned.

'Those Macclesfield students . . .'

'I've got them all filed.'

'Well, you haven't at present: they're here. I want you to take a translation down as I go along; I've got a letter from Malaga here and I can't think in Spanish.'

'One feels like that, sometimes,' said Miss Tripp.

'Ready?' said Emmeline, slightly raising her voice. Omitting the compliments, she dictated slowly a translation of the long letter. It was finished; they paused and looked at each other. 'Just read it through,' said Emmeline. Miss Tripp, with the air of walking a tight-rope, read the translation aloud. Emmeline heard it out with misgivings: this was not what she had dictated, it did not even make sense.

'It sounds odd to me,' said Miss Tripp.

'I'm afraid,' Emmeline suggested, 'it may be the shorthand. Do you think perhaps we had better go through it again?'

'I suppose,' said Miss Tripp tartly, 'they have secretaries in Malaga.'

'I suppose so: why?'

'I suppose a secretary in *Malaga* couldn't make mistakes?'

'I'm afraid no hotel would send off such a silly letter – No, never mind, Miss Tripp; go on with what you were doing; I'll just write down the translation myself.'

Miss Tripp, going scarlet, turned from Emmeline to the fireplace with a convulsive movement, as though she were about to dive up the chimney. 'It seems,' she said, 'I am not a success in this office: nothing I do is right.'

Emmeline felt for a moment they must be engaged in unholy theatricals: such things did not happen this side of the footlights. No one had struck this note in the office before. There sat Miss Tripp, trembling, in a vivid and not pleasing pink spotted frock that had no doubt last summer at Oxford seen happier days. No doubt she had punted in it, making meanwhile clear-headed remarks to recumbent friends in a voice that, penetrating the hawthorns, rang down the curves of the Cher and across the meadows. No doubt she had then been esteemed and admired: *this* seemed too cruel. What had Emmeline done – delaying with Markie, leaving the office unsmiling to clients, Miss Tripp unattended and prey, as it now appeared, to these morbid reflections? Where had she been? – she dared not account for herself. Over her bright day Nemesis fell like an axe. She said faintly: 'Do tell me what is the matter.'

Miss Tripp was quite ready for this. 'The matter is,' she said in a calm, analytical voice, 'simply, that I am human.'

Emmeline, utterly taken aback, stared at her secretary with a surprise that was most unfortunate. 'Yes?' she said.

But Miss Tripp had paused to let this remarkable statement sink in. She was in perfect command of herself: the clock ticked on, evidently some more from Emmeline was expected. 'But why not?' said Emmeline helpless.

'It does not affect you much.'

Emmeline wondered a moment if Miss Tripp had really no money besides their ten shillings, if she was starving.

'Though I dare say,' reflected Miss Tripp, 'that if one died in one's chair, or even just fainted, you might notice.'

'– I hope you are not ill?'

'Oh dear no,' said Miss Tripp, smiling bitterly. 'I find it hard to express my own point of view,' she went on fluently. 'Naturally I should never believe in allowing personal feeling to impinge on business relations: I think that's a fearful mistake. All the same, there are degrees in impersonality.'

'Oh yes . . . yes.'

Not for nothing had the unhappy stenographer said this all over again and again to herself in her bath; it came out with a patness, an impressive conviction that was confounding to Emmeline, for whom – she felt in a flash, with profound contrition – it was as though the very furniture had complained. 'What you really mean,' she said, colouring, 'is, that you find us inhuman?'

Meeting Emmeline's clear and penitent gaze, Miss Tripp who was really quite young, lost her nerve, dropped her voice and began to mumble.

'What did you say?' said Emmeline anxiously.

'I said, that's for you to decide.'

'But I don't understand,' said Emmeline, in despair . . .

From *To the North* by Elizabeth Bowen, 1932

Eight

THE BOSS

No one looms larger in the lives and the mythology – even the demon-ology – of office workers than the awful figure of the Boss. Whereas the clerk is usually portrayed as a ground-down, pathetic creature, the Boss comes across more often than not as a bloated and ruthless tyrant, the dreadfulness of whose deeds and hoped-for come-uppance provide the raw material for outraged and awestruck rumour and speculation. Sur-rounded, in many cases, by frightened courtiers and unalarming and out-wardly unambitious yes-men, who may be competent but pose no threat, office tyrants tend to be harder-working, bolder, brighter and a good deal more aggressive than their colleagues, whom they often find distressingly dim, bored, idle, sceptical or disaffected. Without such human dynamos, for whom life is work and vice versa, the rest of us would sink into an amiable but ineffectual torpor, as soon becomes apparent in most offices when the boss is away: life becomes easier and often a good deal more rational, but without the boss's chiding, fearful presence and fierce if transient passions, much of its zest and vigour drain away – in much the same way that offices which lack a central autocrat tend to become more democratic and so more bureaucratic, with consultative bumph proliferat-ing and a less harried, more egalitarian way of life only partly compensat-ing for the lack of fizz. Human dynamos shame us with their quickness and their concentration: they give their all to their work and get much from it in return, and often regard their milder, less driven colleagues with an understandable and often abrasive impatience. Scornful of compromise or consultation, except of the most severely practical kind, adept at persuading colleagues and the outside world to share – if only for a matter of minutes – their ferocious conviction that a particular product or course of action is of overwhelming urgency and correctness, to doubt which is symptomatic of moral turpitude as well as of pro-fessional incompetence, they bring to office life the same heightened emotions and intensity of feeling that a passionate, ambitious, over-protective parent brings to bear on its children; and whatever their secret doubts in the small hours of the morning, they need to exude a contagious self-confidence and awareness of their worth if they are to activate their sluggish colleagues and staff.

By their very nature, bosses incur – justly or not – fear, dislike and resentment as well as admiration, loyalty, gratitude and affection. Not all bosses, it goes without saying, are raging tyrants, and the thickness of the velvet glove will differ in every case. The ideal is probably the office equivalent of the 18th-century enlightened despot: bosses who are weak, indecisive or over-matey may well end up being ignored or despised, and will almost certainly be speedily replaced. That said, unenlightened despots like James Joyce's abrasive Mr Alleyne or the vespine Sir Roderick Jones make for better anecdotes than more moderate rulers, not least because of the righteous indignation they arouse in those who are told of their crimes, whether in a whisper in the office lavatory or on the printed page: but whereas the bovine Farrington slouches off to lick his wounds and hurl defiance in the pub before taking out his drunken rage and resentment on his wretched child, James Lees-Milne's settling of scores with Sir Roderick will delight all those who have suffered the tyrant's lash.

Unlike Sir Roderick, most bosses share Babbitt's need to be liked by their staff: rather than give a direct but unwelcome answer, the more devious and euphemistic kind of boss may well prefer to employ the technique perfected by Mr Spenlow, whereby blame for one's own decisions can be transferred to intransigent or unsympathetic colleagues. And at home, or in the street outside, the figure of pomp or the despot may cut no ice whatsoever, as Trollope understood and as Mr Pooter discovered, much to his indignation, when he brought up Mr Perkupp's hallowed name at the Lord Mayor's Ball.

Bustling, pompous, insecure, all too well aware of the passing of time and dreaming of his fairy girl, Babbitt is, in his pathos and absurdity, more typical of his kind than most would care to admit. Certainly he's a far more plausible and human figure than the saccharine, do-gooding Cheeryble Brothers: though there's no doubt that had Tim Linkinwater downed tools or demanded a hefty rise, they'd have been quick to keep him firmly in his place.

The Turkey-cock in his Farmyard

On the following morning he received a message, at about one o'clock, by the mouth of the Boardroom messenger, informing him that his presence was required in the Boardroom. 'Sir Raffle Buffle has desired your presence, Mr Eames.'

'My presence, Tupper! what for?' said Johnny, turning upon the messenger almost with dismay.

'Indeed I can't say, Mr Eames; but Sir Raffle Buffle has desired your presence in the Boardroom.'

Such a message as that in official life always strikes awe into the heart of a young man. And yet, young men generally come forth from such interviews without having received any serious damage, and generally talk about the old gentlemen whom they have encountered with a good deal of light-spirited sarcasm, – or chaff, as it is called in the slang phraseology of the day. It is that same 'majesty which doth hedge a king' that does it. The turkey-cock in his own farmyard is master of the occasion, and the thought of him creates fear. A bishop in his lawn, a judge on the bench, a chairman in the big room at the end of a long table, or a policeman with his bull's-eye lamp upon his beat, can all make themselves terrible by means of those appanages of majesty which have been vouchsafed to them. But how mean is the policeman in his own home, and how few thought much of Sir Raffle Buffle as he sat asleep after dinner in his old slippers! How well can I remember the terror created within me by the air of outraged dignity with which a certain fine old gentleman, now long since gone, could rub his hands slowly, one on the other, and look up to the ceiling, slightly shaking his head, as though lost in the contemplation of my iniquities! I would become sick in my stomach, and feel as though my ankles had been broken. That upward turn of the eye unmanned me so completely that I was speechless as regarded any defence. I think that that old man could hardly have known the extent of his own power . . .

From *The Small House at Allington* by Anthony Trollope, 1864

Reggie and C.J.

Reggie strode purposefully across the thick carpet, trying to look unconcerned, as befitted a man starting a new life.

'You wanted to see me, C.J.?' he said.

'Yes. Sit down.'

The pneumatic chair welcomed him to its bosom with a sympathetic sigh.

'Don't forget you're coming to dinner tomorrow evening, C.J.,' he said.

'No. Mrs C.J. and I are looking forward to it immensely.'

'Good.'

'By the way, Reggie, Mrs C.J. doesn't see eye to eye with our piscine friends. I hope that doesn't upset any apple carts.'

'No, C.J.'

'People and their fads, eh?'

'Not at all.'

'Still, if you don't like something, you don't like it.'

'Too true.'

'No use kicking against the pricks.'

'Certainly not, C.J.'

'Neither Mrs C.J. nor myself has ever kicked against a prick.'

'I imagine not, C.J.'

'Now, to business,' said C.J. 'I didn't get where I am today by waffling.'

'No.'

'Never use two words where one will do, that's my motto, that's my axiom, that's the way I look at it.'

'Absolutely, C.J.'

The treble glazing in C.J.'s windows kept out all noise. There was a thick, carpeted silence in the room.

'Would it surprise you, Reggie, to learn that overall sales, across the whole spectrum, were down 0.1 per cent in April?'

'Not altogether, C.J.'

The Francis Bacon stared down as if it knew that C.J. had bought it for tax purposes.

'I don't say to myself: "Oh well, C.J., it's a bad time all round." I say: "C.J., this is intolerable." But I don't say to you: "Pull your socks up, Reggie." I say to you: "Overall sales, across the whole spectrum, were down 0.1 per cent in April." I leave you to draw your own conclusions – and pull your socks up.'

'Yes, C.J.'

'I didn't get where I am today without learning how to handle people.'

'No, C.J.'

'I give them a warning shot across the bows, but I don't let them realize that I'm giving them a warning shot across the bows.'

'Yes, C.J.'

'Not that I want to be entirely surrounded by yes-men.'
'No, C.J.'

From *The Death of Reginald Perrin* by David Nobbs, 1975

The Demon King

The bell rang furiously and, when Miss Parker went to the tube, a furious voice called out in a piercing North of Ireland accent:

'Send Farrington here!'

Miss Parker returned to her machine, saying to a man who was writing at a desk:

'Mr Alleyne wants you upstairs.'

The man muttered '*Blast* him!' under his breath and pushed back his chair to stand up. When he stood up he was tall and of great bulk. He had a hanging face, dark wine-coloured, with fair eyebrows and moustache: his eyes bulged forward slightly and the whites of them were dirty. He lifted up the counter and, passing by the clients, went out of the office with a heavy step.

He went heavily upstairs until he came to the second landing, where a door bore a brass plate with the inscription *Mr Alleyne*. Here he halted, puffing with labour and vexation, and knocked. The shrill voice cried:

'Come in!'

The man entered Mr Alleyne's room. Simultaneously Mr Alleyne, a little man wearing gold-rimmed glasses on a clean-shaven face, shot his head up over a pile of documents. The head itself was so pink and hairless it seemed like a large egg reposing on the papers. Mr Alleyne did not lose a moment:

'Farrington? What is the meaning of this? Why have I always to complain of you? May I ask you why you haven't made a copy of that contract between Bodley and Kirwan? I told you it must be ready by four o'clock.'

'But Mr Shelly said, sir –'

'*Mr Shelly said, sir* ... Kindly attend to what I say and not to what *Mr Shelly says, sir*. You have always some excuse or another for shirking work. Let me tell you that if the contract is not copied before this evening I'll lay the matter before Mr Crosbie ... Do you hear me now?'

'Yes, sir.'

'Do you hear me now? ... Ay and another little matter! I might as well be talking to the wall as talking to you. Understand once for all that you get a half an hour for your lunch and not an hour and a half. How many courses do you want? I'd like to know ... Do you mind me now?'

'Yes, sir.'

Mr Alleyne bent his head again upon his pile of papers. The man stared fixedly at the polished skull which directed the affairs of Crosbie & Alleyne, gauging its fragility. A spasm of rage gripped his throat for a few moments and then passed, leaving after it a sharp sensation of thirst. The man recognized the sensation and felt that he must have a good night's drinking. The middle of the month was passed and, if he could get the copy done in time, Mr Alleyne might give him an order on the cashier. He stood still, gazing fixedly at the head upon the pile of papers. Suddenly Mr Alleyne began to upset all the papers, searching for something. Then, as if he had been unaware of the man's presence till that moment, he shot up his head again, saying:

'Eh? Are you going to stand there all day? Upon my word, Farrington, you take things easy!'

'I was waiting to see . . .'

'Very good, you needn't wait to see. Go downstairs and do your work.'

The man walked heavily towards the door and, as he went out of the room, he heard Mr Alleyne cry after him that if the contract was not copied by evening Mr Crosbie would hear of the matter.

He returned to his desk in the lower office and counted the sheets which remained to be copied. He took up his pen and dipped it in the ink, but he continued to stare stupidly at the last words he had written: *In no case shall the said Bernard Bodley be* . . . The evening was falling and in a few minutes they would be lighting the gas: then he could write. He felt that he must slake the thirst in his throat. He stood up from his desk and, lifting the counter as before, passed out of the office. As he was passing out the chief clerk looked at him inquiringly.

'It's all right, Mr Shelly,' said the man, pointing with his finger to indicate the objective of his journey.

The chief clerk glanced at the hat-rack, but, seeing the row complete, offered no remark. As soon as he was on the landing the man pulled a shepherd's plaid cap out of his pocket, put it on his head and ran quickly down the rickety stairs. From the street door he walked on furtively on the inner side of the path towards the corner and all at once dived into a doorway. He was now safe in the dark snug of O'Neill's shop, and, filling up the little window that looked into the bar with his inflamed face, the colour of dark wine or dark meat, he called out:

'Here, Pat, give us a g.p., like a good fellow.'

The curate brought him a glass of plain porter. The man drank it at a gulp and asked for a caraway seed. He put his penny on the counter and, leaving the curate to grope for it in the gloom, retreated out of the snug as furtively as he had entered it.

Darkness, accompanied by a thick fog, was gaining upon the dusk of February and the lamps in Eustace Street had been lit. The man went up by the houses until he reached the door of the office, wondering whether he could finish his copy in time. On the stairs a moist pungent odour of perfumes saluted his nose: evidently Miss Delacour had come while he was out in O'Neill's. He crammed his cap back again into his pocket and re-entered the office, assuming an air of absent-mindedness.

'Mr Alleyne has been calling for you,' said the chief clerk severely. 'Where were you?'

The man glanced at the two clients who were standing at the counter as if to intimate that their presence prevented him from answering. As the clients were both male the chief clerk allowed himself a laugh.

'I know that game,' he said. 'Five times in one day is a little bit ... Well, you better look sharp and get a copy of our correspondence in the Delacour case for Mr Alleyne.'

This address in the presence of the public, his run upstairs, and the porter he had gulped down so hastily confused the man and, as he sat down at his desk to get what was required, he realized how hopeless was the task of finishing his copy of the contract before half past five. The dark damp night was coming and he longed to spend it in the bars, drinking with his friends amid the glare of gas and the clatter of glasses. He got out the Delacour correspondence and passed out of the office. He hoped Mr Alleyne would not discover that the last two letters were missing.

The moist pungent perfume lay all the way up to Mr Alleyne's room. Miss Delacour was a middle-aged woman of Jewish appearance. Mr Alleyne was said to be sweet on her or on her money. She came to the office often and stayed a long time when she came. She was sitting beside his desk now in an aroma of perfumes, smoothing the handle of her umbrella and nodding the great black feather in her hat. Mr Alleyne had swivelled his chair round to face her and thrown his right foot jauntily upon his left knee. The man put the correspondence on the desk and bowed respectfully, but neither Mr Alleyne nor Miss Delacour took any notice of his bow. Mr Alleyne tapped a finger on the correspondence and then flicked it towards him as if to say: '*That's all right, you can go.*'

The man returned to the lower office and sat down again at his desk. He stared intently at the incomplete phrase: *In no case shall the said Bernard Bodley be* ... and thought how strange it was that the last three words began with the same letter. The chief clerk began to hurry Miss Parker, saying she would never have the letters typed in time for post. The man listened to the clicking of the machine for a few minutes and then set to work to finish his copy. But his head was not clear and his mind wandered away to the glare and rattle of the public-house. It was a night for hot punches. He struggled on with his copy, but when the clock struck five he had still fourteen pages to write. Blast it! He couldn't finish it in time. He longed to execrate aloud, to bring his fist down on something violently. He was so enraged that he wrote *Bernard Bernard* instead of *Bernard Bodley* and had to begin again on a clean sheet.

He felt strong enough to clear out the whole office single-handed. His body ached to do something, to rush out and revel in violence. All the indignities of his life enraged him . . . Could he ask the cashier privately for an advance? No, the cashier was no good, no damn good: he wouldn't give an advance . . . He knew where he would meet the boys: Leonard and O'Halloran and Nosey Flynn. The barometer of his emotional nature was set for a spell of riot.

His imagination had so abstracted him that his name was called twice before he answered. Mr Alleyne and Miss Delacour were standing outside the counter and all the clerks had turned round in anticipation of something. The man got up from his desk. Mr Alleyne began a tirade of abuse, saying that two letters were missing. The man answered that he knew nothing about them, that he had made a faithful copy. The tirade continued: it was so bitter and violent that the man could hardly restrain his fist from descending upon the head of the manikin before him.

'I know nothing about any other two letters,' he said stupidly.

'*You – know – nothing*. Of course you know nothing,' said Mr Alleyne. 'Tell me,' he added, glancing first for approval to the lady beside him, 'do you take me for a fool? Do you think me an utter fool?'

The man glanced from the lady's face to the little egg-shaped head and back again; and, almost before he was aware of it, his tongue had found a felicitous moment:

'I don't think, sir,' he said, 'that that's a fair question to put to me.'

There was a pause in the very breathing of the clerks. Everyone was astounded (the author of the witticism no less than his neighbours) and Miss Delacour, who was a stout amiable person, began to smile broadly. Mr Alleyne flushed to the hue of a wild rose and his mouth twitched with a dwarf's passion. He shook his fist in the man's face till it seemed to vibrate like the knob of some electric machine:

'You impertinent ruffian! You impertinent ruffian! I'll make short work of you! Wait till you see! You'll apologize to me for your impertinence or you'll quit the office instanter! You'll quit this, I'm telling you, or you'll apologize to me!'

He stood in a doorway opposite the office, watching to see if the cashier would come out alone. All the clerks passed out and finally the cashier came out with the chief clerk. It was no use trying to say a word to him when he was with the chief clerk. The man felt that his position was bad enough. He had been obliged to offer an abject apology to Mr Alleyne for his impertinence, but he knew what a hornet's nest the office would be for him. He could remember the way in which Mr Alleyne had hounded little Peake out of the office in order to make room for his own nephew. He felt savage and thirsty and revengeful, annoyed with himself and with everyone else. Mr Alleyne would never give him an hour's rest; his life would be a hell to him. He had made a proper fool of himself this time. Could he not keep his tongue in his cheek? But they had never pulled together from the first, he and Mr Alleyne, ever since the day Mr Alleyne had overheard him mimicking his North of Ireland accent to amuse Higgins and Miss Parker; that had been the beginning of it . . .

From 'Counterparts' in *Dubliners* by James Joyce, 1914

Lord Copper

Twenty minutes later William and Mr Salter passed the first of the great doors which divided Lord Copper's personal quarters from the general office. The carpets were thicker here, the lights softer, the expressions of the inhabitants more careworn. The typewriters were of a special kind; their keys made no more sound than the drumming of a bishop's fingertips on an upholstered prie-dieu; the telephone buzzers were muffled and purred like warm cats. The personal private secretaries padded through the ante-chambers and led them nearer and nearer to the presence. At last they came to massive double doors, encased in New Zealand rose-wood which by their weight, polish, and depravity of design, proclaimed unmistakably, 'Nothing but Us stands between you and Lord Copper.' Mr Salter paused, and pressed a little bell of synthetic ivory. 'It lights a lamp on Lord Copper's own desk,' he said reverently. 'I expect we shall have a long time to wait.'

But almost immediately a green light overhead flashed their permission to enter.

Lord Copper was at his desk. He dismissed some satellites and rose as William came towards him.

From *Scoop* by Evelyn Waugh, 1938

On the Rampage

On a January day the Pemberton office beheld that most terrifying crisis that can come to a hard, slave-driving office. As the office put it, 'The Old Man was on a rampage.'

Mr Pemberton, senior, most hoarily awful of all the big chiefs, had indigestion or a poor balance-sheet. He decided that everything was going wrong. He raged from room to room. He denounced the new poster, the new top for the talcum-powder container, the arrangement of the files, and the whispering in the amen corner of veteran stenographers. He sent out flocks of 'office memos.' Everybody trembled. Mr Pemberton's sons actually did some work; and, as the fire spread and the minor bosses in turn raged among their subordinates, the girls who packed soap down in the works expected to be 'fired.' After a visitation from Mr Pemberton and three raging memos within fifteen minutes, Mr S. Herbert Ross retreated toward the Lafayette Café, and Una was left to face Mr Pemberton's bear-like growls on his next appearance.

When he did appear he seemed to hold her responsible for all the world's long sadness. Meanwhile the printer was telephoning for Mr Ross's O.K. on copy, the engravers wanted to know where the devil was that colour-proof, the advertising agency sarcastically indicated that it was difficult for them to insert an advertisement before they received the order, and a girl from the cashier's office came nagging in about a bill for indian ink.

The memos began to get the range of her desk again, and Mr Pemberton's voice could be heard in a distant part of the office, approaching, menacing, all-pervading.

Una fled. She ran to a wash-room, locked the door, leaned panting against it, as though detectives were pursuing her. She was safe for a moment. They might miss her, but she was insulated from demands of, 'Where's Ross, Miss Golden? Well, why *don't* you know where he is?' from telephone calls, and from memos whose polite 'please' was a gloved threat.

From *The Job* by Sinclair Lewis, 1917

Mr Bickersdyke Blows Up

Mr Bickersdyke sat in his private room at the New Asiatic Bank with a pile of newspapers before him. At least, the casual observer would have said that it was Mr Bickersdyke. In reality, however, it was an active volcano in the shape and clothes of the bank-manager. It was freely admitted in the office that morning that the manager had lowered all records with ease. The staff had known him to be in a bad temper before – frequently; but his frame of mind on all previous occasions had been, compared with his present frame of mind, that of a rather exceptionally good-natured lamb. Within ten minutes of his arrival the entire office was on the jump. The messengers were collected in a pallid group in the basement, discussing the affair in whispers and endeavouring to restore their nerve with about sixpenn'orth of the beverage known as 'unsweet-ened'. The heads of departments, to a man, had bowed before the storm. Within the space of seven minutes and a quarter Mr Bickersdyke had contrived to find some fault with each of them. Inward Bills was out at an A.B.C. shop snatching a hasty cup of coffee, to pull him together again. Outward Bills was sitting at his desk with the glazed stare of one who has been struck in the thorax by a thunderbolt. Mr Rossiter had been torn from Psmith in the middle of a highly technical discussion of the Manchester United match, just as he was showing – with the aid of a ball of paper – how he had once seen Meredith centre to Sandy Turnbull in a Cup match, and was now leaping about like a distracted grasshopper. Mr Waller, head of the Cash Department, had been summoned to the Presence, and after listening meekly to a rush of criticism, had retired to his desk with the air of a beaten spaniel.

From *Psmith in the City* by P. G. Wodehouse, 1910

Spenlow and Jorkins

He [Mr Spenlow] was a little light-haired gentleman, with undeniable boots, and the stiffest of white cravats and shirt-collars. He was buttoned up mighty trim and tight, and must have taken a great deal of pains with his whiskers, which were accurately curled. His gold watch-chain was so massive, that a fancy came across me, that he ought to have a sinewy golden arm, to draw it out with, like those which are put up over the gold-beaters' shops. He was got up with such care, and was so stiff, that he could hardly bend himself; being obliged, when he glanced at some papers on his desk, after sitting down in his chair, to move his whole body, from the bottom of his spine, like Punch.

I had previously been presented by my aunt, and had been courteously received. He now said:

'And so, Mr Copperfield, you think of entering into our profession? I casually mentioned to Miss Trotwood, when I had the pleasure of an interview with her the other day,' – with another inclination of his body – Punch again – 'that there was a vacancy here. Miss Trotwood was good enough to mention that she had a nephew who was her peculiar care, and for whom she was seeking to provide genteelly in life. That nephew, I believe, I have now the pleasure of' – Punch again.

I bowed my acknowledgments, and said, my aunt had mentioned to me that there was that opening, and that I believed I should like it very much. That I was strongly inclined to like it, and had taken immediately to the proposal. That I could not absolutely pledge myself to like it, until I knew something more about it. That although it was little else than a matter of form, I presumed I should have an opportunity of trying how I liked it, before I bound myself to it irrevocably.

'Oh surely! surely!' said Mr Spenlow. 'We always, in this house, propose a month – an initiatory month. I should be happy, myself, to propose two months – three – an indefinite period, in fact – but I have a partner. Mr Jorkins.'

'And the premium, sir,' I returned, 'is a thousand pounds?'

'And the premium, Stamp included, is a thousand pounds,' said Mr Spenlow. 'As I have mentioned to Miss Trotwood, I am actuated by no mercenary considerations; few men are less so, I believe; but Mr Jorkins has his opinions on these subjects, and I am bound to respect Mr Jorkins's opinions. Mr Jorkins thinks a thousand pounds too little, in short.'

'I suppose, sir,' said I, still desiring to spare my aunt, 'that it is not the custom here, if an articled clerk were particularly useful, and made himself a perfect master of his profession –' I could not help blushing, this looked so like praising myself – 'I suppose it is not the custom, in the later years of his time, to allow him any –'

Mr Spenlow, by a great effort, just lifted his head far enough out of his cravat, to shake it, and answered, anticipating the word 'salary.'

'No. I will not say what consideration I might give to that point myself, Mr Copperfield, if I were unfettered. Mr Jorkins is immovable.'

I was quite dismayed by the idea of this terrible Jorkins. But I found out afterwards that he was a mild man of a heavy temperament, whose place in the business was to keep himself in the background, and be constantly exhibited by name as the most obdurate and ruthless of men. If a clerk wanted his salary raised, Mr Jorkins wouldn't listen to such a proposition. If a client were slow to settle his bill of costs, Mr Jorkins was resolved to have it paid; and however painful these things might be (and always were) to the feelings of Mr Spenlow, Mr Jorkins would have his bond. The heart and hand of the good angel Spenlow would have been always open, but for the restraining demon Jorkins. As I have grown older, I think I have had experience of some other houses doing business on the principle of Spenlow and Jorkins! ...

From *David Copperfield* by Charles Dickens, 1850

The Brothers Cheeryble

'Brother Ned,' said Mr Cheeryble, tapping with his knuckles, and stooping to listen: 'are you busy, my dear brother, or can you spare time for a word or two with me?'

'Brother Charles, my dear fellow,' replied a voice from the inside; so like in its tones to that which had just spoken, that Nicholas started, and almost thought it was the same, 'don't ask me such a question, but come in directly.'

They went in, without further parley. What was the amazement of Nicholas when his conductor advanced, and exchanged a warm greeting with another old gentleman, the very type and model of himself – the same face, the same figure, the same coat, waistcoat, and neckcloth, the same breeches and gaiters – nay, there was the very same white hat hanging against the wall!

As they shook each other by the hand – the face of each lighted up by beaming looks of affection, which would have been most delightful to behold in infants, and which, in men so old, was inexpressibly touching – Nicholas could observe that the last old gentleman was something stouter than his brother; this, and a slight additional shade of clumsiness in his gait and stature, formed the only perceptible difference between them. Nobody could have doubted their being twin brothers.

'Brother Ned,' said Nicholas's friend, closing the room-door, 'here is a young friend of mine, whom we must assist. We must make proper inquiries into his statements in justice to him as well as to ourselves, and if they are confirmed – as I feel assured they will be – we must assist him, we must assist him, brother Ned.'

'It is enough, my dear brother, that you say we should,' returned the other. 'When you say that, no further inquiries are needed. He *shall* be assisted. What are his necessities, and what does he require? Where is Tim Linkinwater? Let us have him here.'

Both the brothers, it may be here remarked, had a very emphatic and earnest delivery; but had lost nearly the same teeth, which imparted the same peculiarity to their speech; and both spoke as if, besides possessing the utmost serenity of mind that the kindliest and most unsuspecting nature could bestow, they had, in collecting the plums from Fortune's choicest pudding, retained a few for present use, and kept them in their mouths.

'Where is Tim Linkinwater?' said brother Ned.

'Stop, stop, stop!' said brother Charles, taking the other aside. 'I've a plan, my dear brother, I've a plan. Tim is getting old, and Tim has been a faithful servant, brother Ned, and I don't think pensioning Tim's mother and sister, and buying a little tomb for the family when his poor brother died, was a sufficient recompense for his faithful services.'

'No, no, no,' replied the other. 'Certainly not. Not half enough, not half.'

'If we could lighten Tim's duties,' said the old gentleman, 'and prevail upon him to go into the country, now and then, and sleep in the fresh air, two or three times a-week (which he could, if he began business an hour later in the morning), old Tim Linkinwater would grow young again in time; and he's three good years our senior now. Old Tim Linkinwater young again! Eh, brother Ned, eh? why, I recollect old Tim Linkinwater quite a little boy, don't you? Ha, ha, ha! Poor Tim, poor Tim!'

The fine old fellows laughed pleasantly together: each with a tear of regard for old Tim Linkinwater, standing in his eye.

'But hear this first – hear this first, brother Ned,' said the old man, hastily, placing two chairs, one on each side of Nicholas. 'I'll tell it you myself, brother Ned, because the young gentleman is modest, and is a scholar, Ned, and I shouldn't feel it right that he should tell us his story over and over again as if he was a beggar, or as if we doubted him. No, no, no.'

'No, no, no,' returned the other, nodding his head gravely. 'Very right, my dear brother, very right.'

'He will tell me I'm wrong, if I make a mistake,' said Nicholas's friend. 'But whether I do or not, you'll be very much affected, brother Ned, remembering the time when we were two friendless lads and earned our first shilling in this great city.'

The twins pressed each other's hands in silence; and in his own homely manner, brother Charles related the particulars he had heard from Nicholas. The conversation which ensued, was a long one, and when it was over, a secret conference of almost equal duration took place between brother Ned and Tim Linkinwater in another room. It is no disparagement to Nicholas to say, that before he had been closeted with the two brothers ten minutes, he could only wave his hand at every fresh expression of kindness and sympathy, and sob like a little child.

From *Nicholas Nickleby* by Charles Dickens, 1839

Babbitt Dictates a Letter

He sighed; he read through his mail; he shouted 'Msgoun,' which meant 'Miss McGoun'; and began to dictate.

This was his own version of his first letter:

'Omar Gribble, send it to his office, Miss McGoun, yours of twentieth to hand and in reply would say look here, Gribble, I'm awfully afraid if we go on shilly-shallying like this we'll just naturally lose the Allen sale, I had Allen up on carpet day before yesterday and got right down to cases and think I can assure you – uh, uh, no, change that: all my experience indicates he is all right, means to do business, looked into his financial record which is fine – that sentence seems to be a little balled up, Miss McGoun; make a couple sentences out of it if you have to, period, new paragraph.

'He is perfectly willing to pro rate the special assessment and strikes me, am dead sure there will be no difficulty in getting him to pay for title insurance, so now for heaven's sake let's get busy – no, make that: so now let's go to it and get down – no, that's enough – you can tie those sentences up a little better when you type 'em, Miss McGoun – your sincerely, etcetera.'

This is the version of his letter which he received, typed, from Miss McGoun that afternoon:

BABBITT–THOMPSON REALTY CO.

Homes for Folks

Reeves Bldg., Oberlin Avenue & 3d St., N.E.

Zenith.

Omar Gribble, Esq.,
576 North American Building,
Zenith.

Dear Mr Gribble:

Your letter of the twentieth to hand. I must say I'm awfully afraid that if we go on shilly-shallying like this we'll just naturally lose the Allen sale. I had Allen up on the carpet day before yesterday, and got right down to cases. All my experience indicates that he means to do business. I have also looked into his financial record, which is fine.

He is perfectly willing to pro rate the special assessment, and there will be no difficulty in getting him to pay for title insurance.

So let's go!

Yours sincerely,

As he read and signed it, in his correct flowing business-college hand, Babbitt reflected, 'Now that's a good, strong letter, and clear's a bell. Now what the – I never told McGoun to make a third paragraph there! Wish she'd quit trying to improve on my dictation! But what I can't understand is: why can't Stan Graff or Chet Laylock write a letter like that? With punch! With a kick!'

From *Babbitt* by Sinclair Lewis, 1922

He Wants to be Loved...

With the exception of Brown (whom Kagle hates, fears, and distrusts, and can do nothing about), Kagle tries to like everyone who works for him and to have everyone like him. He is reluctant to discipline his salesmen or reprimand them, even when he (or Brown) catches them cheating on their expense accounts or lying about their sales calls or business trips. (Kagle lies about his own business trips and, like the rest of us, probably cheats at least a little on his expense accounts.) He is unwilling to get rid of people, even those who turn drunkard, like Red Parker, or useless in other ways. This is one of the criticisms heard about him frequently. (It is occasionally made against him by the same people other people want him to get rid of.) He won't, for example, retire Ed Phelps, who wants to hang on. ('I'd throw half those lying sons of bitches right out on their ass,' Brown enjoys bragging out loud to me and Kagle about Kagle's sales force, as though challenging Kagle to do the same. 'And I'd put the other half of those lazy bastards on notice.')

Kagle wants desperately to be popular with all the 'lying sons of bitches' and 'lazy bastards' who work for him, even the clerks, receptionists, and typists, and goes out of his way to make conversation with them; as a result, they despise him. The more they despise him, the better he tries to be to them; the better he is to them, the more they despise him. There are days when his despair is so heavy that he seems almost incapable of stirring from his office or allowing anyone (but me) in to see him. He keeps his door shut for long periods of time, skips lunch entirely rather than allow even his secretary to deliver it, and does everything he can by telephone.

Kagle is comfortable with me (even on his very bad days), and I am comfortable with him. Sometimes he sends for me just to have me confirm or deny rumours he has heard (or made up) and help dispel his anxieties and shame. I do not test or threaten him; I pose no problem; on the contrary, he knows I aid him (or try to) in handling the problems created by others. Kagle trusts me and knows he is safe with me. Kagle doesn't scare me any longer. (In fact, I feel that I could scare him whenever I chose to, that he is weak in relation to me and that I am strong in relation to him, and I have this hideous urge every now and then while he is confiding in me to shock him suddenly and send him reeling forever with some brutal, unexpected insult, or to kick his crippled leg. It's a weird mixture of injured rage and cruel loathing that starts to rise within me and has to be suppressed, and I don't know where it comes from or how long I will be able to master it.) Kagle has lost faith in himself; this could be damaging, for people here, like people everywhere, have little pity for failures, and no affection.

From *Something Happened* by Joseph Heller, 1974

. . . and So Does Babbitt

Babbitt did not often squabble with his employees. He liked to like the people about him; he was dismayed when they did not like him. It was only when they attacked the sacred purse that he was frightened into fury, but then, being a man given to oratory and high principles, he enjoyed the sound of his own vocabulary and the warmth of his own virtue. To-day he had so passionately indulged in self-approval that he wondered whether he had been entirely just:

'After all, Stan isn't a boy any more. Oughtn't to call him so hard. But rats, got to haul folks over the coals now and then for their own good. Unpleasant duty, but – I wonder if Stan is sore? What's he saying to McGoun out there?'

So chill a wind of hatred blew from the outer office that the normal comfort of his evening home-going was ruined. He was distressed by losing that approval of his employees to which an executive is always slave. Ordinarily he left the office with a thousand enjoyable fussy directions to the effect that there would undoubtedly be important tasks to-morrow, and Miss McGoun and Miss Bannigan would do well to be there early, and for heaven's sake remind him to call up Conrad Lyte soon's he came in. To-night he departed with feigned and apologetic liveliness. He was as afraid of his still-faced clerks – of the eyes focused on him, Miss McGoun staring with head lifted from her typing, Miss Bannigan looking over her ledger, Mat Penniman craning around at his desk in the dark alcove, Stanley Graff sullenly expressionless – as a parvenu before the bleak propriety of his butler. He hated to expose his back to their laughter, and in his effort to be casually merry he stammered and was raucously friendly and oozed wretchedly out of the door.

From *Babbitt* by Sinclair Lewis, 1922

A Man-to-man Relationship

Lovebold fetched an expenses chit, while the matter was still fresh in Mounce's mind, and wrote down at random on it two nights' expenses in Wolverhampton, with lunches and entertainment for contacts, adding up to £6 8s 4d. He gave it to Mounce to sign. Mounce folded his hands and closed his eyes.

'For what we are about to receive,' he said, 'may the Lord make us truly thankful.'

A bluff, friendly, man-to-man relationship with your staff, he reflected as he scribbled his signature; that was the way to do it. A bit of bluster – one's staff respected it. A little turning of the old blind eye – they loved you for it. And if they ever took it into their heads to let you down you could always get them the boot for fiddling their exes.

From *Towards the End of the Morning* by Michael Frayn, 1967

Seen out of Context

19 January 1661: And after dinner I ... went to the theatre, where I saw *The Lost Lady*, which doth not please me much. Here I was troubled to be seen by four of our office clerks, which sat in the half-crown box and I in the 1s–6d ...

From the *Diary* of Samuel Pepys, 1661

Mr Perkupp Cuts no Ice

We arrived at the Mansion House too early, which was rather fortunate, for I had an opportunity of speaking to his lordship, who graciously condescended to talk with me some minutes; but I must say I was disappointed to find he did not even know Mr Perkupp, the principal.

From *The Diary of a Nobody* by George and Weedon Grossmith, 1892

Exquisite Revenge

By 1935 it became apparent that I ought to have a permanent job which offered what are called prospects. I could not live indefinitely on a private secretary's salary, agreeable though my actual occupation was. I must earn more money. Lord Lloyd with the kindest intentions got me into Reuters. I left him with heartfelt gratitude and regret.

From the very start I knew that Reuters was not my, and I was not going to be its, cup of tea. My dreamy temperament was hopelessly unsuited to the slick purpose of news scooping. I was far too slow and totally lacking push. Besides, I was absolutely indifferent whether Reuters or the Press Association were first to learn and pass on to the *Daily Sketch* that Swaziland was about to invade Mozambique, or that King Zog was engaged to the daughter of a greengrocer. Neither mattered to me in the very least. Yet it was necessary to suppose it did if one wished to be a success in this distributary of daily incident and sensation.

Because of my recent employment I was made third and junior secretary to the Chairman, Sir Roderick Jones. The appointment was looked upon as a firm rung on the Reuters ladder, albeit the bottom rung of all. Unfortunately Sir Roderick and I were in all respects antipodal. There is no need to expatiate further upon my deficiencies with which by now the reader is all too familiar. Let me then concentrate for a moment on Sir Roderick's. He was in stature a little undersized. He was spruce, and dapper, and perky. I would describe his appearance as that of a sparrow were it not for his waist which, instead of being loose, was tight, pinched in by a conspicuous double-breasted waistcoat which he habitually wore like a corset. This constrictive garment gave him the shape of a magnified wasp. His face too resembled that of a wasp seen under a microscope. It was long and the bulbous nose was proboscis-like. His small eyes darted rapidly in his head in the manner of that insect. They never rested on their victim, yet because of a feverish activity missed nothing. His mouth too was sharp and vespine. His sting was formidable and unlike the bee's could be repeated.

Sir Roderick Jones was intensely proud of the exalted position he occupied in Fleet Street and the world of power. He wished his influence to be felt by the great and humble, particularly the humble. When his Rolls Royce drove up each morning to the main entrance of Reuters a bell rang violently in every room and passage of the building to announce the Chairman's arrival. There was a general scurry and flurry of alarm. When it drove off in the evening another bell rang more softly. There was a contrasting sigh of relief and relaxation of tension.

I have no doubt that Sir Roderick was a loving and loved husband and father. As an employer he was not likeable. He was the very reincarnation of Martinet, without the grisly charm of that French drill-master. He devised an office routine from which no deviation was permissible in any circumstance. He demanded from his underlings the strictest observance of infinitesimal minutiae. For instance, every object on his desk had to be arranged each morning with meticulous exactitude. The edges of the in-tray must be flush with those of the out-tray. The silver calendar, turned for the day, two inches to the left of the clock. Pencils newly sharpened, and clean nibs in pen-holders. The penwiper at right angles to the blotter, freshly filled. Telephones and intercommunicator slightly staggered at an angle of, say, 22½ degrees from the chair. Envelope rack within easy reach without necessitating undue stretching, yet not so close that the elbow had to be unnaturally crooked. If the softest of the three india rubbers was not found on the left-hand side of the row on the allotted tray and adjacent to the red (not blue) sealing-wax, Sir Roderick's displeasure could be terrible.

As third secretary I was responsible for the daily arrangement of Sir Roderick's desk. I also took down and typed out the less important letters he cared to dictate to me. If he detected that a single word had been rubbed out and retyped, the whole page, complete with four carbon copies, was sent back to be done again no matter how late in the evening it was. I was only allowed to draft letters to shops. I once worded a letter to Trumpers as follows: 'Dear Sirs, Will you kindly send me a medium-sized bottle (no. 2) of your "Ecstatic" brilliantine, Yours faithfully (Sgd) Roderick Jones, K.B.E., Chairman and Managing Director of Reuters.' Sir Roderick returned unsigned the typed draft with a pencil line through it and the querulous comment, 'Kindly send is not grammar.' I retyped and submitted a second draft: 'Dear Sirs, Will you send me kindly a medium-sized bottle, etc.' This draft was likewise returned scratched out, with a caustic note, 'Are you trying to be funny, Mr Milne?' Sir Roderick's abbreviation of my surname always nettled me, as it was intended to do. I submitted a third draft: 'Dear Sirs, Will kindly you send me a medium-sized bottle...' Again the sheet was returned, this time torn in half with an angry pencil scrawl, 'You are clearly being insubordinate.' For the fourth time I typed, in capital letters, these words: 'SIRS, SEND ME A SPECIMEN OF YOUR NUMBER 2.' I fired this impertinent missive into Sir Roderick's room and stalked out of the building. Next morning I turned up at Reuters in some trepidation. To my amazement not a word was said by Sir Roderick on the subject.

Often I was kept in the office till 8.30 for perfectly frivolous reasons, such as typing out his children's poetry, to be sent round by special messenger to his London house for the edification of his guests at a dinner party. At eight o'clock he might telephone through to suggest an improvement in the scansion, or direct me to Boots in Piccadilly (open all night), to buy and deliver myself by breakfast time next morning a jar of Cod Liver Oil.

On red letter days I would be despatched to present with Sir Roderick's compliments an enormous bouquet of exotic flowers to Lady So-and-So or the Duchess of This-and-That on the Golden Arrow platform of Victoria station. The departing ladies were always beautiful and sophisticated. I enjoyed these commissions and it was fun trying to guess how much the object of Sir Roderick's attentions reciprocated them. The majority were, I think, more flattered than touched. They were invariably charming and grateful to me just as though I had paid for the expensive flowers. One actually gave me a kiss in the carriage. I rejoiced to think how cross Sir Roderick would be if he knew.

I enjoyed less the luncheon parties he laid on for the editors of foreign and imperial newspapers at the Savoy Hotel. I was not invited to them of course. Instead I was warned the evening before to put on my best suit and above all Old Etonian tie – an important detail – and be in attendance at the restaurant next day. My duty was to show the guests the way to the lavatory and hold out a towel to the most distinguished – they all looked to me alike – as they washed their hands. I would there-upon hold out my hand (I was strictly enjoined not to do this) and sometimes collected several pounds this way. I learned that one should always let the next man see what his predecessor was doing, for tips are as much the fruit of blackmail as of a generous disposition.

Nevertheless I was extremely unhappy at Reuters. It was, with the exception of the War, the most down of all my down periods. It was made worse by an emotional entanglement (I wanted to get married) and the realization that I was being a failure in a job from which the right sort of man would have profited. I was clearly the wrong sort of man. There was no doubt about it whatever. My obvious unsuitability would, I knew, shortly provoke a crisis. Sure enough it came one Friday evening.

Sir Roderick was waiting for the Rolls to take him to Sussex for the weekend. It was incumbent upon me to warn him the moment it arrived. The hall porter rang to tell me the chauffeur was at the door. I forgot to inform Sir Roderick, who was pacing up and down his room watch in hand. Happening to pass the window he looked out and saw the Rolls and the chauffeur, with rug over one arm, standing patiently beside it. He called me into the room. Angrily he demanded why I had not told him. He had already lost five precious minutes which the Empire could ill spare. Was I deliberately obstructive? Or was I merely a fool? He could not decide which. Neither could I. I only knew what he knew, that it was quite unnecessary for him to be told, because neither the Rolls nor he was ever one split second behind the pre-ordained time.

Sir Roderick worked himself into a towering rage. The slanting sun was pouring into the room. He had his back to it, looking no longer like a magnified wasp but a plethoric turkey cock. Very unprepossessing he was too. But the fine particles of his spit caught in the evening sunlight made a fanlike spray which issued with the velocity and subsided on to the pile carpet with the delicacy of the great Apollo Fountain at Versailles. Though the display was in miniature it was no less remarkable than the beautiful prototype of Le Nôtre's contriving. I was so fascinated by this performance which was being repeated for my benefit with each torrent of invective that I paid no heed to what Sir Roderick was saying, and sat blandly smiling. A cloud passed over the sun, the Apollo Fountain was switched off, and I heard the turkey cock splutter, 'Well, I can't stop to argue about it any further now, Mr Milne. We will discuss the matter again on Monday.'

It was thus rudely brought to my intelligence that on Monday I would most probably be given the sack. This would certainly not do. It would be like being sent down from Eton without one's leaving book. I would never be able to get another job. My father would be triumphant. Lord Lloyd would be distressed. Every friend would be deceived in me. Besides, I would starve. What was I to do? I racked my brain all that night to no avail. Sooner than I could have hoped for advice came from an unexpected quarter – conveniently enough, from the Prime Minister . . .

. . . 'And now about yourself?' Mr Baldwin asked as he sidestepped unexpectedly into a concealed path which led off the ride we had been smartly pacing down. He dragged me after him behind a tree. The bowler hats, grunting and grumbling, passed unobserving within a few feet of us in straight pursuit of what was not. 'Lord FitzAlan mentioned that you are now working at Reuters.' I told him I was junior secretary to Sir Roderick Jones. 'That's grave,' said Mr Baldwin. Encouraged by the pejorative tone of his word 'grave' and the sudden warmth of his manner I poured out everything, how bad I was at my job, how much I hated it, how entirely dependent on it I was, and that tomorrow I was almost certainly going to be sacked. Before I had finished I thought how intolerable it was to bore with my paltry woes the Prime Minister of Great Britain who at this time was wrestling with every conceivable issue of national and international importance. Who was I, practically unknown to him, to spoil his one morning's relaxation in the week from the cares of his onerous office? I felt very ashamed. I need not have been. He expressed a most fatherly concern and was extremely sympathetic.

He stopped abruptly to bang his stick on the ground. The two bowler hats, who were hot on our heels again, practically knocked us down. Mr

Baldwin reflected. 'What you must do,' he said with emphasis, 'is this. You must get your notice in first. Immediately, without delay. Tomorrow morning. This will take the wind out of his sails. Having done so you must not repine. Friends will come to your rescue. Do not have silly scruples about accepting help and money which you cannot repay. At your age you are bound to get a job you like eventually, doubtless sooner than you expect. Remember that lean times never last for ever.' This was simple, straightforward stuff, hackneyed if you like. How I treasured and acted upon his advice. I never met Mr Baldwin again. But I have loved him ever since.

Next morning I left a note on Sir Roderick Jones's writing-table asking for an interview as soon as possible. 'Yes, you certainly may see me now,' he shouted down the intercommunicator in a menacing fashion soon after he reached the office. I went into his room. What I knew to be my last vision of him – *in cathedra* so to speak, because for years afterwards I used to see him in my club, where we never spoke to one another – did not alarm me. It strengthened my resolve. 'Well, Mr Milne,' he began, 'there is something further I have to say to you.' He paused, licking his chops – there is no other term for it. 'There is something I have to say to you first, Sir Roderick,' I broke in rather offensively. 'I know I was to blame for not telling you on Friday what of course you knew already, namely that your Rolls Royce had arrived. I merely forgot. I'm sorry. But I am not sorry to tell you how much, how extremely much I have disliked working for you. I wish to give you notice. I am leaving now.'

'Oh, are you indeed? And who, I would like to know, has advised you to do this foolish thing?' he said with a sneer.

'The Prime Minister, Sir Roderick,' I answered swelling with self-satisfaction. 'And if you don't believe me, you can ask him. Good-bye!' I turned and left him, and Reuters, for good and all.

I daresay I lacked discretion and taste in bringing Mr Baldwin's name into this altercation. I just could not resist it. I guessed Sir Roderick was unlikely to check the truth of what I had said. I knew too that he knew it to be the truth.

From *Another Self* by James Lees-Milne, 1970

Nine

GETTING DOWN
TO WORK

As for the work itself – the *raison d'être* for all this noise and bustle – the new arrival soon discovers that, more often than not, it takes up only a modest proportion of the eight hours or so that are devoted to it every day. Most office work could probably be done in a morning, but given the social and ritualistic nature of office life that's hardly the point. Quite apart from coffee-drinking, gossip and over-long lunches – and allowing for the fact that at least half the work-force is bound to be relatively slow-witted and slow-moving – much time has to be set aside for quasi- or para-work: attending long, verbose and usually unnecessary meetings, which allow key participants to relish their own jokes and the sound of their own voices, while the rest of the company is so dazed by the tedium of it all, and so fearful lest they are fixed with an eagle eye, that they are left feeling that a hard day's work has been done and a very great deal achieved; the writing, distribution and reading of equally unnecessary memoranda and consultative documents, the proliferation of which has been exacerbated by computers, photocopiers and gestures of sham democracy; a general shuffling of papers and thoughtful scratching of heads; and – most satisfactory of all – the postponement of difficult or tedious work by the writing of lists, to be acted on or further delayed at some time in the future. (All these manoeuvres – variations on his classic statement of how 'Work expands to fill the time available for its completion' – have been spelt out, wittily and in much detail, by C. Northcote Parkinson, while strategies of delay and 'the art of perceiving – HOW NOT TO DO IT' were famously elaborated by Dickens in his account of the Circumlocution Office.

But it doesn't do to be too cynical. Despite Messrs Pepys and Jerome, much work does get done, often at a frenzied and hysterical rate. Workaholics who put in late hours and hump papers home at the weekend may often, in fact, confuse or conflate work and social life – much so-called working late consists in fact of chewing the fat with cronies, feet up on the desk and a glass of whisky to hand – while idler souls like to justify their indolence by suggesting, sagely, that too much work may be, in some way, an escape from life: be that as it may, what may seem to the rest of us the most tedious and soul-destroying labour may give genuine delight and fascination to those who – like Messrs Curlydown and Bagwax – have devoted their lives to it; what Roy Fuller has described, apropos a fictional building society official, as 'that sense of perfect knowledge and mastery of procedure that was one of the chief pleasures of his life'.

Nothing to Do till Lunch

As they reached the desk, a little man with short, black whiskers buzzed out from behind a glass screen, where there was another desk.

'Where have you been, Bannister, where have you been? You must not leave your work in this way. There are several letters waiting to be entered. Where have you been?'

'Mr Bickersdyke sent for me,' said Bannister, with the calm triumph of one who trumps an ace.

'Oh! Ah! Oh! Yes, very well. I see. But get to work, get to work. Who is this?'

'This is a new man. He's taking my place. I've been moved on to the cash.'

'Oh! Ah! Is your name Smith?' asked Mr Rossiter, turning to Mike.

Mike corrected the rash guess, and gave his name. It struck him as a curious coincidence that he should be asked if his name were Smith, of all others. Not that it is an uncommon name.

'Mr Bickersdyke told me to expect a Mr Smith. Well, well, perhaps there are two new men. Mr Bickersdyke knows we are short-handed in this department. But, come along, Bannister, come along. Show Jackson what he has to do. We must get on. There is no time to waste.'

He buzzed back to his lair. Bannister grinned at Mike. He was a cheerful youth. His normal expression was a grin.

'That's a sample of Rossiter,' he said. 'You'd think from the fuss he's made that the business of the place was at a standstill till we got to work. Perfect rot! There's never anything to do here till after lunch, except checking the stamps and petty cash, and I've done that ages ago. There are three letters. You may as well enter them. It all looks like work. But you'll find the best way is to wait till you get a couple of dozen or so, and then work them off in a batch. But if you see Rossiter about, then start stamping something or writing something, or he'll run you in for neglecting your job. He's a nut. I'm jolly glad I'm under old Waller now. He's the pick of the bunch. The other heads of departments are all nuts, and Bickersdyke's the nuttiest of the lot. Now, look here. This is all you've got to do. I'll just show you, and then you can manage for yourself. I shall have to be shunting off to my own work in a minute.'

From *Psmith in the City* by P. G. Wodehouse, 1910

Keeping One's Nose to the Grindstone

13 January 1660: To my office, where nothing to do ...

14 January: Nothing to do at our office ...

23 January: To my office and there did nothing but make up my balances ...

11 February: This morning I lay long abed; and then to my office, where I read all the morning my Spanish book of Rome ...

From the *Diary* of Samuel Pepys, 1660

The Work of a Lifetime

Curlydown and Bagwax occupied the same room at the office in St Martin's-le-Grand; and there it was their fate in life to arrange, inspect, and generally attend to those apparently unintelligible hieroglyphics with which the outside coverings of our correspondence are generally bedaubed. Curlydown's hair had fallen from his head, and his face had become puckered with wrinkles, through anxiety to make these markings legible and intelligible. The popular newspaper, the popular member of Parliament, and the popular novelist, – the name of Charles Dickens will of course present itself to the reader who remembers the Circumlocution office, – have had it impressed on their several minds, – and have endeavoured to impress the same idea on the minds of the public generally, – that the normal Government clerk is quite indifferent to his work. No greater mistake was ever made, or one showing less observation of human nature. It is the nature of a man to appreciate his own work. The felon who is made simply to move shot, perishes because he knows his work is without aim. The fault lies on the other side. The policeman is ambitious of arresting everybody. The lawyer would rather make your will for you gratis than let you make your own. The General can believe in nothing but in well-trained troops. Curlydown would willingly have expended the whole net revenue of the post-office, – and his own, – in improving the machinery for stamping letters ...

Bagwax was a man who, in his official zeal and official capacity, had exercised his intellect far beyond the matters to which he was bound to apply himself in the mere performance of his duties. Post-marks were his business; and had he given all his mind to post-marks, he would have sufficiently carried out that great doctrine of doing the duty which England expects from every man. But he had travelled beyond post-marks, and had looked into many things. Among other matters he had looked into penny stamps, twopenny stamps, and other stamps. In post-office phraseology there is sometimes a confusion because the affixed effigy of her Majesty's head, which represents the postage paid, is called a stamp, and the post-marks or impressions indicating the names of towns are also called stamps. Those post-marks or impressions had been the work of Bagwax's life; but his zeal, his joy in his office, and the general energy of his disposition, had opened up to him also all the mysteries of the queen's heads.

From *John Caldigate* by Anthony Trollope, 1879

Petty Cash

A bad day today. LW came into the office and helped himself to some of the petty cash. Then, as always, he very deliberately took out his Onoto fountain pen and with a trembling hand entered the sum in the little red cash book.

He asked Miss B what 6d 'toilet requisites' was for and she blushed. Ma C said rather crossly, 'Toilet paper, Mr Woolf.'

He finished adding up the petty cash book and checked it with the money in the little metal money box. Suddenly he gave a cry of vexation and tore out the pages of the book and threw them at me, shouting 'This is totally inaccurate!'

My writing has become so like his that Ma C and Miss B can't tell the difference, especially as I've managed to introduce a wobble into it. This has led to some pretty acrimonious disputes in the office with Ma C accusing LW of making false entries in the ledgers, when the slip-up has been made by me. These mistakes usually happen on a Saturday morning when I am alone in the office. I find it easy to make mistakes when the telephone is ringing and Gordon & Gotch are demanding a selection of books that have to be searched for.

The system employed is that when a book is sold the money is entered in the Petty Cash book and then the cash ledger. An entry is made against the book in a third ledger which has five columns: the date, the name of the purchaser, number of copies sold, total number of copies of the book sold, including the sale just recorded and the amount of money taken.

From *A Boy at the Hogarth Press* by Richard Kennedy, 1972

'I file all letters'

He is loyally determined to complete the filing with extraordinary speed and skill. Besides, he thoroughly enjoys opening a mail – that is, tearing open large, expensive envelopes and throwing them on the floor. This gives him a sense of the wealth and glory of the Empire and he becomes part of it. Reading official letters is a pleasure to him, for it makes him feel like part of His Majesty's Government, and he even enjoys filing so long as he has to deal with established correspondence – that is, letters headed 'In answer to your 174.19.32,' because then he has only to attach them to the cover of file 19. They carry his own file number and he is able to feel at once the pleasure of important and necessary duties and confidence in the results.

What always puzzles him are letters referring to two different subjects; or to new subjects. For instance, here is one in which the first paragraph refers to the new police barracks; and the second to a cow claimed by the company sergeant-major at the provincial capital, Dorua, from a policeman in Fada. Johnson stares at this with blank eyes, while barracks, cows and sergeant-majors perform a sort of witches' dance in his brain. He feels alarmed and depressed and gets more confused every moment. He puts the letter down and grabs another. This is about native tobacco. His eyes grow round. He has never before seen any official reference to native tobacco. What shall he do about it? Why should such a letter come to him just now? He feels a sense of injustice and bewilderment, as if the bottom of the world has dropped out. Nothing can be trusted any more; certainly not intelligence. He takes up the police letter again and finds that it is even more incomprehensible. Finally, he rushes at the heap of files, turns them over, reads odd titles and waits for inspiration. He does not know why at last with deep relief he discovers two upon which he can get rid of the difficult letters. He puts these two at the bottom of the heap, and takes the whole file into the next office.

Rudbeck is not in the office. He is standing in the sun just beyond the stoop, with the plane table set up on its tripod, taking a bearing with the new compass. The whole staff of messengers and several petitioners stand respectfully round him, as they have stood with the same respectful faces, a month before, round Blore while he lays out a putting course. For them the two operations are equally important.

'De mail, sah – I file all letters,' Johnson says.

Adamu answers indignantly, 'Be silent, clerk – the lord is busy.'

Rudbeck murmurs, 'Just a minute.'

In fact, he is only taking a few sights across the station for the pleasure of the thing. He cannot deny himself the delight of handling his new compass.

Johnson goes back to the office and happily writes up the votes ledger. It seems to him now that he has not a single care in the world...

From *Mister Johnson* by Joyce Cary, 1939

A Long Day Ahead

When Tom returned to Hopkins' outer office, the first thing he saw was a pile of about fifteen thick leather-bound books on his desk.

'Mr Hopkins asked me to give you those,' Miss MacDonald said. 'They're the company's annual reports – there are two to a volume. He said he thought you'd like to go through them.'

'Thanks,' Tom said. He sat down, picked up one of the books, and leafed through it. The pages were full of graphs and statistics showing the progress of United Broadcasting. Of course, he thought – I should be studying these. I should have asked for them myself. I bet Hopkins knows these by heart. Anyone who seriously intended to make this company his career should study its history. I should be spending every spare minute on these. He tried to read one of the pages describing a complicated division of stock. His mind wandered – it was difficult material. I should be getting that work on the mental-health committee done first, he thought – my background reading should be done on evenings and week-ends. Work in the office on Saturdays and do your background reading on Sundays – hundreds do it. He glanced at his watch. It was only eleven o'clock. Suddenly he longed for the day to be over – he was ashamed to find that for no particular reason he felt exhausted, and he wanted to go home and relax. An hour and a half until lunch, and then another five and a half hours before he could reasonably catch the train to South Bay. The big sweep hand on his wrist watch seemed to crawl with maddening slowness. Hopkins rarely left his office before seven o'clock, and Tom had sensed he was annoyed to find that Tom usually left earlier. It was embarrassing to have to compete with Hopkins' hours – it was like taking a Sunday-afternoon walk with a long-distance runner. The stereotyped notion of the earnest young man arriving early and leaving late, and the complacent boss dropping in for a few hours in the middle of the day to see how things were going was completely reversed.

From *The Man in the Gray Flannel Suit* by Sloan Wilson, 1956

Humming under his Breath

I was working over some figures with Tiny at the Ministry; it was a figure code. Tiny sighed and hummed under his breath.

Oh, Tiny, don't hum.

Well, all right. Or I can go into the next room. Or you can.

We can't very well do that. I leaned over Tiny and whispered in his ear. We can't very well do that because Clem is there.

Oh Lord, I keep forgetting. Oh how I wish they hadn't moved him into Section V. Oh dear, oh dear.

Well as long as we *remember*, we can think of something else. These cablegrams, for instance. I sighed. What do you make of number seven?

Yes, said Tiny, there's something about figures.

Something like work, I said. Only don't hum, Tiny, that spoils it, that we can do without.

I think our colleagues Eleanor and Constance are awfully nice women, said Tiny with such a generous beaming look.

Why, Tiny, you do look happy. It is the figures that make you feel that way about Eleanor and Constance. They always seem so occupied, those two, especially Eleanor seems so occupied.

We were born under a no-grip star, said Tiny.

Yes, that's it, I said, we are lucky to be in this room together, that is something one might not have looked for.

When I see old Eleanor crashing about with that concentrated look on her face, you would think the whole of the post-war hung up on her. It is like the Saki lady who was in touch with all the Governments of Europe before breakfast . . .

Now, Tiny, I said, that is not quite in the mood.

What do *you* make of Number Seven? said Tiny.

I took it over to the window and began singing 'From Greenland's Icy Mountains' to myself.

You've got the words mixed up, said Tiny crossly, I don't see that that is very much better than my humming.

From *The Holiday* by Stevie Smith, 1949

Mr Smeeth Dictates a Letter

'Now where's that letter from Poppett and Sons?' he demanded. 'It was on this desk an hour ago, I'll swear. It's a letter about their account, and

I told one of you this morning we'd have to answer it to-day. It was you, wasn't it, Miss Sellers? Well, have you taken their letter away, then? Just see if you have? Yes, there you are – that's it. Bring it here and I'll answer it now. Poppett and Sons, Poppett and Sons,' Mr Smeeth repeated idly as he re-read their letter. 'Ye-es. Are you ready? No, half a minute, though – my mistake. I'll have to check that figure. Fi-fifty fo-our pounds, thi-irte-een shillings – yes, yes, that's all right. Now then –' And here Mr Smeeth adjusted his eye-glasses and cleared his throat, giving a faintly pompous little cough. Even now, the thought that he, Herbert Norman Smeeth, was sitting there, a cashier, dictating letters to this firm and that, gave him a thrill. ' – er – We are in receipt of your – er – communication – put the date in there, Miss Sellers – respecting our statement of account dated so-and-so – and beg to point out that this account was quite in order. You asked us to send down the goods by special road delivery and agreed that the extra carriage, paid by us, should be added to our account – no, just a minute – extra carriage, which had to be paid by us in the first place, should be charged to you, and this we accordingly did. We refer you to your letter – I have a note of that letter – ah! here it is – to your letter of the 4th of December last –'

Mr Smeeth rounded off his letter and Miss Sellers hurried it away to her machine.

From *Angel Pavement* by J. B. Priestley, 1930

The Pressure of Work

'Oh God!' said Dyson. He had a staff – Bob and old Eddy Moulton were his staff – and he had to jump up and down all the time switching the lights on and off himself! No wonder he was overwhelmed by work. No wonder that by four o'clock in the afternoon he would be literally dizzy, literally overcome by a sensation of drowning in work, so that he had to loosen his tie and undo his collar. Now that he had put the lights on he could see clearly just how much work there was waiting on his desk. There was copy waiting to be subbed, galley proofs waiting to be corrected. There were complimentary tickets for the National Provincial Bank's performance of *The Pirates of Penzance*, and for an undergraduate production of *Sweeney Agonistes*, passed on to him by the Reviews Editor in case he was interested. There were invitations to Citizenship Forums and Cheese Tastings passed on to him by the News Editor and the Features Editor, and invitations to try new golf-training machines and indoor ski slopes, sent along by the Sports Editor. Dyson's department was the drain into which the last spent dregs of the world's commercial largesse fell after being sieved and filtered by everyone else on the paper, so that it was Dyson who had the labour of writing the letters of refusal. He did not like to tell his colleagues to stop passing on their unwanted perquisites, because occasionally they involved free airline trips abroad, which he and his department accepted.

Most urgent of all, there were notes and memoranda scribbled on pieces of coarse office copy paper. They were from himself to himself. 'Ring Muller abt t buzzards piece,' they said. 'Ask Sims abt t libel poss of sayg chem frtlisr klls hdghgs.' 'Check w Straker on immac concep VM.' 'RING MORLEY FIND OUT WHRE T HELL COPY FOR FRI IS.'

But how could he ring Morley to find out where the hell his copy for Friday was? Every time he stretched out his hand to pick up the phone it rang in his face.

'Hello,' he sighed into it; 'Dyson ... Yes ... Good ... Bless you ... Bless you, bless you ... Wonderful ... Perfect ... Bless you.'

And scarcely had he had time to put it down and mutter 'Silly tit' before it was ringing again. It was an awfully bad day for Dyson, as he told Bob from time to time, when he had a moment.

'Somebody wouldn't like to ring Morley, would they,' he pleaded, 'and find out where the hell his copy for Friday is?'

The words broadcast themselves about the empty air, their urgency fading by the inverse square of the distance.

'Bob!' he said.

'John,' said Bob politely.

'I said somebody wouldn't like to ring Morley, would they, Bob?'

Bob slipped another toffee into his mouth. Reg Mounce, the appalling Reg Mounce, was just crossing the Court, kicking sourly at the paving stones as he went, just in case inanimate matter was in some way capable of sensation.

'I'm a bit tied up at the moment, John,' said Bob absently. 'Got some writing to do in a minute.'

Dyson stood up, trying to get the work on his desk into perspective by gazing down upon it from a great height. Supposing the phone didn't ring for a minute; whom should he call first? Morley, perhaps – then Sims might be back from court ... No, he'd have to ring Straker, because this was the day Straker had a committee at twelve. But Straker would go on for at least ten minutes about immaculate conception, and he would probably miss Morley.

The phone rang again.

'Oh God,' he groaned. 'Hello; Dyson ... Ah, I've been trying to get hold of you all morning ... Yes – I've been trying to get hold of you all morning . . . Exactly – I've been trying to get hold of you all morning . . .'

By the time he put the phone down he couldn't remember what it was he had been worrying about before. The state of the rack, no doubt; that was what he worried about most of the time. He looked anxiously at the rack of galley proofs behind him. He had only seven 'The Country Day by Day' columns in print, and he had sworn never to let the Countries drop below twelve. He had a 'Meditation' column for each of the next three days – unless Winters had made a cock-up about immaculate conception, in which case he had only two-and-a-half pieces – but he should have had a running stock of fourteen Meditations. He would have a blitz on Countries; he would have a blitz on Meditations. But then what about the crosswords? He counted them up miserably. God Almighty, he was down to his last eight cross-words! Day by day the presses hounded him; with failing strength he fed them the hard-won pieces of copy which delayed them so briefly. On and on they came! They were catching him up!

He sank back into his chair and banged the palms of his hands against his forehead.

'I honestly sometimes wonder how I'm expected to carry on,' he said. 'I slave and slave to keep this department going! I work my guts out doing three men's work! I literally work myself into the ground! But what happens? I get no co-operation! I have to try and stagger through with half the staff I need! I have to share a secretary with Boyle and Mounce and Brent-Williamson and half the paper's specialists! I honestly sometimes think I'm heading for a crack-up!'

Bob put the bag of toffees away in his pocket.

'All right, John,' he said. 'I'll give Morley a buzz if you like.'

Dyson stopped heading for a crack-up.

'Bless you, Bob!' he said. 'You're a poppet, you really are. I'm sorry I went on about it like that. I know how busy you are. We're all busy. We're all under strain. I'm sorry, Bob.'

From *Towards the End of the Morning* by Michael Frayn, 1967

Yuppies at Work

He turned the corner, and there it was: the bond trading room of Pierce & Pierce. It was a vast space, perhaps sixty by eighty feet, but with the same eight-foot ceiling bearing down on your head. It was an oppressive space with a ferocious glare, writhing silhouettes, and the roar. The glare came from a wall of plate glass that faced south, looking out over New York Harbor, the Statue of Liberty, Staten Island, and the Brooklyn and

New Jersey shores. The writhing silhouettes were the arms and torsos of young men, few of them older than forty. They had their suit jackets off. They were moving about in an agitated manner and sweating early in the morning and shouting, which created the roar. It was the sound of well-educated young white men baying for money on the bond market.

'Pick up the fucking phone, please!' a chubby, pink-faced member of the Harvard Class of 1976 screamed at someone two rows of desks away. The room was like a newspaper city room in that there were no partitions and no signs of visible rank. Everyone sat at light gray metal desks in front of veal-colored computer terminals with black screens. Rows of green-diode letters and numbers came skidding across.

'I said please pick up the fucking phone! I mean holy shit!' There were dark half-moons in the armpits of his shirt, and the day had just begun.

A member of the Yale Class of 1973 with a neck that seemed to protrude twelve inches out of his shirt stared at a screen and screamed over the telephone at a broker in Paris: 'If you can't see the fucking screen ... Oh, for Christ's sake, Jean-Pierre, that's the *buy*er's five million! The *buy*er's! Nothing further's coming in!'

Then he covered the telephone with his hand and looked straight up at the ceiling and said out loud to no one, except Mammon, 'The frogs! The fucking frogs!'

Four desks away, a member of the Stanford Class of 1979 was sitting down, staring at a sheet of paper on his desk and holding a telephone to his ear. His right foot was up on the stirrup of a portable shoeshine stand, and a black man named Felix, who was about fifty – or was he about sixty? – was humped over his foot, stropping his shoe with a high-shine rag. All day long Felix moved from desk to desk, shining the shoes of young bond traders and salesmen as they worked, at three dollars per, counting the tip. Seldom was a word exchanged; Felix scarcely registered on their maculae. Just then Stanford '79 rose from his chair, his eyes still fastened on the sheet of paper, the telephone still at his ear – and his right foot still on the shoeshine stirrup – and he shouted: 'Well then, why do you think everybody's stripping the fucking twenty-years?'

Never took his foot off the shoeshine stand! What powerful legs he must have! thought Sherman. Sherman sat down before his own telephone and computer terminals. The shouts, the imprecations, the gesticulations, the fucking fear and greed, enveloped him, and he loved it. He was the number one bond salesman, 'the biggest producer,' as the phrase went, in the bond trading room of Pierce & Pierce on the fiftieth floor, and he loved the very roar of the storm.

'This Goldman order really fucked things up good!'

' – step up to the fucking plate and –'

'– bid 8½ –'

'I'm away by two thirty-seconds!'

'Somebody's painting you a fucking picture! Can't you see that?'

'I'll take an order and buy 'em at 6-plus!'

'Hit the five-year!'

'Sell five!'

'You couldn't do ten?'

'You think this thing continues up?'

'Strip fever in the twenty-year! That's all these jerks keep talking about!'

'– a hundred million July-nineties at the buck –'

'– naked short –'

'Jesus Christ, what's going on?'

'I don't fucking believe this!'

'Holy fucking shit!' shouted the Yale men and the Harvard men and the Stanford men. 'Ho-lee fuc-king shit.'

How these sons of the great universities, these legatees of Jefferson, Emerson, Thoreau, William James, Frederick Jackson Turner, William Lyons Phelps, Samuel Flagg Bemis, and the other three-name giants of American scholarship – how these inheritors of the *lux* and the *veritas* now flocked to Wall Street and to the bond trading room of Pierce & Pierce!

From *The Bonfire of the Vanities* by Tom Wolfe, 1988

A Restful Occupation

George goes to sleep at a bank from ten to four each day, except Saturdays, when they wake him up and put him outside at two.

From *Three Men in a Boat* by Jerome K. Jerome, 1889

More of the Same

He [Harold Ross] later had to have a couch put in his own office, for his doctors had ordered him to rest after lunch, and whenever he could, between tasks. Andy White, who has always had a couch, still preserves a note from Ross which he found one day in his typewriter when he woke up from a nap. It read: 'Drop in on me when you wake up. I never disturb a sleeping man.' Ross never disturbed a man if he was typing, either, or if there was, God forbid, a woman in his office.

From *The Years with Ross*, by James Thurber, 1959

First Things First

Blake's office, on the other hand, was almost completely functional: sound teak desk, canvas chairs, wire trays for papers. His only concessions to luxurious living were a miniature cocktail cabinet, which played a yodelling song when you opened the lid, and a small refectory-style table, at which he sometimes entertained the more important buyers to lunch (and what greater honour could they expect?).

And here he retired after the boardroom meeting. Naturally he was not going to Charlie Ammon until somebody came to fetch him – nor would Charlie have expected it. He deliberately ignored the flashes on the intercom buzzer. When in due course Miss Henderson appeared, with the message that he was required immediately, he told her that he had some important telephone calls to make first. He in fact rang his local Off Licence at Rillington, partly to have a chat with Barney Naughton, its proprietor, leading up to an order for a couple of barrels of beer as his own personal gift towards the Old Folks' social on New Year's Eve, partly to make sure that Barney realised that this very order depended on whether he, Barney, cast the right vote at the next Borough Council meeting. Then he drafted a letter to all pensioners of the firm offering them ten per cent over the market price for any Ammon and Foreshearing shares they happened to be holding.

From *The Big Tomato* by Raleigh Trevelyan, 1966

In Search of Scissors

On one of the many days on which there was little that I could profitably do sitting at my desk, I was sent out to buy a pair of scissors. I went to Selfridge's department store, which I felt that I understood. It was thence that my tuck had been sent to me at boarding school. I bought some scissors for five shillings. When I returned and told the girl who kept the petty cash book how much they had cost, she became distraught. 'I can't put down "Scissors, five shillings",' she wailed. 'You can buy a pair in Woolworth's for sixpence.' I tried to calm her by enumerating the ways in which the article I had bought was superior to anything sold by Woolworth's. While doing this, I happened to utter the words 'paper shears'. Her ivory brow smoothed out immediately. 'Oh,' she sighed, 'I can put down "Paper shears, five shillings". That's quite all right.'

From *The Naked Civil Servant* by Quentin Crisp, 1968

Caught on the Hop

The Vice-Chairman took off the mean little spectacles he wore for reading and said, without emphasis: 'Your valuation is slightly above half what it was in 1946, Blackledge?'

'If you read the beginning of my report, Sir Harold,' Blackledge began. 'I don't pretend to understand the science of valuation – or is it an art? – but I do know a little about figures. £33,000 has apparently vanished into thin air.'

'No, Sir Harold, the society only stands to lose –'

'I know that, man,' Sir Harold spoke testily for the first time, and the colour leapt to Blackledge's face. '£8,750 with the current interest – if your valuation is to be relied on.'

'I'm sorry, Sir Harold. I thought you were referring to the difference –'

Sir Harold interrupted him again. 'What the Board will want to know, Blackledge, is how you and Powell in 1946 arrived at what seems now to be the astronomical figure of £70,000 as the value of the freehold.'

'Well, Sir Harold, the company paid £72,000 –'

'I never thought that purchase price had more than an adventitious relationship to value,' said Sir Harold. 'But this is hardly the time for generalizations: you will have to try to make your peace with the Board at a later date, Blackledge.'

The bastard, Blackledge was thinking; the smug bastard. Had he himself never been guilty of a bloomer? Blackledge felt the sweat gumming his shirt to his back and the blood throbbing in his temples, conscious that the General Manager and Gerson had, during his grilling, only emphasized their surprise and interest by their elaborately assumed air of unconcern and needless study of the documents they had before them . . .

From *Image of a Society* by Roy Fuller, 1956

A Sense of Proportion

It is a cheerful all-round bustling job, and Tiny and I, in our room together, are very happy when we are in the middle of jobs. It is only when one pauses for a moment, or when one catches sight of the friends Eleanor and Constance, with the important look on their faces, that one begins to feel a little uncertain. For what does it all add up to, and what is this work that is so bustling and so cosy? What is this? compared with

Libya and Russia, and compared with the men who were sailing backwards and forwards to Russia, sailing upon the deadly Murmansk route? And these men had sailed that way before; they knew what it was. Eh, what are we up to, compared with the victory they got us?

From *The Holiday* by Stevie Smith, 1949

Feet of Clay

The first thing Tom did when he got back to his office the next day was to call Hopkins on the interoffice communication box.

'Glad you're back!' Hopkins said cheerily, as though Tom had just returned from a voyage around the world. 'Have a good trip?'

'Fine,' Tom said. 'Did you want to see me?'

'Yes,' Hopkins replied. 'I'll send a girl down with the latest draft of my speech for Atlantic City. Let's have lunch tomorrow, and you can tell me what you think of it. Would one o'clock be all right?'

So that's all he wanted, Tom thought. He said, 'Fine! I'll meet you in your office tomorrow at one.'

An hour later an exceptionally pretty office girl arrived and with a dazzling smile handed Tom a large manila envelope from Hopkins. Tom opened it and extracted the speech, which had grown and changed since he had worked on it. 'It's a real pleasure to be here this evening,' he read. 'I tremendously appreciate this opportunity to discuss with this distinguished gathering what I believe to be the most crucial problem facing the world today.' Having made this point, the speech went on – in fact, it went on and on and on for thirty pages, saying over and over again in different ways that mental health is important. The last ten pages were devoted to the thought that mental-health problems affect the economy of the nation. 'Our wealth depends on mental health,' this section concluded. 'Yes, our wealth depends on mental health!'

Tom put the speech down, feeling slightly ill. Good Lord, he thought, they're going to sell mental health the way they sell cigarettes! He left the speech on his desk, walked over to the window, and stared out over the city. Standing there, he shrugged his shoulders in an oddly hopeless way.

'Let's have lunch tomorrow, and you can tell me what you think of it,' Hopkins had said.

'*Well, of course I'm just talking off the top of my head, but I think this draft has some fine things in it, and, on the other hand, I have some reservations,*' Tom imagined himself saying. That was the way it was done – always feel the boss out to find what he thinks before committing yourself. Tell the man what he wants to hear.

'I'm sorry, but I think this speech is absurd. It's an endless repetition of the obvious fact that mental health is important. You've said that over and over again and finally turned it into a cheap advertising slogan. If you want to form a mental-health committee, why don't you find out what needs to be done and offer to help do it?'

A few years ago I would have said that, Tom thought. Be honest, be yourself. If the man asks you what you think of his speech, tell him. Don't be afraid. Give him your frank opinion.

That sounds so easy when you're young, Tom thought. It sounds so easy before you learn that your frank opinion often leads directly to the street. What if Hopkins really likes this speech?

Tom shrugged again. The thing to remember is this, he thought: Hopkins would want me to be honest. But when you come right down to it, why does he hire me? To help him do what he wants to do – obviously that's why any man hires another. And if he finds that I disagree with everything he wants to do, what good am I to him? I should quit if I don't like what he does, but I want to eat, and so, like a half million other guys in gray flannel suits, I'll always pretend to agree, until I get big enough to be honest without being hurt. That's not being crooked, it's just being smart.

But it doesn't make you feel very good, Tom thought. It makes you feel lousy. For the third time, he shrugged. How strangely it all works out, he thought. The pretty girl smiles as she hands me the innocuous manila envelope with the speech. I'll go with my boss for luncheon to a nice restaurant somewhere, with music playing in the background, perhaps, and people laughing all around, and the waiters will bow, and my boss will be polite, and I'll be tactful, and there in such delicate surroundings, I'll not be rude enough to say a stupid speech is stupid. How smoothly one becomes, not a cheat, exactly, not really a liar, just a man who'll say anything for pay.

From *The Man in the Gray Flannel Suit* by Sloan Wilson, 1956

The Heart of the Matter

It was three o'clock, and the afternoon sun reddened the western windows of one of the busiest of Government offices. In an airy room on the third floor Richard Dale was batting. Standing in front of the coal-box with the fire-shovel in his hands, he was a model of the strenuous young Englishman; and as for the third time he turned the Government india-rubber neatly in the direction of square leg, and so completed his fifty, the bowler could hardly repress a sigh of envious admiration. Even the reserved Matthews, who was too old for cricket, looked up a moment from his putting, and said, 'Well played, Dick!'

The fourth occupant of the room was busy at his desk, as if to give the lie to the thoughtless accusation that the Civil Service cultivates the body at the expense of the mind. The eager shouts of the players seemed to annoy him, for he frowned and bit his pen, or else passed his fingers restlessly through his hair.

'How the dickens you expect any one to think in this confounded noise,' he cried suddenly.

'What's the matter, Ashby?'

'You're the matter. How am I going to get these verses done for the *Evening Surprise* if you make such a row? Why don't you go out to tea?'

'Good idea. Come on, Dale. You coming, Matthews?' They went out, leaving the room to Ashby.

On his return to England, Harold found that time had wrought many changes. To begin with, the editor of the *Evening Surprise* had passed on to the *Morning Exclamation*.

'You had better take his place,' said the ducal proprietor to Harold.

'Right,' said Harold. 'I suppose I shall have to resign my post at the office?'

'Just as you like. I don't see why you should.'

'I should miss the cricket,' said Harold wistfully, 'and the salary. I'll go round and see what I can arrange.'

But there were also changes at the office. Harold had been rising steadily in salary and seniority during his absence, and he found to his delight that he was now a Principal Clerk. He found, too, that he had acquired quite a reputation in the office for quickness and efficiency in his new work.

The first thing to arrange about was his holiday. He had had no holiday for more than a year, and there were some eight weeks owing to him.

'Hullo,' said the Assistant Secretary, as Harold came in, 'you're looking well. I suppose you manage to get away for the week-ends?'

'I've been away on sick leave for some time,' said Harold pathetically.

'Have you? You've kept it very secret. Come out and have lunch with me, and we'll do a *matinée* afterwards.'

Harold went out with him happily. It would be pleasant to accept the editorship of the *Evening Surprise* without giving up the governmental work which was so dear to him, and the Assistant Secretary's words made this possible for a year or so anyhow. Then, when his absence from the office first began to be noticed, it would be time to think of retiring on an adequate pension.

From 'The Civil Servant' in *Those Were the Days* by A. A. Milne, 1929

Ten

OFFICE POLITICS

Gripping if observed from a distance but often hellish for those involved, unless of a carnivorous or byzantine turn of mind, office politics represent the stern reality of office gossip, in which livelihoods and reputations are at stake. Offices are, invariably, hierarchies: more than the rest of us, office politicians are intensely aware of, and anxious about, their status, the respect due to them, and their relationship to the ultimate source of power. Office politics, like politics in the world at large or some mediaeval court, are peopled by a familiar cast of characters: the tyrant, the usurper, the loyal lieutenant (who may turn out to be less loyal than one thought), the heir apparent (sometimes there because he presents no real threat), the stooge, the plodder, the knight errant, the sycophant, the reject and the loyal retainer. Power is abandoned reluctantly and often bloodily, and deposed tyrants will often do all they can to foul the nest for their successors. Even the wiliest and most worldly of office politicians tend to believe that they are exempt from the rules that govern the rest of us: quite forgetting everything they have learned in a lifetime of scheming and stabbing, they remain – when their turn comes – convinced of their own indispensability, that they will be called back in triumph to sort out the mess the usurper has made, and that they can sell their companies for large sums of money and continue as before. It would be a mistake, however, to assume that the rewards go only to the ruthless and the over-bearing: those of a milder disposition may work their ways to the top, or preserve their positions, by knowing the business inside out, oiling the wheels and keeping a keen eye on the way the wind is blowing.

Office Hierarchies

The office politics bred caste. Caste at Pemberton's was as clearly defined as ranks in an army.

At the top were the big chiefs, the officers of the company, and the heads of departments – Mr Pemberton and his sons, the treasurer, the general manager, the purchasing-agent, the superintendents of the soda-fountain-syrup factory, of the soap-works, of the drug-laboratories, of the toilet-accessories shops, the sales-manager, and Mr S. Herbert Ross. The Olympian council were they; divinities to whom the lesser clerks had never dared to speak. When there were rumours of 'a change,' of 'a cut-down in the force,' every person on the office floor watched the chiefs as they assembled to go out to lunch together – big, florid, shaven, large-chinned men, talking easily, healthy from motoring and golf, able in a moment's conference at lunch to 'shift the policy' and to bring instant poverty to the families of forty clerks or four hundred workmen in the shops. When they jovially entered the elevator together, some high-strung stenographer would rush over to one of the older women to weep and be comforted . . . An hour from now her tiny job might be gone.

Even the chiefs' outside associates were tremendous, buyers and diplomatic representatives; big-chested men with watch-chains across their beautiful tight waistcoats. And like envoys-extraordinary were the efficiency experts whom Mr Pemberton occasionally had in to speed up the work a bit more beyond the point of human endurance . . . One of these experts, a smiling and pale-haired young man who talked to Mr Ross about the new poetry, arranged to have office-boys go about with trays of water-glasses at ten, twelve, two, and four. Thitherto, the stenographers had wasted a great deal of time in trotting to the battery of water-coolers, in actually being human and relaxed and gossipy for ten minutes a day. After the visitation of the expert the girls were so efficient that they never for a second stopped their work – except when one of them would explode in hysteria and be hurried off to the rest-room. But no expert was able to keep them from jumping at the chance to marry anyone who would condescend to take them out of this efficient atmosphere.

Just beneath the chiefs was the caste of bright young men who would some day have the chance to be beatified into chiefs. They believed enormously in the virtue of spreading the blessings of Pemberton's patent medicines; they worshipped the house policy. Once a month they met at what they called 'punch lunches,' and listened to electrifying addresses by Mr S. Herbert Ross or some other inspirer, and turned fresh, excited eyes on one another, and vowed to adhere to the true faith of Pemberton's, and not waste their evenings in making love, or reading fiction, or hearing music, but to read diligently about soap and syrups and window displays, and to keep firmly before them the vision of fifteen thousand dollars a year. They had quite the best time of anyone at Pemberton's, the bright young men. They sat, in silk shirts and new ties, at shiny, flat-topped desks in rows; they answered the telephone with an air; they talked about tennis and business conditions, and were never, never bored.

Intermingled with this caste were the petty chiefs, the office-managers and book-keepers, who were velvety to those placed in power over them, but twangily nagging to the girls and young men under them. Failures themselves, they eyed sourly the stenographers who desired two dollars more a week, and assured them that while *personally* they would be *very* glad to obtain the advance for them, it would be 'unfair to the other girls.' They were very strong on the subject of not being unfair to the other girls, and their own salaries were based on 'keeping down overhead.' Oldish men they were, wearing last-year hats and smoking Virginia cigarettes at lunch; always gossiping about the big chiefs, and at night disappearing to homes and families in New Jersey or Harlem. Awe-encircled as the very chiefs they appeared when they lectured stenographers, but they cowered when the chiefs spoke to them, and tremblingly fingered their frayed cuffs.

Such were the castes above the buzzer-line.

Una's caste, made up of private secretaries to the chiefs, was not above the buzzer. She had to leap to the rattlesnake tattoo, when Mr Ross summoned her, as quickly as did the newest Jewish stenographer. But hers was a staff corps, small and exclusive and out of the regular line. On the one hand she could not associate with the chiefs; on the other, it was expected of her, in her capacity as daily confidante to one of the gods, that she should not be friendly, in coat-room or rest-room or elevator, with the unrecognized horde of girls who merely copied or took the bright young men's dictation of letters to drug-stores. These girls of the common herd were expected to call the secretaries 'Miss,' no matter what street-corner impertinences they used to one another.

There was no caste, though there was much factional rivalry, among the slaves beneath – the stenographers, copyists, clerks, waiting-room attendants, office-boys, elevator-boys. They were expected to keep clean and be quick-moving; beyond that they were as unimportant to the larger phases of office politics as frogs to a summer hotel. Only the cashier's card index could remember their names ... Though they were not deprived of the chief human satisfaction and vice – feeling superior. The most snuffle-nosed little mailing-girl on the office floor felt superior to all of the factory workers, even the foremen, quite as negro house-servants look down on poor white trash.

Jealousy of position, cattishness, envy of social standing – these were as evident among the office-women as they are in a woman's club; and Una had to admit that woman's cruelty to woman often justified the prejudices of executives against the employment of women in business; that women were the worst foes of Woman.

To Una's sympathies, the office proletarians were her own poor relations. She sighed over the cheap jackets, with silesia linings and ravelled buttonholes, which nameless copyists tried to make attractive by the clean embroidered linen collars which they themselves laundered in wash-bowls in the evening. She discovered that even after years of experience with actual office-boys and elevator-boys, Mr Ross still saw them only as slangy, comic-paper devils.

From *The Job* by Sinclair Lewis, 1917

Mr Carker the Manager

Between Mr Dombey and the common world, as it was accessible through the medium of the outer office – to which Mr Dombey's presence in his own room may be said to have struck like damp, or cold air – there were two degrees of descent. Mr Carker in his own office was the first step; Mr Morfin, in *his* own office, was the second. Each of these gentlemen occupied a little chamber like a bath-room, opening from the passage outside Mr Dombey's door. Mr Carker, as Grand Vizier, inhabited the room that was nearest to the Sultan. Mr Morfin, as an officer of inferior state, inhabited the room that was nearest to the clerks.

The gentleman last mentioned was a cheerful-looking, hazel-eyed elderly bachelor: gravely attired, as to his upper man, in black; and as to his legs, in pepper-and-salt colour. His dark hair was just touched here and there with specks of grey, as though the tread of Time had splashed it; and his whiskers were already white. He had a mighty respect for Mr Dombey, and rendered him due homage; but as he was of a genial temper himself, and never wholly at his ease in that stately presence, he was disquieted by no jealousy of the many conferences enjoyed by Mr Carker, and felt a secret satisfaction in having duties to discharge, which rarely exposed him to be singled out for such distinction. He was a great musical amateur in his way – after business; and had a paternal affection for his violoncello, which was once in every week transported from Islington, his place of abode, to a certain club-room hard by the Bank, where quartettes of the most tormenting and excruciating nature were executed every Wednesday evening by a private party.

Mr Carker was a gentleman thirty-eight or forty years old, of a florid complexion, and with two unbroken rows of glistening teeth, whose regularity and whiteness were quite distressing. It was impossible to escape the observation of them, for he showed them whenever he spoke; and bore so wide a smile upon his countenance (a smile, however, very rarely, indeed, extending beyond his mouth), that there was something in it like the snarl of a cat. He affected a stiff white cravat, after the example of his principal, and was always closely buttoned up and tightly dressed. His manner towards Mr Dombey was deeply conceived and perfectly expressed. He was familiar with him, in the very extremity of his sense of the distance between them. 'Mr Dombey, to a man in your position from a man in mine, there is no show of subservience compatible with the transaction of business between us, that I should think sufficient. I frankly tell you, Sir, I give it up altogether. I feel that I could not satisfy my own mind; and Heaven knows, Mr Dombey, you can afford to dispense with the endeavour.' If he had carried these words about with him, printed on a placard, and had constantly offered it to Mr Dombey's perusal on the breast of his coat, he could not have been more explicit than he was.

This was Carker the Manager. Mr Carker the Junior, Walter's friend, was his brother; two or three years older than he, but widely removed in station. The younger brother's post was on the top of the official ladder; the elder brother's at the bottom. The elder brother never gained a stave, or raised his foot to mount one. Young men passed above his head, and rose and rose; but he was always at the bottom. He was quite resigned to occupy that low condition: never complained of it: and certainly never hoped to escape from it.

'How do you do this morning?' said Mr Carker the Manager, entering Mr Dombey's room soon after his arrival one day: with a bundle of papers in his hand.

'How do you do, Carker?' said Mr Dombey, rising from his chair, and standing with his back to the fire. 'Have you anything there for me?'

'I don't know that I need trouble you,' returned Carker, turning over the papers in his hand. 'You have a committee to-day at three, you know.'

'And one at three, three-quarters,' added Mr Dombey.

'Catch you forgetting anything!' exclaimed Carker, still turning over his papers. 'If Mr Paul inherits your memory, he'll be a troublesome customer in the house. One of you is enough.'

'You have an accurate memory of your own,' said Mr Dombey.

'Oh! *I!*' returned the manager. 'It's the only capital of a man like *me*.'

Mr Dombey did not look less pompous or at all displeased, as he stood leaning against the chimneypiece, surveying his (of course unconscious) clerk, from head to foot. The stiffness and nicety of Mr Carker's dress, and a certain arrogance of manner, either natural to him or imitated from a pattern not far off, gave great additional effect to his humility. He seemed a man who would contend against the power that vanquished him, if he could, but who was utterly borne down by the greatness and superiority of Mr Dombey.

'Is Morfin here?' asked Mr Dombey after a short pause, during which Mr Carker had been fluttering his papers, and muttering little abstracts of their contents to himself.

'Morfin's here,' he answered, looking up with his widest and most sudden smile; 'humming musical recollections – of his last night's quartette party, I suppose – through the walls between us and driving me half mad. I wish he'd make a bonfire of his violoncello, and burn his music-books in it.'

'You respect nobody, Carker, I think,' said Mr Dombey.

'No?' inquired Carker, with another wide and most feline show of his teeth. 'Well! Not many people, I believe. I wouldn't answer perhaps,' he murmured, as if he were only thinking it, 'for more than one.'

A dangerous quality, if real; and a not less dangerous one, if feigned. But Mr Dombey hardly seemed to think so, as he still stood with his back to the fire, drawn up to his full height, and looking at his head-clerk with a dignified composure, in which there seemed to lurk a stronger latent sense of power than usual.

Mr Carker the Manager sat at his desk, smooth and soft as usual, reading those letters which were reserved for him to open, backing them occasionally with such memoranda and references as their business purport required, and parcelling them out into little heaps for distribution through the several departments of the House. The post had come in heavy that morning, and Mr Carker the Manager had a good deal to do.

The general action of a man so engaged – pausing to look over a bundle of papers in his hand, dealing them round in various portions, taking up another bundle and examining its contents with knitted brows and pursed-out lips – dealing, and sorting, and pondering by turns – would easily suggest some whimsical resemblance to a player at cards. The face of Mr Carker the Manager was in good keeping with such a fancy. It was the face of a man who studied his play, warily; who made himself master of all the strong and weak points of the game: who registered the cards in his mind as they fell about him, knew exactly what was on them, what they missed, and what they made: who was crafty to find out what the other players held, and who never betrayed his own hand.

The letters were in various languages, but Mr Carker the Manager read them all. If there had been anything in the offices of Dombey and Son that he could *not* read, there would have been a card wanting in the pack. He read almost at a glance, and made combinations of one letter with another and one business with another as he went on, adding new matter to the heaps – much as a man would know the cards at sight, and work out their combinations in his mind after they were turned. Something too deep for a partner, and much too deep for an adversary, Mr Carker the Manager sat in the rays of the sun that came down slanting on him through the skylight, playing his game alone.

And although it is not among the instincts wild or domestic of the cat tribe to play at cards, feline from sole to crown was Mr Carker the Manager, as he basked in the strip of summer-light and warmth that shone upon his table and the ground as if they were a crooked dial-plate, and himself the only figure on it. With hair and whiskers deficient in colour at all times but feebler than common in the rich sunshine, and more like the coat of a sandy tortoise-shell cat; with long nails, nicely pared and sharpened; with a natural antipathy to any speck of dirt, which made him pause sometimes and watch the falling motes of dust, and rub them off his smooth white hand or glossy linen: Mr Carker the Manager, sly of manner, sharp of tooth, soft of foot, watchful of eye, oily of tongue, cruel of heart, nice of habit, sat with a dainty steadfastness and patience at his work, as if he were waiting at a mouse's hole.

From *Dombey and Son* by Charles Dickens, 1848

Garage Spaces

At Saddleford House the Correspondence Department staff came half an hour earlier in the morning than the rest so that the post was already sorted at the start of the working day. Blackledge's letters, like those of all the senior executives, were delivered to his secretary. By the time he arrived they were on his desk with their relevant files.

He was not the first of the senior executives to arrive: Gerson was always there before him. Once this had quite perturbed him, as though in some ill-defined way it gave Gerson an advantage over him. But it was really utterly inappropriate for him to arrive before the post was on his desk, to make his way through the crowded and noisy corridors which marked the arrival of the ordinary staff, and soon he had come to regard Gerson's unnecessary punctuality as a disadvantage to Gerson, denoting a barren home life, an insecurity of position, a character he had once seen described in a magazine as anal-erotic, whatever that obviously derogatory term might mean. There was a sane and balanced practice in these matters: one ought to demonstrate that one was not the slave of the clock, at the same time making sure that Matheson did not inquire for one in vain.

Blackledge put his hat and gloves in the wardrobe in his office and ran the brush he kept there over his hair. Then he sat at his desk, filled his pipe and got it thoroughly going. The files and their relevant letters were piled at his right hand. On the heavy leather bound blotter in front of him were the circulars, the memoranda, the letters, which were new or had no file to be assigned to. He took the well-sharpened red pencil he always used for annotating and for which he knew he was famous, and read rapidly through an information sheet from the Building Societies' Alliance about income tax, and a cyclostyled memorandum from the Premises Manager about the change of address of the society's branch office in Birmingham. Underneath the latter was another cyclostyled memorandum from the Premises Manager headed 'Garage Spaces'. It said that the enlarged garage would be available for use as from the following Monday and then gave, opposite their respective numbers, the names of the twelve executives who had been allocated spaces. Number 1 was Matheson, 2 Gerson, 3 Blackledge.

Blackledge was stunned. He had read the first few places at a glance and now tried to read them slowly and separately in the hope that his eyes had deceived him. A great rage filled his chest and throat and he snatched off the receiver of his internal telephone and dialled the Premises Manager.

'Blackledge here,' he said. 'I've just got your memo about the garage spaces.'

'Oh yes,' said the Premises Manager. He seemed unaware of the emotion which Blackledge himself heard modulating and strangling his voice.

'Didn't Ramsden pass on to you the note I made allocating the spaces?'

'Was that some weeks ago, Mr Blackledge?' The Premises Manager was large, without guile, and slow-speaking.

'Yes, of course,' said Blackledge.

'Well, Mr Blackledge, there was a lot of argument about who should have the new spaces. I couldn't get the chaps concerned to agree so I had a word with the General Manager and he took the whole thing out of my hands.'

'But this is your memo.'

'It's the G.M.'s numbers, Mr Blackledge.'

'Didn't you compare them with my list?'

'No. Naturally not, Mr Blackledge, after the G.M. –'

'It should never have been a matter for Mr Matheson,' interrupted Blackledge. 'Far too trivial.'

'Well, Mr Blackledge, in the ordinary way I shouldn't have dreamt of going to see Mr Matheson, naturally, but there seemed to be a deadlock about these new spaces –'

Blackledge put down his receiver and sat for a moment staring into a chasm that yawned just beyond his desk. Then he took up the offending memorandum, walked rapidly out of the room and along the corridor, and burst into the General Manager's room almost without knocking.

It was empty. The desk and its fittings were as uncluttered as though Matheson were on a long holiday, except that in his 'In' tray there was a copy of *Illustrated*. Of course, he had not yet arrived, and when he did all he would do would be to interfere in trivia – and trivia which did not really concern him. Blackledge turned on his heel and went back to his own room.

Half past nine: there was probably another quarter of an hour to wait. Blackledge could not face the papers on his desk: he looked out into the square, chalky-grey in the morning sunshine, his fingers in his trousers pocket automatically counting his change. The first shock of his anger began to recede and he thought how the others who would receive the memorandum – who at this moment were probably reading it – would at first be surprised and then gleeful at the vital numbers, as one is always gleeful at the catastrophe which does not involve oneself. Not that they wanted to see him discomfited, Blackledge thought, for he had always taken pains, where pains were necessary, to make himself popular with the staff – except Gerson. He was certainly not liked by Gerson and Gerson would desire more than anything to see him done down – provided that did not involve Gerson himself in any risky action. Had Gerson had anything to do with the memorandum, or was it entirely Matheson's thoughtlessness?

Blackledge tried to imagine Gerson working on the General Manager to obtain for himself the second garage space, but the picture failed to focus. And it surely could not be that all these years he had been underestimating, misconceiving, Gerson's character. He heard the door open and whirled round from the window, his pulses throbbing, thinking, confusedly, that it must be the General Manager, his mind as full of the memorandum as Blackledge's own. But it was his secretary, and quickly he said to her: 'I'm not ready for you yet, Maureen.'

'Will you ring, Mr Blackledge?' she asked.

He said he would, remembering even in this hateful instant to bestow upon her what he knew was his charming smile, and she went out. He gave her a few moments to get away from the 'quarter-deck' and then went out himself. But now he had lost the impetus of rage and by the time he had reached the General Manager's door he was halted by the thought that perhaps it would be quite impossible to change the offending numbers. And if it were impossible, protest was more than useless – it was damaging. Was the thing, after all, of no real importance to the rest of the society – a not uncharacteristic product of Matheson's dream world, scarcely remarked on, quickly forgotten?

He stood for a second in front of the General Manager's door, paralysed by the choice of the two courses before him. Then, after glancing round to make sure he was not observed, he strode back to his own room. As soon as he had made this decision he felt a regret that hurt him physically, a gnawing sense of permanently-missed opportunity, a consciousness of defeat that he could not remember experiencing since the weakness of his childhood. He picked up his red pencil and found that his hand was sweating . . .

From *Image of a Society* by Roy Fuller, 1956

A Fight to the Death

Cyril Y. Snaggs (the Y stood for Yeatman, a family name) was a burly man with patches of red on his cheeks that might have been painted there, a horse's wide nostrils through which he blew angrily or eagerly, a large box mouth in which false teeth emphatically clicked, and hairy capable hands. His voice was loud, his manner choleric, his handshake painfully firm. He gripped my hand at our first meeting and said that he would be relying on me for all the help I could give him. Mr Budette had told him about my registration as a conscientious objector and also about the verse magazine that I edited mostly in office time, and he seemed to feel that in some mysterious way the two activities cancelled out each other. 'I tell you frankly, I detest your politics,' he said with what I came to know as a characteristic glare. 'We won't talk about them, if you don't mind, least said soonest mended.' Then he went on to say something about understanding that people mixed up with poetry were a funny lot and that it was not his business anyway. 'We'll be working in harness, got to pull together. If we make a team we'll get on.'

Snaggs was in his middle forties, one of Mr Budette's drinking companions at the Albert. He had had a dozen jobs of one kind and another in the years before the war, all of them as a salesman. I never found out how somebody with no administrative experience had landed this job with Midlands Paint Sprayers – perhaps his downright manner impressed them at an interview – but he started out with immense energy to get the London office established. A stream of applicants came in for the post of travelling representative and two were taken on the payroll. They were known by their initials – Snaggs was a great man for initials, which he equated with brisk efficiency – as L.P.U. and G.W. Enquiries, requests for catalogues, and then orders ensued. I was busier than I had ever been in the V.L.D. days, and Snaggs clicked away in satisfaction at the system I evolved for separating one area from another, cataloguing clients, using different colour cards for enquiries, follow ups, service calls, orders, complaints. Head Office expressed approval, clearly we were making a team.

Such smooth progress delighted Snaggs in a way, but it did not satisfy him emotionally. Metaphysical fire was always shooting out of his nostrils, he was a quarrelsome man who needed an enemy. He found one soon enough in the director we dealt with in Birmingham, a man named Jenkins, who wrote memoranda in what he obviously thought a highly literary style. We would receive notes reading: 'In reply to your memo 181 B anent delivery to Southern Factors, we are doing our best but this line is out of stock and in present conditions I fear a diuturnity may elapse before maturation is possible.' Snagg's irritation at receiving such notes was reasonable, his expression of it excessive. We had no telex to Birmingham, and telephone calls from London were not encouraged except on urgent matters, but Snaggs was on the line in a moment asking how long a diuturnity lasted and whether maturation had anything to do with maternity. Afterwards he would click his teeth at me, breathing hard as though he had just won a race. 'I think we showed our friend just where he got off, Symons, eh?' Within a short time he was on such bad terms with Jenkins that I handled most of the calls from Head Office direct. 'It's that man again,' Snaggs would say, and add without bothering to put his hand over the telephone receiver: 'Little Hitler. Talk to him, will you?'

His relations with L.P.U. also deteriorated quickly. G.W. was mild-mannered and totally harmless, but L.P.U., a hard-drinking red nosed traveller of the old school, was always difficult to reach at home with urgent messages, rarely 'phoned in, and sometimes even failed to attend the Thursday travellers' conference at which calls were arranged for the following week. When Snaggs did reach him on the telephone he would ask, in a tone heavy with sarcasm, whether L.P.U. could spare time to look in at the office. Occasionally L.P.U., a man not easily put down and insusceptible to sarcasm, would say that he was too busy, and then Snaggs would roar: 'I want to see you. Tomorrow at ten thirty. Is that clear?' Slamming down the telephone he would say to me: 'Our friend's got to learn that he can't do that there 'ere.' L.P.U. would arrive, red nosed and cheerful, and the quarrel would be resolved by a drinking session.

. . . Mr Budette was a good-natured man, but he felt an affinity for failure rather than success, and found it natural to view business as a battle of wits rather than an affair of effortful striving. He was himself what he sometimes called a self-made man, and Snaggs's frequent references to his prep school and minor public school annoyed him. The Colonel, as he once said to Snaggs, had been at Eton but didn't make a bloody song and dance about it. Beyond this he was irritated by Snaggs's boastfully busy manner, and by his success in setting up the London office. Mr Budette must unconsciously have compared this success with the declining fortunes of V.L.D., which existed at this time on orders for electric lamps and other odds and ends given us by firms like Watney Combe Reid. In these transactions he acted simply as a middleman, taking his discount merely for passing on an order. I had far more work to do for Midlands Paint Sprayers than for V.L.D. and the Colonel combined, and this annoyed him too.

'I tell you what our friend Snaggs is made of,' he said. 'Piss and wind, he's all piss and wind.' Returning one day from the Albert in company with the Colonel he asked me to tell Snaggs that an outside call had come through, and then connect the two of them through our internal switchboard. Using an undefined regional accent quite unlike his own voice, Mr Budette then played the role of a dissatisfied client. Snaggs loved the telephone and was proud of his technique in dealing with customers, but irascibility soon replaced his 'Can we be of service to you?' manner under the stress of what was in effect personal abuse.

'I've been on to your Mr Jenkins and he told me to get in touch with you', Mr Budette said. 'I told him your machines won't work, they're no bloody good.'

'Very sorry to hear you're having trouble,' Snaggs replied. 'Our aim is to give service. Just tell me where you are, I'll get a man along immediately.'

'He told me to ask for Cyril Y. Snaggs.'

'Snaggs speaking.'

'And I said to him, Snaggs I said, we've got enough snags already, is he like his name? And he said, I wouldn't be surprised.'

Teeth clicked. 'Who is that speaking, I didn't get the name.'

Mr Budette rattled off something unintelligible. 'I told Jenkins, if he's no better than his stupid name I don't want him messing about with my equipment.'

'What is your name?' Snaggs shouted.

'It won't be Snaggs who looks at your machines, Jenkins said, confidentially he doesn't know his arse from his elbow, but we've got some qualified engineers.'

'*Jenkins said that?*' False teeth clattered like a monkey's.

The encounter went on for another couple of minutes and ended with Snaggs slamming down the receiver. He rushed in to tell Mr Budette about the call, found the three of us helpless with laughter, and realised what had happened. His relationship with Mr Budette was restored after a couple of days, but I remained unforgiven. 'I shan't forget this,' he said, and he never did. Rather more strangely, the incident exacerbated his feelings against Jenkins, as though he really had been responsible for the words attributed to him.

But Snaggs's star was in the descendant. Jenkins came down from Birmingham, and was not pleased by what he found. He was a short-haired, brisk executive, whose appearance could not at all be reconciled with those wordy memos. He had a couple of drinks in the Albert, but then made it clear that it was time to leave and get back to work. He thought quite rightly that the rent paid for the crane room was altogether excessive (I always suspected that Mr Budette had made some typical private deal by which a percentage of the rent went to Snaggs), expressed dissatisfaction with the service given to customers by the travellers, said he wanted a twice-weekly report on paper of all London activities, and talked vaguely about taking a larger London office. The warning signs were clear, but Snaggs refused to read them. He embarked on long drinking bouts with Mr Budette, the Colonel and others, which began at the Albert and continued in clubs, so that often he was out during the whole afternoon, returning at five o'clock purplish and breathing hard through distended nostrils. 'What does the little tyke want now?' he would ask, reading with glazed eyes a memo from Birmingham. The air raids on London had begun, and I thought of him staggering home to the ladylike little woman in Sanderstead. Did they go down to sleep in the air raid shelter when the bombs started to fall? Somehow I could not imagine it.

A few days later the blow fell. Snaggs was told that a new and larger office had been found just round the corner in Victoria Street, and that Mr F. G. R. Remnant would be coming down from Birmingham to take charge of it. The firm greatly appreciated the help Snaggs had given in setting up London office, but felt that travelling representation ought to be increased and suggested that he should cover the London area, thus joining L.P.U. and G.W. and become C.Y.S. The letter was signed by the managing director, but Snaggs rightly saw in it Jenkins's vile hand. The news can't exactly have been unexpected, and in a sense he had provoked a struggle which he could only lose, but he took it very hard.

To my surprise he accepted the demotion from Cyril Y. Snaggs, London Manager, to C.Y.S., London rep, but he blamed almost everybody involved, in particular Jenkins and me.

Blame for me was universal. Jenkins had rung Mr Budette from Birmingham and arranged that I should spend four days a week working for them and one for him, and that they would pay the whole of my wages. Mr Budette also squeezed three months' rent from them as notice for leaving the crane room. The whole arrangement was financially profitable to him, and convenient too, but he felt cheated by it, rather as though Midlands Paint Sprayers and I had combined to put over on him some extremely sharp deal. I think he felt that I was in a way his property, and that four-fifths of this property had been stolen from him. This feeling was somehow deepened by the fact that I was a conscientious objector and that Remnant, the new manager, was a dapper mild-mannered liberal who felt considerable sympathy for anybody trying to avoid military service. 'I don't mind telling you that you're absolutely indispensable to our war effort,' he said to me with a wink in Mr Budette's presence. Snaggs, who had come to detest me almost as much as he hated Jenkins, expressed his feelings openly as he had never done before by saying: 'They're going to catch up with all you bloody conchies soon.'

We moved into the new offices, which were by the standards of the time luxurious. A girl typist was engaged. Memos flowed, business flourished. Bombing continued. Against the developing pattern of the war, threatened invasion, tightened belts, a sharpening of patriotic propaganda, Snaggs moved towards his doom.

From *Notes from Another Country* by Julian Symons, 1972

Knowing the Ropes

The morning sun came round and struck through the window of Arnold Gerson's office. He put his pen down, rose, and carefully adjusted the blind so that his desk was shielded from the glare. Then he sat down again in his unupholstered swivel chair – the sort of chair that even those with the smallest pretensions in the society possessed. The walls of the room were distempered cream, and, except for a calendar from some missionary organization, completely bare. Gerson took up his pen and dipped it in the ink – he had never used a fountain pen.

It was quite unconsciously that he exercised the same parsimony with the society's money as with his own. A universal principle governed his life – that of provident management. It was axiomatic that a substantial part of both his own and the society's income should be put to reserve. He had taught his children likewise to save a fixed proportion of their Saturday allowances. Family outings were budgeted for and planned long in advance. He took the *Daily Mail* at home and read at the office the society's copy of *The Times*.

He had not, as he knew, a very good brain, and so he had trained himself to a pitch of almost terrifying scrupulousness. With the patience of Job he checked and double checked all his figures, wrote several drafts of important letters and memoranda, scrutinized and signed every communication that went out of his large department, kept an elaborate diary of reminders and anniversaries, saw that he had authority for any action that had the least likelihood of being questioned. His working day merged almost imperceptibly into his evening's leisure. He was always the last of the executives to leave the office and before he put on his hat and coat he would walk to the General Manager's room, knock on the door and open it discreetly to make sure that Matheson had really gone and would not require him again. Gerson loved the quiet, dimly-lit corridors of Saddleford House at that moment of the day: he permitted himself to relax, walk rather slowly, hum a little tune. Then he would pack some work into his brief case, walk down to the garage, start his pre-war Morris on the handle to save the battery, and drive cautiously home. The evening meal was high tea, which his children shared: over it he questioned them about their day's work and told them and his wife something of his own. Afterwards he took his briefcase to the quiet of the breakfast room.

He had married his wife in the humble days of his career, when he was a junior clerk in a chartered accountant's office. His progress had filled her with awe and she completely accepted his domination of the family's life – a domination, however, which was exercised by a code of conduct so ancient and so natural to him that as a husband and father he exuded only mildness and reason. Very occasionally Mrs Gerson was shocked by what she initially regarded as an outburst of daring extravagance in her husband, but which she grew to see as a far-sighted economy or tactical or social advantage: such was his first purchase of a car and, at the time the eldest child won a scholarship to a grammar school, of the *Encyclopaedia Britannica*. These things were a mark of Arnold's superiority.

From *Image of a Society* by Roy Fuller, 1956

Baxter's Chair

It was the chair, inevitably, that came to characterize Baxter for us all. Its introduction took me by surprise. I had detected hardness in the man when we met, ambition, even ruthlessness. But not paranoia.

He was, inevitably, one of the assertive new grade of managers, honed to tougher marketing, almost fanatically orientated to profit, being pushed up by new systems of selection and training. They seemed to me to be like mercenaries, and one of their martial arts was commercial aggression . . .

Our department was open-plan but Baxter's first act was to replace the clear glass in his partition windows with glazed glass. At the same time he issued an edict saying that no glazed glass was to be used elsewhere, thus establishing that an area that is unique in its seclusion must be supremely important.

He re-orientated his suite so that it extended into a structural corner of the building – no one could get round the back of him. And then he created a modest labyrinth of rooms – filing, conference, secretary, and deputy's room (mine) – so that it was really quite hard even to get through to him.

The 'keep' of this fortification was, of course, his office where he arranged his desk across one corner so that it faced the door.

In other parts of the large room were some mock Chippendales, a bookcase and a pot plant of Andean proportions whose leaves his secretary polished every day.

In front of the desk, facing Baxter, was *the chair*, a large, semi-formal swivel.

Anyone penetrating his defence system efficiently enough to have conversation with him, would be waved toward this.

But, whoever sat there invariably found, with reactions varying from amazement to consternation, that the *swivel chair did not swivel*.

It was fixed rigidly to the floor and its swivelling mechanism had been locked off.

The occupant could not, without contorting himself, change the direction in which his body was facing, and found therefore that he had the utmost difficulty in conferring, by word or expression, with his colleagues who were generally situated to left, right or behind him.

When you sat in the chair it seemed as if it gripped you physically. Whatever feelings of self-confidence you might have had when you sat down diminished markedly during the first thirty seconds.

I found myself watching mesmerically for the moment when the luckless occupant of the chair first found himself restrained by the inertia of the mediaeval contraption.

I like to think my feelings were compounded partly of compassion but I am sure they were not without an element of discreditable amusement. The emotions evoked made me feel guilty, as if I was watching some sucker caught by a 'candid camera' in a demeaning dilemma and at whose plight I smirked because the sucker was not me.

Baxter never showed any signs of his own reactions but always moved quickly into the discussion while the visitor was still wondering how he had got trapped like this.

Whenever I went in to see him, which was often, I used and accepted the chair as some kind of Disneyland gimmick and showed my amusement at it in little ways. I know he was not comfortable with this but it served to raise my self-esteem. Lesser members of the department feared it and I was told on several occasions that it was colloquially referred to as 'the electric' chair. Whether Baxter was aware of this, I do not know.

From 'Swivel' by James Thurlby, 1986

The Velvet Glove

John Hobday sat on the edge of his desk and swung his left leg with characteristic boyishness. He waited for the staff to get settled in their seats and then spoke with careful informality.

'I know how frightfully busy you are. As a matter of fact I am myself,' he said with the half-humorous urchin smile that he used for such jokes. Only his secretary, Veronica, gave the helpful laugh expected. It was not going to be an easy meeting, he decided. 'So I'm not going to waste your time with a lot of talk,' he went on, 'I just thought . . .' He paused and beat with his pencil against the desk whilst Mrs Scrutton moved her chair fussily out of the sunlight. 'Ready?' he asked with an over-elaborate smile. 'Right. Then we'll start again. As I was saying, we're all very busy, but all the same I thought it was time we had a little meeting. I've been here a week now and although I've had some very helpful chats with each of you in turn, we've never had a chance to get together and outline our plans.' None of the three who formed his audience made any response. Veronica, who remembered him taking over new departments at the Ministry during the war, thought he hasn't got the right tone, he doesn't realize that he's coming up against deeper loyalties with these people,

[208]

loyalties to scholarship and ideas. She almost felt like letting him fend for himself, but old habits were too strong.

'I'm sure it's what everybody's been wanting,' she said in her deep voice. She had gauged rightly, his moment of uncertainty had gone, her faithful bark had guided him at the crucial moment. Mrs Scrutton tried to discomfort him. She rustled the papers on her lap and whispered audibly to Major Sarson, 'Our plans. *His* plans for us would be more honest.' But it was too late, she had missed her chance. John merely frowned at the interruption and it was Mrs Scrutton who was left with burning cheeks, hiding her embarrassment by lighting a fresh cigarette.

'As you know,' John went on, and Veronica could tell by the loud, trumpeting, rhetorical note of his voice that he was once more the confident salesman lost in the dream world of the grandiose schemes he was putting before them, 'I've got some very big ideas for the Gallery. I'm not an expert in any way as you people are, but I think that's possibly why Sir Harold's executors chose me for the job. They felt the Gallery had already got its full weight of scholars and experts, what it needed was a man with administrative experience, whose training had led him to take an overall view of things, to think, shall I say, widely rather than deeply. That's why they got me in. But I'm going to be absolutely frank with you,' tossing a lock of brown, wavy hair from his forehead, he stared at the audience with a wide-eyed appeal, 'I need *your* help, without my staff I can get nowhere'...

From 'Realpolitik' in *The Wrong Set* by Angus Wilson, 1949

Keeping up Appearances

He is, I think, as big a coward as I am; yet, he is the only person in the company with enough courage to behave badly. I envy that: I am cordial and considerate to many people I detest (I am cordial and considerate to just about *everybody*, I think, except former girl friends and the members of my family); I trade jokes convivially with several salesmen who annoy the hell out of me and make me waste much of my time with their frantic and contradictory requests; I get drunk with others who bore and irritate me and join them at orgiastic parties with secretaries, waitresses, sales-girls, housewives, nurses, models from Oklahoma, and airline steward-esses from Pennsylvania and Texas; I have two men in my department I'd like to fire and one girl, and there are days when I would truly like to be rid of them all; but I try not to show how I feel, and I'll probably never do anything about any of them, except keep hoping sullenly that they'll disappear on their own; I'm glad that Martha, our crazy typist, isn't going crazy in my department, because I know that I wouldn't have the nerve or competence to do anything about her before she finally falls apart; there's a fellow executive in the Merchandising Department I have lunch with once or twice a month who I sincerely wish would drop dead. (Once a year we have him to dinner, always with a lot of other people, and once each spring he has us to lunch on his God-damned boat.) I know so many people I want to be mean to, but I just don't have the character.

Green, on the other hand, is notorious for being frank and unkind (he is frank, I suspect, *just* to be unkind). He would rather make a bad impression than no impression. He tries extremely hard to be inconsiderate to people on his own level and lower. He creates tension, terror, and uneasiness in an organization that values harmony, dreads disagreements, conceals failure, and disguises conflict and personal dislike. He is aggressive and defensive. He attacks others and is sorry for himself.

People in the company, for example, do their best to minimize friction (we are encouraged to revolve around each other eight hours a day like self-lubricating ball bearings, careful not to jar or scrape) and to avoid quarreling with each other openly. It is considered much better form to wage our battles sneakily behind each other's back than to confront each other directly with any semblance of complaint. (The secret attack can be denied, lied about, or reduced in significance, but the open dispute is witnessed and has to be dealt with by somebody who finds the whole situation deplorable.) We are all on a congenial, first-name basis, especially with people we loathe (the more we loathe them, the more congenial we try to be), and our wives and children are always inquired about familiarly by their first names, even by people who have never met them or met them only once. The right to this pose of comfortable intimacy does not extend downward to secretaries, typists, or mail boys, or more than two levels upward through the executive hierarchy. I can call Jack Green Jack and Andy Kagle Andy and even Arthur Baron Art, but I would not call anyone higher than Arthur Baron anything but mister. That would be not only dangerous but rude, and I am always hesitant about being rude (to anyone but the members of my family) even when it isn't dangerous. Even Jane in the Art Department still calls me Mr Slocum respectfully when we meet (sometimes by telephone appointment when I am feeling especially frivolous) and kid around in one of the back corridors, and Jane and I have gone pretty far with each other by now in conversation. I used to encourage the girls I was after to call me by my first name, but I've learned from experience that it's always better, and

safer, and more effective, to preserve the distinction between executive
and subordinate, employer and employee, even in bed. (*Especially* in bed.)

From *Something Happened* by Joseph Heller, 1974

A Major Irritant

The new year did not bring Mr Stone the reassurance he had been half
expecting. There was nothing new to excite or absorb him, and much of
the work he was called upon to do was simple routine. So, barring the
discussions with Whymper about the Round Table dinner, it had been
for many weeks past; but now, with his new eyes, he thought he saw his
own position more clearly. He was in the office what he had been in
the library, a gentle, endearing man nearing retirement, of no particular
consequence. Now he saw how often in a crisis the instinct of the 'staff'
was to turn to Whymper, for Whymper's quick thinking, his ability to
see his way out of a jam, was legendary – 'ladies in the bower' had already
become an office story – and though not liked, he was respected. He saw
that he was entrusted with what might be considered safe: the supervision
of lists, the overlooking of accounts. He had declined into 'staff' himself.
To this assumption there was nothing with which he could reply. He did
not have Whymper's restless mind; he had no new idea to offer; he was
unable to handle the public relations – and this aspect of the Unit's work
had grown more important since the publicity – with Whymper's skill.
He became snappish in the office; he became rude. And there occurred a
row with Whymper over a typist of Polish origin.

Enraged by her inadequate grammar, sloppy dress and what he thought
was her insolence, he had quarrelled with her in public and gone so far
as to refer to her as 'that D.P. girl.' He was in his office scourging himself
for his behaviour when Whymper entered in a tremendous temper, his
eyes narrow, his lips quivering, Whymper of all people, the man who
during those lunchtime walks had spoken with so much feeling about
'foreigners cluttering up the place'. His performance was melodramatic
and self-appraising from start to finish, from 'What's this I hear, Stone?'
to 'Don't you dare talk to any of the staff like that again, do you hear?'
Mr Stone saw through it all but was none the less cowed. It occurred to
him that the girl might be Whymper's new mistress, and several replies
to Whymper's threat came into his head. But he had the lucidity to remain
silent.

He thought, however, to revenge himself on them the following day.
The girl had typed 'artillery' for 'itinerary' in a letter to a distinguished

Knight Companion. He did not point out the error to her. Instead, he put an asterisk after the word and wrote a footnote: 'I leave this in because I feel that this example of our typists' literacy will amuse you. The word should, of course, be "itinery".' It was a heavy joke, made at the end of the day; perhaps the judgement of early morning might have shown him as much. Two days later the reply came: 'It seems that typists' literacy is catching. By "itinery" I imagine you mean "itinerary".' Now he knew very well how the word ought to be spelt; and in this swift rebuke he saw some sort of judgement, which made him desist from his war against the girl and made him less anxious to impose himself in the office.

In the routine of the office, as in the rhythm of the seasons, he could no longer participate. It all went without reference to himself. Soon it would go on without his presence. His earlier petulance – 'Why do you ask *me*? Why don't you ask Mr Whymper?' At which the ridiculous young man from Yorkshire with the ridiculous clothes had actually sniggered, and reported that 'Pop', the foolish and common nickname which that foolish and common boy had succeeded in popularizing, wasn't in a good mood that morning – his earlier petulance had given way to weariness and indifference and then at last to a distaste for the office which was like fear.

There were days when the office was made unbearable for him by the knowledge that Whymper was present. He felt that Whymper's indifference had turned to contempt, of the sort which follows affection; he thought it conveyed reassessment, rejection and offended disgust. There were times when he felt that he had brought this contempt on himself, that his own revulsion and hostility had been divined by Whymper, who was demonstrating his disregard for the judgement by an exaggerated heartiness with the other members of the staff. He had certainly unbent considerably towards them in these last weeks, and the Whymperish gambit of joviality followed by coldness was less in evidence. 'Tell them a joke,' Whymper used to say in the early days. 'They will laugh. The fresh ones will try to tell you a joke in return. You don't laugh.'

The young accountant had frequently fallen victim to this tactic. Now, fortified by Whymper's friendship – he was Whymper's new lunch companion – he attempted to use it on more junior staff. He also tried to embarrass typists by staring at their foreheads, an 'executive's' gambit which Mr Stone had heard of but had never seen practised. The detestable young man now tapped his cigarettes – it was his affectation to smoke nothing but Lambert and Butler's Straight Cut, with the striped paper – in the Whymper manner. And – these young men appeared to be having an effect on one another – Whymper came back to the office one afternoon wearing an outrageous bowtie: the junior accountant sometimes wore bowties. Mr Stone could imagine the abrupt decision, the marching off to the shop with the young accountant, the determined yet slack-jawed expression as Whymper bought perhaps half a dozen. Thereafter Whymper always wore bowties; and, since he was Whymper, they were invariably askew. Mr Stone thought they looked a perfectly ridiculous pair of young men, particularly on Saturday mornings, when the young accountant came to work in a 'county' outfit, with a hat far above his station. The hat Mr Stone especially loathed. It was green, with a green feather, as though the boy might at any moment be setting off across the moors.

On calmer days Mr Stone felt that Whymper might only be reacting against his former indiscretions, though he was convinced that these indiscretions and perhaps others were being repeated to the junior accountant. He also saw in Whymper's strange behaviour proof of the now persistent rumour that Whymper was soon going to leave the Unit and might indeed be resigning from Excal.

Altogether, it was a relief when Whymper left for his holiday, though the presence of his familiar never ceased to be irritating.

From *Mr Stone and the Knights Companion* by V. S. Naipaul, 1963

Winning Them Round

Ramsden's house telephone rang. He put down the remains of his jam puff and picked up the receiver.

'Hello,' he said shortly. Then his tone changed to one of efficient sweetness. 'Yes, Mr Blackledge,' he said. 'Yes, right away.' He put the receiver back, looked at Willie and then at his scarcely-touched mug of tea. 'God's perishing teeth,' he said. 'Why do they always want me at tea time?'

'Shall I go and get you another mug of tea, Mr Ramsden?' asked Willie.

'No, Willie. Don't know how long I'll be.' Ramsden walked over to the lift, got in, and pressed a button.

This was the lift shaft at the rear of the building: it cut through a series of similar and undistinguished corridors lined with the staff lockers. At the ground floor level Ramsden glimpsed, through glazed doors, the clerks at work in the vast hinterland behind the banking hall. As he swam upwards through the first floor one of his own staff passed carrying a bucket and wearing a safety belt, on the unending task of cleaning Saddleford House's 374 windows. The lift stopped at the second floor and

Ramsden made his way round the corridor to the front of the building. Here, the final section of the corridor was barred at either end with swing doors marked 'Private': Ramsden always referred to it as the quarter-deck. Cream distemper gave way to a dark glossy panelling, plastic floor covering to carpet, the wall lights were someone's dream of a baronial hall. Off the corridor were the offices of the principal executives, at the end of it the board-room. Ramsden, removing with his finger nail a raspberry jam seed from a tooth and wondering if an opportunity would occur now to broach the question of his undignified quarters, knocked on the door of Blackledge's room . . .

'Very good, sir. And if the Premises Manager asks me –'

Blackledge cut him short. 'If the Premises Manager has any questions he must come and see me.'

Ramsden shuffled his feet and half turned to go. Blackledge's voice brought him round again – a voice now pitched lower, slightly honeyed, warm.

'Ramsden,' said Blackledge, 'you're an expert. I'm thinking of buying some rose bushes: what kind ought I to get?'

Ramsden came a little nearer to the desk. 'Didn't know you were a gardener, Mr Blackledge,' he said.

Blackledge let himself be patronized. 'I'm not. Far from it. Beginning to get interested though. Now those rose bushes –'

'Well, sir,' said Ramsden, 'it all depends on what you want. But why don't you go in for these hybrid polyantha . . .'

Blackledge permitted Ramsden to speak enthusiastically for several minutes and then suddenly looked at his watch. 'Good Lord!' he said. 'I must go and talk to those children. Thank you, Ramsden. Most valuable. I won't forget what you've told me.'

Ramsden marched along the corridor with the glow of a man who has done himself conversational justice. And then, as he descended in the lift to his cold tea and the remains of the jam puff, he said to himself: I wouldn't trust that bastard as far as I could throw him.

From *Image of a Society* by Roy Fuller, 1956

Eleven

A FEARFUL BUSINESS

Offices, as Jonathan Gathorne-Hardy points out, are 'founded on fear': fear of the sack, fear of the boss, fear of making a fool of oneself, fear of letting down one's family or colleagues, fear of failure, fear of poverty, fear of retirement, fear of being forgotten. No one is immune, from the most domineering dynamo to the most diffident new arrival: for in the last resort office life, like life itself, is about the struggle to survive, and that is a fearful business.

Founded on Fear

Offices provide security. But this truism conceals a rather curious paradox.

More than most social units, offices are founded on fear. This fear operates outside and inside. Outside, offices fear other offices. They fear competition and takeover, they are afraid their products will become out of date, or that they themselves will. As a result they grow bigger and bigger to fight more effectively. Or smaller and smaller, desperately struggling, till they disappear. They diversify. They call in management consultants or indulge in ruthless purges. Even when they've grown so big and so diverse they haven't any rivals, they are still afraid. The Gas Industry is afraid of the Electrical and Coal Industries and the Government. ICI is afraid of Dupont and of itself (very large, near monopolistic organisations are always afraid of the inertia of their size. Quite rightly.).

But this tendency to grow – here, as elsewhere, the distinguishing mark of our century – of course makes an office still more frightening to those inside it. If my huge office is capable of smashing or defending itself against those other huge offices, what is it not capable of doing to me? Size leads to impersonality and eventually, for most of the inmates, invisibility. 'Morning, Martin,' the Chairman says. 'Henry, sir,' murmurs Henry inaudibly, although he's been there ten years and is expected to be on the board in two more. However convincing their contract, no-one in an office feels they may not be sacked tomorrow.

From *The Office* by Jonathan Gathorne-Hardy, 1970

The Balance of Terror

In the office in which I work there are five people of whom I am afraid. Each of these five people is afraid of four people (excluding overlaps), for a total of twenty, and each of these twenty people is afraid of six people, making a total of one hundred and twenty people who are feared by at least one person. Each of these one hundred and twenty people is afraid of the other one hundred and nineteen, and all of these one hundred and forty-five people are afraid of the twelve men at the top who helped found and build the company and now own and direct it.

All these twelve men are elderly now and drained by time and success of energy and ambition. Many have spent their whole lives here. They seem friendly, slow, and content when I come upon them in the halls (they seem dead) and are always courteous and mute when they ride with others in the public elevators. They no longer work hard. They hold meetings, make promotions, and allow their names to be used on announcements that are prepared and issued by somebody else. Nobody is sure anymore who really runs the company (not even the people who are credited with running it), but the company does run. Sometimes these twelve men at the top work for the government for a little while. They don't seem interested in doing much more. Two of them know what I do and recognize me, because I have helped them in the past, and they have been kind enough to remember me, although not, I'm sure, by name. They inevitably smile when they see me and say: 'How are you?' (I inevitably nod and respond: 'Fine.') Since I have little contact with these twelve men at the top and see them seldom, I am not really afraid of them. But most of the people I am afraid of in the company are.

Just about everybody in the company is afraid of somebody else in the company . . .

In my department, there are six people who are afraid of me, and one small secretary who is afraid of all of us. I have one other person working for me who is not afraid of anyone, not even me, and I would fire him quickly, but I'm afraid of him.

From *Something Happened* by Joseph Heller, 1974

A Summons from Above

He pressed the house telephone and told the girl to get him Tony's firm on the line. While he waited, the buzzer went. He lifted a switch: it was Miss Reeves, the Chairman's secretary.

'Good morning, Mr Bissel.'

'Good morning, Miss Reeves.' How high does one have to go not to feel a qualm when she rang, Leonard wondered.

'The Chairman would like to see you in his office in fifteen minutes, please.'

'Thank you.'

Leonard dropped the buzzer into place, then glanced up at the electric clock over the door. He jotted the precise time on a pad by his side, added on fifteen minutes and wrote the total in large figures . . .

*

Ten minutes after Miss Reeves had telephoned, he left his office. In the directors' washroom he adjusted his tie and checked his hair; his hands and nails were spotless as usual. Then he continued down the corridor, past the front door to the office at the end. Miss Reeves smiled as he entered, asked him to sit and disappeared through a door marked 'Chairman'. Leonard thought it strange how the Miss Reeves of this world were never frightened of the great men they served. It was the directors and managers, seemingly so powerful to outsiders, who could never approach them without slight trepidation . . .

From *The Youngest Director* by Martyn Goff, 1961

Sheer Terror

'I think good people become good ghosts and bad fellows – I dread to contemplate what kind of ghost he will turn out to be when our general manager dies.'

'Who is he?'

'Edward Shilling – a huge fellow, made of beef and whisky. He keeps a bottle even in his office room. I am his personal clerk. God! What terror it strikes in me when the buzzer sounds. I fear some day he is going to strike me dead. He explodes "Damn", "Damn" every few minutes. If there is the slightest mistake in taking dictation, he bangs the table, my heart flutters like a –' He went on talking thus, and Srinivas learnt to leave him alone and go through his business uninterrupted. At first he sat listening sympathetically; but later found that this was unpractical. Though the man had numerous dependants, he had less to say about them than about his beefy master. His master seemed to possess his soul completely, so that the young man was incapable of thinking of anything else, night or day. He seemed to have grown emaciated and dazed through this spiritual oppression. Srinivas had learnt all that was to be learnt about him within the first two or three days of his talk with him. So, though he felt much sympathy for him, he felt it unnecessary to interrupt his normal occupation for the sake of hearing a variation of a single theme.

From *Mr Sampath* by R. K. Narayan, 1949

Revealed at Last

I have a feeling that someone nearby is soon going to find out something about me that will mean the end, although I can't imagine what that something is.

From *Something Happened* by Joseph Heller, 1974

Twelve

TEDIUM VITAE

Boredom, like fear, is a recurrent *motif* of office life – and with it a sense of impotent resentment, of life dribbling away on tedious, humdrum tasks in a place of dismal confinement. As our eager new arrival soon discovers, much to his chagrin and surprise, much of the work done, especially at junior levels, in even the most congenial and glamorous of trades is, by its very nature, routine and repetitive – so much so that, on dog days, neither office friendships nor office gossip can lift the pall of *tedium vitae*. Even the most diligent will spend more time than they should gazing out of the window or wishing they had the courage to produce the paperback lurking in the briefcase and read it under the desk rather than fill in the long hours making unnecessary work so as to assuage feelings of fear and guilt. Men and women of a literary bent – like Nirad Chaudhuri or the Puzzleheaded Girl – tend to combine contempt for the dim restraints of office life with a sense (arrogant, as some may see it) that they are destined for better and for higher things; common to us all, even to go-getting New York journalists, are dreams of escape, of getting away from it all.

'It isn't living at all'

As Bannister had said, the work in the postage department was not intricate. There was nothing much to do except enter and stamp letters, and, at intervals, take them down to the post office at the end of the street. The nature of the work gave Mike plenty of time for reflection.

His thoughts became gloomy again. All this was very far removed from the life to which he had looked forward. There are some people who take naturally to a life of commerce. Mike was not of these. To him the restraint of the business was irksome. He had been used to an open-air life, and a life, in its way, of excitement. He gathered that he would not be free till five o'clock, and that on the following day he would come at ten and go at five, and the same every day, except Saturdays and Sundays, all the year round, with a ten days' holiday. The monotony of the prospect appalled him. He was not old enough to know what a narcotic is Habit, and that one can become attached to and interested in the most unpromising jobs. He worked away dismally at his letters till he had finished them. Then there was nothing to do except sit and wait for more.

He looked through the letters he had stamped, and re-read the addresses. Some of them were directed to people living in the country, one to a house which he knew quite well, near to his own home in Shropshire. It made him home-sick, conjuring up visions of shady gardens and country sounds and smells, and the silver Severn gleaming in the distance through the trees. About now, if he were not in this dismal place, he would be lying in the shade in the garden with a book, or wandering down to the river to boat or bathe. That envelope addressed to the man in Shropshire gave him the worst moment he had experienced that day.

From *Psmith in the City* by P. G. Wodehouse, 1910

Casting Around for Things to Do

My day's work at the office was monotonous, like family life. For if my new Uncle Belton and Mr Phillimore were husband and wife, I was the only child who strays listlessly from room to room trying to find something to do. I stuck on stamps, I copied letters. I put clean water in the flower-bowl which Mr Phillimore kept filled. They were a love-offering. I took messages. I went across the road to buy buns for the typist, or my uncle would send me out to collect a shirt from a shop or to buy a bottle of hair-cream at his barber's.

From 'It May Never Happen' in *It May Never Happen* by
V. S. Pritchett, 1945

Filling in the Long Hours

The long vacation saunters on towards term-time, like an idle river very leisurely strolling down a flat country to the sea. Mr Guppy saunters along with it congenially. He has blunted the blade of his penknife, and broken the point off, by sticking that instrument into his desk in every direction. Not that he bears the desk any ill-will, but he must do something, and it must be something of an unexciting nature, which will lay neither his physical nor his intellectual energies under too heavy contribution. He finds that nothing agrees with him so well, as to make little gyrations on one leg of his stool, and stab his desk, and gape.

From *Bleak House* by Charles Dickens, 1853

Dry Drudgery

Who first invented work, and bound the free
And holyday-rejoicing spirit down
To the ever-haunting importunity
Of business in the green fields, and the town –
To plough, loom, anvil, spade – and (oh most sad!)
To that dry drudgery at the desk's dead wood? ...

From 'Work' by Charles Lamb, 1818

Dull Peacefulness

The three-fourths of Una employed in the office of Mr Troy Wilkins was going through one of those periods of unchanging routine when all past drama seems unreal, when nothing novel happens nor apparently ever will happen – such a time of dull peacefulness as makes up the major part of our lives.

Her only definite impressions were the details of daily work, the physical aspects of the office, and the presence of the 'Boss.'

From *The Job* by Sinclair Lewis, 1917

Child's Play

But my work was dull. The terrible thing was that it was simple and mechanical; far, far less difficult than work at school. This was a humiliation and, even now, the simplicity of most of the work in offices, factories and warehouses depresses me. It is also all trite child's play and repetition and the correcting of an infinitude of silly mistakes, compared with intellectual or professional labour. Most people seemed to me, then, and even now, chained to a dulling routine of systematised and tolerated carelessness and error. Whatever was going to happen to me, I knew I must escape from this easy, unthinking world and I understood my father's dogged efforts to be on his own, and his own master.

From *A Cab at the Door* by V. S. Pritchett, 1968

A Great Pursuit!

Mr Micawber was extremely glad to see me, but a little confused too. He would have conducted me immediately into the presence of Uriah, but I declined.

'I know the house of old, you recollect,' said I, 'and will find my way up-stairs. How do you like the law, Mr Micawber?'

'My dear Copperfield,' he replied. 'To a man possessed of the higher imaginative powers, the objection to legal studies is the amount of detail which they involve. Even in our professional correspondence,' said Mr Micawber, glancing at some letters he was writing, 'the mind is not at liberty to soar to any exalted form of expression. Still, it is a great pursuit. A great pursuit!'

From *David Copperfield* by Charles Dickens, 1850

Bored at the Pru

Eileen was even unhappier at the Pru than she had anticipated. The girl clerks were utterly uninteresting to her, and as for niceness they were mostly the daughters of small tradesmen and bank clerks. They thought Eileen a mass of affectation with her unmanicured hands and her poetry books and high-brow novels. They themselves scarcely noticed the names of authors and eagerly followed the serial in the daily paper their fathers took in; they even discussed the heroines in Sweetheart Novelettes and other orange-covered booklets that until now Eileen had never seen anywhere but in the drawer of the kitchen dresser. For six months the only work entrusted to her was the copying of names, addresses, and policy numbers out of dirty ledgers into clean ones, omitting heavily erased cancelled policies. If she made the slightest slip, the supervisor tore the whole page out of the ledger without a word. Later she was given letters to type, teaching herself as she worked from the company book of instructions. For one week a month everyone had to take a turn at the loathed addressograph.

From *She Knew She was Right* by Ivy Litvinov, 1971

Unworthy of Mankind

Their business was growing. They added carbide to their commodities and were selling it in quantities in coal-mining districts. They had to buy more office machines, including a Moon book-keeping machine. An instructor was sent along with it. Debrett thought this a good chance for Miss Lawrence to earn more money. She had been with them all the winter; cold spring had come, and she had added very little to her office clothing; the cape but no coat, the same shoes, often sodden, and her hair worn simply as a little girl. Debrett called in Maria Magna, who set the girl to the machine. She learned quickly and got it right in an hour or so. Tom Zero, coming into the office, glanced over her shoulder and said to Maria Magna, 'I see the new girl is getting to work on the book-keeping.' 'Yes, I think she'll do it,' said Maria Magna, a little warmth in her voice for the first time. But when the instructor had gone, Miss Lawrence rose from the machine and, going over to Miss Magna, said she could learn the machine, but she would not, she would have nothing to do with accounts, money machines and sales. 'I came here to make a living, but I won't mix in business.'

Miss Magna bustled in to Mr Debrett with this story. 'Tell her to come in.' She appeared at once.

'I understand that you're good on the new machine but you don't want to work it?'

'No. I won't do it.'

'Why?'

'I have to earn my living in an office, but I won't mix in business. I hate and despise business and anything to do with making money.'

'Do you think it's wrong?'

'It is the enemy of art.'

'And you feel yourself an artist?'

'No. But I want to live with artists and live like them. I don't want to be like those earthy girls out there, like Maria Magna and Vera Day. I prefer to die of hunger. Or go away.'

'But you have no money.'

'No. But it doesn't matter. I can get along without money. In the Village, artists get along without money. They all help each other. It's a different kind of living. This is a terrible world here, everyone working for money, no one working for anything good.'

'My God, I think so myself. Things ought to be different; and one day they will be.' But, as always, when a word was said that was, however remotely, challenging on social matters, she shut her mind. 'You don't think so?' She raised her brown head in its childish hair and he saw the maiden breasts move as she drew in a breath. 'You don't think so?'

'I don't think so,' she said primly.

'Well, you must feel you're an artist; that you have some other plan for living,' he pressed her.

'I don't know; I don't know what these things are,' she said vaguely. Tears came into her eyes. 'I don't know why I am here.'

'You're a good girl,' he said getting up and about to go to her, but glancing at the half-glazed partitions which divided the offices. 'Well, go out now and do your work. You do your work well.'

'Yes, but I hate it,' she said, frowning. She had dried her tears. 'It's unworthy. It's not worthy of man.'

'Man?'

'Mankind, people. Artists don't think like this; artists don't fight for money.'

'That's the old Bostonian highmindedness,' he said respectfully. 'You don't meet it often in Manhattan'...

From *The Puzzleheaded Girl* by Christina Stead, 1968

Condemned to a Living Death

From the beginning of May I was given leave for two months to prepare for my examination. But instead of reading the Regulations and manuals of book-keeping, I read literature, and had my 'enlightenment' or 'conversion'. I do not know how it happened that although I had read a good deal of Matthew Arnold's prose, including even *Culture and Anarchy*, I had never read any of his poems. I read these then, and, above all, I read 'The Scholar Gypsy'. The poem clinched the matter for me.

As I read

> Thou hast not lived, why should'st thou perish so?
>   Thou hadst *one* aim, *one* business, *one* desire;
>   Else wert thou long since number'd with the dead!
>   Else hadst thou spent, like other men, thy fire!

I realized in a flash that I was giving up, not only my vocation, but even my life. One futility from which my mind has always recoiled is to sacrifice life for livelihood. I read on:

For early didst thou leave the world, with powers
Fresh, undiverted to the world without,
    Firm to their mark, not spent on other things;
    Free from the sick fatigue, the languid doubt,
Which much to have tried, in much been baffled, brings.

I felt I should be condemned to a living death if I remained in the
Military Accounts Department for the sake of worldly security.

From *Thy Hand, Great Anarch!* by N. C. Chaudhuri, 1987

Dogsbody

Finally, looking back, I marvel somewhat at facing the plod of being
second-in-command – inevitably dogsbodyish – of what was quite a large
solicitor's office. Though a lawyer like the Kafkaesque Philip Witt in
Image of a Society must not be envisaged, my heart was not in many of
the matters that came my way. Instructions for a lease or purchase of
premises for the Society often resulted in a series of moves as boring as
those of an early-drawn chess game.

From *Spanner and Pen* by Roy Fuller, 1991

A Life of Compromise

And then his internal telephone would buzz and he would guiltily lift the
receiver, hearing at the other end the General Manager's mild voice – the
deceptive mildness, it seemed to him, of a father which at any time
might change to a righteous indignation against which his inferior status
afforded him no defence. That no one in Saddleford House ever directed
anger against him gave no reassurance of the comfort and dignity of his
position. With his nominal superiors – the directors and the General
Manager – he exerted all his concern to assure them of his conscientiousness, and not the least element of acting in this was his private
knowledge that really he was not conscientious. His relationship with
men like Blackledge held uneasily within itself the seeds of their possible
future power. Nor were his feelings in all these connexions altered in the
slightest by his clear realization that he despised his work and fundamen-
tally despised all those who had surrendered to it more than superficial
allegiance. Years ago he had thought that the sanctions and coercions of
his professional life could never touch the realities of his existence – his

writing, his reading, his private morality. Now he knew, though in a fashion he continued to struggle against the knowledge, that merely to get one's bread in the world of Hepworths and Gersons, let alone achieve butter on it, meant a life of such compromise as to make it indistinguishable from lives too ignorant and ignoble to know that the problem of compromise could exist.

From *Image of a Society* by Roy Fuller, 1956

Life Leaking Away

He walked down the hall to the stairway, smelling the various office smells – the oiled linoleum of the corridor, the sickeningly scented tobacco of Cameron's pipe, the mimeograph ink of the mail-room, the sucked, stale air of the elevator shaft – all the mosaic of little sensual links that informed him subtly where he was. Their familiarity made him realize how long he had been here or in places like it, how steadily his life was leaking away. On the stairs he met one of the pulp editors and they each dredged up something clever to say in passing – the *politesse* of the office.

From *The Philanderer* by Stanley Kauffmann, 1953

Taking Steps

While these acts and deeds were in progress in and out of the office of Sampson Brass, Richard Swiveller, being often left alone therein, began to find the time hang heavy on his hands. For the better preservation of his cheerfulness therefore, and to prevent his faculties from rusting, he provided himself with a cribbage-board and pack of cards, and accustomed himself to play at cribbage with a dummy, for twenty, thirty, or sometimes even fifty thousand pounds a side, besides many hazardous bets to a considerable amount.

From *The Old Curiosity Shop* by Charles Dickens, 1841

A Sense of Passing Through

Russell knew it was important and knew he ought to listen – he did listen in a way: he could have replied in a snatching, semi-accurate style to a question suddenly thrown at him – but a portion of his mind went travelling. This almost invariably happened when business was under discussion, particularly under serious discussion, particularly when one person was talking at length. He had a basic lack of interest in the business, in his job, in any business – a lack of interest based on the buried belief that he was merely marking time, that this was not his life's work as it was Perry's or Silverman's or Cameron's. He was merely passing through; earning a living while he ripened for some future greatness that lay ahead of him, some undefined, shadowy but superb achievement which would take him over the line of anonymity into fame. There were powers in him (he knew it) which had not been utilized. He could not have named them, but he knew they were there. How else his sensitivity, his perception, his awareness of depth beneath depth in the texture of life around him? How else could all those who knew him well mark him (as he knew they did) as unusual, brilliant, superior? Why else would Madeline have the faith in him that was one of the strong comforts in their marriage? Some day, some rapidly approaching day, the source of that brilliance would be made clear to him, he would recognize the talent or skill or intellectual ability which at present lay dormant in him, signalling its presence only by this radiation of assurance.

He had known all his life that he was going to be clever but he had never been quite sure about what.

From *The Philanderer* by Stanley Kauffmann, 1953

Incarceration

It was nothing to do with the people and only partly to do with the job. Practically all work done in offices is trivial and so was this, but it was bearable. The people, with only one exception, were kind and intelligent. My hatred was an almost physical reaction to the sensation of being shut up, every day, all week, in a box; to the cumulative effect of trivial work, to being exposed for the first time to the humiliations, ambitions and restrictions of office life; and to seeing no possible escape from all this for the rest of my life.

I decided that, in the office system, society had created an aberration which it could not control. It was monstrous that I should submit to it. It was monstrous that that huge me – the world – should submit to it.

From *The Office* by Jonathan Gathorne-Hardy, 1970

Dreams of Escape

Back at the office, your resolution to pursue the facts of the recent French elections has staled. A little nap in one of the upstairs offices would be the thing. But you've got to hang in there. You make yourself a cup of instant espresso with four tablespoons of Maxim. Megan tells you there have been three calls for you: one from the president of the Polar Explorers, one from France and another from your brother Michael.

You go into Clara's office to snag the page proofs but they're not on the desk. You ask Rittenhouse about this, and he tells you that Clara called and asked to have the proofs delivered to Typesetting. She also told him to messenger a photocopy down to her apartment.

'Well,' you say, not sure whether you are horrified or relieved. 'That's that, I guess.'

'Do you have any last-minute changes,' Rittenhouse asks. 'I'm sure there's time for some last-minute changes.'

You shake your head. 'I'd have to go back about three years to make all the necessary changes.'

'I don't suppose you remembered that bagel,' Megan says. 'Not to worry. I'm not really hungry anyway. I shouldn't be eating lunch.'

You apologize. You beg her pardon. You tell her there are so damn many things on your mind. You have a bad memory for details. You can tell her the date of the Spanish Armada, but you couldn't even guess at the balance of your checkbook. Every day you misplace your keys or your wallet. That's one of the reasons you're always late. It's so hard just getting in here every morning, let alone remembering all that you're supposed to do. You can't pay attention when people talk to you. So many little things. The big things – at least the big things declare open combat. But these details ... When you are engaged, life or death, with the main army – then to have these niggardly details sniping at you from the goddamned trees ...

'I'm so sorry, Meg. I'm really, really sorry. I'm just fucking everything up.'

Everyone is looking at you. Megan comes over and puts her arm around your shoulders. She strokes your hair.

'Take it easy,' she says. 'It's only a bagel. Sit down, just sit down and relax. Everything's going to be all right.'

Somebody brings you a glass of water. Along the windows, the potted plants form a jungle skyline, a green tableau of the simple life. You think of islands, palm trees, food-gathering. Escape.

From *Bright Lights, Big City* by Jay McInerney, 1984

'Don't you want to learn the business?' Hopkins asked quietly, but with obvious import.

'Of course . . .' Tom began. Then he paused and took a sip of his drink. The hell with it, he thought. There's no point in pretending. I've played it straight with him so far, and I might as well keep on. Anyway, he's a guy who can't be fooled. He glanced up and saw that Hopkins was smiling at him with great friendliness. Here goes nothing, Tom thought, and the words came with a rush. 'Look, Ralph,' he said, using the first name unconsciously, 'I don't think I do want to learn the business. I don't think I'm the kind of guy who should try to be a big executive. I'll say it frankly: I don't think I have the willingness to make the sacrifices. I don't want to give up the time. I'm trying to be honest about this. I want the money. Nobody likes money better than I do. But I'm just not the kind of guy who can work evenings and week-ends and all the rest of it for ever. I guess there's even more to it than that. I'm not the kind of person who can get all wrapped up in a job – I can't get myself convinced that my work is the most important thing in the world. I've been through one war. Maybe another one's coming. If one is, I want to be able to look back and figure I spent the time between wars with my family, the way it should have been spent. Regardless of war, I want to get the most out of the years I've got left. Maybe that sounds silly. It's just that if I have to bury myself in a job every minute of my life, I don't see any point to it. And I know that to do the kind of job you want me to do, I'd have to be willing to bury myself in it, and, well, I just don't want to.'

He paused, out of breath, half afraid to look at Hopkins. And then it happened – Hopkins gave a funny, high, indescribable little laugh which rose in the air and was cut off immediately. It was a laugh Tom never forgot, and it was followed by a moment of complete silence. Then Hopkins said in a low voice, 'I'm glad you're honest. I've always appreciated that quality in you.'

It was Tom's turn to laugh nervously. 'Well, there it is,' he said. 'I don't know what I do now. Do you still want me to work for you?'

'Of course,' Hopkins said kindly, getting up and pouring himself another drink. 'There are plenty of good positions where it's not necessary for a man to put in an unusual amount of work. Now it's just a matter of finding the right spot for you.'

'I'm willing to look at it straight,' Tom said. 'There are a lot of contradictions in my own thinking I've got to face. In spite of everything I've said, I'm still ambitious. I want to get ahead as far as I possibly can without sacrificing my entire personal life.'

Hopkins stood with his back turned toward Tom, and when he spoke, his voice sounded curiously remote. 'I think we can find something for you,' he said. 'How would you like to go back to the mental-health committee? That will be developing into a small, permanent organization. I'm thinking of giving my house in South Bay to be its headquarters. That would be quite nice for you – you wouldn't even have any commuting. How would you like to be director of the outfit? That job would pay pretty well. I'd like to think I had a man with your integrity there, and I'll be making all the major decisions.'

'I'd be grateful,' Tom said in a low voice.

Suddenly Hopkins whirled and faced him. '*Somebody has to do the big jobs!*' he said passionately. 'This world was built by men like me! To really do a job, you have to live it, body and soul! You people who just give half your mind to your work are riding on our backs!'

'I know it,' Tom said.

Almost immediately Hopkins regained control of himself. A somewhat forced smile spread over his face. 'Really, I don't know why we're taking all this so seriously,' he said. 'I think you've made a good decision. You don't have to worry about being stuck with a foundation job all your life. I'll be starting other projects. We need men like you – I guess we need a few men who keep a sense of proportion.'

From *The Man in the Gray Flannel Suit* by Sloan Wilson, 1956

'Office'

At night your sleep is a race
down dimly lit passages where
the floor shines up at you,
the corridor never ends.

Each time you're searching
for the office door but when
you find it, it's stuck fast
and through the toughened glass

you can make it all out:
the windows nailed shut,
the phones chirruping,
the desks piled high with paper.

Awake, your eyes feel starched open
and rushing for the number 19 or 5
you check your head for a showercap,
check your feet for slippers.

You join the lift's
conspiracy of silence,
its collision of Chanels,
numbers 19 and 5.

Between coffees and invoices,
questions gather in the in-tray,
are dismissed in the out-tray,
resolved in the bin.

Other people's sadnesses
blow in like dust. Your nose
and ears, your eyes and mouth
are full of them. You write letters

offering hope like a biscuit.
You pour tea to untangle the net
of your colleagues' affairs.
Fear spreads through your gut

To lodge like a knot of fury
that you suck mints to ease
and call indigestion.
You go home lonely and at night

you toss and turn, running down
a corridor that never ends.

From *Explaining Magnetism* by Maura Dooley, 1991

Thirteen

BUCKING THE SYSTEM

However awkward or embarrassing they might be in the flesh, few figures are more pleasing to read or hear about than those rare, insouciant figures – of whom P. G. Wodehouse's Psmith is perhaps the finest example – who make office life impossible by refusing to take it seriously: hierarchies, reputations and rituals are as nothing to those who not only realise, like the rest of us, that *sub specie aeternitatis* (and a good deal shorter than that) the Emperor is wearing no clothes, but are prepared to point it out, loudly and discomfortingly. Less radical but equally difficult to deal with is the polite but firm 'I would prefer not to' of Melville's Bartleby. James Lees-Milne's defiance of Sir Roderick Jones has already been referred to: most of us, however, restrict ourselves to angry rhetoric behind the scenes, like Mr Wrenn or Charley Carpenter, though such modest acts of revolt or criticism as we may mount against the powers-that-be are told and re-told, suitably embellished, to admiring and delighted groups of colleagues, and may even find their way into the folklore of the office ('Then I told him exactly what I thought of him, and I can tell you he didn't like it one little bit . . .').

'I would prefer not to'

Now my original business – that of a conveyancer and title hunter and drawer-up of recondite documents of all sorts – was considerably increased by receiving the Master's office. There was now great work for scriveners. Not only must I push the clerks already with me, but I must have additional help.

In answer to my advertisement, a motionless young man one morning stood upon my office threshold, the door being open, for it was summer. I can see that figure now – pallidly neat, pitiably respectable, incurably forlorn! It was Bartleby.

After a few words touching his qualifications, I engaged him, glad to have among my corps of copyists a man of so singularly sedate an aspect, which I thought might operate beneficially upon the flighty temper of Turkey and the fiery one of Nippers.

I should have stated before that ground-glass folding doors divided my premises into two parts, one of which was occupied by my scriveners, the other by myself. According to my humor, I threw open these doors or closed them. I resolved to assign Bartleby a corner by the folding doors, but on my side of them, so as to have this quiet man within easy call, in case any trifling thing was to be done. I placed his desk close up to a small side window in that part of the room, a window which originally had afforded a lateral view of certain grimy back yards and bricks, but which, owing to subsequent erections, commanded at present no view at all, though it gave some light. Within three feet of the panes was a wall, and the light came down from far above, between two lofty buildings, as from a very small opening in a dome. Still further to a satisfactory arrangement, I procured a high green folding screen, which might entirely isolate Bartleby from my sight, though not remove him from my voice. And thus, in a manner, privacy and society were conjoined.

At first, Bartleby did an extraordinary quantity of writing. As if long famishing for something to copy, he seemed to gorge himself on my documents. There was no pause for digestion. He ran a day and night line, copying by sunlight and by candlelight. I should have been quite delighted with his application, had he been cheerfully industrious. But he wrote on silently, palely, mechanically.

It is, of course, an indispensable part of a scrivener's business to verify the accuracy of his copy, word by word. Where there are two or more scriveners in an office, they assist each other in this examination, one reading from the copy, the other holding the original. It is a very dull, wearisome, and lethargic affair. I can readily imagine that, to some sanguine temperaments, it would be altogether intolerable. For example, I cannot credit that the mettlesome poet, Byron, would have contentedly sat down with Bartleby to examine a law document of, say five hundred pages, closely written in a crimpy hand.

Now and then, in the haste of business, it had been my habit to assist in comparing some brief document myself, calling Turkey or Nippers for this purpose. One object I had in placing Bartleby so handy to me behind the screen was to avail myself of his services on such trivial occasions. It was on the third day, I think, of his being with me, and before any necessity had arisen for having his own writing examined, that, being much hurried to complete a small affair I had in hand, I abruptly called to Bartleby. In my haste and natural expectancy of instant compliance, I sat with my head bent over the original on my desk, and my right hand sideways, and somewhat nervously extended with the copy, so that, immediately upon emerging from his retreat, Bartleby might snatch it and proceed to business without the least delay.

In this very attitude did I sit when I called to him, rapidly stating what it was I wanted him to do – namely, to examine a small paper with me.

Imagine my surprise, nay, my consternation, when, without moving from his privacy, Bartleby, in a singularly mild, firm voice, replied, 'I would prefer not to.'

I sat awhile in perfect silence, rallying my stunned faculties. Immediately it occurred to me that my ears had deceived me, or Bartleby had entirely misunderstood my meaning. I repeated my request in the clearest tone I could assume; but in quite as clear a one came the previous reply, 'I would prefer not to.'

'Prefer not to,' echoed I, rising in high excitement, and crossing the room with a stride. 'What do you mean? Are you moon-struck? I want you to help me compare this sheet here – take it,' and I thrust it towards him.

'I would prefer not to,' said he.

I looked at him steadfastly. His face was leanly composed; his gray eyes dimly calm. Not a wrinkle of agitation rippled him. Had there been the least uneasiness, anger, impatience or impertinence in his manner; in other words, had there been anything ordinarily human about him, doubtless I should have violently dismissed him from the premises. But as it was I should have as soon thought of turning my pale plaster-of-Paris bust of Cicero out of doors. I stood gazing at him awhile, as he went on with his own writing, and then reseated myself at my desk. This is very strange, thought I. What had one best do? But my business hurried me. I concluded to forget the matter for the present, reserving it for my future leisure. So calling Nippers from the other room, the paper was speedily examined.

A few days after this, Bartleby concluded four lengthy documents, being quadruplicates of a week's testimony taken before me in my High Court of Chancery. It became necessary to examine them. It was an important suit, and great accuracy was imperative. Having all things arranged, I called Turkey, Nippers, and Ginger Nut from the next room, meaning to place the four copies in the hands of my four clerks, while I should read from the original. Accordingly, Turkey, Nippers, and Ginger Nut had taken their seats in a row, each with his document in his hand, when I called to Bartleby to join this interesting group.

'Bartleby! quick, I am waiting.'

I heard a slow scrape of his chair legs on the uncarpeted floor, and soon he appeared standing at the entrance of his hermitage.

'What is wanted?' said he, mildly.

'The copies, the copies,' said I, hurriedly. 'We are going to examine them. There' – and I held towards him the fourth quadruplicate.

'I would prefer not to,' he said, and gently disappeared behind the screen.

For a few moments I was turned into a pillar of salt, standing at the head of my seated column of clerks. Recovering myself, I advanced towards the screen and demanded the reason for such extraordinary conduct.

'*Why* do you refuse?'

'I would prefer not to.'

With any other man I should have flown outright into a dreadful passion, scorned all further words, and thrust him ignominiously from my presence. But there was something about Bartleby that not only strangely disarmed me, but, in a wonderful manner, touched and disconcerted me. I began to reason with him.

'These are your own copies we are about to examine. It is labor saving to you, because one examination will answer for your four papers. It is common usage. Every copyist is bound to help examine his copy. Is it not so? Will you not speak? Answer!'

'I prefer not to,' he replied in a flutelike tone. It seemed to me that, while I had been addressing him, he carefully revolved every statement that I made; fully comprehended the meaning; could not gainsay the irresistible conclusion; but, at the same time, some paramount consideration prevailed with him to reply as he did.

'You are decided, then, not to comply with my request – a request made according to common usage and common sense?'

He briefly gave me to understand that on that point my judgment was sound. Yes: his decision was irreversible.

It is not seldom the case that, when a man is browbeaten in some unprecedented and violently unreasonable way, he begins to stagger in his own plainest faith. He begins, as it were, vaguely to surmise that, wonderful as it may be, all the justice and all the reason is on the other side. Accordingly, if any disinterested persons are present, he turns to them for some reinforcement for his own faltering mind.

'Turkey,' said I, 'what do you think of this? Am I not right?'

'With submission, sir,' said Turkey, in his blandest tone, 'I think that you are.'

'Nippers,' said I, 'what do you think of it?'

'I think I should kick him out of the office.'

(The reader of nice perceptions will here perceive that, it being morning, Turkey's answer is couched in polite and tranquil terms, but Nippers replies in ill-tempered ones. Or, to repeat a previous sentence, Nippers's ugly mood was on duty, and Turkey's off.)

'Ginger Nut,' said I, willing to enlist the smallest suffrage in my behalf, 'what do *you* think of it?'

'I think, sir, he's a little *luny*,' replied Ginger Nut, with a grin.

'You hear what they say,' said I, turning towards the screen, 'come forth and do your duty.'

But he vouchsafed no reply. I pondered a moment in sore perplexity. But once more business hurried me. I determined again to postpone the consideration of this dilemma to my future leisure. With a little trouble we made out to examine the papers without Bartleby, though at every page or two Turkey deferentially dropped his opinion that this proceeding was quite out of the common; while Nippers, twitching in his chair with a dyspeptic nervousness, ground out between his set teeth occasional hissing maledictions against the stubborn oaf behind the screen. And for his (Nippers's) part, this was the first and the last time he would do another man's business without pay.

Meanwhile Bartleby sat in his hermitage, oblivious to everything but his own peculiar business there . . .

From *Bartleby* by Herman Melville, 1853

Taking it literally

I recently worked in an office where they had a number of those signs reading 'Think,' the motto of the International Business Machines Corporation, which so many other business firms seem to be adopting. The signs became almost at once a bone of contention between my employer and me, though not because I was not responsive to them; I have always reacted unqualifiedly to wall injunctions, especially the monosyllabic kind. Confronted, for example, with the exhortation 'Smile,' my face becomes wreathed in an expression of felicity that some people find unendurable, and as for 'Keep On Keepin' On,' I mean like one gander at it and it's 'Oh, I will, I will!' The 'Think' signs, one of which was visible from my desk, so I saw it every time I raised my head, were equally effective. As a consequence, by midmorning of my first day on the job I was so immersed in rumination that the boss, a ruddy, heavyset fellow named Harry Bagley, paused on his way past my desk, evidently struck by a remote and glazed look in my eye.

'What's the matter with you?' he asked.

'I was just thinking,' I said, stirring from my concentration.

'What about?'

'Zeno's paradoxes,' I answered. 'The eight paradoxes by which he tries to discredit the belief in plurality and motion, and which have come down to us in the writings of Aristotle and Simplicius. I was recalling particularly the one about Achilles and the tortoise. You remember it. Achilles can never catch up with the tortoise for, while he traverses the distance between his starting point and that of the tortoise, the tortoise advances a certain distance, and while Achilles traverses this distance, the tortoise makes a further advance, and so on ad infinitum. Consequently, Achilles may run ad infinitum without overtaking the tortoise. *Ergo* there is no motion.'

'A fat hell of a lot of good this is doing us,' Bagley said.

'Oh, I know Zeno's old hat and, as you say, fruitless from a practical point of view,' I said. 'But here's the thought I want to leave with you. It's amazing how many of our values are still based on this classic logic, and so maybe the semanticists, under Korzybski and later Hayakawa, have been right in hammering home to us a less absolutistic approach to things.'

'Yes, well, get some of this work off your desk,' Bagley said, gesturing at a mulch of documents that had been thickening there since nine o'clock.

'Right,' I said, and he bustled off.

I fell to with a will, and by noon was pretty well caught up. But as I sat down at my desk after lunch, my eye fell on the admonitory legend dominating the opposite wall, and I was soon again deep in a train of reflections, which, while lacking the abstruseness of my morning cogitations, were nevertheless not wholly without scope and erudition. My face must have betrayed the strain of application once more, for Bagley stopped as he had earlier.

'Now what?' he said.

I put down a paper knife I had been abstractedly bending.

'I've been thinking,' I said, 'that the element of the fantastic in the graphic arts is, historically speaking, so voluminous that it's presumptuous of the Surrealists to pretend that they have any more than given a contemporary label to an established, if not indeed hoary, vein. Take the chimerical detail in much Flemish and Renaissance painting, the dry, horrifying apparitions of Hieronymus Bosch –'

'Get your money,' Bagley said.

'But why? What am I doing but what that sign says?' I protested, pointing to it.

'That sign doesn't mean this kind of thinking,' Bagley said.

'What kind, then? What do you want me to think about?' I asked.

'Think about your work. Think about the product. Anything.'

'All right, I'll try that,' I said. 'I'll try thinking about the product. But which one?' I added, for the firm was a wholesale-food company that handled many kinds of foods. I was at pains to remind Bagley of this. 'So shall I think of food in general, or some particular item?' I asked. 'Or some phase of distribution?'

'Oh, good God, I don't know,' Bagley said impatiently. 'Think of the special we're pushing,' he said, and made off.

The special we were pushing just then was packaged mixed nuts, unshelled. The firm had been trying to ascertain what proportions people liked in mixed nuts – what ratio of walnuts, hazelnuts, almonds, and so on – as reflected in relative sales of varying assortments that the company had been simultaneously putting out in different areas. I didn't see how any thinking on my part could help reach any conclusion about that, the more so because my work, which was checking and collating credit memoranda, offered no data along those lines. So I figured the best thing would be for me to dwell on nuts in a general way, which I did.

Shortly after four o'clock, I was aware of Bagley's bulk over me, and of Bagley looking down at me. 'Well?' he said.

I turned to him in my swivel chair, crossing my legs.

'Nuts, it seems to me, have a quality that makes them unique among foods,' I said. 'I'm not thinking of their more obvious aspect as an autumnal symbol, their poetic association with festive periods. They have something else, a *je ne sais quoi* that has often haunted me while eating them but that I have never quite been able to pin down, despite that effort of imaginative physical identification that is the legitimate province of the senses.'

'You're wearing me thin,' Bagley warned.

'But now I think I've put my finger on the curious quality they have,' I said. '*Nuts are in effect edible wood.*'

'Get your money,' Bagley said.

I rose. 'I don't understand what you want,' I exclaimed. 'Granted the observation is a trifle on the precious side, is that any reason for firing a man? Give me a little time.'

'You've got an hour till quitting time. Your money'll be ready then,' Bagley said.

My money was ready by quitting time. As I took it, I reflected that my wages from this firm consisted almost exclusively of severance pay. Bagley had beefed about having to fork over two weeks' compensation, but he forked it over.

I got another job soon afterward. I still have it. It's with an outfit that doesn't expect you to smile or think or anything like that. Anyhow, I've learned my lesson as far as the second is concerned. If I'm ever again confronted with a sign telling me to think, I'll damn well think twice before I do.

From 'A Hard Day at the Office' in *Without a Stitch in Time* by
Peter de Vries, 1974

Psmith Arrives at the Bank

His three-quarters-of-an-hour absence had led to the accumulation of a small pile of letters on his desk. He sat down and began to work them off. The addresses continued to exercise a fascination for him. He was miles away from the office, speculating on what sort of a man J. B. Garside, Esq, was, and whether he had a good time at his house in Worcestershire, when somebody tapped him on the shoulder.

He looked up.

Standing by his side, immaculately dressed as ever, with his eye-glass fixed and a gentle smile on his face, was Psmith.

Mike stared.

'Commerce,' said Psmith, as he drew off his lavender gloves, 'has claimed me for her own. Comrade of old, I, too, have joined this blighted institution.'

As he spoke, there was a whirring noise in the immediate neighbourhood, and Mr Rossiter buzzed out from his den with the *esprit* and animation of a clockwork toy.

'Who's here?' said Psmith with interest, removing his eyeglass, polishing it, and replacing it in his eye.

'Mr Jackson,' exclaimed Mr Rossiter. 'I really must ask you to be good enough to come in from your lunch at the proper time. It was fully seven minutes to two when you returned, and –'

'That little more,' sighed Psmith, 'and how much is it!'

'Who are you?' snapped Mr Rossiter, turning on him.

'I shall be delighted, Comrade –'

'Rossiter,' said Mike, aside.

'Comrade Rossiter. I shall be delighted to furnish you with particulars of my family history. As follows. Soon after the Norman Conquest, a certain Sieur de Psmith grew tired of work – a family failing, alas! – and settled down in this country to live peacefully for the remainder of his life on what he could extract from the local peasantry. He may be described as the founder of the family which ultimately culminated in Me. Passing on –'

Mr Rossiter refused to pass on.

'What are you doing here? What have you come for?'

'Work,' said Psmith, with simple dignity. 'I am now a member of the staff of this bank. Its interests are my interests. Psmith, the individual, ceases to exist, and there springs into being Psmith, the cog in the wheel of the New Asiatic Bank; Psmith, the link in the bank's chain; Psmith, the Worker. I shall not spare myself,' he proceeded earnestly. 'I shall toil with all the accumulated energy of one who, up till now, has only known what work is like from hearsay. Whose is that form sitting on the steps of the bank in the morning, waiting eagerly for the place to open? It is the form of Psmith, the Worker. Whose is that haggard, drawn face which bends over a ledger long after the other toilers have sped blithely westwards to dine at Lyons' Popular Café? It is the face of Psmith, the Worker.'

'I –' began Mr Rossiter.

'I tell you,' continued Psmith, waving aside the interruption and tapping the head of the department rhythmically in the region of the second waistcoat-button with a long finger, 'I tell *you*, Comrade Rossiter, that you have got hold of a good man. You and I together, not forgetting Comrade Jackson, the pet of the Smart Set, will toil early and late till we boost up this Postage Department into a shining model of what a Postage Department should be. What that is, at present, I do not exactly know. However. Excursion trains will be run from distant shires to see this Postage Department. American visitors to London will do it before going on to the Tower. And now,' he broke off, with a crisp, businesslike intonation, 'I must ask you to excuse me. Much as I have enjoyed this little chat, I fear it must now cease. The time has come to work. Our trade rivals are getting ahead of us. The whisper goes round, "Rossiter and Psmith are talking, not working," and other firms prepare to pinch our business. Let me Work.'

Two minutes later, Mr Rossiter was sitting at his desk with a dazed expression, while Psmith, perched gracefully on a stool, entered figures in a ledger.

Mr Rossiter had discovered Psmith's and Mike's absence about five minutes after they had left the building. Ever since then, he had been popping out of his lair at intervals of three minutes, to see whether they had returned. Constant disappointment in this respect had rendered him decidedly jumpy. When Psmith and Mike reached the desk, he was a kind of human soda-water bottle. He fizzed over with questions, reproofs, and warnings.

'What does it mean? What does it mean?' he cried. 'Where have you been? Where have you been?'

'Poetry,' said Psmith approvingly.

'You have been absent from your places for over half an hour. Why? Why? Why? Where have you been? Where have you been? I cannot have this. It is preposterous. Where have you been? Suppose Mr Bickersdyke had happened to come round here. I should not have known what to say to him.'

'Never an easy man to chat with, Comrade Bickersdyke,' agreed Psmith.

'You must thoroughly understand that you are expected to remain in your places during business hours.'

'Of course,' said Psmith, 'that makes it a little hard for Comrade Jackson to post letters, does it not?'

'Have you been posting letters?'

'We have,' said Psmith. 'You have wronged us. Seeing our absent places you jumped rashly to the conclusion that we were merely gadding about in pursuit of pleasure. Error. All the while we were furthering the bank's best interests by posting letters.'

'You had no business to leave your place. Jackson is on the posting desk.'

'You are very right,' said Psmith, 'and it shall not occur again. It was only because it was the first day. Comrade Jackson is not used to the stir and bustle of the City. His nerve failed him. He shrank from going to the post-office alone. So I volunteered to accompany him. And,' concluded Psmith, impressively, 'we won safely through. Every letter has been posted.'

'That need not have taken you half an hour.'

'True. And the actual work did not. It was carried through swiftly and surely. But the nerve-strain had left us shaken. Before resuming our more ordinary duties we had to refresh. A brief breathing-space, a little coffee and porridge, and here we are, fit for work once more.'

'If it occurs again, I shall report the matter to Mr Bickersdyke.'

'And rightly so,' said Psmith, earnestly. 'Quite rightly so. Discipline, discipline. That is the cry. There must be no shirking of painful duties. Sentiment must play no part in business. Rossiter, the man, may sympathise, but Rossiter, the Departmental head, must be adamant.'

Mr Rossiter pondered over this for a moment, then went off on a side-issue.

'What is the meaning of this foolery?' he asked, pointing to Psmith's gloves and hat. 'Suppose Mr Bickersdyke had come round and seen them, what should I have said?'

'You would have given him a message of cheer. You would have said, "All is well. Psmith has not left us. He will come back." And Comrade Bickersdyke, relieved, would have –'

'You do not seem very busy, Mr Smith.'

Both Psmith and Mr Rossiter were startled.

Mr Rossiter jumped as if somebody had run a gimlet into him, and even Psmith started slightly. They had not heard Mr Bickersdyke approaching. Mike, who had been stolidly entering addresses in his ledger during the latter part of the conversation, was also taken by surprise.

Psmith was the first to recover. Mr Rossiter was still too confused for speech, but Psmith took the situation in hand.

'Apparently no,' he said, swiftly removing his hat from the ruler. 'In reality, yes. Mr Rossiter and I were just scheming out a line of work for me as you came up. If you had arrived a moment later, you would have found me toiling.'

'H'm. I hope I should. We do not encourage idling in this bank.'

'Assuredly not,' said Psmith warmly. 'Most assuredly not. I would not have it otherwise. I am a worker. A bee, not a drone. A *Lusitania*, not a limpet. Perhaps I have not yet that grip on my duties which I shall soon acquire; but it is coming. It is coming. I see daylight.'

'H'm. I have only your word for it.' He turned to Mr Rossiter, who had now recovered himself, and was as nearly calm as it was in his nature to be. 'Do you find Mr Smith's work satisfactory, Mr Rossiter?'

Psmith waited resignedly for an outburst of complaint respecting the small matter that had been under discussion between the head of the department and himself; but to his surprise it did not come.

'Oh – ah – quite, quite, Mr Bickersdyke. I think he will very soon pick things up.'

Mr Bickersdyke turned away. He was a conscientious bank manager, and one can only suppose that Mr Rossiter's tribute to the earnestness of one of his employés was gratifying to him. But for that, one would have said that he was disappointed.

'Oh, Mr Bickersdyke,' said Psmith.

The manager stopped.

'Father sent his kind regards to you,' said Psmith benevolently.

Mr Bickersdyke walked off without comment.

'An uncommonly cheery, companionable feller,' murmured Psmith, as he turned to his work.

From *Psmith in the City* by P. G. Wodehouse, 1910

Hurling Defiance

The April skies glowed with benevolence this Saturday morning. The Metropolitan Tower was singing, bright ivory tipped with gold, uplifted and intensely glad of the morning. The buildings walling in Madison Square were jubilant; the honest red-brick fronts, radiant; the new marble, witty. The sparrows in the middle of Fifth Avenue were all talking at once, scandalously but cleverly. The polished brass of limousines threw off teethy smiles. At least so Mr Wrenn fancied as he whisked up Fifth Avenue, the skirts of his small blue double-breasted coat wagging. He was going blocks out of his way to the office; ready to defy time and eternity, yes, and even the office manager. He had awakened with Defiance as his bedfellow, and throughout breakfast at the Hustler Dairy Lunch sunshine had flickered over the dirty tessellated floor.

He pranced up to the Souvenir Company's brick building, on Twenty-eighth Street near Sixth Avenue. In the office he chuckled at his ink-well and the untorn blotters on his orderly desk. Though he sat under the weary unnatural brilliance of a mercury-vapour light, he dashed into his work, and was too keen about this business of living merrily to be much flustered by the bustle of the lady buyer's superior '*Good* morning.' Even up to ten-thirty he was still slamming down papers on his desk. Just let anyone try to stop his course, his readiness for snapping fingers at The Job; just let them *try* it, that was all he wanted!

Then he was shot out of his chair and four feet along the corridor, in reflex response to the surly 'Bur-r-r-r-r' of the buzzer. Mr Mortimer R. Guilfogle, the manager, desired to see him. He scampered along the corridor and slid decorously through the manager's doorway into the long sun-bright room, ornate with rugs and souvenirs. Seven Novelties glittered on the desk alone, including a large rococo Shakespeare-style glass ink-well containing cloves and a small iron Pittsburg-style one containing ink. Mr Wrenn blinked like a noon-roused owlet in the brilliance. The manager dropped his fist on the desk, glared, smoothed his flowered prairie of waistcoat, and growled, his red jowls quivering:

'Look here, Wrenn, what's the matter with you? The Bronx Emporium order for May Day novelties was filled twice, they write me.'

'They ordered twice, sir. By 'phone,' smiled Mr Wrenn, in an agony of politeness.

'They ordered hell, sir! Twice – the same order?'

'Yes, sir; their buyer was prob –'

'They say they've looked it up. Anyway, they won't pay twice. I know

[247]

'em. We'll have to crawl down graceful, and all because you – I want to know why you ain't more careful!'

The announcement that Mr Wrenn twice wriggled his head, and once tossed it, would not half denote his wrath. At last! It was here – the time for revolt, when he was going to be defiant. He had been careful; old Goglefogle was only barking; but why should *he* be barked at? With his voice palpitating and his heart thudding so that he felt sick he declared:

'I'm *sure*, sir, about that order. I looked it up. Their buyer was drunk!'

It was done. And now would he be discharged? The manager was speaking:

'Probably. You looked it up, eh? Um! Send me in the two order-records. Well. But, anyway, I want you to be more careful after this, Wrenn. You're pretty sloppy. Now get out. Expect me to make firms pay twice for the same order 'cause of your carelessness?'

Mr Wrenn found himself outside in the dark corridor. The manager hadn't seemed much impressed by his revolt.

The manager wasn't. He called a stenographer and dictated:

'Bronx Emporium:

'GENTLEMEN: – Our Mr Wrenn has again (underline that "again," Miss Blaustein), again looked up your order for May Day novelties. As we wrote before, order certainly was duplicated by 'phone. Our Mr Wrenn is thoroughly reliable, and we have his records of these two orders. We shall therefore have to push collection on both –'

After all, Mr Wrenn was thinking, the crafty manager might be merely concealing his hand. Perhaps he had understood the defiance. That gladdened him till after lunch. But at three, when his head was again foggy with work and he had forgotten whether there was still April anywhere, he began to dread what the manager might do to him. Suppose he lost his job; The Job! He worked unnecessarily late, hoping that the manager would learn of it. As he wavered home, drunk with weariness, his fear of losing The Job was almost equal to his desire to resign from The Job.

From *Our Mr Wrenn* by Sinclair Lewis, 1914

Reading at One's Desk

Masters of the Universe! The roar filled Sherman's soul with hope, confidence, esprit de corps, and righteousness. Yes, righteousness! Judy understood none of this, did she? None of it. Oh, he noticed her eyes glazing over when he talked about it. Moving the lever that moves the world was what he was doing – and all she wanted to know was why he never made it home for dinner. When he did make it home for dinner, what did she want to talk about? Her precious interior-decorating business and how she had gotten their apartment into *Architectural Digest*, which, frankly, to a true Wall Streeter was a fucking embarrassment. Did she commend him for the hundreds of thousands of dollars that made her decorating and her lunches and whatever the hell else she did possible? No, she did not. She took it for granted . . .

. . . and so forth and so on. Within ninety seconds, emboldened by the mighty roar of the bond trading room of Pierce & Pierce, Sherman managed to work up a good righteous head of resentment against this woman who had dared make him feel guilty.

He picked up the telephone and was ready to resume work on the greatest coup of his young career, the Giscard, when he spotted something out of the corner of his eye. He *detected* it – righteously! – amid that great bondscape of writhing limbs and torsos. *Arguello was reading a newspaper.*

Ferdinand Arguello was a junior bond salesman, twenty-five or -six years old, from Argentina. He was leaning back in his chair nonchalantly reading a newspaper, and even from here Sherman could see what it was: *The Racing Form. The Racing Form!* The young man looked like a caricature of a South American polo player. He was slender and handsome; he had thick wavy black hair, combed straight back. He was wearing a pair of red silk moiré suspenders. *Silk moiré.* The bond department of Pierce & Pierce was like an Air Force fighter squadron. Sherman knew it even if this young South American didn't. As the number one bond salesman, Sherman had no official rank. Nevertheless, he occupied a moral eminence. You were either capable of doing the job and willing to devote 100 percent to the job, or you got out. The eighty members of the department received a base salary, a safety net, of $120,000 a year each. This was regarded as a laughably small sum. The rest of their income came from commissions and profit-sharing. Sixty-five percent of the department's profits went to Pierce & Pierce. But 35 percent was split among the eighty bond salesmen and traders themselves. All for one and one for all, and lots for oneself! And therefore . . . no slackers allowed! no deadwood! no lightweights! no loafers! You headed straight for your desk, your telephone, and your computer terminal in the morning. The day didn't start with small talk and coffee and perusals of *The Wall Street Journal* and the financial pages of the *Times*, much less *The Racing Form*. You were expected to get on the telephone and start making money. If you left the office, even for lunch, you were expected to give your destination and a telephone number to one of the 'sales assistants,' who were really secretaries, so that you could be summoned immediately if a new issue of bonds came in (and had to be sold fast). If you went out for lunch, it better have something directly to do with selling bonds for Pierce & Pierce. Otherwise – sit here by the telephone and order in from the deli like the rest of the squadron.

Sherman walked to Arguello's desk and stood over him. 'What are you doing, Ferdi?'

From the moment the young man looked up, Sherman could tell he knew what the question meant and that he knew he was wrong. But if there was one thing an Argentine aristocrat knew, it was how to brazen it out.

Arguello locked a level gaze onto Sherman's eyes and said, in a voice just slightly louder than necessary: 'I'm reading *The Racing Form*.'

'What for?'

'What for? Because four of our horses are racing at Lafayette today. That's a track outside of Chicago.'

With this he resumed reading the newspaper . . .

From *The Bonfire of the Vanities* by Tom Wolfe, 1988

Bravado Behind the Scenes

The noon-hour was not The Job's, but his, for exploration of the parlous lands of romance that lie hard by Twenty-eighth Street and Sixth Avenue. But he had to go out to lunch with Charley Carpenter, the assistant book-keeper, that he might tell the news. As for Charley, he needed frequently to have a confidant who knew personally the tyrannous ways of the office manager, Mr Guilfogle.

Mr Wrenn and Charley chose (that is to say, Charley chose) a table at Drübel's Eating House. Mr Wrenn timidly hinted, 'I've got some big news to tell you.'

But Charley interrupted, 'Say, did you hear old Goglefogle light into me this morning? I won't stand for it. Say, did you hear him – the old – '

'What was the trouble, Charley?'

'Trouble? Nothing was the trouble. Except with old Goglefogle. I made one little break in my accounts. Why, if old Gogie had to keep track of seventy-'leven accounts and watch every single last movement of a fool girl that can't even run the adding-machine, why, he'd get green around the gills. He'd never do anything *but* make mistakes! Well, I guess the old codger must have had a bum breakfast this morning. Wanted some exercise to digest it. Me, I was the exercise – I was the goat. He calls me in, and he calls me *down*, and me – well, just lemme tell you, Wrenn, I calls his bluff!'

Charley Carpenter stopped his rapid tirade, delivered with quick head-shakes like those of palsy, to raise his smelly cigarette to his mouth. Midway in this slow gesture the memory of his wrongs again overpowered him. He flung his right hand back on the table, scattering cigarette ashes, jerked back his head with the irritated patience of a nervous martyr, then waved both hands about spasmodically, while he snarled, with his cheaply handsome smooth face more flushed than usual:

'Sure! You can just bet your bottom dollar I let him see from the way I looked at him that I wasn't going to stand for no more monkey business. You bet I did! ... I'll fix him, I will. You just *watch* me. (Hey, Drübel, got any lemon merang? Bring me a hunk, will yuh?) Why, Wrenn, that cross-eyed double-jointed fat old slob, I'll slam him in the slats so hard some day – I will, you just watch my smoke. If it wasn't for that messy wife of mine – I ought to desert her, and I will some day, and –'

From *Our Mr Wrenn* by Sinclair Lewis, 1914

Fourteen

ESCAPING THE OFFICE,
AND EATING LUNCH

Playing truant is, as our new arrival soon discovers, among the illicit pleasures of office life – and one that continues to afford an infantile delight throughout one's working life. Apart from occasional oddities like Mr Fidus Neverbend, few office workers have not, from time to time, rung in to plead a feigned sore throat or a bogus stomach ache – not least on a bright spring day, when the contrast between desk and deck chair seems particularly poignant. Once the deed has been done – the voice low and tremulous, as if bravely battling pain – and the commiserations received ('Now stay in bed and *get well soon*'), the rest of the day stretches ahead to be filled as one wills. Nor are many escapees caught quite as red-handed as the hapless Mr Corkscrew. Licit escape – going on errands, like the youthful V. S. Pritchett, or snoozing fitfully in some heavily carpeted conference centre – is almost as pleasurable, and minus the burden of guilt. Licit or illicit, leaving the office during working hours is always an oddly unsettling business, like moving from one world into another: the escapee comes blinking into the sunlight like some hibernating rodent, surprised and slightly shocked to find that life outside the office goes on much the same as ever.

Consisting more often than not of sandwiches eaten at the desk or a sausage and beer in a crammed and raucous pub, followed by a walk or some shopping or a glance at a museum, the lunch hour is, for most of us, the high point of the working day, the watershed that divides the brightness and the bustle of the morning from the somnolent melancholy of the afternoon. (Given the prevalence of afternoon slumber, enlightened office managers should bow to the inevitable and provide let-down canvas beds, so enabling their employees to give of their best later on.) The traditional office lunch – bibulous, protracted and indiscreet – looms large in the mythology of office life, though Perrier culture, Yuppiedom and recession have done grave damage to its age-old rituals.

The prospect of a long, congenial lunch, in which any business that needs to be aired will be crammed in at the coffee stage after gossip, children and holidays have held the floor, gives the prospective luncher something to look forward to – particularly if the other party is paying, so removing all worries about whether and how such a meal can be justified on expenses. It's advisable to clear one's desk before stepping sharply out in the direction of the edibles: though this in itself is unlikely to protect the late luncher, sneaking in by the back exit at 4.30, his breath hot with alcoholic fumes and his hair in disarray, from a flurry of angry or anxious notes to say that the Boss has been looking for him all afternoon, and is highly unamused. Pausing briefly to straighten his clothing and rinse out his mouth, the late luncher hurries nervously down to the Inner Sanctum, only to discover that the Boss has quite forgotten why it was he needed to see him so badly. As is so often the case in office life, one's presence is what matters, rather than the work itself.

A Glimpse of the Outside World (1)

The thing I liked best was being sent on errands in Bermondsey. They became explorations, and I made every excuse to lengthen them. I pushed down south to the Dun Cow in the Old Kent Road, eastward by side streets and alleyways to Tower Bridge. I had a special pleasure in the rank places like those tunnels and vaults under the railway: the smells above all made me feel importantly a part of this working London. Names like Wilde's Rents, Cherry Garden Street, Jamaica Road, Dockhead and Pickle Herring Street excited and my journeys were not simply street journeys to me: they were like crossing the desert, finding the source of the Niger. . . . I would see other office boys wearing their bowler hats as I wore mine: we were a self-important, cracked-voice little race, sheepish, yet cocky, regarding our firms with childish awe.

From *A Cab at the Door* by V. S. Pritchett, 1968

A Glimpse of the Outside World (2)

I soon discovered that the life of a messenger boy suited me to perfection: indeed, it still seems to me to have been the most entirely enjoyable type of work I have ever done, involving as it did much travelling of a sedate and therapeutic kind, ample opportunities to daydream or read interminable nineteenth-century novels or inspect art galleries and City churches, and – most important of all – a complete absence of responsibility. By far the most frequent and enjoyable trips were to the newspaper offices in Fleet Street. Carrying an advertising block and my book in one hand and my umbrella in the other – the product of the lost property office in Victoria, to which it rapidly found its way once more – I would climb aboard a Number 13 bus, inch my way down Baker Street peacefully reading on the upper deck, sit for at least forty minutes in a mammoth traffic jam in Oxford Street while all about us angry motorists raged and hooted and banged the roofs of their cars, the bus accelerating to something approaching walking speed as we flashed down Regent Street, and – if I'd finished my book or felt like stretching my legs – jump off at the Strand and walk the rest of the way from there. Having gone all that way, it seemed only right to spend a few minutes in the Soane Museum or the Temple Church; after which I re-boarded a Number 13 travelling in the opposite direction, and made my way slowly back to the office.

From *Playing for Time* by Jeremy Lewis, 1987

Caught in the Act

'Oh, here's a regular go,' said Scatterall. 'It's all up with Corkscrew, I believe.'

'Why, what's the cheese now?'

'Oh! it's all about some pork chops, which Screwy had for supper last night.' Screwy was a name of love which among his brother navvies was given to Mr Corkscrew. 'Mr Snape seems to think they did not agree with him.'

'Pork chops in July!' exclaimed Charley.

'Poor Screwy forgot the time of year,' said another navvy; 'he ought to have called it lamb and grass.'

And then the story was told. On the preceding afternoon, Mr Corkscrew had been subjected to the dire temptation of a boating party to the Eel-pie Island for the following day, and a dinner thereon. There were to be at the feast no less than four-and-twenty jolly souls, and it was intimated to Mr Corkscrew that as no soul was esteemed to be more jolly than his own, the party would be considered as very imperfect unless he could join it. Asking for a day's leave Mr Corkscrew knew to be out of the question; he had already taken too many without asking. He was therefore driven to take another in the same way, and had to look about for some excuse which might support him in his difficulty. An excuse it must be, not only new, but very valid; one so strong that it could not be overset; one so well avouched that it could not be doubted. Accordingly, after mature consideration, he sat down after leaving his office, and wrote the following letter, before he started on an evening cruising expedition with some others of the party to prepare for the next day's festivities.

'MY DEAR SIR,

'I write from my bed where I am suffering a most tremendous indigges-
tion, last night I eat a stunning supper off pork chopps and never
remembered that pork chopps always does disagree with me, but I was
very indiscrete and am now teetotally unable to rise my throbing head from
off my pillar, I have took four blu pills and some salts and sena, plenty of
that, and shall be the thing to-morrow morning no doubt, just at present I
feel just as if I had a mill stone inside my stomac – Pray be so kind as to
make it all right with Mr Oldeschole and believe me to remain,

'Your faithful and obedient servant,
'VERAX CORKSCREW.

'Thomas Snape, Esq., &c.,
'Internal Navigation Office, Somerset House.'

Having composed this letter of excuse, and not intending to return to
his lodgings that evening, he had to make provision for its safely reaching
the hands of Mr Snape in due time on the following morning. This he
did, by giving it to the boy who came to clean the lodging-house boots,
with sundry injunctions that if he did not deliver it at the office by ten
o'clock on the following morning, the sixpence accruing to him would
never be paid. Mr Corkscrew, however, said nothing as to the letter not
being delivered before ten the next morning, and as other business took
the boy along the Strand the same evening, he saw no reason why he
should not then execute his commission. He accordingly did so, and duly
delivered the letter into the hands of a servant girl, who was cleaning the
passages of the office.

Fortune on this occasion was blind to the merits of Mr Corkscrew, and
threw him over most unmercifully. It so happened that Mr Snape had
been summoned to an evening conference with Mr Oldeschole and the
other pundits of the office, to discuss with them, or rather to hear discussed, some measure which they began to think it necessary to introduce,
for amending the discipline of the department.

'We are getting a bad name, whether we deserve it or not,' said Mr
Oldeschole. 'That fellow Hardlines has put us into his blue-book, and
now there's an article in the *Times*!'

Just at this moment, a messenger brought in to Mr Snape the unfortunate letter of which we have given a copy.

'What's that?' said Mr Oldeschole.

'A note from Mr Corkscrew, sir,' said Snape.

'He's the worst of the whole lot,' said Mr Oldeschole.

'He is very bad,' said Snape; 'but I rather think that perhaps, sir, Mr
Tudor is the worst of all.'

'Well, I don't know,' said the Secretary, muttering *sotto voce* to the

Under-Secretary, while Mr Snape read the letter – 'Tudor, at any rate, is a gentleman.'

Mr Snape read the letter, and his face grew very long. There was a sort of sneaking civility about Corkscrew, not prevalent indeed at all times, but which chiefly showed itself when he and Mr Snape were alone together, which somewhat endeared him to the elder clerk. He would have screened the sinner had he had either the necessary presence of mind or the necessary pluck. But he had neither. He did not know how to account for the letter but by the truth, and he feared to conceal so flagrant a breach of discipline at the moment of the present discussion.

Things at any rate so turned out that Mr Corkscrew's letter was read in full conclave in the board-room of the office, just as he was describing the excellence of his manoeuvre with great glee to four or five other jolly souls at the 'Magpie and Stump.'

At first it was impossible to prevent a fit of laughter, in which even Mr Snape joined; but very shortly the laughter gave way to the serious considerations to which such an epistle was sure to give rise at such a moment. What if Sir Gregory Hardlines should get hold of it and put it into his blue-book! What if the *Times* should print it and send it over the whole world, accompanied by a few of its most venomous touches, to the eternal disgrace of the Internal Navigation, and probably utter annihilation of Mr Oldeschole's official career! An example must be made!

From *The Three Clerks* by Anthony Trollope, 1858

Varieties of Lunch

... the lunch-hour and the catalogue of what she was so vulgar as to eat were of importance in Una's history, because that hour broke the routine, gave her for an hour a deceptive freedom of will, of choice between Boston beans and – New York beans. And her triumphant common sense was demonstrated, for she chose light, digestible food, and kept her head clear for the afternoon, while her overlord, Mr Troy Wilkins, like vast numbers of his fellow business men, crammed himself with beefsteak-and-kidney pudding, drugged himself with cigar smoke and pots of strong coffee and shop-talk, spoke earnestly of the wickedness of drunkenness, and then, drunk with food and tobacco and coffee and talk, came back dizzy, blur-eyed, slow-nerved; and for two hours tried to get down to work.

From *The Job* by Sinclair Lewis, 1917

The Coffee Pot

Emmeline lunched not far from Woburn Place at a shop called 'The Coffee Pot,' with Peter Lewis, her partner. She read a book about Poland, he blue-pencilled a manuscript; they ate poached eggs on spinach, each paid for their own lunches and did not speak to each other. The place was full of pleasant young men and women, secretaries of the surrounding learned societies, lunching elbow to elbow. Young women in more of a hurry ate salad up at a counter, perched on high scarlet stools: young men are seldom in such a hurry as all that ...

From *To the North* by Elizabeth Bowen, 1932

Getting Ready for Lunch

Babbitt's preparations for leaving the office to its feeble self during the hour and a half of his lunch-period were somewhat less elaborate than the plans for a general European war.

He fretted to Miss McGoun, 'What time you going to lunch? Well, make sure Miss Bannigan is in then. Explain to her that if Wiedenfeldt calls up, she's to tell him I'm already having the title traced. And oh, b' the way, remind me to-morrow to have Penniman trace it. Now if anybody comes in looking for a cheap house, remember we got to shove that Bangor Road place off onto somebody. If you need me, I'll be at the Athletic Club. And – uh – And – uh – I'll be back by two.'

He dusted the cigar-ashes off his waistcoat. He placed a difficult unanswered letter on the pile of unfinished work, that he might not fail to attend to it that afternoon. (For three noons, now, he had placed the same letter on the unfinished pile.) He scrawled on a sheet of yellow backing-paper the memorandum: 'See abt apt h drs,' which gave him an agreeable feeling of having already seen about the apartment house doors.

He discovered that he was smoking another cigar. He threw it away, protesting, 'Darn it, I thought you'd quit this darn smoking!' He courageously returned the cigar-box to the correspondence file, locked it up, hid the key in a more difficult place, and raged, 'Ought to take care of myself. And need more exercise – walk to the club, every single noon – just what I'll do – every noon – cut out this motoring all the time.'

The resolution made him feel exemplary. Immediately after it he decided that this noon it was too late to walk.

It took but little more time to start his car and edge it into the traffic than it would have taken to walk the three and a half blocks to the club.

From *Babbitt* by Sinclair Lewis, 1922

Alcoholic Interlude

Turkey was a short, pursy Englishman, of about my own age – that is, somewhere not far from sixty. In the morning, one might say, his face was of a fine florid hue, but after twelve o'clock, meridian – his dinner hour – it blazed like a grate full of Christmas coals; and continued blazing – but, as it were, with a gradual wane – till six o'clock, p.m., or thereabouts; after which I saw no more of the proprietor of the face, which, gaining its meridian with the sun, seemed to set with it, to rise, culminate, and decline the following day, with the like regularity and undiminished glory. There are many singular coincidences I have known in the course of my life, not the least among which was the fact, that, exactly when Turkey displayed his fullest beams from his red and radiant countenance, just then, too, at that critical moment, began the daily period when I considered his business capacities as seriously disturbed for the remainder of the twenty-four hours. Not that he was absolutely idle or averse to business then; far from it. The difficulty was, he was apt to be altogether too energetic. There was a strange, inflamed, flurried, flighty recklessness of activity about him. He would be incautious in dipping his pen into his inkstand. All his blots upon my documents were dropped there after twelve o'clock, meridian. Indeed, not only would he be reckless and sadly given to making blots in the afternoon, but some days he went further and was rather noisy. At such times, too, his face flamed with augmented blazonry, as if cannel coal had been heaped on anthracite. He made an unpleasant racket with his chair; spilled his sandbox; in mending his pens, impatiently split them all to pieces and threw them on the floor in a sudden passion; stood up and leaned over his table, boxing his papers about in a most indecorous manner, very sad to behold in an elderly man like him. Nevertheless, as he was in many ways a most valuable person to me, and all the time before twelve o'clock, meridian, was the quickest, steadiest creature, too, accomplishing a great deal of work in a style not easily to be matched – for these reasons I was willing to overlook his eccentricities, though indeed, occasionally, I remonstrated with him. I did this very gently, however, because, though the civilest, nay, the blandest and most reverential of men in the morning, yet, in the afternoon he was disposed, upon provocation, to be slightly rash with his tongue – in fact, insolent. Now, valuing his morning services as I did, and resolved not to lose them – yet, at the same time, made uncomfortable by his inflamed ways after twelve o'clock – and being a man of peace, unwilling by my admonitions to call forth unseemly retorts from him, I took upon me one Saturday noon (he was always worse on Saturdays) to hint to him, very kindly, that perhaps, now that he was growing old, it might be well to abridge his labors; in short, he need not come to my chambers after twelve o'clock, but, dinner over, had best go home to his lodgings and rest himself till teatime. But no; he insisted upon his afternoon devotions. His countenance became intolerably fervid, as he oratorically assured me – gesticulating with a long ruler at the other end of the room – that if his services in the morning were useful, how indispensable, then, in the afternoon?

'With submission, sir,' said Turkey, on this occasion, 'I consider myself your right-hand man. In the morning I but marshal and deploy my columns, but in the afternoon I put myself at their head, and gallantly charge the foe, thus' – and he made a violent thrust with the ruler.

'But the blots, Turkey,' intimated I.

'True; but, with submission, sir, behold these hairs! I am getting old. Surely, sir, a blot or two of a warm afternoon is not to be severely urged against gray hairs. Old age – even if it blot the page – is honorable. With submission, sir, we *both* are getting old.'

This appeal to my fellow feeling was hardly to be resisted. At all events, I saw that go he would not. So I made up my mind to let him stay, resolving, nevertheless, to see to it that, during the afternoon, he had to do with my less important papers.

From *Bartleby* by Herman Melville, 1853

'Mind if I join you?'

'Where are you headed?'

'Lunch,' you say, before you can think better of it. The last time you told Alex you were on your way to lunch you needed a stretcher to get you back to the office.

He consults his watch. 'Not a bad idea. Mind if I join you?'

By the time you compose an excuse it seems too late, indeed rude, to say that you're meeting a friend. You don't have to match him drink for drink. You don't have to drink anything, although one wouldn't kill you. One pop would cut neatly through this headache. You'll just tell him you've got a big piece going to press. He'll understand. You could use a friendly presence. You might even confide in him. Tell him some of your problems. Alex is a man familiar with trouble.

From *Bright Lights, Big City* by Jay McInerney, 1984

Reeling Back

Nothing further passed up to Mr Swiveller's dinner-time, which was at three o'clock, and seemed about three weeks in coming. At the first stroke of the hour, the new clerk disappeared. At the last stroke of five, he reappeared, and the office, as if by magic, became fragrant with the smell of gin and water and lemon-peel.

From *The Old Curiosity Shop* by Charles Dickens, 1841

When the Cat's Away . . .

. . . At half-past twelve Father called to me and we went out for lunch.

'Will you be back, Mr Day?' the cashier asked respectfully, but eagerly too. On days when Father said yes, all the clerks looked disappointed. They bent over their desks, saying nothing, till Father went out of the door, but if I lingered behind for a moment I heard them slamming their ledgers about. Not only did they and the office-boys all have to stay, but the rule was that they couldn't even smoke until Father had gone home for the day.

To-day he said no, however. I saw them getting out their sulphur matches as he was crossing the threshold, and the instant he stepped into the hall they struck them on the seats of their pants.

From *Life with Father* by Clarence Day, 1936

Appearance and Reality

Nick – Nick Lee – shared Sefton's office but hadn't been seen for months. He kept a briefcase permanently on his desk and one of his jackets permanently over his chair so that by re-arranging them three or four times a day Sefton was able to make it appear that Nick was around somewhere but had just popped out – in all probability to the library. Nick and Sefton had not come to any formal agreement about this – and indeed, if Nick could have been found to be asked, he would have been as insistent to Sefton as to anyone that he had been in the Polytechnic all day and had just popped out momentarily to the library – but Sefton acted out of some automatic loyalty to him. And he was not the only one. Somehow or other essays were collected from Nick's desk and returned marked; notes and messages from Nick to his students were pinned to the door; and every week or so a new jacket appeared on the back of his chair. Without ever being there Nick Lee was much more up to date with his work than Sefton was.

From *Coming from Behind* by Howard Jacobson, 1983

Fifteen

GETTING AWAY FROM
IT ALL

Truancy and four-hour lunches are all very well, but escape is in fact to hand every evening of the working week: nothing is sweeter than the bustle of departure, the gathering up of coats and briefcases, the covering over of office equipment and the turning out of lights, the shouts of 'Good night' or – better still, if it's a Friday – 'Have a good weekend' or – best of all – 'Have a good holiday.' Evenings, weekends and even holidays may be blighted and overcast by worries about impending horrors at work, but nothing can take away the immediate pleasure of departure and escape. Once away on holiday, it seems hard to believe one will ever return: but then, all too suddenly, only a week remains, and the old familiar anxieties come back to haunt us at night. Yet part of us longs to know what has happened in our absence; and by the end of the first morning back it's difficult to remember one had ever been away.

Closing Time

A bank's day ends gradually, reluctantly, as it were. At about five there is a sort of stir, not unlike the stir in a theatre when the curtain is on the point of falling. Ledgers are closed with a bang. Men stand about and talk for a moment or two before going to the basement for their hats and coats. Then, at irregular intervals, forms pass down the central aisle and out through the swing doors. There is an air of relaxation over the place, though some departments are still working as hard as ever under a blaze of electric light. Somebody begins to sing, and an instant chorus of protests and maledictions rises from all sides. Gradually, however, the electric lights go out. The procession down the centre aisle becomes more regular; and eventually the place is left to darkness and the night watchman.

From *Psmith in the City* by P. G. Wodehouse, 1910

Working Late (1)

7 November 1668:
Up, and at the office all morning; and so to it again after dinner and there

busy late, choosing to imploy myself rather than go home to trouble with my wife ...

From the *Diary* of Samuel Pepys, 1668

Working Late (2)

Those benefactors of the species linger yet, though office hours be past; that they may give for every day, some good account at last.

From *Bleak House* by Charles Dickens, 1853

Homeward Bound

We worked until seven in the evening. On Saturdays we left between two and four, this depending on the mail. In the evenings I went home from London Bridge Station. In *The Waste Land* T. S. Eliot wrote of the strange morning and evening sight of those thousands of men, all wearing bowlers and carrying umbrellas, crossing London Bridge in long, dull regiments and pouring into that ugly, but to me most affecting, railway station which for years I used. I was captivated by it as I suppose every office worker is by the station in the great city that rules his life. Penn Station in New York, St Lazare in Paris, Waterloo, Paddington and Liverpool Street, are printed on the pages of a lifetime's grind at the office desk. Each is a quotidian frontier, splitting a life, a temple of the inexorable. The distinction of London Bridge Station, on the Chatham side, is that it is not a terminus but a junction where lives begin to fade and then blossom again as they swap trains in the rush hours and make for all the regions of South London and the towns of Kent. The trains come in and go out over those miles of rolling brick arches that run across South London like a massive Roman wall. There were no indicators on the platforms in my day and the confusion had to be sorted out by stentorian porters who called out the long litanies of stations in a hoarse London bawl and with a style of their own. They stood on the crowded platform edge, detected the identifying lights on the incoming engine and then sang out. To myself, at that age, all places I did not know, seemed romantic and the lists of names were, if not Miltonic, at any rate as evocative as those names with which the Georgian poets filled up their lines. I would stare admiringly, even enviously, at the porter who would have to chant the long line to Bexley Heath; or the man who, beginning with the blunt and challenging football names of Charlton and Woolwich would go on to comic Plumstead and then flow forward over his long list till his voice fell to the finality of Greenhythe, Northfleet and Gravesend; or the softer tones of St Johns, Lewisham, and Blackheath. And to stir us up were the powerful trains – travelling to distances that seemed as remote as Istanbul to me – expresses that went to Margate, Herne Bay, Rochester and Chatham. I saw nothing dingy in this. The pleasure of my life as an office boy lay in being one of the London crowd and I actually enjoyed standing in a compartment packed with fifteen people on my way to Bromley North. How pleasant it was, in the war years, to stop dead outside Tower Bridge and to see a maroon go off in an air-raid warning and, even better, for a sentimentalist, to be stuck in one of those curry powder fogs that came up from the river and squashed London flat in its windless marsh. One listened to the fog signals and saw the fires of the watchmen; there was a sinister quiet as the train stood outside the Surrey Docks. And when, very late, the train got to Bromley North and one groped one's way home, seeing the conductors with flares in their hands walking ahead of the buses, or cars lost and askew on the wrong side of the road, and heard footsteps but saw no person until he was upon you and asking where he was, one swanked to oneself that at last one had had a load of the traditional muck on one's chest.

From *A Cab at the Door* by V. S. Pritchett, 1968

The Weekend Awaits

Very soon the City itself would be standing over until Monday: the crowds of brokers and cashiers and clerks and typists and hawkers would have vanished from its pavements, the bars would be forlorn, the teashops nearly empty or closed; its trams and buses, no longer clamouring for a few more yards of space, would come gliding easily through misty blue vacancies like ships going down London River; and the whole place, populated only by caretakers and policemen among the living, would sink slowly into quietness; the very bank-rate would be forgotten; and it would be left to drown itself in reverie, with a drift of smoke and light fog across its old stones like the return of an army of ghosts. Until – with a clatter, a clang, a sudden raw awakening – Monday.

Papers were swept into drawers, letters were stamped in rows, blotters were shut, turned over, put away, ledgers and petty cash boxes were locked up, typewriters were covered, noses were powdered, cigarettes and pipes were lit, doors were banged, and stairs were noisy with hasty feet. The week was done. Out they came in their thousands into Angel Pavement, London Wall, Moorgate Street, Cornhill and Cheapside. They were so thick along Finsbury Pavement that the Moorgate Tube Station seemed like a monster sucking them down into its hot rank inside. Among these vanishing mites was one with a large but not masterful nose, full brown eyes, a slightly open mouth, and a drooping chin. This was Turgis going home.

He had to stand all the way, and though there were at least five nice-looking girls in the same compartment – and one was very close to him, and two of the others he had noticed several times before – not one of them showed the slightest interest in him.

From *Angel Pavement* by J. B. Priestley, 1930

The Importance of Golf

Every Saturday afternoon he hustled out to his country club and hustled through nine holes of golf as a rest after the week's hustle.

In Zenith it was as necessary for a Successful Man to belong to a country club as it was to wear a linen collar. Babbitt's was the Outing Golf and Country Club, a pleasant grey-shingled building with a broad porch, on a daisy-starred cliff above Lake Kennepoose. There was another, the Tonawanda Country Club, to which belonged Charles McKelvey, Horace Updike, and the other rich men who lunched not at the Athletic but at the Union Club. Babbitt explained with frequency, 'You couldn't hire me to join the Tonawanda, even if I did have a hundred and eighty bucks to throw away on the initiation fee. At the Outing we've got a bunch of real human fellows, and the finest lot of little women in town – just as good at joshing as the men – but at the Tonawanda there's nothing but these would-be's in New York get-ups, drinking tea! Too much dog altogether. Why, I wouldn't join the Tonawanda even if they – I wouldn't join it on a bet!'

When he had played four or five holes, he relaxed a bit, his tobacco-fluttering heart beat more normally, and his voice slowed to the drawling of his hundred generations of peasant ancestors.

From *Babbitt* by Sinclair Lewis, 1922

Christmas Revels

An abrupt noise of singing, as if a loud radio-van was passing – a pub door had swung open and was now held wide by Christmas drinkers almost tumbled out by the crowd inside. She stopped dead. It was like suddenly looking into an electric night from day, carnival night with lights blazing and packed faces swaying and singing. You could hardly see the streamers for the smoke. Mackintoshes, duffle-coats, glasses, beer, moustaches, red lips. Packed clerks with pale faces roared and drank like giants, flushed typists brimming with crème de menthe and Cherry Heering shrieked with laughter, purse-free old men sweated red-faced, wedged in a beery heaven, happy as lark-puddings.

Sandra stood on the cold pavement and gazed in not like the poor child left out, for a millionaire could not have found room inside – they were packed closer than the rush-hour whose temporary cessation they celebrated – she simply gazed in wonder.

She did not see Ralph Mansford and Hearst wedged between glee-singing chartered accountants and a pin-table, nobody could have.

From *The Last Hours of Sandra Lee* by William Sansom, 1961

On the Eve

But the garden looked sad and sorry this dripping September afternoon. It had begun to rain quite early in the morning: it was spotting when she came out of the butcher's, soon after eleven; and now, at five o'clock, a silent, listless rain was filling the hollows of the paths. She was distressed and miserable. The night before they left home for their holidays was always one of family celebration. When Dick and Mary had been children it was a night that rose almost to the height of Christmas Eve: a night, voted sometimes, as the best of all the holiday, although it was spent at home and the sea was still sixty miles away.

But the sea would always be calling them that evening; and when Mr Stevens took his after-supper stroll in the garden he could almost taste the saltness in the air. It was a habit of Mr Stevens to linger in the garden longer than usual on that night before they went away: the Office was behind him: he had slammed the lid of his desk for fifteen splendid days, and he liked to feel the holiday had begun that evening. On the little lawn outside – in the dusk – he would open his chest and breathe the air. Then he would go to his bedroom and lay out the clothes he would wear at the sea, his grey flannel trousers, tweed sports jacket, stout brown boots, and soft tweed cap. But he would seldom wear the cap. For a whole fortnight his thin brown hair would blow in the sunlight and the breeze.

Again Mrs Stevens peered out. If only the rain would stop! The whole holiday would be damped if they were cheated out of this first evening – sweet because it was stolen: because it was not, officially, a part of the holiday at all.

A special supper always marked the evening, too. This year it was boiled beef, because it made good sandwiches for the train journey, and was easy to wash up, giving more leisure for the final packing afterwards. Then there were apple dumplings, Mr Stevens' favourite sweet.

From *The Fortnight in September* by R. C. Sherriff, 1931

Babbitt in Maine

Their launch rounded the bend; at the head of the lake, under a mountain slope, they saw the little central dining-shack of their hotel and the crescent of squat log cottages which served as bedrooms. They landed, and endured the critical examination of the habitués who had been at the hotel for a whole week. In their cottage, with its high stone fireplace, they hastened, as Babbitt expressed it, to 'get into some regular he-togs.' They came out; Paul in an old grey suit and soft white shirt; Babbitt in khaki shirt and vest and flapping khaki trousers. It was excessively new khaki; his rimless spectacles belonged to a city office; and his face was not tanned, but a city pink. He made a discordant noise in the place. But with infinite satisfaction he slapped his legs and crowed, 'Say, this is getting back home, eh?'

They stood on the wharf before the hotel. He winked at Paul and drew from his back pocket a plug of chewing-tobacco, a vulgarism forbidden in the Babbitt home. He took a chew, beaming and wagging his head as he tugged at it. 'Um! Um! Maybe I haven't been hungry for a wad of eating-tobacco! Have some?'

They looked at each other in a grin of understanding. Paul took the plug, gnawed at it. They stood quiet, their jaws working. They solemnly spat, one after the other, into the placid water. They stretched voluptuously, with lifted arms and arched backs. From beyond the mountains came the shuffling sound of a far-off train. A trout leaped, and fell back in a silver circle. They sighed together.

From *Babbitt* by Sinclair Lewis, 1922

A Lifeline

But besides Sundays I had a day at Easter, and a day at Christmas, with a full week in the summer to go and air myself in my native fields of Hertfordshire. This last was a great indulgence; and the prospect of its recurrence, I believe, alone kept me up through the year, and made my durance tolerable. But when the week came round, did the glittering phantom of the distance keep touch with me? Or rather was it not a series of seven uneasy days, spent in restless pursuit of pleasure, and a wearisome anxiety to find out how to make the most of them? Where was the quiet, where the promised rest? Before I had a taste of it, it was vanished. I was at the desk again, counting upon the fifty-one tedious weeks that must intervene before such another snatch would come. Still the prospect of its coming threw something of an illumination upon the darker side of my captivity. Without it, as I have said, I could scarcely have sustained my thraldom.

From 'The Superannuated Man' in *Essays of Elia* by Charles Lamb, 1818

The Office Casts Its Shadow

On Saturday night – as Mr Stevens sat back in his favourite chair before knocking out his pipe and going to bed, it came to him with a sigh of regret that half the holiday had gone. Gone it seemed, in no time – in a flash, for though their last morning in Corunna Road might easily have been a year ago, it seemed scarcely a day since he had sat in this same chair on the evening of their arrival, thinking of the unbroken holiday ahead.

Still, there was a whole week yet: Sunday – Monday – Tuesday, Wednesday – Thursday: five clear days at least before they need think of packing. But even as he reviewed the days remaining, a pile of ragged invoice ledgers loomed out from where, a few days ago – only the sea, and the downs had lain. He had to blink, and give his head a shake before the dusty, unpalatable vision would fade away. He was letting an attack of the blues get hold of him – a futile thing to allow –

That order form from Warrington's! Why couldn't he forget the beastly thing? It had arrived just as he was clearing up to go on his last evening before the holiday: he was almost certain he put it on Mr Rogers' desk to be dealt with in the morning; he'd stuck a pin through it to prevent it fluttering to the ground and being swept up by the charwoman. And yet just as definitely he remembered it lying on his blotting pad beside some papers he was to put in his desk to be dealt with on his return. Supposing he had shut the order in the pad? It might be lying in his desk, unattended to – a big order – and Warrington's were just the sort of people who would kick up a row. It had occurred to him on his way home on the bus, but his thoughts had been too full of the holiday to worry then. And now the confounded thing kept intruding itself – again and again – even when he was undressing for his bathe that morning. He ought to have dropped Rogers a line – just to make sure – but it was too late now: Warrington's would have been fuming on the telephone early last week – probably cancelling all their business. It would mean a black mark against his name – possibly something worse. Again he shook his head to get rid of it: of course he'd put it on Rogers' desk: it was probably quite all right – and here he was worrying himself to death over nothing.

From *The Fortnight in September* by R. C. Sherriff, 1931

First Day Back

The first day they were back in the office was the second of January. None of them had really needed New Year's Day to recover from the celebrations of the night before because none of them had been to a party, but there had always been grumblings when in the past they had been obliged to work on the day. Now, of course, the extended holiday had seemed a little too long and they were all glad to be back to work.

'Or what passes for work,' as Norman remarked, tilting back in his chair and drumming his fingers on his empty table.

'It's always a bit slack at this time,' Letty said. 'One tries to get things done before Christmas.'

'To clear one's desk,' said Marcia importantly, using a phrase from long ago that had little or no reality in their present situation.

'And when you get back there's nothing on it,' said Norman peevishly. He was bored now that the first interest of hearing about other people's Christmases had evaporated.

From *Quartet in Autumn* by Barbara Pym, 1977

Sixteen

HOME AND THE
OFFICE

Few men have had a shrewder understanding of office life than Wemmick, Mr Jaggers's clerk in *Great Expectations*; and the sensible office worker soon realises that, as Wemmick put it, 'Walworth is one place, and this office is another. Much as the Aged is one person, and Mr Jaggers another. They must not be confounded together. My Walworth sentiments must be taken at Walworth; none but my official sentiments can be taken in this office.' Consciously or not, we adopt different personae and play different parts at home and in the office: confusing the two can lead to trouble, and the irruption of home life and domestic affairs into the very different world of the office can prove unwelcome and embarrassing, as Charley Tudor discovered when the landlady of the Cat and Whistle hoved up in the Internal Navigation Office to quiz him about his intentions *vis-à-vis* Norah Geraghty. Though most office workers make full and shameless use of the office telephone and the office franking machine in pursuit of domestic concerns, care must be taken to keep the spheres in their proper places. The obligatory family photographs, however endearing or consoling, often seem oddly furtive, vulnerable and uneasy; while the appearance of a spouse at a party or an office function may be greeted with an uncomfortable mixture of resentment and amazement, as though the office worker had gone and done something uncalled for while his or her colleagues were engaged elsewhere. And a glimpse of the boss at home may be equally disruptive – a man or woman like any other, treated very differently, perhaps, by disrespectful children or an aggravated spouse than by the awestruck minions in the office. Small wonder that – faced with nappies or an angry wife – many men spin out the working day, gossiping in pubs or someone else's office; or that the office can come to seem a refuge and a consolation, the loss of which leaves them stranded and exposed, all power and dignity suddenly drained away.

Wemmick's Philosophy

'Is it [the Castle, Wemmick's home in Walworth, where he lives with his father, the Aged P] your own, Mr Wemmick?'

'O yes,' said Wemmick. 'I have got hold of it, a bit at a time. It's a freehold, by George!'

'Is it, indeed? I hope Mr Jaggers admires it?'

'Never seen it,' said Wemmick. 'Never heard of it. Never seen the Aged. Never heard of him. No; the office is one thing, and private life is another. When I go to the office, I leave the Castle behind me, and when I come into the Castle, I leave the office behind me. If it's not in any way disagreeable to you, you'll oblige me by doing the same. I don't want it professionally spoken about.'

. . . seeing that Mr Jaggers stood quite still and silent, and apparently quite obdurate, under this appeal, I turned to Wemmick, and said, 'Wemmick, I know you to be a man with a gentle heart. I have seen your pleasant home, and your old father, and all the innocent cheerful playful ways with which you refresh your business life. And I entreat you to say a word for me to Mr Jaggers, and to represent to him that, all circumstances considered, he ought to be more open with me!'

I have never seen two men look more oddly at one another than Mr Jaggers and Wemmick did after this apostrophe. At first, a misgiving crossed me that Wemmick would be instantly dismissed from his employment; but, it melted as I saw Mr Jaggers relax into something like a smile, and Wemmick become bolder.

'What's all this?' said Mr Jaggers. 'You with an old father, and you with pleasant and playful ways?'

'Well!' returned Wemmick. 'If I don't bring 'em here, what does it matter?'

'Pip,' said Mr Jaggers, laying his hand upon my arm, and smiling openly, 'this man must be the most cunning impostor in all London.'

'Not a bit of it,' returned Wemmick, growing bolder and bolder. 'I think you're another.'

Again they exchanged their former odd looks, each apparently still distrustful that the other was taking him in.

'*You* with a pleasant home?' said Mr Jaggers.

'Since it don't interfere with business,' returned Wemmick, 'let it be so. Now, I look at you, sir, I shouldn't wonder if *you* might be planning and contriving to have a pleasant home of your own, one of these days, when you're tired of all this work.'

From Great Expectations by Charles Dickens, 1861

An Embarrassing Irruption

A messenger came up and informed him that a lady was waiting to see him.

'A lady!' said Charley: 'what lady?' and he immediately began thinking of the Woodwards, whom he was to meet that afternoon at Chiswick.

'I'm sure I can't say, sir: all that she said was that she was a lady,' answered the messenger, falsely, for he well knew that the woman was Mrs Davis, of the 'Cat and Whistle.'

Now the clerks at the Internal Navigation were badly off for a waiting-room; and in no respect can the different ranks of different public offices be more plainly seen than in the presence or absence of such little items of accommodation as this. At the Weights and Measures there was an elegant little chamber, carpeted, furnished with leathern-bottomed chairs, and a clock, supplied with cream-laid note-paper, new pens, and the *Times* newspaper, quite a little Elysium, in which to pass half an hour, while the Secretary, whom one had called to see, was completing his last calculation on the matter of the decimal coinage. But there were no such comforts at the Internal Navigation. There was, indeed, a little room at the top of the stairs, in which visitors were requested to sit down; but even here two men were always at work – at work, or else at play.

Into this room Mrs Davis was shown, and there Charley found her. Long and intimately as the young navvy had been acquainted with the landlady of the 'Cat and Whistle,' he had never before seen her arrayed for the outer world. It may be doubted whether Sir John Falstaff would, at the first glance, have known even Dame Quickly in her bonnet, that is, if Dame Quickly in those days had had a bonnet. At any rate Charley was at fault for a moment, and was shaking hands with the landlady before he quite recognized who she was.

The men in the room, however, had recognized her, and Charley well knew that they had done so.

'Mr Tudor,' she began, not a bit abashed, 'I want to know what it is you are a-going to do?'

Though she was not abashed, Charley was, and very much so. However, he contrived to get her out of the room, so that he might speak to her somewhat more privately in the passage. The gentlemen at the Internal

Navigation were well accustomed to this mode of colloquy, as their trades-men not unfrequently called, with the view of having a little conversation, which could not conveniently be held in the public room.

'And, Mr Tudor, what are you a-going to do about that poor girl there?' said Mrs Davis, as soon as she found herself in the passage, and saw that Charley was comfortably settled with his back against the wall.

'She may go to Hong-Kong for me.' That is what Charley should have said. But he did not say it. He had neither the sternness of heart nor the moral courage to enable him to do so. He was very anxious, it is true, to get altogether quit of Norah Geraghty; but his present immediate care was confined to a desire of getting Mrs Davis out of the office.

'Do!' said Charley. 'Oh, I don't know; I'll come and settle something some of these days; let me see when – say next Tuesday.'

'Settle something,' said Mrs Davis. 'If you are an honest man, as I take you, there is only one thing to settle; when do you mean to marry her?'

'Hush!' said Charley; for, as she was speaking, Mr Snape came down the passage leading from Mr Oldeschole's room. 'Hush!' Mr Snape as he passed walked very slowly, and looked curiously round into the widow's face. 'I'll be even with you, old fellow, for that,' said Charley to himself; and it may be taken for granted that he kept his word before long.

'Oh! it is no good hushing any more,' said Mrs Davis, hardly waiting till Mr Snape's erect ears were out of hearing. 'Hushing won't do no good; there's that girl a-dying, and her grave'll be a-top of your head, Mr Tudor; mind I tell you that fairly; so now I want to know what it is you're a-going to do.' And then Mrs Davis lifted up the lid of a market basket which hung on her left arm, took out her pocket-handkerchief, and began to wipe her eyes.

Unfortunate Charley! An idea occurred to him that he might bolt and leave her. But then the chances were that she would make her way into his very room, and tell her story there, out before them all. He well knew that this woman was capable of many things if her temper were fairly roused. And yet what could he say to her to induce her to go out from that building, and leave him alone to his lesser misfortunes?

'She's a-dying, I tell you, Mr Tudor,' continued the landlady, 'and if she do die, be sure of this, I won't be slow to tell the truth about it. I'm the only friend she's got, and I'm not going to see her put upon. So just tell me this in two words – what is it you're a-going to do?' And then Mrs Davis replaced her kerchief in the basket, stood boldly erect in the middle of the passage, waiting for Charley's answer.

Just at this moment Mr Snape again appeared in the passage, going towards Mr Oldeschole's room. The pernicious old man! He hated Charley Tudor; and, to tell the truth, there was no love lost between them. Charley, afflicted and out of spirits as he was at the moment, could not resist the opportunity of being impertinent to his old foe: 'I'm afraid you'll make yourself very tired, Mr Snape, if you walk about so much,' said he. Mr Snape merely looked at him, and then hard at Mrs Davis, and passed on to Mr Oldeschole's room.

'Well, Mr Tudor, will you be so good as to tell me what it is you're going to do about this poor girl?'

'My goodness, Mrs Davis, you know how I am situated – how can you expect me to give an answer to such a question in such a place as this? I'll come to the "Cat and Whistle" on Tuesday.'

'Gammon!' said the eloquent lady. 'You know you means gammon.'

Charley, perhaps, did mean gammon; but he protested that he had never been more truthfully in earnest in his life. Mr Oldeschole's door opened, and Mrs Davis perceiving it, whipped out her handkerchief in haste, and again began wiping her eyes, not without audible sobs. 'Confound the woman!' said Charley to himself; 'what on earth shall I do with her?'

Mr Oldeschole's door opened, and out of it came Mr Oldeschole, and Mr Snape following him. What means the clerk had used to bring forth the Secretary need not now be inquired. Forth they both came, and passed along the passage, brushing close by Charley and Mrs Davis; Mr Oldeschole, when he saw that one of the clerks was talking to a woman who apparently was crying, looked very intently on the ground, and passed by with a quick step; Mr Snape looked as intently at the woman, and passed very slowly. Each acted according to his lights.

'I don't mean gammon at all, Mrs Davis – indeed, I don't – I'll be there on Tuesday night certainly, if not sooner – I will indeed – I shall be in a desperate scrape if they see me here talking to you any longer; there is a rule against women being in the office at all.'

'And there's a rule against the clerks marrying, I suppose,' said Mrs Davis.

The colloquy ended in Charley promising to spend the Saturday evening at the 'Cat and Whistle,' with the view of then and there settling what he meant to do about 'that there girl'; nothing short of such an undertaking on his part would induce Mrs Davis to budge. Had she known her advantage she might have made even better terms. He would almost rather have given her a written promise to marry her barmaid, than have suffered her to remain there till Mr Oldeschole should return and see her there again. So Mrs Davis, with her basket and pocket-handkerchief, went her way about her marketing, and Charley, as he returned to his room, gave the strictest injunctions to the messenger that not, on any ground or excuse whatever, was any woman to be again allowed to see him at the office.

From The Three Clerks by Anthony Trollope, 1858

More Important Matters

The ringing of the external telephone broke in on his uncomprehending reading of a staff surveyor's report. His mind automatically framed what his response should be to some demand for an explanation of how Gerson appeared to be his senior, in immediate succession to Matheson. He lifted the receiver and said: 'Mortgage Manager.'

'Stuart, a terrible thing's happened,' said Rose. Her voice was unfamiliarly deep and broken.

'Rosie, what on earth's the matter?' he said, fearful.

'The bird's been killed.'

His mind returned immediately to the memorandum. 'What a shame!' he said.

'It was my fault.'

'I'm sure it wasn't, darling,' he said.

'After you left, the mother bird got in the conservatory through the top window. It made a terrific noise, chirping. And in the end the little bird came out of the rockery. It couldn't really fly, but the mother bird fluttered over it and encouraged it. In fact, showed it the way out through the garden door. And at last it got out, on the step outside the door, and crouched there, you know, looking round.'

Blackledge found that his pencil was making a nervous, heavy design on his scribbling pad: while Rose had been speaking he had completely changed his mind about the memorandum. He had decided that he could not let it rest, that he must see Matheson, and soon.

'I watched it through the side window,' Rose said. 'The other birds were on the conservatory gutter, very noisy, and the mother had just come out and kept flying down to it. Then just for a moment I went away, only for a cigarette. I came straight back and saw Ludo with the bird in his mouth. I banged on the window but he ran off with it into the bushes. I couldn't find him – he must have gone through the fence.'

'Well, darling,' he said, trying tactfully to cut her short, 'how can you say it was your fault? Cats do go after birds.'

'Ludo got into the garden through the sitting-room window – I'd forgotten it was open. And then going for a cigarette . . .'

'Rosie, don't upset yourself like this about it.'

'It's so pathetic, Stuart. When Ludo had it all the others were making a tremendous chirping and two of them even fluttered over him trying to drive him away. And now the mother keeps coming down to the step, looking, and there's still that noise going on.'

'Rosie, please. It's only a bird.' But in his mind was the uneasy thought that perhaps it was not only a bird: in the year after their marriage she had had a child that had only survived three days and she had never wanted another.

'. . . so helpless,' she was saying, 'just crouching there . . . And then how terrible for it to see Ludo and –'

'Darling, you must try to forget it,' he interrupted.

'I'll never forget it,' she said.

Matheson must certainly be in now, he thought, and soon he would be having his stream of callers. 'Look, darling,' he said, 'I'm frightfully busy. I'll ring you up when I get back from lunch, shall I?'

She said: 'You don't realize how terrible it was.'

'I do,' he said, shifting round in anticipation of returning the receiver to its cradle. 'Keep your pecker up, darling. I must go now. Good-bye.' He waited for a moment or two, but she said nothing. Half guiltily, half exasperatedly, he put the receiver down. What a time for her to telephone him, he thought: as though he had nothing better to do than talk about the phenomenon of cats eating birds!

From *Image of a Society* by Roy Fuller, 1956

Each in its Proper Place

Vic Wilcox is in a meeting with his Marketing Director, Brian Everthorpe, who answered Vic's summons at 9.30, complaining of contraflow holdups on the motorway, and whom Vic, himself dictating letters at 9.30, told to come back at eleven. He is a big man, which in itself doesn't endear him to Vic, with bushy sideboards and RAF-style moustache. He wears a three-piece suit with an old-fashioned watch-chain looped across his waistcoated paunch. He is the most senior, and the most complacent, member of the management team Vic inherited.

'You should live in the city, like me, Brian,' says Vic. 'Not thirty miles away.'

'Oh, you know what Beryl is like,' says Brian Everthorpe, with a smile designed to seem rueful.

Vic doesn't know. He has never met Beryl, said to be Everthorpe's second wife, and formerly his secretary. As far as he knows, Beryl may not even exist, except as an excuse for Brian Everthorpe's delinquencies. *Beryl says the kids need country air. Beryl was poorly this morning and I had to run her to the doctor's. Beryl sends her apologies – she forgot to give me your message.* One day, quite soon in fact, Brian Everthorpe is going to have to concentrate his mind on the difference between a wife and an employer.

From *Nice Work* by David Lodge, 1988

The Public and the Private Face

I was surprised when one day Snaggs invited me to dinner at his house, and distinctly disconcerted to find that I had been asked not in my business capacity but as a writer (even though Snaggs had read nothing I had written), conscientious objector, holder of heretical opinions. We drove out one evening to his bungalow at Sanderstead. There I found again with surprise, although this is the kind of shock to which I have long since become inured, that Snaggs too had a public and a private face.

Mrs Snaggs was a dainty little lady of great gentility, and the bungalow was dainty too. In her presence Snaggs the roarer was a sucking dove. She gently reproved him for offering spirits before dinner, saying that she was sure Mr Symons would sooner have a glass of sherry. During the meal he was constantly up and about, taking dishes to the kitchen, offering to help, being criticised for the inefficiency of his carving. While we ate she plied me lightly with questions about the latest novels she had got from the local Boot's or Smith's libraries, and I could feel my status sinking as I said that I had read none of them. Things brightened up a little when she touched on my conscientious objection. 'Cyril doesn't approve, but I told him that he must try to understand.' She spoke of her unusually silent husband as though he were not there. 'I think all war is very hateful, very terrible.' Snaggs broke in at this to ask what would happen if everybody took that attitude, did she want Hitler to trample all over us? Mrs Snaggs looked to me for a gesture of solidarity, but I was unable to make it. What would have been the point of explaining that my objections were political, that I believed only a near-Fascist government could successfully oppose Fascism, and opposed the war in the name of a revolution which would sweep away all Snaggses and their bungalows?

Later Snaggs and I played chess, his moves punctuated by grunts and clicks, while Mrs Snaggs first cleared away, and then maintained mild conversation with me. The uneasy evening came to an end which I might have foreseen when she produced a sheaf of her poems and asked me to take them away and give me a frank opinion of their merits. In vain I said that my little magazine had been suspended for the duration. The poems were pressed on me, and I departed with them. I cannot remember what they were like, or what anodyne words I wrote to her. Snaggs never referred to the visit afterwards, but there was some change in his manner towards me. The evening marked the high point of our relationship, which afterwards steeply declined.

From *Notes from Another Country* by Julian Symons, 1972

Seventeen

OFFICE PARTIES

Every now and then – more often than not around Christmas – the monotony of office life is broken by an office party. Such parties tend to begin stiffly – the bosses strenuously jocular, the underlings tongue-tied and timid, and everyone even more uneasily aware than usual of differences in rank and status – and end in riot and debauchery. Once the drink begins to flow, much that lies beneath the surface of office life comes seething to the surface. Things are said and jokes are made that would never be dared in normal life; hitherto unsuspected hands sneak round waists that have long been admired from a distance, while men of maturer years find themselves – much to their embarrassment next morning – out of control on staircases or in stationery cupboards; inhibitions evaporate as the dancing begins, the sober and the dutiful wend their way home to bed, and the topers, the lechers and the jokers prepare to inherit the earth, for an hour or two at least. So potent and so touching are these uneasy bacchanalia that William Sansom devoted an entire novel to an office party, small slices of which are served up here. Drink and sex are the twin hazards of all office parties, and both of them are liable to lead the participant astray, not least in the eyes of his or her spouse: Peter de Vries provides a cunning variant on an all too familiar theme . . .

Coconut Kisses

By Christmas afternoon the Establishment Room had been quite transformed, and everything was ready for the tea party. Each plywood table was covered with a lace-edged cloth, and right across the centre of the big middle table, where the adding machines usually stood, ran a row of little pots of holly made so cleverly from tinfoil and decorated with little cut-out black cats in bedsocks. A whole collection of 'In' and 'Out' trays had been lined with paper doilies and filled with every sort of delicious cake and sandwich – Thea's sausage rolls and Penelope's dainty bridge rolls filled with sandwich spread, Helen's raspberry fingers and little pyramids of chocolate powder and post toasties that Joan Fowler called 'Coconut Kisses'; the extra sugar ration of months had gone into the display. Caricatures of everybody were pinned on the walls, and some drawings of cuties modelled on 'Jane' from the *Daily Mirror*, but less sexy and more whimsical. It had proved very difficult to fit the branches of holly and evergreen to the blue tubular lighting, but by a united effort it had been done; whilst from the central hanging light there swung an enormous and rather menacing bunch of mistletoe. Stephanie had brought six bottles of peaches in brandy from Fortnum's and they stood in uncompromisingly lavish display on the table by the window, until at the last minute Joan Fowler decided to decorate them with crackers and some silver 'stardust' that flew all over the room and stuck to everyone's clothes. At four sharp visitors from other rooms and sections began to arrive.

Never was the dissimilarity, the lack of basic compatibility of the staff of the Bureau more apparent than on such customarily festive occasions as Christmas. Compelled by convention to put aside 'shop' talk and the gossip of personalities which surrounded their working hours, the tightly welded machine parts soon collapsed into a motley collection of totally disparate individuals. The service officers found it impossible to continue to suggest that they were really intellectuals; the businessmen's service talk creaked badly; whilst the assumption of business toughness among the dons and schoolmasters was patently laughable. The women of all ages and classes, who so outnumbered the men at the Bureau, glimpsed with shame something of their failure to preserve the standards of glamour and charm normally offered to the other sex; they saw for a moment that in their fatigue and absorption with routine they had forgotten to turn the males out of the dressing room before it was too late. Everywhere in the room the regulation masks of brightness and competence were slipping . . .

From 'Christmas Day at the Workhouse' in *Such Darling Dodos* by
Angus Wilson, 1950

The Ultimate Office Party

. . . It was the day of the Office Party. The afternoon would be a rout, a riot. Already it was absurd to call the office grey, for round each desk and in drawers everywhere there lay parcels and tissue-wrapped bottles, and where these touched a radiator the heat sent out festive crackle-sounds of crinkly paper, red and green Christmas crackle . . .

'Man the lifeboats!' H. J. called.

'And splice the mainbrace,' boomed Mavis and there was a renewed clinking and gurgling as glasses and cups were refilled. They began to leave their chairs to perch on corners of desks, or on the lowest filing cabinets, and H. J. sent Monica in for a half dozen claret he had ready, for he had thought this to be the best available solvent for the diversity about – a Cherry Heering and a British Port from the Mailing Department already lay beneath his surgical belt.

It began to look for the first time as if a party was in progress. The lights were switched on, and turned the darkening room abrupt yellow. Festive tissues and coloured wrappings lay everywhere. Bottles and sweets and bits of food winked among typewriters and folders and files. There was a fuzz of smoke. Tin-lid ash-trays were already full, ash was getting among the paper-clips.

Yet they were still in everyday office clothes – and this struck a note both abandoned and dreary at the same time.

There would soon be a coming and going between departments, people drifting here and there with bottles in their hands. Shop talk fell away, Christmas was in the air, and snatches of talk came to Sandra, through the growing buzz, as she wondered whom to speak with . . .

. . . the mailing clerk Bossom came dancing in with his friend, Bone, to complete a short step routine by the door.

'A glass of po-ort?' these two ended, in close harmony.

Everyone turned in wonder.

Messrs Bone and Bossom stood poised as if carrying straw hat and cane. Jollily tipsy, they were at the stage that likes to pretend it is drunk.

H. J. on the far side of the room clapped his jovial hands, and nodded to Monica to give them a couple of glasses. Bone crumpled with shyness. Even Bossom flinched, but then regained himself and took his glass with a fine theatrical bow. They were a well-known double-act in the office. Bone was like a fleshy shadow attached to the virile Bossom, and it was Bone who was so hopelessly in love with Sandra. She now went straight to him, panicking from Monica, and slipped her arm in his. He seemed to glisten brighter with youthful oils, and he turned a shade paler. This had never, never happened before. Tiny Hearst laboriously helped them out with:

'Entrez, Mr Outray. And the outrageous Mr Intray!'

'Happy as bank-larks,' Mark tried.

For a moment the solstice was forgotten. Sandra herself had drunk much more than usual, and on top of a good lunch. Monica might be dangerous – but for the moment she chose to forget that too. Much more important was Bun's imminent arrival: and a certain change that had come over the party.

It was definitely easing. Glasses were balancing on round ink-erasers, bottles were leaving rings on buff manila files – and people were showing the edges of their mantelpieces. Mavis Cook had come into the clear battling for H. J., and H. J. himself had relaxed from twinkling to become like any other big tired man, heavy-jowled, like a weary boxer-dog. And Monica was fussing him like an equal – confirming many a suspicion.

Then Sandra saw that Jill had slung a rope of pearls beneath her flushed face, and now gazed at Mark Deane between bruised-looking eyelids! Ralph Mansford was looking more worried than ever, and drinking like a real father-to-be. And here was Tiny Hearst edging his huge bulk up against H. J., standing with hands in pockets and telling him exactly what he, personally, Hearst himself thought about the commissionaire Bletch below taking half an hour off for tea just when the lift was needed most . . .

'Oh, she'll be all right,' his voice faded away down the passage.

Sandra opened the door, and hurried Mavis along to the Red Hell.

In that place, in the rose-reflected mirror, Mavis saw her face and shrieked, 'Oh, what a sight!' quickly losing her grief in a patting of hair and wiping of eyes. But to Sandra she had looked little different from usual.

'Would you think this was the same office?' she said for the sake of talking. 'Mavis, it's all a kind of dream really, everyone taking a drop too much, and tomorrow they'll all never believe it happened . . . if they even remember' . . .

Just then H. J. came back into the room, wiping his forehead with a handkerchief, although there was no sweat there. Monica went straight over to him.

'I don't know, I don't know,' he was saying, 'there's Mansford retching outside the lavatory and the hyacinths in a dreadful state, and I go myself' – he prodded his chest – '*myself* down to get Bletch to come up with a cloth and of course there's no lift and no Bletch, only a strong smell of rum. Things are getting out of hand' . . .

'Here we go gathering NUTS IN MAY!' shouted the transistor.

'With Jimmy and Mona and Tom and Hilda and Ron and Don and Esther –' it shouted on, while Sandra leaned forward coughing, but still clutching her chest, and Bossom thumped her on the back dislodging the clasp, and she pressed harder, the pin dug itself further in, and she stumbled, not from this small pain but because now she was drunk.

'Here we go gathering Nuts in May!' yelled the Pool, joining hands, 'Nuts in May, Boing de Boing –' they sang.

Instinctively the line of suspects joined hands. And nobody saw Sandra slip back behind them and lurch to the glass partition leading to H. J.'s room. Carefully keeping an eye on Monica's back, she staggered through the opening in the glass and on into the inner office. She swung his door in a slam behind her – but even then caught it in time, closing it softly just as the Pool danced forward chanting Nuts-in-May and Mark's line stepped out joyfully to meet it.

H. J. suddenly forgot his troubles – he surged forward towards the Pool singing strongly, for Nuts-in-May was something he understood. Gone the awkwardness of talk, forgotten for a moment that damnable clasp and Monica's rising temper – this was the party spirit, parties should have games and Nuts-in-May was a great leveller . . .

From *The Last Hours of Sandra Lee* by William Sansom, 1961

Keeping in Touch

As he trampled her insteps to the strains of 'The Tennessee Waltz,' which he seemed to regard as a fox-trot, he hummed the tune in a manner suggesting a tin ear as well, and he would occasionally disengage himself and snap his fingers, to emphasize a democratic rapport with his employees.

From *Sauce for the Gander* by Peter de Vries, 1982

'Sonnet: The Days and the Nights to Come'

An immense ballroom. Thirties style. And hired
by an immense Company: annual Dinner Dance.
The girls are young and beautiful, so beautiful
you could light a cigar at them. They burn,
some hundreds of them, with traditional ardour;
    flaming youth.
Hairstyles; and tits displayed, old salesmen's jokes:
make a clean breast of it. They shake in joy,
so loving it all, so loving the young men

and (most) themselves. Give it just fifteen years –
or ten. They're kitchen-sinking. Eyes are underlined,
what love did once is now the old routine;
the joint is jumping, sizzling. It's a gas.

The kids have spread that body like a quilt,
A sad negro sings: 'It's a wonderful world!'

From *The Gavin Ewart Show* by Gavin Ewart, 1971

Ripples of Girlish Laughter

The dinner was due to begin at half-past six. By four o'clock all work
had ended so far as the female staff, Miss Henderson excepted, was
concerned. Rhona Peters and the crime lady went home, by separate routes,
to change, but the rest packed themselves into the anteroom. A perpetual
ripple of girlish laughs, interrupted by occasional shrieks (surprise, ecstasy,
disaster, pain?), could be heard from behind the closed door. An amalgam
of scents, dominated by Delphine's lily of the valley, the bottle of which
had been smashed on the basement stairs, filtered gradually up to the highest floor of the building. Sometimes the door would be flung open, by design
no doubt, in case a wandering male might be lurking in the passageway,
and the shrieks would be intensified, as though a bunch of Persephones had
discovered a swarthy, naked Pluto hidden in their midst. There would be
glimpses then, for whoever cared to look, of orchid-coloured chiffon, silver
heels, bare backs and powdered shoulders.

By and large the men waited at their desks, afraid of descending into
the basement in case some encounter would result in having to spend
money on a taxi. Indeed, long before the girls emerged, agog for pleasure,
jewel-eyed, dainty as any ballerinas, most of the men had slipped out
through the back entrance. Ammon's Daimler, however, was at their
disposal, and Captain Runche, ever gallant, was ready to transport a
twittering contingent. Someone produced a sprig of mistletoe and, to the
accompaniment of yet more shrieks, held it over Gloria's head as Runche
helped her into the seat beside him.

Toby had not been warned of the danger of lingering on the premises.
He was spied by Runche, who commissioned him to hire a taxi. When it
was discovered that he had asked Miss Henderson to be one of his passengers, each girl whom he invited to join them said that she had made
alternative arrangements.

In the end Toby and Miss Henderson shared their taxi with Jupes and
his secretary. For Jupes, apart from Runche, was virtually the only man
who made a point of staying on at the office expressly in order to travel
with the girls; the trouble was that the girls, much as they hoped for male
company, knew far too well what to expect if they found themselves
wedged next to him in a taxi.

Jupes's secretary, on the other hand, normally so timid that Toby always thought of her as a shell-shocked mouse with too much lipstick, revealed herself as possessing very few inhibitions. In fact she and Jupes remained glued to one another the whole journey. Miss Henderson appeared not to notice and rattled on to Toby about the option clause in some book or other, the standard of the typing of the May blurbs, some galley proofs that were overdue and a possible strike in the paper-mills. Toby, for his part, was rehearsing his speech in his head. Indeed, he only spoke once and then found that they were at cross-purposes – either that, or she had not even listened.

Some of the girls who had declined to join them, and who had failed to find other free transport, were already labouring out of the Tube station, when the taxi drew up at the De Grey Hotel, ballroom entrance. The rush hour was on. The faery creatures had a hard time of it struggling against the crowds. The packed, illuminated buses, double-layered aquariums, trundled by unheeding. There was not one wistful glance from under the umbrellas in the queues. Shops were closing; lights were being switched off behind the Christmas trees, the reindeer with the funny faces, the witch-balls and the tinselly cotton-wool. Wasn't there anyone, oh anyone, who envied the glamorous night ahead for these silver-shod girls, battling against the rain along grimy pavements towards the Egyptian porticos of the De Grey Hotel?

Pensioners of the firm, in white silk scarves and brown felt hats, had also made the journey by Tube. Their wives all wore evening dresses, lifted knee-high because of the rain; gold or sequined reticules dangled from furry gloves. But only those guests who came by car or taxi were noticed by the commissionaire and had the privilege of his massive blue and mauve umbrella . . .

Now came the moment for the Warehouse Nightingale to sing another aria or two. When she had finished, the meal was in theory half-way through. In theory, because a great deal more entertainment was still to come before the speeches. Some boys from the trade counter acted a sketch of apparently dubious taste, full of jokes which kept their colleagues convulsed but which meant little to the rest of the audience. There followed an hilarious brains trust between the firm's oldest pensioner and its newest recruit, the girl who did the labels in Cash Register, with Captain Runche as question-master. Moneyfield won a prize for being the only man in the room wearing one sock-suspender . . .

There was a feeling of expectancy now. Any moment Captain Runche would call for silence and the speeches would begin. Not that people were especially looking forward to them – the speeches were the most tedious part of the whole evening. When one reached that stage, however, it meant a stage nearer freedom: freedom to buy or cadge (as in the case of Ernie Skinton) a drink; freedom to shake off a neighbour (as in the case of Mrs Barminster and the labels girl); freedom to rush down to the gentlemen's cloakroom (as in the case of Moneyfield); freedom to escape home (as in the case of the crime lady, who had decided that she could not bear the risk of finding herself opposite the Educational Director in a Paul Jones); freedom to make passes (as in the case of Jupes, who was tired of the labels girl and was only fumbling her now because he knew it embarrassed her); freedom to get at the warehouse boys (as in the case of Olivia Quantock, despite the fact that she herself was now definitely to be one of the speech-makers).

From *The Big Tomato* by Raleigh Trevelyan, 1966

'Office Party'

We were throwing out small-talk
On the smoke-weary air,
When the girl with the squeaker
Came passing each chair.
She was wearing a white dress,
Her paper-hat was a blue
Crown with a red tassel,
And to every man who

Glanced up at her, she leant over
And blew down the hole,
So the squeaker inflated
And began to unroll.

She stopped them all talking
With this trickery,
And she didn't leave out anyone
Until she came to me.

I looked up and she met me
With a half-teasing eye
And she took a mild breath and

[293]

Went carefully by,

And with cold concentration
To the next man she went,
And squawked out the instrument
To its fullest extent.

And whether she passed me
Thinking that it would show
Too much favour to mock me
I never did know –

Or whether her withholding
Was her cruelty,
And it was that she despised me,
I couldn't quite see –

So it could have been discretion,
And it could have been disgust,
But it was quite unequivocal,
And suffer it I must:

All I know was: she passed me,
Which I did not expect
– And I'd never so craved for
Some crude disrespect.

From *The Lions' Mouths* by Alan Brownjohn, 1967

A Spanish Evening

The office Christmas party was held on a particularly fine foggy night that year. It was, the notice boards informed us, to be a Spanish evening: we were all to dress up as pallid, washed-out looking señors and señoritas, and the office wags spent the days before the great event drumming their heels on the ground and clicking their fingers above their heads. Even Robert – a more improbable Spaniard than most – temporarily abandoned some careful teeing-off with the upside-down umbrella in favour of a preparatory stamping of the foot and narrow-eyed tossing of the head, causing his curious cone of hair to bob to and fro like the windsock at Northolt Aerodrome. The very idea of dressing up as a toreador filled me with a nameless dread, and I had a strong suspicion that I would prove as inept with the castanets as I was with bat and ball or the parcels of breakables which Robert still sent spinning in my direction; so that although I was diffident and self-conscious to a ludicrous degree I resolved to defy the notice boards and go as something else. I was living at the time with some friends of my parents in a large house in Ladbroke Square, and when I explained my predicament they hurried to be of help. Between them they unearthed some ancient, musty-smelling Chinese garments, gave me a pair of slit eyes with which to peer through my horn-rims, glued a cotton wool beard to my granitic, unChinese-like chin, pinned a paper skullcap and a black woollen pigtail to my even less oriental hair, ordered up a taxi, and sent me stumbling out into the night.

The party was to be held in a large house, since demolished, at the bottom of Park Lane. As I sped towards the office party, I suddenly realized that I had quite forgotten to bring with me the roneoed note – with castanets in each corner, a Mexican hat in the middle, and embellished with many a '*Caramba!*' and '*Olé!*' – ordering all staff to be present in Spanish dress, and giving the exact address to which I should be heading. All I knew was that I should look out for a large house at the bottom of Park Lane, so I ordered the taxi to stop somewhere behind Apsley House, and set out through the fog towards the sound of revelry. By now I was beginning to regret having come as a Chinaman: the ancient clothes were poor protection against the cold, my appearance seemed to excite little confidence in those I encountered in the gloom, and my spirit of defiance – never strong except at a distance – was quickly beginning to wilt.

Eventually I stumbled upon what seemed a large enough house, wandered in through the open front door and, finding no one about, strolled up a great flight of stairs, along interminable corridors and round dark and gloomy wells, expecting at any moment to hear the clack of the castanet and a mighty drumming sound as a great army of clerks hurled themselves into the fandango. But not a sound was to be heard in this empty, echoing house; and at last I came across a bent and elderly occupant who, politely disguising any surprise he may have felt at coming across a complete stranger very badly disguised as a Chinaman, suggested I try further up Park Lane, and kindly escorted me back to the front door.

As for the office party itself, I felt wretchedly conspicuous and ill-at-ease in my musty Chinese dressing gown and pigtail: still more so since most of my fellow-workers had, very sensibly, made the most perfunctory gesture in the direction of Spain and had turned up in shirts and jeans, with the odd pair of castanets or papier mâché sombrero as a way of showing willing. Sid and Alf were sitting with a clutch of cheerful-looking cleaning ladies and people from Accounts; their hair was full of streamers, and the table in front of them was stiff with empty bottles of pale ale. Sid, I noticed, was wearing a large red-and-white spotted handkerchief tied about his head, which gave him a vaguely piratical look, appropriate to the Spanish Main; Alf, on the other hand, had on a maroon cardigan, a pale green shirt, grey flannel trousers held up with braces and (or so I liked to think) a pair of check Pirelli slippers, and I could only assume that he had cunningly disguised himself as a Spanish office packer enjoying an evening out. My friend the personnel officer seemed to have muddled Germany with Spain, and was striding jovially about in a pork pie hat and a pair of knee-length shorts; while far away, in the middle of the dance floor, Robert – fully togged out as a toreador by courtesy of a firm of theatrical costumiers – twisted and strutted in a wild and sensuous flamenco with the girl from the canteen with the Bardot lips, a three-cornered hat uneasily balanced on his unusual cone of hair. My colleagues were understandably baffled by my unpersuasive stab at Spanish national dress, and I spent much of the evening fending off cross or puzzled enquiries about what I was supposed to *be*; I resolved that, if I were to try to buck the system in future, I should do so in a slightly subtler and more devious way.

From *Playing for Time* by Jeremy Lewis, 1987

Disgraceful Scenes

A party was being organized by the directors in honour of Dorothy Sayers, who had been a copywriter in the Agency before the War. It was rumoured that the guest list for employees would sort out the trainee sheep from the goats. Those who were invited could take this mark of favour as an indication that they were, in some sense, 'regularized'. Those who weren't would still have to regard themselves as on probation. I found that I was the only one from the trainees or juniors to be honoured with an invitation.

The party took the form, first, of the unveiling of a plaque on the spiral staircase which had figured so prominently in Dorothy Sayers's *Murder Must Advertise*. Then everyone moved to a studio overlooking the corner of Kingsway and Great Queen Street. Drink flowed in large quantities. Most of it was Pimm's, one of the products which the Agency's advertisements had made famous. Even more famous, of course, was Guinness, and there was plenty of that there, too. I looked out over the depressing architecture of Kingsway, a grey, inhibited version of the imperial grandeur of New Delhi, in which I had lived for nearly the whole of 1943. I wasn't likely to be sent anywhere as exotic as that again, I thought. Nevertheless, I was cockahoop at being invited to this party and at hob-nobbing with directors, account managers and other senior staff and their wives. I don't think I actually spoke to Dorothy Sayers, but I remember her as a large lady in chiffon with lots of beads.

This Pimm's was pretty innocuous stuff, I decided. I must step up my intake, in order to take full advantage of the free and plentiful supplies. It occurred to me a little later that in the crowded, noisy bustle of the room I could afford to have a tankard of Pimm's in each hand. People would merely think that I was taking one of them to my wife or some other female in the throng. I spoiled this impression by explaining my idea to everyone I talked to. The party began to thin out. I didn't care. I was going to stay right to the end. Finally, one of the directors took away from me the bunch of grapes I was waving in the air like a toy balloon. He ushered me gently towards the lift. 'Come on, Mellors,' he said, 'the party's over.' There was an account manager in the lift. 'You're going to have trouble with him,' he told my wife. 'Where do you live?' 'Putney.' 'I'll see if I can get you a cab.' The first two taxis hailed refused to take me. 'Had one like that the other night,' said one driver, grimly. 'Never again.' 'Sall right,' I said, 'we'll go by tube.' I tottered into Holborn Underground Station and tried to walk down the up escalator. It rejected me in a tangle of arms and legs. Obviously, a complicated journey under-ground was quite beyond me. At last, an unobservant taxi driver accepted me. I wasn't sick until after Phoebe had somehow pulled and pushed me into the friends' house at Putney where we had left our baby.

I decided the next morning, or perhaps it was decided for me, that I was far too ill to go into the office. Phoebe telephoned. 'They didn't seem surprised,' she reported. Oh God, I thought. I've done it now. They'll give me my cards for sure. When I did go in I found that some joker had put on my desk a book called *The Effects of Alcohol on Man*. No other comment was made. I kept out of the directors' sight as much as possible for the next few days.

From *Memoirs of an Advertising Man* by John Mellors, 1976

'Who's the Woman?'

The office where Frisbie worked as vice-president in charge of purchases had its Christmas party a week early, because the head of the corporation was leaving for Miami, but otherwise it was like any other Christmas party. Everyone stood around self-consciously at first, drinking whiskey from paper cups, then bandied intramural jokes as the liquor thawed them, and ended up by slinging arms around one another in general camaraderie. Frisbie found himself dancing (to music from a radio that had been left in the office since the World Series) with a Mrs Diblanda, hired temporarily for the Christmas rush. He left with Mrs Diblanda when the party broke up, and they stopped at a neighboring bar for another drink. Frisbie had told his wife not to figure on him for dinner, as there was no way of knowing how long the party would last or how substantial the refreshments would be. There had been loads of canapés, so little edge was left on his appetite, but when, calling a cab, he offered to drop Mrs Diblanda off at her apartment and she invited him up for a last drink and maybe a bite of supper, he accepted. They had a couple of drinks, and then – quite naturally, it seemed – Frisbie kissed her. Mrs Diblanda, a divorced woman of about thirty who lived alone, transmitted a clear sense of readiness for anything, but just at that moment the image of Mrs Frisbie interposed itself between him and Mrs Diblanda, and he rose, got his hat and coat, excused himself, and left.

Now, this forbearance struck Frisbie as a fine thing. How many men he knew – fellows at the office, say – tempted by an isolated pleasure that could have been enjoyed and forgotten with no complications whatever, would have denied themselves? Damn few, probably. The more he thought of it the more gratifying his conduct seemed, and, presently, the more his satisfaction struck him as worth sharing with his wife, not for the light the incident put him in but as a certification of their bond. Superimposed upon the good spirits in which the drinks had left him, his moral exhilaration mounted. There were no cabs outside Mrs Diblanda's apartment house, and, hurrying on foot through a cool, needling drizzle that he found ravishing to his face, Frisbie tried to put himself in a woman's place, and couldn't imagine a wife not grateful for the knowledge of her husband's loyalty. By the time he reached home, he had decided to tell Mrs Frisbie of his.

It was twenty minutes to ten when Frisbie entered the house. He greeted his wife with a jovial hoot from the hall when she called from upstairs to ask if it was he. He hung up his coat and hat and went on up to the bedroom, where Mrs Frisbie was sitting in bed, filing her fingernails with an emery board. He answered a few questions about what the party had been like, and then took off his coat and vest and carried them into his closet. 'Guess what,' he said from there. 'I had a chance to have an affair.'

The sound of the emery board, which he could hear behind him, stopped, then resumed more slowly. 'I say I had a chance to sleep with someone. A woman,' he said. He reached for a wire hanger and knocked two or three to the floor in a tangle. He stooped to retrieve one, slipped his coat and vest onto it, and hung them up. 'But I declined,' he said, attempting to strike a humorous note.

The sound of the emery board stopped altogether. 'Who's the woman?' Mrs Frisbie asked in a tone slightly lower than normal . . .

From 'Flesh and the Devil' in *Without a Stitch in Time* by
Peter de Vries, 1974

Eighteen

LOVE AMONG
THE FILING
CABINETS

Even without the stimulus of office parties, love and sex are bound to flourish in offices: between people of the same and the opposite sexes, between the old and the young, between the married and the unmarried. Office workers spend more time with their colleagues than with family and friends, and these colleagues can all too easily loom larger in their private as well as their personal lives than those they have left behind; and because offices, like schools or nunneries, are closed and self-contained communities, folly and obsessions tend to fester in their airless halls. Brought low by a gaze from under a hat or the touch of a wrist, a happily married man may find himself besotted by someone half his age; the office wolf, with his flattery and bogus chat lines, stalks every new arrival;* the office vamp and the office tart go briskly about their business, while admiration for an older colleague may blossom into love; more timid souls may hope to catch glimpses of the beloved (or the lusted after) in lifts or corridors, bridle at the attentions and the triumphs of cruder, more confident opponents, and – with luck – eventually advance their causes at the annual office party. Since offices are public places, where even the inner sanctum may be disturbed by a knock on the door and a sudden, unwelcome presence, the physical manifestations of love in the office tend to be furtive and uneasy: kissing couples caught in the act will spring apart as though on elastic and explain, red-faced and standing far too close, how they were examining, in some detail, the latest set of sales figures, while love among the filing cabinets is by definition an uncomfortable, unsatisfactory business, with both parties listening tremulously for the slam of a door or the tread of a cleaning woman, much frenzied pulling on and off of clothes, and various parts of the anatomy scraped on the haircord carpet. Once in the office, it's probably wiser to retain a formal, even distant relationship with those with whom one is in love or has recently been in bed. Office affairs between the married and the single, or between people of very different ages, are invariably dishonest and dispiriting, involving elaborate deceits and misleading phone calls home about having to work late: yet sexual tension and attraction, and the gossip that ensues, are inevitable and pervasive elements of office life that

---

* One subject not dealt with here is sexual harassment – Peter de Vries's *Sauce for the Gander*, in which the heroine sets out in search of office pests, proving resistant to extraction, alas.

few of us would care to do without, however badly we may burn ourselves in the process.

'Office Friendships'

Eve is madly in love with Hugh
And Hugh is keen on Jim.
Charles is in love with very few
And few are in love with him.

Myra sits typing notes of love
With romantic pianist's fingers.
Dick turns his eyes to the heavens above
Where Fran's divine perfume lingers.

Nicky is rolling eyes and tits
And flaunting her wiggly walk.
Everybody is thrilled to bits
By Clive's suggestive talk.

Sex suppressed will go berserk,
But it keeps us all alive.
It's a wonderful change from wives and work
And it ends at half past five.

From *Pleasures of the Flesh* by Gavin Ewart, 1966

Dewy Eyes

. . . I worked most of one morning on this letter and being known for bad handwriting, I re-wrote it several times and took it to him. I stood waiting and looking at his new secretary. She had lovely dewy eyes and one of them quivered, almost with a wink, as she smiled with a terrible lack of innocence at me. She was very small. She leaned towards me for her pencil and as she did so I could see her breasts in her low blouse. I gazed helplessly at them and she, pleased by the effect she was having on me, looked up. In these few seconds Mr James had taken out his pen which had green ink in it and was saying:

'Why is it, I wonder, you never dot your "i"s?'

And was dotting them in green. He turned to look at me, I was startled by his voice. I couldn't speak. I began to sway, the room seemed to spin.

'He's fainting', said the girl archly.

I was. I clutched at the desk. Mr James jumped up and held me. Quickly the colour came back to my face and I was stuttering and blushing.

'Have you been smoking?' said Mr James to me with a sly glance at the girl.

'I don't smoke, sir', I said.

Mr James let go of me, gave me back the letter and sent me away. A delightful laugh came from behind the frosted glass of his door after I had left.

From *A Cab at the Door* by V. S. Pritchett, 1968

'Blondie there is ripe'

And speaking of debauchery ... There is a man at the office who deals with transfers to secondary school, a matter of such concern to the general public that it is necessary for him to have a little box of a room all to himself so that he can interview parents in private. This, at any rate, is the theory he has upheld successfully against all efforts to make him share a larger room, thus releasing his cubbyhole for the duplicator – which machine at present stands at the top of the stairs in such a position that very fat people are discouraged from ever visiting staff in the upper regions. On several occcasions when I have taken Mr Randall his tea, I have found him at work on pen and ink drawings. At first, he was quick to put them to one side, but as he came to recognise my footsteps he ceased to make any effort at concealment.

'Your pictures seem to tell a story,' I said to him one day last week.

'I'm glad of that,' he replied, without looking up, 'I'm a book illustrator. These are preliminary sketches.'

'Why do you work here, then?'

'Because, so underrated is the artist, his work doesn't bring in enough money to keep body and soul together, let alone support a wife and child.'

'Is that why we all had to work late last term, helping you to get the transfer notices out to parents?'

'You could say I know my priorities. Does that shock you?'

'I was shocked when I had to work so late.'

He put his pen down and looked at me. He is one of those pale men with straw hair which merges into ashy skin. His face looks grubby as if he becomes easily discouraged while shaving and his body has that sort of looseness which comes of never having tried very hard at anything.

He gives the impression that however hard you washed him he would never come up looking clean and fresh. Rumour has it he is going into the RAF. One wonders what they will make of him.

'You must be helped to overcome this tendency to be shocked,' he said. 'Otherwise, with your looks, you are going to have an exhausting time.'

I did not return to his office to collect his cup, but later, when I was washing up, he came behind me and put the cup in the basin. The sink is wedged into a corner of the store room and there isn't space for two people to stand side by side, so I didn't think anything of his standing behind me until he slid his hands beneath my breasts. I would not want to tell this to anyone but you, Sheila. The result quite startled me. My body behaved as though it wasn't part of me. While my mind was saying with admirable coolness, 'Hello, what is this?' my stomach muscles knotted and contracted in the most painful way and my breath came through my lips like steam out of a kettle. Then members of the general public came labouring up the stairs and began to negotiate the duplicator. Mr Randall removed his hands, which had wandered to my stomach to be rewarded with yet more surprising spasms, and departed.

The next day, he discovered some civil defence questionnaires which he had neglected to send to the three grammar schools. He asked the Education Officer if I could accompany him to the schools as I was familiar with the work and could help the school secretaries to complete the questionnaire. He said he had overlooked the forms which had to be returned to Head Office at the end of the week. As there was a lot of trouble over the last lot of forms which Mr Randall had overlooked, the Education Officer agreed to his.

The school secretaries did not need any help from me and we had finished distributing the forms before lunch. Mr Randall said that as he lived nearby and we had plenty of time, perhaps I would like to see some of the books he had illustrated. You know your Constance, Sheila. I was flattered as I think I have an eye for a good drawing; and I have to confess I was curious to see how an artist lives and to meet the artist's wife. If my reading is reliable, artists' wives are a very special breed.

As soon as we got into the house I experienced that sense of having gone deaf which I get when I enter empty buildings. 'When does your wife get home?' I asked. He said she was in Dorset, and pushed me into the sitting-room. He kissed me, bending my head back so hard I thought my neck must snap and getting one of his legs in between mine so that we were all tangled up and it was a wonder I didn't topple over with him on top of me. As we lurched round the room in an ungainly tango he contrived to get my dress unbuttoned and my bra unhooked. Had he cursed or implored me by name I would not have been so frightened; but he applied himself to his task as if I were not a person but a Christmas parcel he was endeavouring to tear open, some of the goodies already on view. I was surprised by how well-equipped I was to fight. The body has several sharp joints, each of which I used to some purpose. I also discovered that I had at some stage acquired a knowledge of the male anatomy and it was a shrewd placement of the knee joint which eventually brought an end to our engagement. The realisation that I could handle this situation gave me a feeling I can only describe as pure joy. When I had adjusted my clothing and he had recovered his breath, I said that I would like to see the books now.

He said, 'Never mind that. You'll make your way in life without having to use your head.'

By the time we got back to the office my legs had stopped shaking and I felt quite self-possessed, although one of the School Attendance Officers gave me a quizzing as I passed him in the doorway. Later, in the corridor, I overheard this man say to the Juvenile Employment Officer, 'I reckon Blondie there is ripe,' and he made a sucking noise as if messing with a juicy fruit ...

From *Letters from Constance* by Mary Hocking, 1992

The Effect of Two Martinis

... Possibly I should be proud of myself, because she is, after all, a decent and very attractive young girl of only twenty-four whom I can probably lay whenever I want to. (I have her scheduled vaguely somewhere ahead, probably in the weeks before the convention, when I will be using everybody in the Art Department a great deal.) I don't really know how I am supposed to feel. I do know that girls in their early twenties are easy and sweet. (Girls in their late twenties are easier but sad, and that isn't so sweet.) They are easy, I think, because they are sweet, and they are sweet, I think, because they are dumb.

On days when *I've* had two martinis for lunch, Jane's breast and legs can drive me almost wild as she parks her slender ass against the wall of one of the narrow corridors in the back offices near the Art Department when I stop to kid with her. Jane smiles a lot and is very innocent (she thinks I'm a very nice man, for example), although she is not, of course, without some sex experience, about which she boasts laughingly when I taunt her with being a virgin and denies laughingly when I taunt her with being a whore. I make teasing, rather mechanical and juvenile jokes (I've made them all before to other girls and ladies in one variation or another) about her eye or sweater or the good or bad life I pretend she is leading as I lean down almost slavering toward the front of her skirt (I don't know how she can bear me in these disgusting moments – but she can) and gaze lecherously over the long stretch of her thighs underneath, even though I know already I would probably find her legs a little thin when I had her undressed and would probably describe her as a bit too skinny if I ever spoke about her afterward to anyone . . .

From *Something Happened* by Joseph Heller, 1974

Adjusting his Dress

One January day, a grey shawl of rain came down the Liffey from the west, and I thought to go back early to the office and peck out on one of the typewriters the beginning of a short story. (I started at least one story a week, confident each time that if I could only finish it, Frank O'Connor and Sean O'Faoláin would fold their tents in despair.) As I entered the public office I heard a female voice coming from the alcove where we hung our coats. Evidently, two girls were having a gossip, and it occurred to me to tiptoe over, and leap in front of them with a heart-stopping yell. And so I crept softly to the alcove and made my leap. As for the yell, it hung frozen and unuttered.

Columbia employed a number of 'reps', whose task it was to travel the country hymning the glories of, and taking orders for, Warner Baxter in *Crime Doctor's Strangest Case* and the Three Stooges in *Crash Goes the Hash*. We, the deskbound, envied them as free spirits, and one of them – their doyen, in fact – was at present in the alcove furiously coupling with my bespectacled *vis-à-vis*, the amorphous Dolores.

She was hiccupping as her back thudded against the door leading to the basement. When they saw me, they faltered in their exertions, then quite literally ground to a halt. I stood as if petrified, one forefinger uplifted and my lips still rounded for the 'Boo!' that never came. Probably, I looked like an idiot, but at least I had the consolation that they were not in a mood to say so. As the earth showed no inclination to open beneath my feet, I went to my desk, picked up a pencil and began to scribble on the bare wood without the formality of using a sheet of paper. I was eighteen and almost certainly felt more guilty than they did.

The 'rep' came over to me, and I saw that in adjusting his dress he had skipped a buttonhole so that his flies pointed outwards in a false tumescence. He gave me a raffish Errol Flynn smile.

'Listen,' he said. 'Be a good man and say nothing. You don't want to get the girl into trouble.'

As green as I was, I could still recognise a remark that dictated its own riposte, but even if I had had the audacity to deliver it, there was no time, for he went skipping out into Middle Abbey Street, leaving me with Dolores. She came over, tugging at her skirt, and to my horror I caught a glimpse of old-fashioned pink knickers, mercifully elasticised just above the knees. She sat on her accustomed chair, looked demurely at me through her bottle lenses and said: 'Did you see that fella gone out?'

I nodded, dumbly.

She said: 'Nobody here likes him. He's always trying to talk to me.'

From *Out After Dark* by Hugh Leonard, 1989

Right on the Yellow Carpet

—JILL: You should've seen some of the things that went on in my last office! Honestly, I wasn't sorry to leave. One of the Directors wanted to have me in the lift.

—JANICE: Nothing happens here. It's too big. You never know when someone won't come in. My sister used to work for a publisher. There was this evening when she had to work late and there was no-one else in the office – you wouldn't get that here for a start – and her boy-friend came to see her. He wanted to have her there, at once. She said no, certainly not. You know, it was just cold lino in her office and all full of desks and chairs and typewriters. So he opened the door into the Chairman's office, and said what about here? This has a carpet and lots of room and all. And my sister said she couldn't, not in the Chairman's office! In the end they did, had it off right in the middle, and the next morning she went in and there was this stain right on the yellow carpet. She was so embarrassed! She said she thought everyone would notice and guess what it was, so she stood on it to cover it up.

From *The Office* by Jonathan Gathorne-Hardy, 1970

Getting Laid (Official)

The company has a policy about getting laid. It's okay.

And everybody seems to know that (although it's not spelled out in any of the personnel manuals). Talking about getting laid is even more okay than doing it, but doing it is okay too, although talking about getting laid with your own wife is never okay. (Imagine: 'Boy, what a crazy bang I got from my wife last night!' That wouldn't be nice, not with gentlemen you associate with in business who might know her.) But getting laid with somebody else's wife is very okay, and so is talking about it, provided the husband is not with the company or somebody anybody knows and likes. The company is in favor of getting laid if it is done with a dash of élan, humor, vulgarity, and skill, without emotion, with girls who are young and pretty or women who are older and foreign or glamorous in some other way, without too much noise and with at least some token gesture toward discretion, and without scandal, notoriety, or any of the other serious complications of romance. Falling in love, for example, is *not* usually okay, although marrying someone else right after a divorce is, and neither is 'having an affair,' at least not for a man.

Getting laid (or talking about getting laid) is an important component of each of the company conventions and a decisive consideration in the selection of a convention site; and the salesmen who succeed in getting laid there soonest are likely to turn out to be the social heroes of the convention, though not necessarily the envy. (That will depend on the quality of whom they find to get laid with.) Getting laid at conventions is usually done in groups of three or four (two decide to go out and try and take along one or two others). Just about everybody in the company gets laid (or seems to), or at least talks as though he does (or did). In fact, it has become virtually *comme il faut* at company conventions for even the very top and very old, impotent men in the company – in fact, *especially* those – to allude slyly and boastfully to their own and each other's sexual misconduct in their welcoming addresses, acknowledgements, introductions, and informal preambles to speeches on graver subjects...

From *Something Happened* by Joseph Heller, 1974

'Chamois comes off on a girl's skirt'

About this time, Mr Clark, the sullen invoice clerk, took his pretty assistant up to the chamois room. It was a small warm room with a U-shaped alley between the bins of chamois leather that reached to the ceiling. The clerks were not supposed to leave the office for the warehouse without good reason. Clark, always defiant, before the amazed eyes of all the office, snapped his fingers at the girl and off they went, she pitter-pattering obediently along, up the stairs, into the wobbling lift and up to the room.

'I've got a query', he said as he left the office.

'Four skins short?' Mr Drake, the lewd one, said.

Like the term 'belly splits' or 'let's have a look at the flesh side', this was a daily office joke.

'Hobbs, Hobbs', moaned the cashier. 'I don't like a young girl like that being in the warehouse . . .'

'Quite, sir, certainly, sir. I have to go up anyway'.

In a few minutes he came back with the girl who in a minute or two was followed by Clark. The girl was sent to work at another desk. And Hobbs and Clark sat opposite to each other, staring into each other's eyes. I brought a stock book to Hobbs in the middle of the stare.

'I've been in this trade twelve years and one thing I have learned is that chamois comes off on a girl's skirt', said Hobbs.

'You bastard', said Clark with one of his rare smiles. 'Just in the nick of time'.

'Don't mention it. He saved others, himself he could not save. You owe me a drink'.

The cashier groaned his private gratitude to Hobbs and Hobbs being a thorough man, took the older sister for a ride in the warehouse lift. A ride with Hobbs was always an experience and she came back with a dreamy look in her eyes.

From *A Cab at the Door* by V. S. Pritchett, 1968

'Couples'

Upstairs Mr Goldberg has his secretary over a desk,
Her panties round her ankles . . .

From *The Deceptive Grin of the Gravel Porters* by Gavin Ewart, 1968

'What about tonight?'

Joan came in, pad in hand.

'C. J. wants to see you at eleven,' she said.

'Stuff C. J.,' he said. 'I'm sorry about yesterday, darling.'

'It was one of those things,' she said.

'It did happen, didn't it? You did come to my home yesterday?'

'Well of course I did, silly.'

He held his hand out towards her across his desk and she stroked it briefly. Her skirt was working its way up her leg, but today she didn't pull it down.

It had begun to rain. A train clattered along the embankment.

'We'd better start work,' he said.

'I suppose so.'

He was shy of dictating to her. It seemed so foolish, when you wanted to make love, sending letters about mangoes.

'What about tonight?' he said.

'I suppose I could get a baby-sitter.'

'What about your husband?'

'He's away – on business.'

'Tonight, then.'

'Tonight.'

'I suppose we'd better start, then.'

'I suppose so.'

'Your breasts are wonderful.'

She blushed.

'To the Secretary, Artificial Sweetening Additives Research Council. Dear Sir . . .'

From *The Death of Reginald Perrin* by David Nobbs, 1978

The End of an Affair

. . . A middle-aged man and a middle-aged woman, their food untouched, were deep in an important-seeming discussion. From the woman's miserable expression and the man's haggard one, Gryce deduced a long-running affair that was going sour. That was where a casual glass of wine could lead you if you weren't too careful.

'Love's young dream,' said Pam softly.

'The long-suffering Cargill from Salary Accounts,' murmured Seeds. 'The lady, on the other hand, is definitely not Mrs Cargill, much though her ambitions might lie in that direction.'

'A certain obstacle in the shape of the present Mrs Cargill?' sniggered Gryce. It was good to be privy to office gossip so soon.

'The very substantial shape, from all I gather. Mark you, we can offer you rather more shall we say above-board examples of true love running smooth.'

'Don't be bitchy!' Pam chided, enjoying herself.

From *Office Life* by Keith Waterhouse, 1978

Office Formalities (1)

The boss gave a lift to the head
Of the typing department, and said
  He had rogered her (twice)
  And found it was nice
To be called 'Mr Pritchard' in bed.

Richard Usborne (n.d.)

Office Formalities (2)

Hundreds of times, in secret maiden speculations about love, the girl Una
had surmised that it would be embarrassing to meet a man the morning
after you had yielded to his caress. It had been perplexing – one of those
mysteries of love over which virgins brood between chapters of novels,
of which they diffidently whisper to other girls when young married
friends are amazingly going to have a baby. But she found it natural to
smile up at Walter . . . In this varnished, daytime office neither of them
admitted their madness of meeting hands.

He merely stooped over her desk and said sketchily, 'Mornin', little
Goldie.'

Then for hours he seemed to avoid her.

From *The Job* by Sinclair Lewis, 1917

Delayed in the Office

They entered a public house at the corner of a street. It was warm there,
and crowded, and quite attractively noisy. Fairy lights were draped on a
Christmas tree just inside the door because Christmas was less than six
weeks away. Men like Tommy Blyth, in overcoats with furred collars and
with reddish faces, were standing by a coal fire with glasses in their
hands. One of them had his right arm round the waist of C.S. and E.'s
black-haired receptionist.

'What's your poison, Angela?' Gordon Spelle asked, and she said she'd
like some sherry.

'Dry?'

'Oh, it doesn't matter – well, medium, actually.'

He didn't approach the bar but led her into a far corner and sat her down at a table. It was less crowded there and rather dimly lit. He said he wouldn't be a minute.

People were standing at the bar, animatedly talking. Some of the men had taken off their overcoats. All of them were wearing suits, most of them grey or blue but a few of a more extravagant shade, like Gordon Spelle's. Occasionally a particular man, older and stouter than his companions, laughed raucously, swaying backwards on his heels. On a bar-stool to this man's right, in a red wool dress with a chiffon scarf at her throat, sat Miss Ivygale. The red wool coat that had been hanging just inside the outer office door all day hung on the arm of the raucous man: Miss Ivygale, Angela deduced, was intent on staying a while, or at least as long as the man was agreeable to looking after her coat for her. 'You'll find it friendly at C.S. and E.,' Miss Ivygale had said. 'A generous firm.' Miss Ivygale looked as though she'd sat on her barstool every night for the past twenty-three years, which was the length of time she'd been at C.S. and E.

'Alec Hemp,' Gordon Spelle said, indicating the man who had Miss Ivygale's coat on his arm.

The name occurred on C.S. and E.'s stationery: *A. R. Hemp*. It was there with other names, all of them in discreet italics, strung out along the bottom of the writing paper that had *C.S. and E.* and the address at the top: *S. P. Bakewell, T. P. Cooke, N. N. E. Govier, I. D. Jackson, A. F. Norris, P. Onniman, A. R. Hemp*, the directors of the C.S. and E. board.

'That's been going on for years,' Gordon Spelle said. He handed her her sherry and placed on the table in front of him a glass of gin and Britvic orange juice. His droopy eye had closed, as if tired. His other, all on its own, looked a little beady.

'Sorry?'

'Pam Ivygale and Alec Hemp.'

'Oh.'

'It's why she never married anyone else.'

'I see.'

Miss Ivygale's brisk manner in the office and her efficient probing when she'd interviewed Angela had given Angela the impression that she'd lived entirely for her work. There was no hint of a private life about Miss Ivygale, and certainly no hint of any love affair beyond a love affair with C.S. and E.

'Alec,' Gordon Spelle said, 'has a wife and four children in Brighton.'

'I see.'

'Office romance.' His droopy eye opened and gazed bleakly at her, contrasting oddly with the busyness of the other eye. He said it was disgraceful that all this should be so, that a woman should be messed up the way Mr Hemp for twenty-three years had messed up Miss Ivygale. Everyone knew, he said, that Alec Hemp had no intention of divorcing his wife: he was stringing Miss Ivygale along. 'Mind you, though,' he added, 'she's tricky.'

'She seems very nice –'

'Oh, Pam's all right. Now, tell me all about yourself' . . .

He insisted on buying her another drink and while he was at the bar she wondered when, or if, she was going to meet the people he'd mentioned, the other employees of C.S. and E. Miss Ivygale had narrowed her eyes in her direction and then had looked away, as if she couldn't quite place her. The black-haired receptionist had naturally not remembered her face when she'd come into the bar with the two men. The only person Gordon Spelle had so far introduced her to was the man called Tommy Blyth, who had joined the group around the fire and was holding the hand of a girl.

'It's the C.S. and E. pub,' Gordon Spelle said when he returned with the drinks. 'There isn't a soul here who isn't on the strength.' He smiled at her, his bad eye twitching. 'I like you, you know.' She smiled back at him, not knowing how to reply. He picked up her left hand and briefly squeezed it.

'Don't trust that man, Angela,' Miss Ivygale said, passing their table on her way to the Ladies. She stroked the back of Gordon Spelle's neck. 'Terrible man,' she said . . .'

In the lavatory Gordon Spelle swore as he urinated. Typical of bloody Pam Ivygale to go nosing in like that. He wouldn't have brought the girl to the Arms at all if he'd thought Ivygale would be soaked to the gills, hurling abuse about like bloody snowballs. God alone knew what kind of a type the girl thought he was now. Girls like that had a way of thinking you a sexual maniac if you so much as took their arm to cross a street. There'd been one he'd known before who'd come from the same kind of area, Plymouth or Bristol or somewhere. Bigger girl actually, five foot ten she must have been, fattish. 'Touch of the West Countries', he'd said when she'd opened her mouth, the first time he'd used the expression. Tamar Dymond she'd been called, messy bloody creature.

Gordon Spelle combed his hair and then decided that his tie needed to be reknotted. He removed his pepper-coloured jacket and his waistcoat and took the tie off, cocking up the collar of his striped blue shirt in order to make the operation easier. His wife, Peggy, would probably be reading a story to the younger of their two children, since she generally did so at about seven o'clock. As he reknotted his tie, he imagined his wife sitting by the child's bed reading a Topsy and Tim book.

'Oh, say you're going to Luton,' Miss Ivygale said. 'Tell her it's all just cropped up in the last fifteen minutes.'

Mr Hemp shook his head. He pointed out that rather often recently he'd telephoned his wife at seven o'clock to say that what had cropped up in the last fifteen minutes was the fact that unexpectedly he had to go to Luton. Mr Hemp had moved away from the man called Dil, closer to Miss Ivygale. They were speaking privately, Mr Hemp in a lower voice than Miss Ivygale. The man called Dil was talking to another man.

Standing by herself and not being spoken to by anyone, Angela was feeling happy. It didn't matter that no one was speaking to her, or paying her any other kind of attention. She felt warm and friendly, quite happy to be on her own while Gordon Spelle was in the Gents and Mr Hemp and Miss Ivygale talked to each other privately. She liked him, she thought as she stood there: she liked his old-fashioned manners and the way he'd whistled 'Smoke Gets in Your Eyes', and his sympathy over her being new. She smiled at him when he returned from the Gents. It was all much nicer than the German wine firm, or the laminates firm.

'Hullo,' he said in a whisper, staring at her.

'It was nice of you to bring me here,' she said, whispering also.

'Nice for me, too,' said Gordon Spelle.

Mr Hemp went away to telephone his wife. The telephone was behind Angela, in a little booth against the wall. The booth was shaped like a sedan chair, except that it didn't have any shafts to carry it by. Angela had noticed it when she'd been sitting down with Gordon Spelle. She hadn't known then that it contained a telephone and had wondered at the presence of a sedan chair in a bar. But several times since then people had entered it and each time a light had come on, revealing a telephone and a pile of directories.

'Because they only told me ten minutes ago,' Mr Hemp was saying. 'Because the bloody fools couldn't make their minds up, if you can call them minds.'

Gordon Spelle squeezed her hand and Angela squeezed back because it seemed a friendly thing to do. She felt sorry for him because he had only one good eye. It was the single defect in his handsome face. It gave him a tired look, and suggested suffering.

'I wish you'd see it my way,' Mr Hemp was saying crossly in the sedan chair. 'God damn it, I don't *want* to go to the bloody place.'

'I really must go,' Angela murmured, but Gordon Spelle continued to hold her hand . . .

From 'Office Romances' in *Angels at the Ritz* by William Trevor, 1975

'Are you married?'

'And what about you? Are you married?'

'Oh, very much so.'

They were in the Pressings wine bar, on the Friday evening. Gryce, sipping his second glass of Soave (he should have ordered a bottle and been done with it) congratulated himself again on the speed at which this first clandestine rendezvous had been arrived at. Nor was he in any doubt that clandestine was the right word: it was Pam, not he, who had headed for the discreet corner under the stairs.

He still couldn't believe it. Only four days, well, four and a half days, had gone by since that lunch they'd had with Seeds in the Buttery, yet here they were with their hands practically touching across a table made out of a sherry barrel, in a whitewashed cellar off the beaten track, discussing every subject under the sun. Including the fact that Pam had a husband called Peter who often worked far into the night, or laid claim to working far into the night more like, as an inspector of listed buildings for the Department of the Environment. Ideal.

So however discouraging – or anyway not actively encouraging, in fact quite cool really – Pam might have been in the relatively anonymous territory of the seventh floor, once within the vertical cloisters of the lift-shaft she was camaraderie itself. Gryce had not yet had the pleasure of travelling up with her in the morning – she was a notorious late-arriver, indeed it was a standing joke that Mrs Rashman would sing out, 'Here comes the early bird!' when she rolled in at ten past nine – but he seized with both hands the opportunity of travelling down with her in the evening. While Pam might be the last to arrive each day it could be said in her favour that she was also the last to leave. Gryce found that by loitering at the glass doors of the seventh floor foyer until he saw her gathering up her handbag, then summoning the lift and keeping his finger pressed on the 'Open' button, he had every chance of inducing her to run for it. This she did with the scuttering, crab-like movement common to all last-minute lift passengers. To recover her composure, as the lift descended to ground level and Gryce slid his shoulderblades up and down against the vinyl panelling, Pam would peer into her handbag and ruminate: 'Now what have I forgotten?' Gryce took to saying: 'Door key? Purse? Season ticket? Adequate supply of the firm's ballpoint pens?' and thus a bond between them was forged.

Gryce shared the lift with Pam four times in his first working week:

[316]

not bad going. It would have been five but for his over-zealousness on Tuesday when he had found himself stranded in Catering (Administration); he wondered if Pam had been disappointed not to see a certain familiar figure holding the lift-doors open.

But they had made up for that. On one occasion – yesterday, Thursday, red-letter day – she had been so slow in clearing her desk that the building had just about emptied and they had had the lift to themselves. Gryce had been able to push the frontiers of their relationship forward a little by remarking, after they had enjoyed the familiar exchange about what Pam might have forgotten, 'You know, I'll swear these lifts are centrally-heated!' To which Pam had replied, 'It's air-conditioning, so-called. They pump in hot air all through the summer and cold air in winter.' Gryce had then made a great show of wiping imaginary beads of sweat from his brow. Pam had responded by puckering her lips and exhaling heavily – a genteel version of Beazley blowing up his nostrils – and making a fanning motion with her rolled-up *Evening Standard*. A cosy moment. It was going very well.

Gryce, however, was not one to run before he could walk and failing any luck on the Buttery front next week he was content to let their lift relationship blossom as slowly as might be necessary. He was, after all, in no hurry. It would be his first extra-marital affair, his first affair ever, actually, if you discounted his courtship of Peggy back at Docks and Inland Waterways, and he would just as soon take it slowly . . .

From *Office Life* by Keith Waterhouse, 1978

Literary Love

But within the past three or four weeks, a new factor had arisen to influence his outlook. He was puzzled to know how it had happened (for it had not yet occurred to him that despite a fairly well balanced temperament he was an imaginative and romantic young man), but he was infatuated with Mrs Nanette Hinckson, the chief stenographer and the Manager's secretary. Most of the time he could control himself – he was sure he had successfully concealed his feelings from everyone – but his condition caused him uneasiness, gave him a feeling of uncertainty and instability. Whenever he was in the presence of Mrs Hinckson he was aware of a tenseness and an unnatural inclination to take deep breaths; he felt an ache in his stomach; he stammered and felt his face going hot.

Toward his mother, these past weeks, he had felt a sense of guilt, because he had not been able to tell her of his infatuation; some intuition warned him that his audience would not applaud, that his audience would be unsympathetic, might even subject him to ridicule and contumely. It was a weakness which must be concealed from her, but the very concealment created guilt and a feeling of self-reproach.

He considered that it was foolish of him to have become enamoured of this lady. It was true that she was charming and attractive – physically as well as in manner – but he should have remembered that he was only a black boy, whereas she was a coloured lady of good family. His complexion was dark brown; hers was a pale olive. His hair was kinky; hers was full of large waves and gleaming. He was a poor boy with hardly any education, the son of a cook; she was well off and of good education and good breeding. He was low-class; she was middle-class.

Last night he had done something he considered daring – something which he even regarded as critical. From an old, battered copy of the *Complete Works of Shakespeare* – a volume passed on to him by Peter de Germain, the eldest son of the family – Horace had copied a passage from *As You Like It* which he deemed appropriate as an expression of his feelings.

It was in bed that the really daring idea had taken shape. Why couldn't he leave this quotation on Mrs Hinckson's desk? He would be the first to enter the office from to-morrow morning. No one would see him putting it on her desk. And if he got out of bed now and copied it on another piece of paper in block letters it would be perfectly anonymous. The thought that she would be reading something which his hand had written – words which, though not his own, represented his feelings – would be enough, he knew, to give him a deep satisfaction and relief.

From *A Morning at the Office* by Edgar Mittelholzer, 1950

A Puzzleheaded Girl

One November Saturday afternoon, working overtime, they sent out for lunch; the paper cups were still on the desks when doorman Fisher told Debrett that a girl was waiting for an interview. They still needed a filing clerk. One of the typists, a boyish girl named Charlotte and called Sharlie, went out to look her over. A young seventeen, perhaps, dressed like a poor schoolgirl, she sat reading a small book, her light brown hair over her plain grave face. She looked up, a sweet and wistful expression appeared. Sharlie withdrew, and reported: 'She's just a high-school kid reading art to impress the customers, an innocent – doesn't know she's alive yet.'

Augustus Debrett, a stubby dark man with large hazel eyes, a round head, with pale face turned blue with the winter light, sat between two large windows, behind a big polished desk on which was nothing but a blotter and an inkstand.

She stood for a moment in the doorway looking at the room; the light fell on her. He saw a diffident girl in a plain tan blouse, a tight navy-blue skirt, very short at a time when skirts were not short, round knees, worn walking shoes; she wore no overcoat. 'Miss Lawrence, come in.'

She had a chin dimple and a dimple in her left cheek, a flittering smile; and when the smile went, her face returned to its gravity, its almost sadness. She had a full, youthful figure. She said she was eighteen. She sat down, keeping her knees together and holding her skirt on her knees with her brown purse. The little book she placed on the desk in front of her. It was a book in English on French symbolism. He looked at her face a moment before he began to question her. 'Surely Honor Lawrence is a New England name? It sounds like Beacon Hill,' and he laughed kindly in case it was not Beacon Hill. No answer. She said she had experience and wanted a good wage, and then she named a low wage and said she had no references: 'Only my schoolteacher.' 'Where was your last job?' After a pause, she said, 'I could start now if you liked.' Debrett engaged her. 'Come on Monday. If you've been out of a job for some time, you may be short of money. Do you need money now? I can give you an advance.' 'Oh, no, I have money.' She got up and went to the door. There she turned and said quietly, 'Thank you.' As she was going out, Tom Zero, the young lawyer, one of the partners, entered. He was short, slender, debonair and so swarthy that he was looked at curiously in restaurants in the South, handsome and dark-eyed from two olive-skinned parents from southern Europe, fastidious but with a faint sweet personal odour, like grass and olives; ambitious, bright and selfish.

'I've engaged Miss Lawrence as filing clerk: she's coming on Monday,' said Debrett. Zero looked sharply. 'Have you looked at her references? Can she type?' 'Yes,' said Debrett. The girl looked straight into Zero's eyes and moved away. Later, Debrett thought about her, her poverty and her book . . .

From *The Puzzleheaded Girl* by Christina Stead, 1968

Facing Facts, Alas

He would give the girl up. It was quite absurd to risk his promotion: the Secretaryship could never go to a man who was domestically unsound.

He began to imagine the conversation with Judith when he would tell her that they could not meet again, setting the scene in her room, even adding such superfluous and, indeed, ludicrous, properties as a valedictory bottle of champagne and the wearing of one of the new ties he had bought yesterday. For a moment he found a certain pleasure in this elaborate prefiguring of his loss, but then he thought of leaving her for the last time and the ensuing emptiness of his life. It struck him afresh how miraculous their coming together had been – not only the mechanics of it (for, after all, a man with a nubile son must expect to encounter young girls) but her simple acquiescence. He could never expect to form a relationship again with a girl of this kind – a girl with slim waist and ankles, whose parents respectably lived in Aylesbury, who telephoned and asked him to meet her.

At the beginning of their meetings he had thought – carried away by the long touch of her hand in cinemas, the inexhaustible pleasures at being able to gaze freely at her face, the return of simple, urgent, conspiratorial emotions that he had imagined himself incapable of ever experiencing again or, rather, had totally forgotten could exist – that he had been plunged into a romantic and deepening love affair, and had prepared himself for, welcomed, the prospect of his life being utterly changed. How easily in those days could he have quitted Dorothy and his children, the nexus of house, investments, insurance policies, that now seemed a totally unshiftable anchor to the coral-reef existence he had patiently made for himself over the long years. But the affair had never ripened: it had stayed green, ingrown, deformed; and now he could not tell whether its failure was through Judith's shallowness or his own lack of courage – for he realized that the adolescent dream he had had of giving up 'everything' for her was incapable of being translated into reality. At fifty the ideas governing a man's life cannot be those of romantic love but the realities he has himself created – the fear of his son's scorn, his pity for his wife, his desire to fulfil himself in his work. And so imperceptibly he had moved into a furtive, day-to-day conception of the affair, accepting what crumbs Judith threw him, scarcely attempting to impose his own pattern on it.

He must give the girl up. For a moment he stood at the door of his office, realizing almost with surprise that he could, if he allowed himself, tip over into a paroxysm of self-pity, and feeling already the prick of tears behind his eyes that might become a storm such as he had never experienced since his youth.

From *The Father's Comedy* by Roy Fuller, 1961

True Love

Annie's eyes were bright and her attention was almost painful, but she did not laugh as much as the others. It was not her way. That would not quite do for Sam, and without leaving the rest of them he turned to his right and concentrated his whole attention for a moment on her. She looked back at him fearlessly, sitting solid and composed in her peculiar white dress.

'Are you enjoying yourself?'

Annie nodded, but that was not enough for him.

'You know, I've remembered now what it is, I mean who it is, you remind me of, Annie. It's a French picture by Monet, or Manet, it doesn't really matter which, a girl, or perhaps a boy, dressed in white, and sitting at a café table, all in shade, under a striped awning, but there's very bright sunshine beyond that, and there's some older people at the table too, with glasses of something in front of them, wine I suppose, but none of them are really looking at each other.'

'I'm sorry you don't know whether it was a boy or a girl,' said Annie mildly. He saw that she had not given in.

'You haven't been with us as long as the others. I should like . . .' He was improvising. 'I should like to give you a present. The best! There's no point at all in a present unless it's the best one can give.'

'I don't know what the best would be, Mr Brooks.' She was not worried.

It was a game.

'I shall give you a ring.'

They had all of them been with him in the studio and knew how dexterous he was, but none of them would have believed that he could take the inch of gold wire still dangling from the champagne bottle, pierce the end through one of the red currants and give it three twists or flicks so that the currant was transfixed, a jewel on which the blond light shone. His broad fingers held the wire as neatly as a pair of pliers.

'Well, Annie.'

Annie had been keeping her hands under the table, but now she spread them out on the stiff-feeling tablecloth. They were pinkish and freckled, but delicate, not piano-player's hands, not indeed as practical as one would have expected, thin and tender. After some hesitation, as though making a difficult selection, Sam Brooks picked up the left hand and most ingeniously put the currant ring onto the third finger, compressing it to make it fit exactly.

The others watched in silence. Annie did not know what to say or do, so she said nothing, and left her hand where it was on the table. Something inside her seemed to move and unclose ...

'I'm not leaving because of the overtime, Mr Brooks. I'm leaving because I love you.'

Halted on the half turn, he looked almost frightened.

'Do you mean you're in love with me?'

'No, I didn't say that. I said I loved you.'

So deep was his habit of demanding and complaining that he scarecely knew what to do with such a gift. Something had to be done, of course. 'You're very young,' he attempted. 'For some reason Establishment never bothered to tell me anything about when they took you on, but I know you're very young. In a few years' time you'll meet someone your own age –'

'You've read that some time in some book or paper,' Annie interrupted. 'You can't just quite think which one it is at the moment, but it'll come back to you sooner or later.'

He took off his glasses. It was capitulation. He stood reproved now by a delicate blur, the mere shape of a girl.

'I had no idea,' he said.

'That's what I was getting at. You've no idea about others, and you don't notice what makes them suffer. Do you remember the ring with the red currant?'

Sam floundered. 'Did you have one? I think I remember your having one.'

'You gave it me.'

'Have you kept it, then?'

'I would have done, if it hadn't begun to go off.'

She almost felt like asking him to put his glasses back. Otherwise, she wouldn't be able to go on much longer without touching him.

'Dear Annie,' he said to her, 'I don't think I can talk to you here. I want to take you out with me somewhere. There's only one café open now that's the Demos. We'll go and have a drink and start from the beginning.'

Her happiness was greater than she could bear.

'That'll be very nice.'

'It won't be all that nice,' said Sam, feeling compunction, and amazement at himself for feeling it. Annie, for her part, knew that unlike many in BH he wasn't given to feeling he needed a drink. Their lives were shaking into pieces. 'What are we going to do, Annie?' he asked in bewilderment. She put her arms round. Good-bye, Asra, she thought. God knows what's going to become of you now.

From *Human Voices* by Penelope Fitzgerald, 1980

[322]

Nineteen

ODDS AND SODS

Because ritual and repetition are such important ingredients of office life, matters like going to the lavatory – as much to gossip or escape as for anything else – the arrival of morning coffee or taking a stroll down the corridor loom large in the daily round, breaking the monotony and lending some kind of shape or pattern to the day. The nuts and bolts of office life – taking the lift, waiting one's turn for the photocopier, coping with the telephone (confidently, the receiver tucked under the chin, the hands scribbling or sorting through papers; timidly, as though it were a serpent coiled to strike) – all produce their own elaborate rites, familiar emollients to elevate the tedious and make palatable the passing of time.

'She's in a meeting'

Authors – they wanted to know why publication date was always being postponed. The phone would ring. Whereupon Ivy, in her highly affected drawing-room accent, would loudly reply above the auditory effects of our office, 'Mrs Hawkins is in a meeting, I'm afraid. Can I take a message? No, I don't know when she'll be back. No I can't disturb her, she's in a meeting.' I discovered, after enquiring, that it was an old tradition of the firm, started by Martin York, to say 'in' a meeting, not 'at' a meeting. I supposed 'in' sounded more immersed and not to be disturbed. Ivy had the knack of making 'in a meeting' sound indignant right from the start, as if the very idea of telephoning merely to ask for someone who was thus occupied was an outrage ...

From *A Far Cry from Kensington* by Muriel Spark, 1988

'Kin I 'elp yew?'

Everthorpe left, and Robyn sat down. The two women behind the reception desk avoided her eye. One was typing and the other was operating the switchboard. Every minute or so the telephone operator intoned in a bored sing-song, 'J. Pringle & Sons good morning kin I 'elp yew?', and then, 'Puttin' yew threw,' or 'Sorree, there's no reply.' Between calls she murmured inaudibly to her companion and stroked her platinum-blonde hair-do as if it were an ailing pet. Robyn looked around the room. There were framed photographs and testimonials on the panelled walls, and some bits of polished machinery in a glass case. On a low table in front of her were some engineering trade magazines and a copy of the *Financial Times*. It seemed to her that the world could not possibly contain a more boring room.

From *Nice Work* by David Lodge, 1988

Platinum-throated

Her phone had begun ringing; she excused herself by raising her hand. Then, in a voice that was suddenly sweet, efficient, platinum-throated, slightly breathy, she said,

'Good morning, Donald Vanci's office? I'm sorry, Don's stepped away from his desk. May I take your number and have him get back to you?' Smoothly disengaging her pen from my fingers, she located her While You Were Out pad and wrote down a name. Then, repeating product codes and amounts, she began to take a complex message. I wanted slightly to leave, but it would have been brusque to do so. What with Ray's poster and the roasting chicken, our interchange had passed just barely beyond office civility into the realm of human conversation, and thus had to be terminated conversationally: etiquette required me to wait until her phone duty was done in order to exchange one last sentence with her, unless the message she was taking was clearly going to go on for more than three minutes, in which case Tina, who knew the conventions well, would release me – cued first by some 'Gee, I'm taking off now' movement from me (pulling up the pants, checking for my wallet, a joke salute) – with a mouthed 'Bye!' . . .

From *The Mezzanine* by Nicholson Baker, 1988

'Karl Marx here'

There were about ten people in the room when the telephone rang. I answered it. A man with a thick accent, the origin of which I could not determine, asked for Mr Bevan. I asked who was speaking. 'Karl Marx here.' Karl Marx? 'Sorry,' I said, 'I didn't catch the name. Who?' 'Karl Marx.' I couldn't possibly interrupt the meeting and tell Bevan that Karl

Marx was on the line for him. Was it a hoax? 'Who?' I asked again, desperately; this could go on all morning. Bevan evidently felt the same. He got up and snatched the telephone from me. Everyone else stared at me. I felt like a man in a Bateman cartoon: The Man Who Thought Karl Marx Was On The Telephone. 'Bevan here. Who? Oh, Car Mart. Yes. Good. I'll send my driver round this afternoon.' 'Who did you think it was?' Bevan asked me. 'Well, it sounded to me like Karl Marx,' I said shamefacedly. Bevan grunted. I tried to sink through the floor. The Copy Director saved me. 'I had that chap on the 'phone the other day,' he said, 'and I could hardly understand a word.'

From *Memoirs of an Advertising Man* by John Mellors, 1976

Mistaken for a Man

Then my boss offered to take me into the firm as a full-time member of her staff of one. I accepted gladly though for me no job could ever be more than a seaside romance with respectability.

My duties as a permanent employee were different from the free-lance work. I made cocoa and washed up the cups; I added up my wages and subtracted my income tax. I typed letters and filed the replies; I answered the telephone and learned how odd my voice sounded to other people. A telephone conversation with an unknown woman client with a baritone voice ended in her saying, 'Your voice is very deep. It's almost as low as mine and I'm frequently taken for a man – over the 'phone, I mean.'

After that, I tried to round out my voice and pitch it lower. I never found a way of eliminating its jangling quality as of a ruined piano that I noticed when I later heard myself speak on a tape-recorder. Almost immediately I began to be offered appointments with fear over the telephone. These were less sinister than the calls I received at home. Receptionists of other firms, who had originally dialled our number in error, rang a second time from a switchboard on which other people were listening.

From *The Naked Civil Servant* by Quentin Crisp, 1968

Solzhenitsyn Strikes

I had been at work for about a week when, to my horror, the telephone on my desk – which had been mercifully silent hitherto – began to ring in a loud, insistent way. I had lost none of my old dread of the telephone in the intervening years: I jolted back in my seat, like a man who has touched an electric fence; my heart began to pound; I stared at the loathsome instrument as though it were a serpent coiled upon my desk before eventually picking it up. 'A Mr Solzhenitsyn wishes to speak to you,' the lady on the switchboard informed me in a disapproving voice: 'He sounds like a foreign gentleman.' In those days the bearded sage was not yet the household name he has since become, but he did ring bells of a kind. 'Put him through,' I commanded in my most impressive tones, after which a guttural-sounding voice began to tell me at great length about his next book, and to ask if we might be interested in publishing it. Dimly aware that I had been plunged straight into the heart of the publishing business, and that I might, in my first week, be about to pull off the coup of a lifetime, I asked the great man to hold on and, clamping my hand over the receiver, turned to my room-mate for advice, my eyes revolving in their sockets with excitement. 'I've got that chap Soljey-something on the line,' I said. 'Isn't he one of those Russians who write about prison camps and people standing around with snow on their boots? What should I tell him?' 'Never heard of him,' my colleague replied, busily buffing his nails, one leg crooked over the arm of his chair: 'I should get rid of him if you can. He's almost certainly a maniac. Put him through to editorial.' Anxiously I turned back to work – only to find Solzhenitsyn inexplicably convulsed with mirth. The brute turned out to be my old friend Tom, who was now working in the City, and for whom impersonation of distinguished Russian writers was an agreeable way of filling in the long hours of office life. Was this the shape of things to come?

From *Playing for Time* by Jeremy Lewis, 1987

Telephone Techniques

I should explain that all through that period of my life telephones rang constantly. My memories of those times are so often of waiting for someone to cease speaking into a telephone that, as other people may attempt to vet the long and golden summers of their youth to see if the days were as bright and rainless as their recollections suggest, now I try to remember if it was true that phones rang all the time.

They did.

On my first day I sat and waited for nearly a quarter of an hour while Bob Basnett talked steadily into the telephone. Then he ushered me into Vince Marcus's office where there was a repeat of this performance – Vince too had the receiver jammed against his ear. He looked up as I entered, nodded at Bob's brief introduction from the door, then muttered 'LA' to me while pointing at a chair.

For several minutes I studied the desktop before me. Then I started to look around as Vince continued talking, unperturbed, completely absorbed with his telephone conversation. He spoke quickly. There were short pauses, interspersed with brief questions, terse comments, rapid double-checks. He put his head to one side so he could grip the phone between his neck and his shoulder while he made notes . . .

From *The Story of the Year of 1912 in the Village of Elza Darzins*
by Thea Welsh, 1990

'Come on, lift'

Lifts, so Gryce had noticed in some of his previous billets, were very intimate places in their way. People behaved in them in a private, idiosyncratic manner not all that very far removed from pulling faces in the bathroom mirror. Beazley, as an example, was in the habit of jutting out his lower lip and blowing hard up his nostrils, while Grant-Peignton would make tocking noises as if in imitation of a grandfather clock. Neither would have dreamed of making such a public exhibition of himself outside the confines of the lift. Seeds, whenever he was a fellow passenger, was given to humming the opening bars of an obscure song called 'I'm Happy When I'm Hiking', it was the only instance in which he evidenced an interest in music. Among other behaviour patterns noted by Gryce was that Copeland would sigh heavily as the lift stopped at each floor, swivelling up his eyeballs to invite collusion with his impatience from whoever was standing next to him; and Mrs Rashman, possibly in sympathy with Copeland, would bend slightly at the knees, while imploring, 'Come on, lift.'

For Gryce's own part, he was a bit out of touch with such rituals because at Comform he had worked on the ground floor of what was in any case a low-rise building. But quite quickly he managed to establish his own particular style. Riding to the seventh floor each morning and down again each evening, he took to levering himself up on the balls of his feet, at the same time sliding his back against the vinyl panelling of the lift and constricting his shoulder blades so that they almost met. This seemed an acceptable enough arrangement to the other lift regulars, and Gryce was able to feel almost from the start that he was of their company. It was, he told himself, a bit like joining the freemasons.

From *Office Life* by Keith Waterhouse, 1978

Rituals of Coffee-drinking

'Thank you, Doris,' said the General Manager as the tray was put conveniently on the desk to his right hand. Even in this moment he observed with satisfaction that the biscuits this morning were coated with milk chocolate. He stole a glance at the *Daily Mail* to confirm it was still there to accompany the coffee-drinking rite. All he had to do to enjoy the next twenty minutes was to dismiss Arnold Gerson.

From *Image of a Society* by Roy Fuller, 1956

Elevenses

At eleven o'clock there was a sound like a traction engine mounting a steep hill and Mrs Smithers, an enormous woman as short as Lola was long, with great brawny forearms, came grunting up the stairs from the cellar bearing a tray loaded with 'elevenses' – tea and whatever else she had been able to obtain on the special ration that was allowed to businesses such as ours. The traction engine simile was banished by her actual appearance. Mrs Smithers' husband had gone down at the battle of Coronel and she herself retained an air that had something naval about it. With her bulges encased in a whale-bone corset that was as solid as armour plate she resembled a great sea-going monitor.

'Morning all,' she said. 'Let me have the tray back when you've finished, there's a dear.' This to Lola who had immediately 'perked up' (as Miss Webb said) at the sight of food, as though Pavlov himself had rung a bell in the laboratory for mittagessen.

As Mrs Smithers and her ancient aides mounted the stairs with more and more trays of strong, brown tea and grisly pastries, the sounds of activity, the whirring noises from the workrooms on the upper floors and the sounds of typewriters beating out the monthly statements in the Counting House died away and Lane and Newby's ground to a standstill.

From *Something Wholesale* by Eric Newby, 1962

The Contents of a Drawer

Mr Bredon, left alone, did not immediately attack the subject of margarine. Like a cat, which, in his soft-footed inquisitiveness, he rather resembled, he proceeded to make himself acquainted with his new home. There was not very much to see in it. He opened the drawer in his writing-table and found a notched and inky ruler, some bitten-looking pieces of india-rubber, a number of bright thoughts on tea and margarine scribbled on scraps of paper, and a broken fountain-pen. The book-case contained a dictionary, a repellent volume entitled *Directory of Directors*, a novel by Edgar Wallace, a pleasingly got-up booklet called *All about Cocoa*, *Alice in Wonderland*, Bartlett's *Familiar Quotations*, the *Globe* edition of the *Works of Wm. Shakespeare*, and five odd numbers of the *Children's Encyclopaedia*. The interior of the sloping desk offered more scope for inquiry; it was filled with ancient and dusty papers, including a Government Report on the Preservatives in Food (Restrictions) Act of 1926, a quantity of rather (in every sense) rude sketches by an amateur hand, a bundle of pulls of advertisements for Dairyfields commodities, some private correspondence and some old bills. Mr Bredon, dusting fastidious fingers, turned from this receptacle, inventoried a hook and a coat-hanger on the wall and a battered paper-file in a corner, and sat down in the revolving-chair before the table. Here, after a brief glance at a paste-pot, a pair of scissors, a new pencil and a blotting-pad, two scribbling-blocks and a grubby card-board box-lid full of oddments, he propped up the Dairyfields guard-book before him, and fell to studying his predecessor's masterpieces on the subject of Green Pastures Margarine.

From *Murder Must Advertise* by Dorothy L. Sayers, 1933

Draining the Rooster

For new-hires, the number of visits [to the office lavatories] can go as high as eight or nine a day, because the corporate bathroom is the one place in the whole office where you understand completely what is expected of you. Other parts of your job are unclear: you have been given a pile of xeroxed documents and files to read; you have tentatively probed the supply cabinet and found that they don't stock the kind of pen you prefer; relative positions of power are not immediately obvious; your office is bare and unwelcoming; you have no nameplate on the door yet, no business cards printed; and you know that the people who are friendliest to you in the first weeks are almost never the people you will end up liking and respecting, yet you can't help but think of them as central figures in the office simply because they have ingratiated them-selves, even if others seem to avoid them for reasons you can't yet grasp. But in the men's room, you are a seasoned professional; you let your hand drop casually on the flush handle with as much of an air of careless familiarity as men who have been with the company for years. Once I took a new-hire to lunch, and though he asked not-quite-to-the-point questions as we ate our sandwiches, and nodded without comprehension or comeback at my answers, when we reached the hallway to the men's room, he suddenly made a knowing, one-man-to-another face and said, 'I've got to drain the rooster. See you later. Thanks again.' I said, 'Yip, take it easy,' and walked on, even though I too needed to go, for reasons that will become clearer soon.

From *The Mezzanine* by Nicholson Baker, 1988

Lavatory Rites

... When I first joined an office I remember the lavatory as one of the only places I could hide to regain my equilibrium. Much of the gossip takes place in the women's lavatory. And even in the men's there are embarrassing exchanges, heavy *badinage*. There are some people you only see in the lavatory. You can tell something from the minute rituals (shaken crossed fingers, spitting) they surreptitiously carry out to ward off the evil eye or primitive contagion they obscurely feel they may catch by peeing where someone else has pee'd. You can tell something, or think you can, from whether they wash their hands, or don't, or comb their hair, or whistle, from the way they stand and shake themselves.

From *The Office* by Jonathan Gathorne-Hardy, 1970

Deference in Ditto

In the Directors' and Senior Executives' lavatory two men were washing their hands. The younger was a blond man in his forties, wearing horn-rimmed spectacles with thick lenses which rested on a snub, insignificant nose and almost completely masked his expression. He spoke to the other man in deferential tones and even, out of deference, accommodated the tempo of his ablutions to his companion's, so that he reached out for a towel a moment after the other. This man was Arnold Gerson, the Accounts Manager of the society.

The other man was much older, though his hair, combed very close to his scalp like an extra skin, was still black. He had a sallow face, bilious

[331]

brown eyes, and a slight paunch. He was the society's vice-chairman, Harold Ashton. Both were chartered accountants.

'I quite agree, Sir Harold,' Gerson was saying.

'Admittedly there is full employment at the moment' – Sir Harold looked in the mirror and passed a brush over his skull to flatten a quite imaginary out-of-place hair – 'but that is still a consequence of the aftermath of the war. No thanks to these Labour chaps.'

'I agree completely, Sir Harold,' said Gerson, watching the other intently as though learning from him the secret of successful grooming.

From *Image of a Society* by Roy Fuller, 1956

Sounds from the Stalls

From the men's room came the roar of a flushed urinal, followed immediately by 'I'm a Yankee Doodle Dandy' whistled with infectious cheerfulness and lots of rococo tricks – most notably the difficult yodel-trill technique, used here on the 'ee' of 'dandy,' in which the whistler gets his lips to flip the sound binarily between the base tone and a higher pitch that is I think somewhere between a major third and a perfect fourth above it (why it is not a true harmonic but rather perceptibly out of tune has puzzled me often – something to do with the physics of pursed lips?): a display of virtuosity forgivable only in the men's room, and not, as some of the salesmen seemed to think, in the relative silence of working areas, where people froze, hate exuding from suspended Razor Points, as the whistler passed. Tunes sometimes lived all day in the men's room, sustained by successive users, or remembered by a previous user as soon as he reentered the tiled liveness of the room. Once, hopped-up after several cups of coffee, I loudly whistled the bouncy opening of the tune that starts out, 'All I want is a room somewhere,' and then stopped, embarrassed, because I realized that I had unknowingly interrupted someone else's quieter and more masterly whistling of a soft-rock standard with my toneless, aerated tweets; later that day, though, I heard a stylishly embellished version of my tune whistled at the copying machine by someone who must have been in one of the stalls during my earlier roughshod interruption of the soft-rocker.

I leaned quite hard into the men's room door to open it, startling the Doodle Dandy man, who was on his way out, and who turned out to be Alan Pilna from International Service Marketing – his face, when the opening door revealed it, was not formed in the fruity whistler's pout, but had a momentary flinch of surprise on it.

He said, 'Oop!'

I said, 'Oop!' and then, as he stood aside, holding the door for me to enter, 'Thanks, Alan'...

I was just on the point of relaxing into a state of urination when two things happened. Don Vanci swept into position two urinals over from me, and then, a moment later, Les Guster turned off his tap. In the sudden quiet you could hear a wide variety of sounds coming from the stalls: long, dejected, exhausted sighs; manipulations of toilet paper; newspapers folded and batted into place; and of course the utterly carefree noise of the main activity: mind-boggling pressurized spatterings followed by sudden urgent farts that sounded like air blown over the mouth of a beer bottle.*

I sometimes tried in passing to glance into the women's corporate bathroom when by chance someone was opening the door, wanting even at the age of twenty-five to glimpse the row of sinks and the women leaning over them toward the mirror to adjust their shoulder pads or put on lip gloss, wanting to see a woman drawing her lower lip tight over her lower teeth à la William F. Buckley, Jr, and then, holding the screwed-out stick of gloss motionless, slide the lip from side to side under it and press her mouth together and then moue it outward, because the sight of this in a corporate setting gave an exotic overlay to memories of my beloved darling getting ready for parties: – the arousing skin-smell of her recent shower, the knowledge that she was putting on makeup to be attractive to other people, the sight of her wearing the holy expression that women have only for themselves in mirrors: slightly raised eyebrows, opened throat, very slightly flared nostrils.

* The absence of stealth or shame that men, colleagues of mine, displayed about their misfortunes in the toilet stall had been an unexpected surprise of business life. I admired their forthrightness, in a way; and perhaps in fifteen years I too would be spending twenty-minute stretches in similar corporate stalls, making sounds that I had once believed were made only by people in the extremity of the flu or by bums beyond caring in urban library bathrooms. But for now, I used the stalls as little as possible, never really at ease reading the sports section left there by an earlier occupant, not happy about the prewarmed seat. One time, while I was locked behind a stall, I did unintentionally interrupt the conversation between a member of senior management and an important visitor with a loud curt fart like the rap of a bongo drum. The two paused momentarily; and then recovered without dropping a stitch – 'Oh, she is a very, very capable young woman, I'm quite clear on that.' 'She is a sponge, a sponge, she soaks up information everywhere she goes.' 'She really is. And she's tough, that's the thing. She's got armor.' 'She's a major asset to us.' Etc. Unfortunately, the grotesque intrusion of my fart struck me as funny, and I sat on the toilet containing my laughter with the back of my palate – this pressure of containment forced a further, smaller fart. Silently I pounded my knee, squinting and maroon-colored from suppressed hysteria.

This suggestion of domesticity, come to think of it, contributes a characteristic tone to the inventions found in the corporate bathroom: these inventions are grander, more heroic variants of machines central to our life away from work – the sink, soap dish, mirror, and toilet of home bathrooms. In home bathrooms, the toilet seats are complete ovals, while in corporate bathrooms the seats are horseshoe-shaped; I suppose the gap lessens the problem of low-energy drops of urine falling on the seat when some scofflaw thoughtlessly goes standing up without first lifting the seat. There may be several other reasons for the horseshoe shape, having to do with accessibility, I'm not sure. But I am pleased that someone gave this subject thought, adapting what his company manufactured to deal with the realities of actual behavior. (Until I learned how to raise the seat with my shoe I myself sometimes urinated into toilets with the seat down, and because I am tall, I almost always was inaccurate.) Unlike home rolls, the toilet paper here was housed in a locked device that paid out the frames of paper with a certain amount of resistance, so that you had to pull slowly and carefully in order to keep the paper from tearing on one of the perforations, discouraging waste, and when one roll was spent, a second dropped into place. I was willing to have my wastefulness discouraged, to some degree – before that invention, I had sometimes felt a qualm when I was able to make the roll trundle momentumously around the spindle, reeling off a great drape of unnecessary paper:

From *The Mezzanine* by Nicholson Baker, 1988

The Tonsorial Touch

The office was kept pretty clean by Bill Christian, a barber who had got the job of building superintendent because Colonel Cunningham, the managing editor, liked his tonsorial touch. Bill was allergic to work himself, but he rode herd diligently on his staff of colored scavengers, and the whole editorial floor was strangely spick and span for that time. Even the colonel's own den was excavated at least twice a month, and its accumulation of discarded newspapers hauled out. Bill failed, however, to make any progress against the army of giant cockroaches that had moved in when the building was opened, three or four years before. On dull nights the copy-readers would detail office-boys to corral half a dozen of these monsters, and then race them across the city-room floor, guiding them with walking-sticks. The sport required some skill, for if a jockey pressed his nag too hard he was apt to knock off its hind legs.

From *Newspaper Days* by H. L. Mencken, 1941

Signing the Card

'Have you signed the poster for Ray?' said Tina, rolling out in her chair. Tina had lots of hair, moussed out impressively around a small smart face; she was probably at her most alert just then, because she was watching the phones for Deanne and Julie, the other secretaries in my department, until they returned from lunch after one. In the more private area of her cube, in the shadow of the shelf under the unused fluorescent light, she had pinned up shots of a stripe-shirted husband, some nephews and nieces, Barbra Streisand, and a multiply xeroxed sentiment in Gothic type that read, 'If You Can't Get Out of It, Get Into It!' I would love sometime to trace the progress of these support-staff sayings through the offices of the city; Deanne had another one pushpinned to a wall of her cube, its capitals in crumbling ruins under the distortion of so many copies of copies; it said, 'YOU MEAN YOU WANT ME TO RUSH THE RUSH JOB I'M RUSHING TO RUSH?'

'What's happened to old Ray?' I said; Ray being the man responsible for emptying the trash in each office and cubicle and restocking the bathroom supplies, but not for vacuuming, which was done by an outside company. He was about forty-five, proud of his kids, wore plaid shirts – he was always associated for me with the feeling of working late, because I could hear the gradual approach of distant papery crashes and the slinkier sounds of sheet plastic as Ray worked his way down the row toward my office, emptying each wastebasket liner into a gray triangular plastic push-dumpster, and thereby defining that day as truly over for that office, even though you might still be working in it, because anything you now threw out was *tomorrow's trash*. Before he draped a new plastic liner in a wastebasket, he left a second, folded one cached in the bottom for the next day, saving himself a few motions on every stop; and he tied a very fast knot in the plastic so that it wouldn't be pulled in, effectively becoming trash itself, as soon as you discarded something big like a newspaper.

'He hurt his back last weekend while trying to move a swimming pool,' said Tina.

I winced in office sympathy. 'An above-ground pool, I hope.'

'A toddler's pool for his grandniece. He may be out for a while.'

'That explains why for the last few days, whenever I throw out my coffee cup, I've had to lower it through this puffy cushion of plastic. The person who's been taking Ray's place doesn't know how to get rid of the trapped air. I've been kind of enjoying the effect, though – a pillow effect.'

'I'll bet you enjoy the pillow effect,' she said, flirting mechanically. She led me to a poster laid out on the desk of a research assistant who had called in sick.

'I sign where?'

'Anywhere. Here's a pen.'

I had already half pulled out my shirt-pocket pen, but not wanting to refuse her offer, I hesitated; at the same time, she saw that I already had a pen, and with an 'Oh' began to retract hers from the proffering position; meanwhile I had decided to accept hers and had let go of the one in my pocket, not registering until it was too late that she had withdrawn the offer; she, seeing that I was now beginning to reach for her pen, canceled her retraction, but meanwhile I, processing her earlier corrective movement, had gone back to reaching for my own pen – so we went through a little foilwork that was like the mutual bobbings you exchange with an oncoming pedestrian, as both of you lurch to indicate whether you are going to pass to the right or to the left. Finally I took her pen and studied the poster; it depicted, in felt-tip colors, a vase holding five large, loopy outlined flowers. On the vase was the legend, in A+ cursive handwriting, 'Ray, missing you, hoping you come back to work soon! From your Co-Workers.' And on the petals of the felt-tip flowers were the neat, nearly identical signatures of many secretaries from the mezzanine, all of them signed at different angles. Intermixed with these were the more varied signatures of a few of the managers and research assistants. I made an exclamation about its beauty: it *was* beautiful.

'Julie did the vase, I did the flowers,' said Tina.

I found an unobtrusive petal of the fourth flower: not too prominent, because I had a feeling that I might have been a little on the cool side to Ray recently – you go through inevitable cycles of office friendliness – and I wanted him to see signatures of people whose sentiments he would be absolutely sure of first. I almost signed, and then luckily I noticed that my boss Abelardo's tall and horizontally compressed conquistador signature, with lots of overloops and proud flourishes, was located one petal over on the very same flower I had chosen. To sign my name so near his would have been vaguely wrong: it might be construed as the assertion of a special alliance (my signature being closer than Dave's or Sue's or Steve's, who also worked for Abelardo), or it might seem to imply that I was seeking out my boss's name because I wanted to be near another exempt person's name, avoiding the secretarial signatures. I had signed enough office farewell and birthday and get-well cards by that time to have developed an unhealthy sensitivity to the nuances of signature placement. I moved over to an antipodal flower's petal, near Deanne's name, and signed at what I hoped was an original angle. 'Ray will sob with joy when he sees this poster, Tina,' I said.

From *The Mezzanine* by Nicholson Baker, 1988

To Sign, or not to Sign?

Mrs Rashman was leaving. Officially, of course, she was supposed to work until the end of the week but she did have two days of her compassionate leave concession owing, and taking that into consideration and the fact that there were no desks to work at, Copeland had used his discretion to release her at lunch-time. There was to be a presentation.

Gryce found himself in a quandary. He had been asked to add his signature to the giant-sized card – of a cartoon elephant woozily imbibing a glass of champagne: not at all suitable, considering Mrs Rashman's girth and her well-known proclivity for wine-bars – which Pam had bought at one of the many greetings-cards shops near the office. (It bore the caption 'Don't forget to write', which at least could be said to justify the elephant motif, and most of the signatories had touched on this theme in their parting quips – 'If you have time!!!', 'After the honeymoon natch!!!' etc. Gryce, not being on familiar terms with the woman, had contented himself with a chaste, 'Best wishes, C. Gryce.') But he had not been asked to chip in to the collection which Beazley had surreptitiously made under the pretext of selling supplementary raffle tickets. Quite right too: Gryce had been sweating on the top line on that one. But it did place him in the position of having to decide whether to attend the presentation ceremony or not. A fruit cake had been bought with the few shillings left over from the set of teak-handled steak knives that was to be Mrs Rashman's leaving present. If Thelma could find it again in the jumble of filing cabinets out in the foyer, it was to be sliced and consumed during coffee break when Copeland would make a speech. Could Gryce eat cake that he had not subscribed towards? Could he look suitably bashful, along with the others, when Copeland spoke of 'a little something to remember us all by'?

Much as Gryce enjoyed a good leaving thrash, he came to the reluctant conclusion that he would be better off out of it. Accordingly, when Thelma began whispering audibly to Pam about paper plates, he discreetly absented himself, pretending to be heading for the lavatory but instead wheeling off sharply into the furniture-infested foyer. It was not as if there was any work to be getting on with. No one would miss him.

From *Office Life* by Keith Waterhouse, 1978

Exes

'I've been looking at your expense account, Brian,' says Vic, turning over a small pile of bills and receipts.

'Yes?' Brian Everthorpe stiffens slightly.

'It's very modest.'

Everthorpe relaxes. 'Thank you.'

'I didn't mean it as a compliment.'

Everthorpe looks puzzled. 'Sorry.'

'I'd expect the Marketing Director of a firm this size to claim twice as much for overnight stays.'

'Ah, well, you see, Beryl doesn't like being on her own in the house at night.'

'But she has your kids with her.'

'Not during term, old man. We send them away to school – have to, living in the depths of the country. So I prefer to drive back home after a meeting, no matter how far it is.'

'Your mileage is pretty modest, too, isn't it?'

'Is it?' Brian Everthorpe, beginning to get the message, stiffens again.

From *Nice Work* by David Lodge, 1988

Twenty

GETTING THE SACK

It goes without saying that the sack makes for more entertaining reading than promotion, just as congenial rogues often prove more sympathetic than the dutifully good; quite apart from which, diffidence and a natural modesty should inhibit too much beating of one's private drum on the part of the autobiographer. Most sackings are probably kinder and milder affairs than they are subsequently made out to be, with much awkward clearing of throats and beating about the bush involved: the victim – who has almost certainly seen it coming, and is none too fussed either way – may even hurry forward to relieve the executioner, nodding agreement with all that is said and even adding some additional failings or wrong-doings so as to make the prosecution case entirely watertight. Less amen-able souls, however, may use the occasion to settle old scores and make their own views felt, brushing aside the sacker's well-meant attempts to sweeten the pill and persuade the victim that he has his best interests at heart. Whether kindly or ferocious, the straightforward sack is vastly preferable to 'constructive dismissal', an office euphemism for inching out the unwanted by hint and rumour, by isolation and the gradual removal of their jobs and their self-respect: more often than not the victim, unable or unwilling to bear it any longer, will offer to resign, so forfeiting the compensations of the sack. Resignation on grounds of pique or principle is almost always a mistake, reflecting an over-inflated sense of one's own importance and an alarming lack of realism. We like to think of ourselves as indispensable, and we tell ourselves that without us the old firm will grind to a halt, and that within weeks they will be begging us to return: yet office life is a ruthless, unsentimental affair, and the departure of even the most flamboyant, forceful figures often causes only momentary disruption. Within days the waters have closed over and it is as though they had never been, lingering on in the memories of those who worked with them before being forgotten altogether.

Pooter and Promotion

JANUARY 1. I had intended concluding my diary last week; but a most important event has happened, so I shall continue for a little while longer on the fly-leaves attached to the end of my last year's diary. It had just struck half-past one, and I was on the point of leaving the office to have my dinner, when I received a message that Mr Perkupp desired to see me at once. I must confess that my heart commenced to beat and I had most serious misgivings.

Mr Perkupp was in his room writing, and he said: 'Take a seat, Mr Pooter, I shall not be a moment.'

I replied: 'No, thank you, sir; I'll stand.' I watched the clock on the mantelpiece, and I was waiting quite twenty minutes; but it seemed hours. Mr Perkupp at last got up himself.

I said: 'I hope there is nothing wrong, sir?'

He replied: 'Oh dear, no! quite the reverse, I hope.' What a weight off my mind! My breath seemed to come back again in an instant.

Mr Perkupp said: 'Mr Buckling is going to retire, and there will be some slight changes in the office. You have been with us nearly twenty-one years, and, in consequence of your conduct during that period, we intend making a special promotion in your favour. We have not quite decided how you will be placed; but in any case there will be a considerable increase in your salary, which, it is quite unnecessary for me to say, you fully deserve. I have an appointment at two; but you shall hear more tomorrow.'

He then left the room quickly, and I was not even allowed time or thought to express a single word of grateful thanks to him. I need not say how dear Carrie received this joyful news. With perfect simplicity she said: 'At last we shall be able to have a chimney-glass for the back drawing-room, which we always wanted.' I added: 'Yes, and at last you shall have that little costume which you saw at Peter Robinson's so cheap.'

JANUARY 2. I was in a great state of suspense all day at the office. I did not like to worry Mr Perkupp; but as he did not send for me, and mentioned yesterday that he would see me again today, I thought it better, perhaps, to go to him. I knocked at his door, and on entering, Mr Perkupp said: 'Oh, it's you, Mr Pooter; do you want to see me?' I said: 'No, sir, I thought you wanted to see me!' 'Oh!' he replied, 'I remember. Well, I am very busy today; I will see you tomorrow.'

JANUARY 3. Still in a state of anxiety and excitement, which was not alleviated by ascertaining that Mr Perkupp sent word he should not be at the office today ...

JANUARY 4. Mr Perkupp sent for me and told me that my position would be that of one of the senior clerks. I was more than overjoyed. Mr Perkupp added, he would let me know tomorrow what the salary would be. This means another day's anxiety; I don't mind, for it is anxiety of the right sort ...

JANUARY 5. I can scarcely write the news. Mr Perkupp told me my salary would be raised £100! I stood gaping for a moment unable to realize it. I annually get £10 rise, and I thought it might be £15 or even £20; but £100 surpasses all belief.

From *The Diary of a Nobody* by George and Weedon Grossmith, 1892

A Break, All Right

Suddenly Russell got his first clear picture – a sharp image of what the new job would be like. He saw a mahogany desk instead of his scarred old second-hand monstrosity; a leather chair instead of his squeaky wreck; thick carpet instead of linoleum. He could feel the arm of the chair under his hand; he could smell the leather and good wood. He took in the prospect through his senses instead of his mind and instantly felt a flush of pleasure and anxiety. Certainly he'd like the job. Why, there'd even be more money.

And Madeline would laugh when he told her, as if she had expected it all along, and would be very proud.

'Yep. It's a break, all right.'

From *The Philanderer* by Stanley Kauffmann, 1953

Instant Dismissal

The advent of Miss Grig, of course, considerably agitated the office and in particular the small room, two of whose occupants had never seen the principal of whose capacity for sustained effort they had heard such wonderful and frightening tales.

At nine-thirty that Thursday morning it was reported in both rooms that Miss Grig had re-entered her fortress. Nobody had seen her, but ears had heard her, and, moreover, it was mystically known by certain signs, as, for example, the reversal of a doormat which had been out of position for a week, that a higher presence was immanent in the place and that the presence could be none other than Miss Grig. Everybody became an exemplar of assiduity, amiability, and entire conscientiousness. Everybody prepared a smile; and there was a universal wish for the day to be over.

Shortly after ten o'clock Miss Grig visited the small room, shook hands with Lilian and Millicent, and permitted the two new typists to be presented to her. Millicent spoke first and was so effusive in the expression of the delight induced in her by the spectacle of Miss Grig and of her sympathy for the past and hope for the future of Miss Grig's health, that Lilian, who nevertheless did her best to be winning, could not possibly compete with her. Miss Grig had a purified and chastened air, as of one detached by suffering from the grossness and folly of the world, and existing henceforth in the world solely from a cold, passionate sense of duty. Her hair was greyer, her mild equable voice more soft, and her burning eyes had a brighter and more unearthly lustre. She said that she was perfectly restored, let fall that Mr Grig had gone away at her request for a short, much-needed holiday, and then passed smoothly on to the large room.

After a while a little flapper of a beginner came to tell Millicent that Miss Grig wanted her. Millicent, who had had charge of the petty cash during the interregnum, was absent for forty minutes. When she returned, flushed but smiling, to her expectant colleagues, she informed Lilian that Miss Grig desired to see her at twelve o'clock.

'I notice there's an account here under the name of Lord Mackworth,' Miss Grig began, having allowed Lilian to stand for a few seconds before looking up from the ledger and other books in which she was apparently absorbed. She spoke with the utmost gentleness, and fixed her oppressive deep eyes on Lilian's.

'Yes, Miss Grig?'

'It hasn't been paid.'

'Oh!' Lilian against an intense volition began to blush.

'Didn't you know?'

'I didn't,' said Lilian.

'But you've been having something to do with the books during my absence.'

'I did a little at first,' Lilian admitted. 'Then Mr Grig saw to them.'

'Miss Merrislate tells me that you had quite a lot to do with them, and I see your handwriting in a number of places here.'

'I've had nothing to do with them for about three weeks, and – and of course I expected the bill would be paid by this time.'

'But you never asked?'

'No. It never occurred to me.'

This statement was inaccurate. Lilian had often wondered whether Lord Mackworth had paid his bill, but, from some obscurely caused self-consciousness, she had not dared to make any inquiry . . .

'But can't we send in the account again?' Lilian weakly suggested; she was overthrown by the charge of fast-living against Lord Mackworth, yet she had always in her heart assumed that he was a fast liver.

'I've just telephoned to 6a St James's Street, and I needn't say that Lord Mackworth is no longer there, and they don't know where he is. You see what comes of disobeying rules.'

Lilian lifted her head: 'Well, Miss Grig, the bill isn't so very big, and if you'll please deduct it from my wages on Saturday I hope that will be the end of that.'

It was plain that the bewildered creature had but an excessively imperfect notion of how to be an employee. She had taken to the vocation too late in life.

Miss Grig put her hand to the support of her forehead, and paused.

'I can tolerate many things,' said she, with great benignity, 'but not insolence.'

'I didn't mean to be insolent.'

'You did. And I think you had better accept a week's notice from Saturday. No. On second thoughts, I'll pay your wages up to Saturday week now and you can go at once.' She smiled kindly. 'That will give you time to turn round.'

'Oh! Very well, if it's like that!'

Miss Grig unlocked a drawer; and while she was counting the money Lilian thought despairingly that if Mr Grig, or even if the nice Gertie, had been in the office, the disaster could not have occurred.

Miss Grig shook hands with her and wished her well.

'Where are you going to? It's not one o'clock yet,' asked Millicent in the small room as Lilian silently unhooked her hat and jacket from the clothes-cupboard.

'Out.'

'What for?'

'For Miss G., if you want to know.'

And she left. Except her clothes, not a thing in the office belonged to her. She had no lien, no attachment. The departure was as simple and complete as leaving a Tube train. No word! No good-bye! Merely a disappearance.

From *Lilian* by Arnold Bennett, 1922

'I assume I'm fired'

From the window to Clara's office is a very short distance. Much too short. You are there. She slams the door from the inside, takes the seat in front of the desk and stares you down. She doesn't ask you to sit, so you do. This is shaping up even worse than you anticipated. Still, you feel a measure of detachment, as if you had suffered everything already and this were just a flashback. You wish that you had paid more attention when a woman you met at Heartbreak told you about Zen meditation. Think of all of this as an illusion. She can't hurt you. Nothing can hurt the samurai who enters combat fully resolved to die. You have already accepted the inevitability of termination, as they say. Still, you'd rather not have to sit through this.

'I would like to know what happened.'

A dumb question. Far too general. You draw a good breath. 'I screwed up.' You might add that the writer of the piece in question really screwed up, that you improved the thing immeasurably, and that the change of scheduling was ill-advised. But you don't.

'You screwed up.'

You nod. It's true. In this case, however, honesty doesn't make you feel a whole lot better. You're having trouble meeting her glare.

'May I be so bold as to ask for a little elaboration? Really, I'm interested.'

Sarcasm now.

'Just *how* did you screw up, exactly?'

More ways than you can say.

'Well?'

You're already gone. You are out the window with the pigeons. You try to alleviate the terror by thinking how ridiculous her French braids look, like spinnakers on a tugboat. You suspect that deep down she enjoys this. She's been looking forward to it for a long time.

'Do you realize just how serious this is?' she demands. 'You have endangered the reputation of this magazine. We have built a reputation for scrupulous accuracy with regard to matters of fact. Our readers depend on us for the truth.'

You would like to say, Whoa! Block that jump from facts to truth, but she is off and running.

'Every time this magazine goes to press that reputation is on the line, and when the current issue hits the stands you will have compromised that reputation, perhaps irretrievably. Do you know that in fifty years of publication there has only been one printed retraction?'

Yes, you know.

'Have you considered that everyone on the staff will suffer as a result of your carelessness?'

Clara's office is none too large under the best of circumstances, and it is getting smaller by the minute. You raise your hand. 'Can I ask what errors you have found?'

She has the list ready to hand: Two accents reversed, an electoral district in central France incorrectly identified as northern, a minister ascribed to the wrong department. 'This is just what I've been able to find so far. I'm scared to death of what I'll uncover as I go along. The proofs are a mess. I can't tell what you've verified and what you haven't. The point is, you have not followed standard procedure, which by this time should be second nature to you, which procedure is thoroughly outlined in your manual, which procedure is the net result of many years of collective labor, and proper application of which ensures that, insofar as possible, errors of fact do not appear in this magazine.'

Clara is red in the face. Although Wade claims she has recently taken up jogging, her wind is lousy.

'Do you have anything to say for yourself?'

'I don't think so.'

'This isn't the first time. I've given you the benefit of the doubt before. You seem unable to perform the duties required for this job.'

You're not about to take issue with anything she says. You would confess to all of the crimes detailed in the *Post* today in exchange for an exit visa. You nod your head gravely.

'I'd like to hear what you have to say.'

'I assume I'm fired.'

She looks surprised. She drums her fingers on the desk and glowers. You're pleased that her hands are shaking. 'That's correct,' she says at last. 'Effective immediately.'

'Anything else?' you say, and when she doesn't answer you stand up to go. Your legs are trembling, but you don't think she notices.

'I'm sorry,' she says as you open the door.

From *Bright Lights, Big City* by Jay McInerney, 1984

Expelled from the Hogarth Press

CATASTROPHE

LW has returned from Rodmell in a towering rage. Apparently the whole Uniform Edition project has been ruined by me because I have unwittingly instructed Spalding & Hodge to cut the paper the wrong size.

LW brought back a number of sacks of apples and potatoes from Rodmell and I tried to help him hump them up the stairs, but he would not accept any assistance from me. He refuses to speak to me. He had Gossling in and gave him a terrific tongue lashing. Gossling's cheeks went quite pale.

I suppose I have really got the sack. LW says I can't be trusted to do anything but wrap up parcels and that I am the most frightful idiot he has ever had the privilege of meeting in a long career of suffering fools.

CATASTROPHE CONT'D

Wrapped up parcels all day. LW is still irate and glares at me.

Mrs C tells me that LW and Mrs W have invited a new author to tea and if she comes to the Press she must be shown upstairs. I asked who the author was.

'It's a lady called Miss Burnett.'

'Not Ivy Compton-Burnett! I must tell LW at once.'

When he came down at lunchtime he didn't give me an opportunity to speak to him so I ran after him and caught him on the stairs going up to his flat. I tried to tell him that we had refused Ivy Compton-Burnett's first book, but he looked at me quite uncomprehendingly and ran his hand through his hair.

'Never mind now, Richard,' he said in quite a kindly voice.

Well, I suppose it doesn't really matter. I'm leaving at the end of the month.

From *A Boy at the Hogarth Press* by Richard Kennedy, 1972

Giving One's Notice

'Give notice? Is that what you said, Miss Sely?'

'Yes, Mr Riddle.' Nell's voice had begun as a squeak but she impatiently pulled it down again; she was only giving notice, wasn't she? Thousands of people must give notice in London every day.

'But why? What for? Your work is quite satisfactory.'

'Thank you, Mr Riddle.'

'Then why do you want to leave us? What reason could there possibly be?' Then, before she could bring out the tactful arguments which she had assembled –

'This is a very nice firm to work for, you know. There are Prospects, if you work hard (Miss Driver will be getting married one day, of course), and you know all about our Pensions Fund and the Canteen. Next year we hope to have a Firm's Dance. It isn't what I care about myself, Mrs Riddle not being fond of dancing and in any case my dancing days being over, but young people like dancing. *You* like dancing, Miss Sely, don't you?'

Nell moved her gaze from his face, which was beginning to unnerve her, to the floor. Was she expected to toil year in and year out with Akkro Products for the reward of one evening's hopping about during the twelvemonth?

'Don't you, Miss Sely?'

'It isn't anything to do with the firm, Mr Riddle.'

She tried to add something about having been very happy there, but rebelled. Why should she lie to Mr Riddle? She had disliked every moment of it.

'Then what ... I suppose you want more – er – money?'

'I do want more money but it isn't only that. Mr Riddle, if you could tell me whom I give in my notice to, I could do it this morning. Before lunch.'

From *Here Be Dragons* by Stella Gibbons, 1956

Ritualistic Firing

People in the company are almost never fired; if they grow inadequate or obsolete ahead of schedule, they are encouraged to retire early or are eased aside into hollow, insignificant, newly created positions with fake functions and no authority, where they are sheepish and unhappy for as long as they remain; nearly always, they must occupy a small and less convenient office, sometimes one with another person already in it; or, if they are still young, they are simply encouraged directly (though with courtesy) to find better jobs with other companies and then resign. Even the wide-awake young branch manager with the brilliant future who got drunk and sick one afternoon and threw up into the hotel swimming pool during the company convention in Florida two years ago wasn't fired, although everyone knew he would not be permitted to remain. He knew it, too. Probably nothing was ever said to him. But he knew it. And four weeks after the convention ended, he found a better job with another company and resigned.

Green, on the other hand, does fire people, at least two or three people every year, and makes no secret of it; in fact, he makes it a point to let everyone know immediately after he *has* fired someone. Often, he will fire someone for no better reason than to cause discussion about himself or to wake the rest of us up for a while. Most of us who won't ever amount to anything really big here, including Green, do tend to sink into lethargy and coast along sluggishly on the energy and new ideas that helped us make it safely through the year before. That's one of the reasons we won't ever amount to anything much. Most of the men who do make it toward the top are persistent hard workers if they are nothing else (and they are frequently nothing else. Ha, ha).

Sometimes the people Green fires are people he likes personally whose work is good enough (that may, in fact, be just the reason he does fire them – that he has no reason). Then he will grow compassionate and become seriously concerned with their plight (as though he were not the one who created it). He will begin an earnest effort to find other jobs for them somewhere else in the company. He is usually not successful, for his zest for catty advantage quickly replaces his original (and uncharacteristic) good intention, and his approach turns malicious and self-defeating.

'He'd be perfect for you,' is one method Green likes to use in recommending someone in his department to someone who is the head of another department. 'He just isn't good enough for me.'

Once he has made this point in enough places, he soon forgets about the people he has fired, and they go away.

From *Something Happened* by Joseph Heller, 1974

'Caprice'

I sat only two tables from the one I was sacked at,
    Just three years ago,
And here was another meringue like the one which I hacked at
    When pride was brought low
And the coffee arrived – the place which she had to use tact at
    For striking the blow.

'I'm making some changes next week in the organisation
   And though I admire
Your work for me, John, yet the need to increase circulation
   Means you must retire:
An outlook more global than yours is the qualification
   I really require.'

Oh sickness of sudden betrayal! Oh purblind Creator!
   Oh friendship denied!
I stood on the pavement and wondered which loss was the greater –
   The cash or the pride.
Explanations to make to subordinates, bills to pay later
   Churned up my inside.

From *High and Low* by John Betjeman, 1966

The Biter Bit

... He had to discharge Graff, and this was a part of office routine which he feared. He liked people so much, he so much wanted them to like him, that he could not bear insulting them.

Miss McGoun dashed in to whisper, with the excitement of an approaching scene, 'He's here!'

'Mr Graff? Ask him to come in.'

He tried to make himself heavy and calm in his chair, and to keep his eyes expressionless. Graff stalked in – a man of thirty-five, dapper, eye-glassed, with a foppish moustache.

'Want me?' said Graff.

'Yes. Sit down.'

Graff continued to stand, grunting, 'I suppose that old nut Varney has been in to see you. Let me explain about him. He's a regular tightwad, and he sticks out for every cent, and he practically lied to me about his ability to pay the rent – I found that out just after we signed up. And then another fellow comes along with a better offer for the house, and I felt it was my duty to the firm to get rid of Varney, and I was so worried about it I skun up there and got back the lease. Honest, Mr Babbitt, I didn't intend to pull anything crooked. I just wanted the firm to have all the commis –'

'Wait now, Stan. This may all be true, but I've been having a lot of complaints about you. Now I don't s'pose you ever mean to do wrong, and I think if you just get a good lesson that'll jog you up a little, you'll turn out a first-class realtor yet. But I don't see how I can keep you on.'

Graff leaned against the filing-cabinet, his hands in his pockets, and laughed. 'So I'm fired! Well, old Vision and Ethics, I'm tickled to death! But I don't want you to think you can get away with any holier-than-thou stuff. Sure I've pulled some raw stuff – a little of it – but how could I help it, in this office?'

'Now, by God, young man –'

'Tut, tut! Keep the naughty temper down, and don't holler, because everybody in the outside office will hear you. They're probably listening right now. Babbitt, old dear, you're crooked in the first place and a damn skinflint in the second. If you paid me a decent salary I wouldn't have to steal pennies off a blind man to keep my wife from starving. Us married just five months, and her the nicest girl living, and you keeping us flat broke all the time, you damned old thief, so you can put money away for your saphead of a son and your wishywashy fool of a daughter! Wait, now! You'll by God take it, or I'll bellow so the whole office will hear it! And crooked – Say, if I told the prosecuting attorney what I know about this last Street Traction option steal, both you and me would go to prison, along with some nice, clean, pious, high-up traction guns!'

From *Babbitt* by Sinclair Lewis, 1922

This is going to hurt me . . .

Having to sack Jupes was a bit awkward for Ammon at the moment. He was not quite ready for it, especially with the holiday season under way. Racoon Worrell had definitely been got rid of, for good and all, and that had been a relief, although there had been difficulty in finding a replacement for him. It would have been easier, therefore, to have been able to wait just a little longer before going to all the additional worry and fuss of choosing someone else suitable for Jupes's post as Publicity Manager.

Racoon had made the mistake of applying for a job at Willett, Ransome's. Of course 'Grandpa' Willett had been only too delighted to tell Ammon that one of the staff of Ammon and Foreshearing had approached him. He had encouraged Racoon, before turning him down (a foregone conclusion), to be entirely frank about his grievances against Ammon personally – all of which had been faithfully passed on.

When Racoon had been summoned to London by Charlie Ammon, he had been quite excited. Maybe Charlie had relented and was hankering after the old times. Why not suggest a piss-up in that very City pub where they used to drink together and gaze at those gorgeous tits belonging to the barmaid, Agnes Elsie Blood?

'Wifelet wants fur coatlet, don't forget,' were the cheery farewell words at Oswestry station. Both Racoon and his wife well knew that all the money from his rise must go towards painting the outside of their house, now already overdue under the terms of their lease.

At first everything had gone swimmingly. They had chatted about the Outing and Charlie had complimented him on getting on so well with Max Lucas over the Martin Foreshearing memorial bust, a real tribute to Racoon's forward-looking ideas on contemporary art. Then Charlie said that this year he had decided to give Venning, the foreman of Stereo, the job of organising the entertainments at the Outing, so that Racoon could have the chance of a rest. Secretly, of course, Racoon was disappointed about this, although at that time he thought Charlie meant it kindly; he liked organising the Outing, it was his big moment. Then they talked, with utter frankness, about the weaknesses in character of other personalities in the firm, including directors. Racoon found himself saying some very sharp and witty things, all in the drawling, dead-pan voice that in pre-war days Charlie used to find so funny.

Somehow or other they got round to the subject of salaries.

'I understand, Worrell,' Charlie said, 'that you feel badly treated at having been made to accept a lower salary when you were moved up to Oswestry.'

Racoon agreed eagerly.

'Well, we don't like having people working for us who feel they've been badly treated –'

From *The Big Tomato* by Raleigh Trevelyan, 1966

The Circuitous Approach

Reg Mounce marched into Dyson's department, kicking the door open in front of him.

'Oh, it's you,' he said to Tessa, looking sourly round the room. 'Both at the wake, are they?'

He hesitated, frowning at a sheet of paper he was holding.

'It was one or the other of your bright boy-friends who sent me this, was it?' he demanded, tossing the paper down in front of her. She picked it up and read it.

Editor to R. Mounce. PRIVATE AND CONFIDENTIAL.
I cannot trace any acknowledgement from you of the memorandum I

sent you on the twelfth of this month, regarding your talents and the scope for them in this office. Since the matter is important, I wonder if you would take the trouble to write to me again, indicating particularly whether such other arrangements as you will be making are likely to commence at an earlier date than one might otherwise suppose. Certain other arrangements which *I* must make naturally turn upon this.

I trust that your own other arrangements are proceeding satisfactorily.

'Some sort of joke, is it?' demanded Mounce bitterly.

'I'm afraid I don't know. It looks as if it's from the Editor.'

'Oh, it *looks* as if it's from the Editor,' said Mounce ironically.

'It says it's from the Editor.'

'Oh, it *says* it's from the Editor. The last one *said* it was from the Editor. But it wasn't. It was just a load of crap that some joker had sent. All this crap about "other arrangements"! It's just crap.'

'Is it?' said Tessa, wondering if perhaps it was. She tried to focus her mind on the words. 'Other arrangements' – well, other arrangements were alternative dispositions. And alternative dispositions were – well, they were other arrangements. But somehow, she felt, the words had passed right through her mind without leaving any deposit of meaning behind.

'Well, isn't it?' said Mounce. 'People aren't asked to make other arrangements on this paper, are they? Have you ever heard of anyone in this office being asked to make other arrangements?'

'Well, no . . .'

'So it's obviously a load of crap. Everyone saw that. This isn't the *Express*, after all.'

He took the note out of Tessa's hands and began to read it through again, rubbing his chin uneasily.

'I mean,' he said, 'you don't think this *is* from the Editor, do you?'

'I've honestly no idea.'

'I mean, this is just the sort of shit the Editor would write. "Other arrangements" – that's just the sort of stinking thing he'd say.'

'I thought,' said Tessa timidly, 'that you said people weren't asked to make other arrangements on this paper?'

'No, but what I mean is, if they *were* asked to make other arrangements, making other arrangements is just what the stinking Editor would call it.'

Mounce held the note up to the light, as if looking for a watermark.

'I wonder,' he said gloomily. 'Now you've put doubts in my mind.'

'I suppose you could ring the Editor's secretary and check . . .' suggested Tessa hesitantly.

Mounce stared at her absently, pushing his lower lip up.

'I suppose I could . . .' he said. He read through the note again, frowning. Then he went over to the window, and gazed down into Hand and Ball Court for several minutes, frowning and pushing his lower lip up alternately.

'I suppose that would be one way of tackling it,' he said. He took another look at the note, putting a finger into his mouth and trying to dislodge some irritating morsel of lunch from between his back teeth. Slowly, still rereading the note and still working on his teeth, he wandered out of the room.

'I'll bear it in mind,' he said gloomily, without turning his head, as he went through the door.

From *Towards the End of the Morning* by Michael Frayn, 1967

A Helping Hand

By now it must have been apparent to my boss with the empurpled features and the warhorse that I was not the stuff of which aspiring advertising agents are made. No one could deny that I had made a first-rate job of pasting advertisements into scrap-books, but beyond that, it seemed, I had alarmingly little to offer. I showed no interest whatsoever in the work upon which I was bent; my mind was obviously elsewhere; not only did I spurn the cricket pitch and make heavy weather of incoming telephone calls, but I jumped whenever spoken to, spoke in an incomprehensible rumble, and moved with strange, convulsive jerks, like a puppet whose master had taken to the bottle or had trouble in working out which string was which. One sunny morning the purple-faced one called me into his office and asked me to close the door behind me. Placing his elbows on his G-plan desk, and interlacing his fingers like a housemaster preparing to admonish in a firm but kindly way, he asked me what I was reading and how I spent my evenings. Had I been a bright or ambitious youth I would have told him that I had just finished a work by Marshall McLuhan or *The Affluent Society*, and that after work I hurried away to learn about typography and block-making at the London College of Printing, or browse through the literature at the Institute of Practitioners in Advertising; instead, I thought hard and long before revealing that I had just finished *Barnaby Rudge* and was wondering whether to move on to *Little Dorrit* or *Our Mutual Friend* – perhaps he had views on the matter? – and that I had spent the last three evenings in a tiny cinema in Westbourne Grove seeing what must in fact have been one of the last ever showings of Marcel Pagnol's masterly trilogy about the adventures of César and Marius in Marseilles between the wars.

At this my boss sighed heavily and gazed at the ceiling with the pensive look of one who was about to embark on an unpleasant but unavoidable course of action, and was anxious to choose exactly the right words before setting forth; and after half a minute or so he asked me, in the most considerate and helpful way, whether I felt I was altogether suited to the cut and thrust of advertising life, and whether I shouldn't perhaps give some serious thought to the future ... So touched was I by his air of concern, and by the delicate, roundabout route he was taking to the moment of dismissal that I hastened to cut him short, and set his mind at rest. I was sure he was right, I said; I had been coming to much the same conclusion myself; he *must* not worry himself on my behalf; only the other day I had, in fact, decided to take advantage of the £10 assisted passage, and make a new life for myself in Australia (I sometimes filled in the long hours after delivering a 'telephone' message to Fleet Street by reading the papers in Australia House, and some unusually quick thinking enabled me to come up with this implausible version of my future). A look of intense relief suffused my boss's benevolent, bloodshot features; it was hard to know which of us was the more delighted by the outcome; without going so far as to forgive me for reading at my desk, he shook me warmly by the hand, assured me that I had made the right decision, and told me that of course I could stay on to the end of the month; and with that my career in advertising was over.

From *Playing for Time* by Jeremy Lewis, 1987

Lupin Disgraced

MAY 13. A terrible misfortune has happened. Lupin is discharged from Mr Perkupp's office, and I scarcely know how I am writing my diary. I was away from office last Sat., the first time I have been absent through illness for twenty years. I believe I was poisoned by some lobster. Mr Perkupp was also absent, as Fate would have it; and our most valued customer, Mr Crowbillon, went to the office in a rage, and withdrew his custom. My boy Lupin not only had the assurance to receive him, but recommended him the firm of Gylterson, Sons and Co., Ltd. In my own humble judgement, and though I have to say it against my own son, this seems an act of treachery.

This morning I receive a letter from Perkupp, informing me that Lupin's services are no longer required, and an interview with me is desired at eleven o'clock. I went down to the office with an aching heart, dreading an interview with Mr Perkupp, with whom I have never had a word. I saw nothing of Lupin in the morning. He had not got up when it was time for me to leave, and Carrie said I should do no good by disturbing him. My mind wandered so at the office that I could not do my work properly.

As I expected, I was sent for by Mr Perkupp, and the following conversation ensued as nearly as I can remember it.

Mr Perkupp said: 'Good morning, Mr Pooter! This is a very serious business. I am not referring so much to the dismissal of your son, for I knew we should have to part sooner or later. *I* am the head of this old, influential, and much-respected firm; and when *I* consider the time has come to revolutionize the business, *I* will do it myself.'

I could see my good master was somewhat affected, and I said: 'I hope, sir, you do not imagine that I have in any way countenanced my son's unwarrantable interference?' Mr Perkupp rose from his seat and took my hand and said: 'Mr Pooter, I would as soon suspect myself as suspect you.' I was so agitated that in the confusion, to show my gratitude, I very nearly called him a 'grand old man'.

Fortunately I checked myself in time, and said he was a 'grand old master'. I was so unaccountable for my actions that I sat down, leaving him standing. Of course, I at once rose, but Mr Perkupp bade me sit down, which I was very pleased to do. Mr Perkupp, resuming, said: 'You will understand, Mr Pooter, that the high-standing nature of our firm will not admit of our bending to anybody. If Mr Crowbillon chooses to put his work into other hands: – I may add, less experienced hands – it is not for us to bend and beg back his custom.' 'You *shall* not do it, sir,' I said with indignation. 'Exactly,' replied Mr Perkupp; 'I shall *not* do it. But I was thinking this, Mr Pooter. Mr Crowbillion is our most valued client, and I will even confess – for I know this will not go beyond ourselves – that we cannot afford very well to lose him, especially in these times, which are not of the brightest. Now, I fancy you can be of service.'

I replied: 'Mr Perkupp, I will work day and night to serve you!'

Mr Perkupp said: 'I know you will. Now, what I should like you to do is this. You yourself might write to Mr Crowbillon – you must not, of course, lead him to suppose I know anything about your doing so – and explain to him that your son was only taken on as a clerk – quite an inexperienced one in fact – out of the respect the firm had for you, Mr Pooter. This is, of course, a fact. I don't suggest that you should speak in too strong terms of your son's conduct; but I may add, that had he been a son of mine, I should have condemned his interference with no measured terms. That I leave to you. I think the result will be that Mr Crowbillon will see the force of the foolish step he has taken, and our firm will neither suffer in dignity nor in pocket.'

I could not help thinking what a noble gentleman Mr Perkupp is. His manners and his way of speaking seem to almost thrill one with respect.

I said: 'Would you like to see the letter before I send it?'

Mr Perkupp said: 'Oh no! I had better not. I am supposed to know nothing about it, and I have every confidence in you. You must write the letter carefully. We are not very busy; you had better take the morning tomorrow, or the whole day if you like. I shall be here myself all day tomorrow, in fact all the week, in case Mr Crowbillon should call.'

I went home a little more cheerful, but I left word with Sarah that I could not see either Gowing or Cummings, nor in fact anybody, if they called in the evening. Lupin came into the parlour for a moment with a new hat on, and asked my opinion of it. I said I was not in the mood to judge of hats, and I did not think he was in a position to buy a new one. Lupin replied carelessly: 'I didn't buy it; it was a present.'

I have such terrible suspicions of Lupin now that I scarcely like to ask him questions, as I dread the answers so. He, however, saved me the trouble.

He said: 'I met a friend, an old friend, that I did not quite think a friend at the time, but it's all right. As he wisely said, "all is fair in love and war", and there was no reason why we should not be friends still. He's a jolly good, all-round sort of fellow, and a very different stamp from that inflated fool of a Perkupp.'

I said: 'Hush, Lupin! Do not pray add insult to injury.'

Lupin said: 'What do you mean by injury? I repeat, I have done no injury. Crowbillon is simply tired of a stagnant stick-in-the-mud firm, and made the change on his own account. I simply recommended the new firm as a matter of biz – good old biz!'

I said quietly: 'I don't understand your slang, and at my time of life have no desire to learn it; so, Lupin, my boy, let us change the subject' . . .

MAY 14. Lupin came down late, and seeing me at home all the morning, asked the reason of it. Carrie and I both agreed it was better to say nothing to him about the letter I was writing, so I evaded the question.

Lupin went out, saying he was going to lunch with Murray Posh in the City. I said I hoped Mr Posh would provide him with a berth. Lupin went out laughing, saying: 'I don't mind *wearing* Posh's one-priced hats, but I am not going to *sell* them.' Poor boy, I fear he is perfectly hopeless.

It took me nearly the whole day to write to Mr Crowbillon. Once or twice I asked Carrie for suggestions; and although it seems ungrateful, her suggestions were none of them to the point, while one or two were absolutely idiotic. Of course I did not tell her so. I got the letter off, and took it down to the office for Mr Perkupp to see, but he again repeated that he could trust me.

Gowing called in the evening, and I was obliged to tell him about Lupin and Mr Perkupp; and, to my surprise, he was quite inclined to side with Lupin. Carrie joined in, and said she thought I was taking much too melancholy a view of it. Gowing produced a pint sample-bottle of Madeira, which had been given him, which he said would get rid of the blues. I dare say it would have done so if there had been more of it; but as Gowing helped himself to three glasses, it did not leave much for Carrie and me to get rid of the blues with.

MAY 15. A day of great anxiety, for I expected every moment a letter from Mr Crowbillon. Two letters came in the evening – one for me, with 'Crowbillon Hall' printed in large gold-and-red letters on the back of the envelope; the other for Lupin, which I felt inclined to open and read, as it had 'Gylterson, Sons, and Co Limited', which was the recommended firm. I trembled as I opened Mr Crowbillon's letter. I wrote him sixteen pages, closely written; he wrote me less than sixteen lines.

His letter was: 'Sir, – I totally disagree with you. Your son, in the course of five minutes' conversation, displayed more intelligence than your firm has done during the last five years. – Yours faithfully, Gilbert E. Gillam O. Crowbillon.'

What am I to do? Here is a letter that I dare not show to Mr Perkupp, and would not show to Lupin for anything. The crisis had yet to come; for Lupin arrived, and, opening his letter, showed a cheque for £25 as a commission for the recommendation of Mr Crowbillon, whose custom to Mr Perkupp is evidently lost for ever. Cummings and Gowing both called, and both took Lupin's part. Cummings went so far as to say that Lupin would make a name yet. I suppose I was melancholy, for I could only ask: 'Yes, but what sort of a name?'

MAY 16. I told Mr Perkupp the contents of the letter in a modified form, but Mr Perkupp said: 'Pray don't discuss the matter; it is at an end. Your son will bring his punishment upon himself.' I went home in the evening, thinking of the hopeless future of Lupin. I found him in most extravagant spirits and in evening dress. He threw a letter on the table for me to read.

To my amazement, I read that Gylterson and Sons had absolutely engaged Lupin at a salary of £200 a year, with other advantages. I read the letter through three times and thought it must have been for me. But there it was – Lupin Pooter – plain enough. I was silent. Lupin said: 'What price Perkupp now? You take my tip, Guv. – "off" with Perkupp and freeze on to Gylterson, the firm of the future! Perkupp's firm? The stagnant dummies have been standing still for years, and now are moving back. I want to go *on*. In fact I must go off, as I am dining with the Murray Poshes tonight.'

In the exuberance of his spirits he hit his hat with his stick, gave a loud war 'Whoo-oop,' jumped over a chair, and took the liberty of rumpling my hair all over my forehead, and bounced out of the room, giving me no chance of reminding him of his age and the respect which was due to his parent. Gowing and Cummings came in the evening, and positively cheered me up with congratulations respecting Lupin.

Gowing said: 'I always said he would get on, and, take my word, he has more in his head than we three put together.'

Carrie said: 'He is a second Hardfur Huttle.'

From *The Diary of a Nobody* by George and Weedon Grossmith, 1892

Expelled from Eden

As he walked down the hall, he felt suddenly alien. A few minutes ago he had been part of this sprawling organism, seeing it from within; now he was outside. The very floors seemed unfriendly, the door-knobs grudging. He had done it to himself but still, unsatisfactory as this group was, he was no longer one of them. The next two weeks would be filled with embarrassed sufferance on the part of the others. The lunch-hour poker in the art department, the after-work cocktails in the bar downstairs, the baseball chatter in the elevator, all would seem different now.

From *The Philanderer* by Stanley Kauffmann, 1953

A Daring Deed

Mrs Yerger bullied us all. In a little while, nearly all of the file clerks quit, a few of the older ones to go into the army or navy, the rest of us for better jobs. I left for a job that turned out to be worse. It took nerve to give notice I was quitting, and it always has. (I rehearsed my resignation speech for days, building up the courage to deliver it, and formulated earnest self-righteous answers to accusing questions about my reasons for leaving that neither Mrs Yerger not anyone else even bothered to ask.) I have this thing about authority, about walking right up to it and looking it squarely in the eye, about speaking right out to it bravely and defiantly, even when I know I am right and safe. (I can never make myself believe I *am* safe.) I just don't trust it.

From *Something Happened* by Joseph Heller, 1974

A Uniform Farewell

Our new American managing director was affable, enthusiastic, conscientious, knowledgeable about all the nuts and bolts of advertising – and completely out of his depth, I thought. When we had our 'getting to know you' drink together in a pub in Esher one Sunday morning and he asked me what my ambition was in the Agency I said that now it was to leave, if they would add to my small pension entitlement that began the next year when I was fifty. He was unflatteringly unshocked and took me up on my suggestion six months later. Roger Lloyd and I shared a leaving party. It was in a hotel where they carved the roast beef in slices as thick as rump steak. Roger and I each received a flowery telegram from our colleagues in the States. Unfortunately, they were identically worded, which rather spoiled the effect. It was like being bidden farewell in a mailing shot designed by a computer.

From *Memoirs of an Advertising Man* by John Mellors, 1976

Twenty-One

THE END OF
THE ROAD

Some forty years after the opening interview – having survived, in one place or another, the sack, assorted managing directors, the depredations of the office wolf or the office vamp, innumerable office parties and canteen salmonella – even the greenest of new arrivals will reach, in the fullness of time, the moment of retirement. The attendant ceremonies are almost as embarrassing as the early stages of the office party: the whip-round for some appropriate item of glass- or silverware, to be suitably engraved; the giant leaving card, every inch of which will be sprawled with waggish or effusive greetings of farewell (trying to think what to say on such occasions is the major literary hazard of office life); the uneasy farewell drinks-cum-presentation, at which the senior member present says a few familiar words to mark the end of a lifetime ('Life here will never be quite the same again' and 'However shall we cope without you?') – all of which are flattering enough but, life being the way it is, manifestly untrue.

Retirement itself lies beyond the scope of this book. For a while the names and reputations of office tyrants and office characters live on in memory and folklore; for a while they return to haunt the scenes of their past. But every time there are fewer left who knew them, and less and less to say; in the end the connection is broken, and nothing more remains.

'Takeover' –

And what's more, you'll have your own quill
And what's more, you'll have your own stool
And what's more, you'll have your own desk
And what's more, you'll have your own phone
And what's more, you'll have your own secretary
And what's more, you'll have your own personal computer
And what's more, you'll have your own redundancy payment
    and your own farewell party

From *Under the Circumstances* by D. J. Enright, 1991

A Last Time

'There's a last time for everything.'

It was not his habit to talk to himself, he was rounding up and tidying away a sickness of heart, some universal heart of the matter. He hoped his own feelings had not become distorted, this was supposed to be a happy occasion. This, he remembered, putting his key into the lock, was a moment people cherished. He himself was marking the occasion with thought, certainly he did not feel one way or the other.

The habit of a lifetime was about to be broken. He could say so, but the habit would not break now, nor tomorrow, nor next week. It would scarcely break at all, it would wither and starve and hang on in shreds. The human spirit being what it was, he must from time to time expect to find himself ready to go through the hoops.

Trying, he thought, that will be very trying. He would have preferred a clean finish on the other side of the door mat. From then on he might say he was his own master, he was free – which he had never been before. Before, it was all to do, he owed a living. Now he was paid up and the living was his own. What was left of it.

The time of day prompted that last thought, he was tired, therefore he was inclined to pessimism. When the daylight ran out it took a long wick of youth to burn up against the dark.

He wiped his feet on the mat. As far as he was concerned it was finished and if any of it went on it must be regarded as reflex action, a nervous twitch. The sickness was not in his heart.

Habit suffered its first fracture: he did not hang up his bowler and his umbrella, he lifted the lid of the hall chest and laid them away. He then took out an old grey felt and put it on the peg which his City hat had always occupied.

Charlotte, coming from the kitchen, saw the grey felt and her prepared face, not prepared for that, pursed, then brightened defensively. 'Oh, it's you,' she said, thus making her distinction because it would hardly be anyone else and because she always at this time said, 'Hallo, dear.' 'Hallo, dear,' at five past seven, for going on forty years, with one break – one small break it seemed now – of the war years. She looked at him – with pride, was it, compunction, or disquiet? – before she reached up to kiss his cheek bone. 'I thought you would be later.'

'Why?' He knew, but sensed more preparation, a going-gently, against possible disappointment, snub, hurt, or even something enough to corrode and undermine the forty years. 'We did have a bit of a gathering. Colonel Rayburn is off to the States tonight so it had to be early.'

'Why, that was nice!' She sounded relieved.

'One or two people came in to say goodbye.' At five o'clock, when they all had the week's work to wind up and leave ready coiled for Monday, cutting out of the legitimate day an aimless and uncomfortable hour of holding glasses, cigarettes and sweet French biscuits and trying not to catch, let alone hold, anyone's glance. 'Sherry doesn't agree with me.'

'And Colonel Rayburn was there – and Langley? Did Langley come?'

'And Cyril Ford and Miss Endicott.'

'Even Miss Endicott!'

'Cody's office took it in turns to go down and man the phone.'

'Then it was quite a party, quite a send-off?'

'I'm not going anywhere,' he said, 'unless you count Edensea.' He unstrapped his wrist-watch, as always, to lay aside on his dressing-table when he changed into his house jacket. 'They gave me a clock.'

'A clock?'

'With an inscription. As far as I can remember it reads: "Presented to John Henry Agar by his friends and colleagues on the occasion of his retirement from the Solomon Rayburn Company"!'

'But how nice of them!'

'Eight-day Westminster chime, walnut case, Arabic gold figures, a dignified and reliable piece,' he said, winding his watch. 'They should have given it to me forty years ago, I had more need of time then.'

'Where is it?' Charlotte peered round his shoulder. 'Where's the clock?'

'Cody's bringing it tomorrow in his car. I didn't want it chiming on the Underground.'

'It was a nice gesture, but no more than you deserve.'

She was being too careful, as if he had suffered a bereavement. 'There's a last time for everything,' he said, 'only we don't always know when it's come.'

Charlotte had always known what to do with her hands, she fastened them warmly round his wrists. 'You'll feel it at first, of course. You're bound to. But that will pass –'

'I don't feel it. Why should I? I've done my job, I organised and ran an efficient department and now it's all theirs.' He did not say, as he thought, that now it would go to pieces. 'I'm an old man. I ceased to be useful at 5.30 this p.m.' Watching her face disarrange and crumple, he thought so here was the sickness in her heart, being nursed and softly handled because she thought it must be in his. 'If they were honest they would have told me so at 5.31 instead of pretending it was the end of an era.'

From 'A Question of Identity' in *Lost upon the Roundabouts*
by A. L. Barker, 1964

For the Sake of the Bank

'If one works till sixty, one does very well,' Miss Vernon said.

'You did not think that applicable to me, ma'am,' said the clerk. 'You would not let me give up till I was near seventy.'

'For the sake of the bank – for the sake of the young men. Where would they have been without a guide?'

From *Hester* by Mrs Oliphant, 1883

'How long is it you've been with us, Mr Josser?'

Then Mr Battlebury arrived. Even without his overcoat he was still a big man. He had a broad fleshy face, with heavy dewlaps and a long protruding nose that started too high up his forehead. What remained of his hair was crisp and curly and he wore it cut short except for a little bunch of the stuff that sprang out over each ear. The dome of his head was entirely bald – prematurely bald that is – for Mr Battlebury was only forty-three. Altogether his skull had a smooth glossy appearance as though it were regularly massaged, or even polished. Not that it seemed in the least out of place. Everything about Mr Battlebury was rather highly polished.

'Well, well, well,' he began, rubbing his hands together. 'Are we all ready?'

He surveyed the room with a gratifyingly pleased beam through his horn-rimmed spectacles and then stopped himself abruptly.

'But where's Josser?' he asked.

There was just a trace of irritation in his voice as he put the question. Mr Battlebury, it was apparent, did not like to be kept waiting even on purely social occasions.

He was not kept waiting for long, however. The door from the Counting House reopened and four large ledgers with a pair of striped trousers underneath them came into sight. The ledgers hesitated for a moment and

[365]

then steered a swaying and erratic course toward the big steel safe on the opposite side of the room.

A voice from behind the ledgers said: 'Just coming, sir.'

Everybody gave a little titter. Then, as the walking ledgers passed the centre of the room, the owner of the voice came into sight. He was a small, elderly man with a wisp of white hair that stood straight up like egrets' feathers. Under his black business coat, a blue knitted cardigan showed like an azure body-band along the back and seemed to divide him into two portions. When he finally reached the safe he tilted forward, swung the steel doors together, locked them and took the bunch of keys over to Mr Veritter. There was something oddly mechanical about the whole operation. It was like that of an actor who has rehearsed a small part so thoroughly that he has forgotten what it is all about. It was obvious that Mr Josser could have carried it all through blindfolded.

As soon as he had handed over the keys he began dusting his hands one against the other and addressed himself again to Mr Battlebury.

'Sorry to keep you waiting, sir,' he said.

Two of the young ladies exchanged glances. They were Miss Heyland who hammered away for nearly eight hours a day at the invoicing machine and Miss Woodman who was Mr Veritter's secretary.

'Isn't that just like old Josser?' Miss Heyland observed. 'Still working.'

'He *is* rather a *pet*,' Miss Woodman admitted.

'Won't he miss it – after all this time,' Miss Heyland remarked sentimentally.

'Oh I don't know,' replied Miss Woodman. 'Would you?'

Meanwhile, Mr Battlebury was smiling again, now that he discovered that he wasn't to be kept waiting after all.

'Ah Josser,' he said. 'Nothing like clearing up, is there?'

'No, sir,' Mr Josser replied dutifully.

'Well,' said Mr Battlebury. 'We mustn't take up too much time because everybody wants to be off home. I'm sure that I do, and I'm sure Mr Josser does. But I felt – we all felt – that we couldn't let our old friend go without making some little presentation to him. That's why we're all here now.'

Mr Battlebury paused and began rubbing his hands together again as though he were looking forward to Mr Josser's departure and saw no point in concealing it.

'How long is it you've been with us, Mr Josser?' he asked in the easy, deceptive manner of a counsel trying to draw out an uncommunicative witness.

'Forty-two years, sir,' Mr Josser answered.

The answer came pat because those forty-two years had been in his mind a great deal lately. Ever since his last illness Mr Josser had found himself steadily re-living them. It was as though inside his brain someone were turning over the pages of an old photographic album with smudgy pictures of himself on every page.

But Mr Battlebury had cheerfully taken up the thread of his address again.

'Forty-two,' he remarked heartily. 'Just about my age. Might almost be twins, Mr Josser?'

He was smiling so broadly by now that Mr Josser could see that he was meant to smile as well. He did so obediently even though he didn't feel in the least like smiling.

'So now our old friend is going to have the rest he deserves,' Mr Battlebury rattled on. 'No more running for the early tram, eh Mr Josser? No more waiting about in the rain for the same old tram to take you home again. I'm bound to say I almost envy you.' Here Mr Battlebury shook his head as though the greater part of his life was spent in the rain waiting about for trams. 'But the rest of us,' he went on, 'have got to put in a few more years before we can retire – that's so, isn't it Miss Sweeting.'

Miss Sweeting was eighteen and had just joined Battlebury's straight from a Secretarial College. It seemed that the College had taught her everything about Pitman's Shorthand and touch typewriting, but nothing at all about large hearty men like Mr Battlebury. She was a pretty fair-haired girl and she blushed.

'Definitely,' she said, and tried to look older than she was.

'And now the time has come to make our little presentation to Mr Josser,' Mr Battlebury continued.

He paused and Mr Josser shifted in his chair in embarrassment.

'Thank you, sir,' he said awkwardly.

'No, no,' Mr Battlebury caught him up. 'You don't have to thank me. They only asked me to speak because I've known you longest.'

Mr Battlebury turned abruptly towards the man on his right.

'Got it there, Veritter?' he demanded.

'Here it is, sir,' Mr Veritter answered, rising hurriedly.

He went over to a table at the back of the room, and picked up the big marble clock tenderly, as though it were a large stony baby. Then he placed it openly on the drawing cabinet beside Mr Battlebury and stood back. Up to that moment he had been trying to keep the whole thing out of sight so that he could produce it as a surprise even though Mr Josser had been asked what he wanted and nearly everyone else had helped to choose it.

'Well,' said Mr Battlebury in a rising crescendo of heartiness, 'this is the very handsome time-piece for which your friends have subscribed.

And every time you look at it you can just sit back and remember that the rest of your time's your own.'

'The rest of my time's my own,' Mr Josser found himself repeating silently.

He had got up and come forward. Now that he was standing up beside the majestic form of Mr Battlebury everyone could see how small he was. How small and how shabby. Viewed from the front the effect of the blue woollen cardigan that Mrs Josser had knitted him was even more striking. It buttoned up almost to the throat and made Mr Josser look as though he'd dressed hurriedly and not put on anything underneath. The cuffs of the cardigan which were too long anyhow, had been rolled up and hung down outside the sleeves of the black jacket.

But it was his face at which everyone was looking. Behind the pince-nez glasses which lay aslant upon his nose – one of the springs was broken: it had been broken for years, seven or eight years at least, and Mr Josser had never had it mended – large tears were forming. At last, one of them detached itself and slithered down his cheek on to the ragged grey moustache.

Mr Josser took out his handkerchief and mopped about with it.

'Oh look,' said Miss Woodman. 'He's crying.'

'Sshh!' Miss Heyland replied sharply. 'He'll hear you.'

But Mr Battlebury had picked up the clock by now. Formally and with a little bow, he gave it to Mr Josser. It looked even bigger in Mr Josser's arms than it had done in Mr Battlebury's. Mr Josser sagged right down under the weight of it.

'And now,' said Mr Battlebury, feeling in his pocket, 'here is my own little contribution. I told you that I didn't have anything to do with the clock, that is entirely from the – er – staff.'

He produced a flat white envelope as he spoke, and Mr Josser mechanically caught hold of it.

Then Mr Battlebury held out his hand for a cordial last handshake. But Mr Josser could do nothing about it. The clock had just slipped alarmingly and he now had both arms gripped frantically round it. He seemed to be wrestling with himself. The envelope that Mr Battlebury had given him was crushed and crumpled in his right hand. The other hand was clutching the clock.

And this was a pity: because in all those years of their association this was the first time that Mr Battlebury had ever tried to shake hands with Mr Josser.

It was very quiet now in the counting-house and only one of the lights was still on. The girls had left first, going off down the staircase in twos and threes, all chattering like a company of sparrows, and carrying their mysterious Christmas packages. The men had been rather slower about leaving. They had stood about first in groups, filling their pipes, and savouring the pleasant sensation of not actually doing anything. Then with a lot of cheery talk along familiar lines – 'Have a good time, old man,' 'Don't eat too much,' and 'Be good,' and 'Keep sober' – they, too, had gone. Mr Josser was left standing there.

He had shaken hands with all of them, one after another, until he was sick of shaking hands. He never wanted to see another hand again. And he had said 'Happy Christmas' thirty-two times in all. But it was of neither of these that he was thinking now. He was thinking of the speech that he had just made. Ever since he had known that there was going to be a presentation he had been practising the little address – the few words – that he was going to give them. Among so many young people he suddenly felt like the ancient of the tribe, Old Wise Owl, and there was all manner of deep advice that he wanted to give them.

And what had actually happened? He had simply stood there facing the lot of them – even mere children like Miss Sweeting – and had remained silent, absolutely silent, for what must have been about thirty seconds. Then, in a thick unnatural voice that didn't sound in the least like his own, he had said all in one gulp, 'Thankyouallverymuch,' and had sat down again. Just that. No more.

The door behind him opened suddenly and Mr Veritter stood there. He had got nearly as far as Cannon Street before he had discovered that he had left his reading glasses behind him in his desk. He started when he saw Mr Josser.

'Hullo, Josser,' he said. 'You still here?'

Mr Josser dropped his eyes to avoid Mr Veritter's.

'Yes, I'm still here, sir,' he answered lamely.

'Have all the others gone?'

'Yes sir, they've all gone.'

Mr Veritter stood regarding him for a moment and then went through into his inner office. His glasses were there exactly where he had left them. Mr Veritter shut up his desk once more and came back again into the Counting House.

Mr Josser had not moved and Mr Veritter became apprehensive for a moment – but not too apprehensive as he still meant to have a slap at catching the 5.45.

'Feeling all right, aren't you, Josser?' he asked. 'Chest's not troubling you again?'

Mr Josser drew himself up with a jerk.

'I'm perfectly well, thank you sir,' he replied. And, after a long pause, he added, 'Perfectly well' as though to settle the matter.

Mr Veritter took one last glance at him and one glance at his watch.

'Well, good-bye, Josser,' Mr Veritter said hurriedly. 'Happy Christmas. Come back and see us sometime.'

'Thank you, sir,' Mr Josser answered. 'Same to you, sir. I will.'

Then, when Mr Veritter had left him, he went on standing there as before.

It was the sound of St Mary-Under-Cannon striking the half-hour that roused him. He went over to the hat stand and took down his alpaca office coat. It rolled into quite a small parcel, and he wrapped it up carefully in a copy of the *Star* that someone had left in the waste paper basket. Then he pulled open his drawer – the inside of the drawer that was the nearest that he had ever come to privacy in Battlebury and Son – and removed the things that belonged to him. There was a packet of pipe cleaners, several empty tobacco tins, a collar stud, the end of a pair of braces and a box of iodised pastilles. He threw the tobacco tins and the brace-ends into the waste paper basket, and shovelled the rest into his pocket.

Finally, with a feeling almost like relief, now that the moment had actually come, he put on his raincoat, wound the knitted muffler round his neck – it was blue, like the cardigan: off the same skein in fact – clapped his hat on his head, gathered up the clock that was now back in the wrapping in which the makers had supplied it, took up his umbrella from the corner, turned off the light – with difficulty, because his hands were full – and closed the door behind him.

Mr Josser and the fullness of life had parted company.

From *London Belongs to Me* by Norman Collins, 1945

'You're a gentleman of leisure now'

No one appeared to look with unusual interest at Mr Baldwin as he walked into the office at three o'clock. The Cashiers were busy as they always were on the days following Michaelmas: the telephone was ringing, several clients stood at the rail with papers spread before them – everything was so exactly the same, so normal that he could not avoid a slight sense of disappointment. A day of such consequence to him might at least have sent a ripple across those bowed, working heads.

As Chief Cashier, he occupied a screened-in corner to himself, but glass played so large a part in the screens that the official behind them was always known as the goldfish. His desk was clear of official papers, but it still remained for him to clear out the personal relics that had accumulated there; a strange assortment that had travelled with him from desk to desk in his gradual rise to the screened-in corner; odd things that for some reason or another had not been destroyed or taken home.

For once and for all he had got to decide what to do with his Menu of the Staff Jubilee Dinner, held at Gatti's in 1889. It had been too valuable to destroy but too dangerous to take home, for Denny had been on the staff in those days, and Denny had become a famous black-and-white artist a few years later. Amongst the high-spirited after-dinner scribblings on the Menu card was an authentic, early Denny – unfortunately a somewhat indecent Denny. To rub it out would have been vandalism, to take it home and risk Edith seeing it would have been unthinkable, and so it had lain amongst this jetsam, dusty and fading, for thirty-six years.

It occurred to Mr Baldwin that one of the Juniors might like to have it, but there would be no purpose in giving it away unless he pointed out the reason for its value, and to do that would scarcely be in keeping with his position as Chief Cashier. The card was still creased where he had folded it for his pocket on that distant night: it had been his first Dinner: he had been in the office five years and he was to marry Edith in the summer. Huîtres – Potage Russe – Whitebait – Duckling – somebody had scrawled here, 'Where are you going when this is over?' He tried to decipher the names, and the misty pencil scrawls took misty form – ghosts in high collars – in frock coats that dangled to boot heels hitched to the crossbars of absurdly high stools: flickering gas jets over each office desk, a baking heat from fifty jets when a pea-soup fog demanded lights all day. A curious crowd round the first telephone, touching it as if it were a bomb – a whiskered Messenger screwing down a copying book in a machine that looked like Caxton's printing press – pulling out clammy, sodden letters, folding them and stamping them. The Queen was nearly seventy and they used to wonder how much longer the head of a girl would appear on her lilac postage stamps. The office itself had scarcely changed, except for the central heating and electric light. The Management prided itself upon its old foundation and tried to retain the atmosphere of the past. The door was the same that the merry party had used on their way up West for the Gatti's Dinner, but they had climbed on to a growling iron rimmed omnibus, young Mr Baldwin beside the driver, with a lamp-lit view of a swaying tail and sweating haunches. Everybody above the rank of office boy had worn a top hat in those times, and a woman in the City was as rare as a horse to-day. And the streets themselves: swirls of dust on an August evening; a mire on a winter night; unbelievably quiet when the staff worked late at overtime. Now and then the clip-clop of a hansom, taking a City Magnate to the station ... so near to yesterday that the closing of the eyes brought back the very sounds ...

He lay the Menu card aside, for despite years of indecision he still had a few more minutes to decide its fate. These casually collected relics linked themselves together and formed a panorama. He propped up the lid of his desk, for he did not want anyone to see what he was doing. There were a few picture postcards from men on their holidays: Bexhill, Lowestoft – one from an adventurer who had gone to Guernsey: a report of an Inter-Office Chess Match, kept for its record of 'T. H. Baldwin, 1. F. Cass, 0' – report of an Office Cricket Match: 'Baldwin, run out, 3.' There was a cigarette picture of Mornington Cannon, the jockey, a few fossilised pieces of india-rubber and a sweepstake ticket. Amongst the fluff and cake crumbs in a corner there lay a small splinter of anti-aircraft shell that he had picked up in the doorway of the office. He destroyed the papers but he dropped the splinter into his pocket. There was a musty sentiment about old papers that was best forgotten, but the sentiment of this jagged, glittering piece of steel was of another kind. It conjured up cold starlight nights of loneliness, with whistle and truncheon, when for a few dark hours he had been a different kind of man from the Baldwin who had defeated F. Cass at chess and the Baldwin run out for three in the office cricket match.

He scraped a few nibs and paper clips together, dropped them into an envelope and put them in his pocket. The desk was empty, he lowered the lid and was surprised to see Henslip the Messenger just closing the main doors. He had been dreaming in his desk for over half an hour, but he was glad the time had passed so quickly.

He knew exactly what was going to happen now. Strictly speaking it was a secret shared by the staff and withheld from him alone, but he had shared the secret with the others so many times in the past that it could not hold any surprise for him now.

First of all, Henslip the Messenger disappeared into the Manager's room. Then he emerged, went downstairs and returned with a small brown-paper parcel. After another short disappearance he re-emerged and passed with a furtive importance from one member of the staff to another whispering something to each. Each member of the staff, upon receiving the whisper, glanced curiously towards Mr Baldwin's desk, slid off his stool and disappeared into the Manager's room.

He saw the girls file downstairs from the typewriting rooms and follow the men: gradually the office emptied until Mr Baldwin sat alone behind his glass screen. Then there was a hitch. The telephone rang, Henslip hurried with an impatient grunt to answer it, and called out, 'Mr Robins!

– Somebody wants to report a Fire Claim!' A harassed Junior came out of the Manager's room, and for a few moments Mr Baldwin sat listening to words that seemed now to eddy back from the past – 'Yes – I see – curtain blew into candle flame – have you got your policy number? – Never mind, I'll turn it up. I'll send you a Claim Form. Good-bye.'

Henslip was fidgeting outside the telephone box. He hustled the Junior back to the Manager's room and crossed the silent office to Mr Baldwin's desk.

'Will you come into Mr Wilson's room, sir?'

Mr Baldwin looked up from an almanack with an attempt at surprise. 'Yes. All right. I'll come now.'

He was glad to feel so calm and controlled, for he had been dreading this moment for days. He waited until Henslip had gone, then tore the Gatti's Menu into little squares and threw them into the fire as he passed on his way to the Manager's room. It seemed to be the right and only moment to destroy it.

Mr Wilson had a spacious, cheerful room, flooded with sunlight on fine mornings, for its windows were upon a side street with low buildings opposite. Now the lights were on and above the buildings lay a green strip of smoky sky. On the mantelpiece stood a photograph of Mr Wilson's wife, for it was a custom of successive Managers to have some personal decoration in this room. At one time Mr Baldwin had had visions of a photograph of Edith standing there, but things had not worked out that way.

The whole staff, men and girls, were grouped round the walls, and Mr Wilson stood behind his desk, his tea tray pushed aside to make way for the brown-paper parcel.

'Are we all here?'

'Yes, sir,' said Henslip, closing the door.

It is embarrassing for people who know each other to stand together in a crowd. Young ones, unused to the ceremony, shuffled, looked down at their feet or at their fingernails, older ones gazed with bland smiles at Mr Baldwin, the sort of smiles used at weddings, turned on very carefully to half pressure to prevent them wearing out too soon. Mr Baldwin took up his position a little in front of the rest, like a prisoner about to hear sentence at Court Martial. He smiled feebly at Mr Wilson, then lowered his eyes to the edge of the Manager's desk. Henslip stood nearest him and he caught the slight odour of long-used flannel that always rose from the Messenger's red, polished face. A coal popped in the fire, and there was silence. Then Mr Wilson cleared his throat and began.

'Mr Baldwin. The staff has asked me to hand you this little souvenir on the occasion of your retirement. I need hardly say what a sad occasion it is for us although I'm sure it's a very happy one for you. We shall miss you, for although we may be able to fill your official position we cannot replace your personality.'

There were some appreciative murmurs, and Mr Wilson turned to the staff.

'Mr Baldwin joined the staff of this office in 1884: he has given honourable service for forty-one years. He could tell us some interesting stories of the naughty nineties if he wanted to – even of the eighties, too! There's no need for me to enlarge upon Mr Baldwin's virtues, for they are known to you all. The office will remember him as a loyal and devoted servant: we personally shall remember him as an upright gentleman. We all wish you, Mr Baldwin, many years of the happiness and leisure that you so justly deserve, and we hope you will often come in to see us. We ask you to accept this little present as a token of our esteem.'

Mr Wilson waited for the polite applause to die away, then drew aside the brown paper and revealed a neat square clock in varnished oak. He picked it up with a smile and put it down again on the corner of the desk nearest Mr Baldwin.

It was Mr Baldwin's turn. He took a step forward, his fingers fumbled the clock as he turned to face the staff. He did not feel like Mr Baldwin at all, he was a strange, light-headed person who had had some vague connection with a Mr Baldwin in the past, who began to recite words that this Mr Baldwin had taught him.

'Mr Wilson, Ladies and Gentlemen. I really can't tell you how much I – I value this lovely present. I shall always keep it to remind me of the days in the old office, because they've been good days. I'm sorry they're over, and I'm going to miss you all. It's very kind of you to think of giving me such a beautiful present. Thank you very much . . . very much indeed.'

The short speech, with its abrupt close took everybody by surprise and there was an awkward little silence before Mr Wilson nodded to Henslip to open the door. The telephone began calling out like a spoilt child annoyed at being left alone: someone hurried off to soothe it, the girls and the Juniors edged along the walls and disappeared. Some of the senior men shook hands with Mr Baldwin, others, less senior, nearly did. Gradually the room emptied and Mr Baldwin was alone with the Manager.

He had never felt at ease with Wilson. Five years Mr Wilson's senior, it had been difficult for him when this tall, puckered man arrived from the Head Office to take command.

'Well, Baldwin – you're a gentleman of leisure now!'

'Yes,' said Mr Baldwin with a faint smile.

'What are you going to do with yourself?'

'Oh, there's a good many things been waiting for this to happen. Garden, you know – and books to read – and – and hobbies –'

'That's right. Hobbies are the thing.'

Henslip the Messenger tapped at the door and peeped in.

'Shall I do the clock up for you, Mr Baldwin?'

'Yes, do please – Henslip.'

The Manager himself took the clock across to Henslip and Mr Baldwin followed with the paper and string.

'I'll find a stronger bit of string than that,' said Henslip.

The Manager turned back into the room and offered Mr Baldwin a cigarette.

'Don't forget to look us up sometimes.'

'Certainly,' replied Mr Baldwin, knowing quite well that retired members of the staff were a curse when they came wandering round, wasting people's time.

'Is your wife keeping well?'

'Quite.'

'That's good.'

The Manager's eyes were upon a pile of letters waiting for his signature, and Mr Baldwin held out his hand.

'Well, good-bye, Mr Wilson. Thanks for the nice things you said in that speech.'

Mr Wilson smiled. 'I meant it. Well, good-bye.'

He met one of the Juniors as he went downstairs for his overcoat and hat: a pleasant lad who lived somewhere out in the country and had an hour's train journey to get home. He stopped, flashed a smile at Mr Baldwin and said: 'We're going to miss you a lot, sir – the way you always help us' – the boy played football on Saturday afternoons and Mr Baldwin had sometimes helped him to get away sharp at one o'clock by taking a bundle of letters from him and doing them up himself – 'we've just been saying so downstairs ... how decent you've been to us ... thanks ...' The boy's library book slid from under his arm and clattered on the stairs, there was a dive for it ... a laugh ... a flustered handshake ... a cold hand, still damp from washing. 'Don't be silly,' said Mr Baldwin. 'I've never done anything.'

'You've done lots and we're going to miss you. Don't forget to come in and see us sometimes, sir.' Another smile and the boy was gone. Something flew up and stung Mr Baldwin at the back of his nose and he hastened downstairs to the lavatories.

A little later, with a neat brown parcel under his arm, he rumbled the main door to and joined the broad stream of home-goers. The last moments in the office had seemed unreal to him, but everything was cool and normal here: the same brown, shining street – the same swinging of umbrellas and bobbing of white folded newspapers – the same giant buildings filled with light – the same deep murmur – the same narrow strips of remote, unnoticed sky.

From *Greengates* by R. C. Sherriff, 1936

The Clearing of Drawers

The organization where Letty and Marcia worked regarded it as a duty to provide some kind of retirement party for them, when the time came for them to give up working. Their status as ageing unskilled women did not entitle them to an evening party, but it was felt that a lunchtime gathering, leading only to more than usual drowsiness in the afternoon, would be entirely appropriate. The other advantage of a lunchtime party was that only medium Cyprus sherry need be provided, whereas the evening called for more exotic and expensive drinks, wines and even the occasional carefully concealed bottle of whisky or gin – 'the hard stuff', as Norman called it, in his bitterness at being denied access to it. Also at lunchtime sandwiches could be eaten, so that there was no need to have lunch and it was felt by some that at a time like this it was 'better' to be eating – it gave one something to do.

Retirement was a serious business, to be regarded with respect, though the idea of it was incomprehensible to most of the staff. It was a condition that must be studied and prepared for, certainly – 'researched' they would have said – indeed it had already been the subject of a seminar, though the conclusions reached and the recommendations drawn up had no real bearing on the retirement of Letty and Marcia, which seemed as inevitable as the falling of the leaves in autumn, for which no kind of preparation needed to be made. If the two women feared that the coming of this date might give some clue to their ages, it was not an occasion for embarrassment because nobody else had been in the least interested, both of them having long ago reached ages beyond any kind of speculation. Each would be given a small golden handshake, but the State would provide for their basic needs which could not be all that great. Elderly women did not need much to eat, warmth was more necessary than food, and people like Letty and Marcia probably had either private means or savings, a nest-egg in the Post Office or a Building Society. It was comforting to think on these lines, and even if they had nothing extra, the social services were so much better now, there was no need for anyone to starve or freeze. And if governments failed in their duty there were always the media – continual goadings on television programmes, upsetting articles in the Sunday papers and disturbing pictures in the colour supplements. There was no need to worry about Miss Crowe and Miss Ivory.

The (acting) deputy assistant director, who had been commanded to make the presentation speech, wasn't quite sure what it was that Miss Crowe and Miss Ivory did or had done during their working life. The activities of their department seemed to be shrouded in mystery – something to do with records or filing, it was thought, nobody knew for certain, but it was evidently 'women's work', the kind of thing that could easily be replaced by a computer. The most significant thing about it was that nobody was replacing them, indeed the whole department was being phased out and only being kept on until the men working in it reached retirement age. Yet under the influence of a quick swig of sherry, even this unpromising material could be used to good effect.

The deputy assistant director stepped into the middle of the room and began to speak.

'The point about Miss Crowe and Miss Ivory, whom we are met together to honour today, is that nobody knows exactly, or has ever known exactly, what it is that they do,' he declared boldly. 'They have been – they *are* – the kind of people who work quietly and secretly, doing good by stealth, as it were. *Good*, do I hear you ask? Yes, good, I repeat, and good I mean. In these days of industrial unrest it is people like Miss Ivory and Miss Crowe' – the names seemed to have got reversed, but presumably it didn't matter – 'who are an example to us all. We shall miss them very much, so much so that nobody has been found to replace them, but we would be the last to deny them the rewards of a well earned retirement. It gives me much pleasure on behalf of the company and staff to present each of these ladies with a small token of our appreciation of their long and devoted service, which carries with it our best wishes for their future.'

Letty and Marcia then came forward, each to receive an envelope containing a cheque and a suitably inscribed card, the presenter remembered a luncheon engagement and slipped away, glasses were refilled and a buzz of talk broke out. Conversation had to be made and it did not come very easily once the obvious topics had been exhausted. As the party went on, people divided most easily into everyday working groups. It was the most natural thing then for Letty and Marcia to find themselves with Edwin and Norman, and for the latter to make some comment on the speech and to suggest that from what had been said he supposed they would spend their retirement setting the motor industry to rights.

Letty began clearing out her office drawer, neatly arranging its contents in her shopping bag. There was not much to be taken away – a pair of light slippers for the days when she needed to change her shoes, a box of paper handkerchiefs, writing paper and envelopes, a packet of indigestion tablets. Following Letty's example, Marcia began to do the same, muttering as she did so and stuffing the contents into a large carrier bag. Letty knew that Marcia's drawer was very full although she had never seen inside it properly, only caught glimpses of things bulging out when Marcia opened it. She knew that there was a pair of exercise sandals in which Marcia used to clump around in the days when she had first bought them, but she was surprised to see her take out several tins of food – meat, beans and soups.

'Quite a gourmet feast you've got there,' Norman remarked. 'If only we'd known.'

Marcia smiled but said nothing. Norman seemed to be able to get away with these teasing comments, Letty thought. She had turned aside, not wanting to see what Marcia was taking out of the drawer. It seemed an intrusion into Marcia's private life, something it was better not to know about.

'It will seem funny without you both,' said Edwin awkwardly. He did not really know what to say now that it had come to the point. None of them knew, for it was the kind of occasion that seemed to demand something more than the usual good-bye or good night of the end of an ordinary working day. Perhaps they should have given the women a present of some kind – but *what*? He and Norman had discussed it, but decided in the end that it was altogether too difficult. 'They wouldn't expect it – it would only embarrass them,' they had concluded, 'and it's not as if we were never going to see them again.' In the circumstances it was much easier to assume this but without going into too much detail about it. For of course they *would* all meet again – Letty and Marcia would revisit the office, 'pop in' some time. There might even be meetings outside the office – a kind of get-together for lunch or 'something' . . . even if it was beyond imagining what that something might be, at least it made it easier for them all to go on their separate ways assuming a vague future together.

'I see you've spread yourselves out a bit,' she said, noticing that the men now seemed to occupy all the space that had once accommodated the four of them. Again she experienced the feeling of nothingness, when it was borne in on her so forcibly that she and Marcia had been phased out in this way, as if they had never existed. Looking round the room, her eyes lighted on a spider plant which she had brought one day and not bothered to take away when she left. It had proliferated; many little offshoots were now hanging down until they dangled over the radiator. Was there some significance in this, a proof that she had once existed, that the memory of her lingered on? At least Nature went on, whatever happened to us; she knew that.

'Yes, it's grown, that plant,' Edwin said. 'I've watered it every week.'

'You left a bit of yourself behind,' said Norman, in his chatty way ...

From *Quartet in Autumn* by Barbara Pym, 1977

The Farewell Lunch

The office boy brought in a hand-written envelope and placed it on Jane's desk.

> Miss Jane Broadbent [said the card inside] is cordially invited to the farewell luncheon in honour of Mr Charles Pringle, Director, who is retiring after fifty years' service with the Company.

Jane knew Mr Pringle well. He came in every morning for a couple of hours to keep an eye on the department. He also tempered Caesar's wrath on occasions, but found this tiring. He had his own room, and Jane worked for him. The work was not arduous: she used to dust his desk and change the calendar each day. One morning he dictated a letter. It was to the manager of a famous hotel in Brighton, asking him to forward Mrs Pringle's slippers, which she'd left under the bed the previous weekend.

He was a kindly old man. In his time he must have been as ruthless as the rest, but now he was freewheeling. He had come right up from the bottom: office boy in Birmingham. He was always telling their office boy about it.

From *The Underlings* by Barbara Benson, 1977

The Retirement Clock

Mr Baldwin felt unreasonably self-conscious standing on Broad Street platform with the clock under his arm. Although it was done up in brown paper and nobody could possibly guess what it was, he could not help feeling that a placard reading 'RETIRED!' hung round his neck.

The crowd around him, companions of a thousand journeys, seemed detached and remote from him now. The bond that had held him to them had snapped at four o'clock when the door of the office closed. His spirit was no longer with them, but his body would have to stand amongst them on the platform and sit amongst them in the train until a porter called out 'Brondesbury Park!' He was glad when the train came in, and the clock, with his hat on top of it, lay on the luggage rack above his head.

An elderly man in the far corner had also placed a parcel on the luggage rack, and Mr Baldwin wondered whether he, too, had received a clock that afternoon. Then the man leant forward and began a vigorous conversation with a friend. Mr Baldwin caught the words 'stocktaking next week . . . late evenings . . . more business in the spring,' and he knew that the old man's parcel contained no clock: he could not make him a spiritual companion for the journey home. All these other passengers, the old man included, would go to the City tomorrow morning and be on this train to-morrow night. With a deepening loneliness he opened his evening paper.

The train drew out and side-stepped clumsily across the points. The chilly night had been observed by the railway authorities, and they had caused a stuffy, metallic smell to ooze in warm clouds from beneath the seat and up Mr Baldwin's trouser legs. He watched the familiar electric signs pass by for his last inspection and began to realise how little he had prepared himself for what had happened this afternoon. Freedom – leisure: they were words for inspiration, and he was like an old canary with its cage door open, crouching on the furthest end of its perch. He had made no plans. If he had thought of it at all he had rarely planned anything beyond an extra half hour in bed and a morning in the garden, but mostly he had put the matter uneasily from his mind. Retirement, he had told himself, could take care of itself when it came. It meant decay: the beginning of the end and he had no desire to premeditate it.

But now he began to think as a marooned man might think as he calculates the time his food will last. There was his scrap-book with a good many cuttings waiting to be stuck in: a picture frame to repair and some drawers to clear out: there was the garden: an afternoon walk and books he had been waiting to read. He had been given his reward for forty years of work. He had yearned a thousand times for freedom, and now that it had come he was afraid of it. It was the fear of a man who, having habitually enjoyed two apples a day, is suddenly called upon to eat six in the same period.

He was a man of method; he had planned his leisure in such a way that its whole span was comfortably filled – no part being overcrowded and no part empty. Home usually at six, there was a half-hour's rest and talk with Edith, a walk until dinner-time, his diary, business and books from then until bed, with a visit to the pictures once a week and an occasional theatre in the West End. For Saturday afternoons there was always a football match to watch in the Park and for Sundays there was the garden, tea with friends and some pleasant, aimless pottering. In the past, without a moment's boredom, he had comfortably enjoyed four hours of leisure each day: his problem was how to dispose of twelve. If he were an old man he could doze away the extra hours before the fire, but he was not an old man: he was only fifty-eight . . .

Mr Baldwin hitched the clock firmly under his arm to open the gate. For some months past the front gate had been opening with increasing difficulty, with a resentful squeak that robbed the door-bell of all importance. He made a mental note of the gate as one of the things he would now have time to attend to. He could save a good deal by setting aside half an hour a day for minor repairs.

He heard his wife's familiar 'All right, Ada!' as he rang the bell. The basement stairs had begun to trouble Ada of recent years and they were in the habit of saving her the climb when they knew for certain who was at the door.

Edith stood under the hall light, and Mr Baldwin gave her the traditional kiss. She gave no sign to suggest that this was not just another ordinary homecoming on a late autumn night.

'Was there much fog in the City? It's been coming up here since tea-time.' She looked out for a moment before she closed the door.

'Nothing to speak of,' said Mr Baldwin. 'It began to look bad at lunch-time, but it cleared up. The late trains are going to catch it.'

He hung up his hat, dropped his umbrella into the stand, and with the parcel under his arm went into the dining-room without removing his overcoat. There was a faint perfume: a big fire was blazing, and a smell of warm leather came from the front of the armchair. The room was at its best in the winter warmth, for the sun had a way of pointing out things that the standard lamp forgave. The sun made the purple velvet mantelpiece cover look like a cloak at an open-air pageant: the lamp gave back its dignity.

Mr Baldwin put the parcel on the table beside Edith's work-basket. He stood casually beside it and Edith came and peered at it over her glasses.

'Got your scissors handy?'

'What is it, Tom?'

'Just a little thing the staff gave me. You open it.'

He went into the passage and took longer than usual to remove his overcoat. He wanted her to enjoy the surprise by herself. He heard the rustling of paper, judged his time, and returned.

'Isn't that awfully nice! – it's so neat and simple.'

She put it on the table and stepped back to admire it. The old walnut-wood pendulum clock on the mantelpiece, with its round, keyhole eyes, stared in mild curiosity at the little quick-ticking newcomer – reassured itself and continued its placid beat without further interest. It was a doleful clock at the best of times, but it looked at its worst at twenty-five past six, when its hands gave it a dreary, drooping moustache.

'What an awfully nice thing to have done. Wasn't it a surprise? Weren't you pleased?'

'They all gave something towards it,' said Mr Baldwin. There was no point in telling her that everybody got a clock when they retired.

From *Greengates* by R. C. Sherriff, 1936

Passing out of Time

If peradventure, Reader, it has been thy lot to waste the golden years of thy life – thy shining youth – in the irksome confinement of an office; to have thy prison days prolonged through middle age down to decrepitude and silver hairs, without hope of release or respite; to have lived to forget that there are such things as holidays, or to remember them but as the prerogatives of childhood; then, and then only, will you be able to appreciate my deliverance.

It is now six and thirty years since I took my seat at the desk in Mincing-lane. Melancholy was the transition at fourteen from the abundant play-time, and the frequently-intervening vacations of school days, to the eight, nine, and sometimes ten hours' a-day attendance at a counting-house. But time partly reconciles us to anything. I gradually became content – doggedly contented, as wild animals in cages.

. . . on the evening of the 12th of April, just as I was about quitting my desk to go home (it might be about eight o'clock) I received an awful summons to attend the presence of the whole assembled firm in the formidable back parlour. I thought, now my time is surely come, I have done for myself, I am going to be told that they have no longer occasion for me. L–, I could see, smiled at the terror I was in, which was a little relief to me, – when to my utter astonishment B–, the eldest partner, began a formal harangue to me on the length of my services, my very meritorious conduct during the whole of the time (the deuce, thought I, how did he find out that? I protest I never had the confidence to think as much). He went on to descant on the expediency of retiring at a certain time of life (how my heart panted!) and asking me a few questions as to the amount of my own property, of which I have a little, ended with a proposal, to which his three partners nodded a grave assent, that I should accept from the house, which I had served so well, a pension for life to the amount of two-thirds of my accustomed salary – a magnificent offer! I do not know what I answered between surprise and gratitude, but it was understood that I accepted their proposal, and I was told that I was free from that hour to leave their service. I stammered out a bow, and at just ten minutes after eight I went home – for ever. This noble benefit – gratitude forbids me to conceal their names – I owe to the kindness of the most munificent firm in the world – the house of Boldero, Merryweather, Bosanquet, and Lacy.

Esto perpetua!

For the first day or two I felt stunned, overwhelmed. I could only apprehend my felicity; I was too confused to taste it sincerely. I wandered about, thinking I was happy, and knowing that I was not. I was in the condition of a prisoner in the old Bastile, suddenly let loose after a forty years' confinement. I could scarce trust myself with myself. It was like passing out of Time into Eternity – for it is a sort of Eternity for a man to have his Time all to himself . . .

A fortnight has passed since the day of my first communication. At that period I was approaching to tranquillity, but had not reached it. I boasted of a calm indeed, but it was comparative only. Something of the first flutter was left; an unsettling sense of novelty; the dazzle to weak eyes of unaccustomed light. I missed my old chains, forsooth, as if they had been some necessary part of my apparel. I was a poor Carthusian, from strict cellular discipline suddenly by some revolution returned upon the world. I am now as if I had never been other than my own master. It is natural to me to go where I please, to do what I please. I find myself at eleven o'clock in the day in Bond-street, and it seems to me that I have been sauntering there at that very hour for years past. I digress into Soho, to explore a book-stall. Methinks I have been thirty years a collector. There is nothing strange nor new in it. I find myself before a fine picture in a morning. Was it ever otherwise? What is become of Fish-street Hill? Where is Fenchurch-street? Stones of old Mincing-lane, which I have worn with my daily pilgrimage for six and thirty years, to the footsteps of what toil-worn clerk are your everlasting flints now vocal? I indent the gayer flags of Pall Mall. It is Change time, and I am strangely among the *Elgin marbles*. It was no hyperbole when I ventured to compare the change in my condition to a passing into another world. Time stands still in a manner to me. I have lost all distinction of season. I do not know the day of the week, or of the month. Each day used to be individually felt by me in its reference to the foreign post days; in its distance from, or propinquity to, the next Sunday. I had my Wednesday feelings, my Saturday night's sensations. The genius of each day was upon me distinctly during the whole of it, affecting my appetite, spirits, &c. The phantom of the next day, with the dreary five to follow, sate as a load upon my poor Sabbath recreations. What charm has washed that *Ethiop* white? What is gone of Black Monday? All days are the same. Sunday itself – that unfortunate failure of a holyday as it too often proved, what with my sense of its fugitiveness, and over-care to get the greatest quantity of pleasure out of it – is melted down into a week day. I can spare to go to church now, without grudging the huge cantle which it used to seem to cut out of the holyday. I have Time for everything. I can visit a sick friend. I can interrupt the man of much occupation when he is busiest. I can *insult* over him with an invitation to take a day's pleasure with me to Windsor this fine May-morning. It is Lucretian pleasure to behold the poor drudges, whom I have left behind in the world, carking and caring; like horses in a mill, drudging on in the same eternal round – and what is it all for? A man can never have too much Time to himself, nor too little to do. Had I a little son, I would christen him NOTHING-TO-DO; he should do nothing. Man, I verily believe, is out of his element as long as he is operative. I am altogether for the life contemplative. Will no kindly earthquake come and swallow up those accursed cotton mills? Take me that lumber of a desk there, and bowl it down

As low as to the fiends.

I am no longer ******, clerk to the Firm of &c. I am Retired Leisure. I am to be met with in trim gardens. I am already come to be known by my vacant face and careless gesture, perambulating, at no fixed pace, nor with any settled purpose. I walk about; not to and from. They tell me, a certain *cum dignitate* air, that has been buried so long with my other good parts, has begun to shoot forth in my person. I grow into gentility perceptibly. When I take up a newspaper, it is to read the state of the opera. *Opus operatum est.* I have done all that I came into this world to do. I have worked task work, and have the rest of the day to myself.

From 'The Superannuated Man' in *Essays of Elia* by Charles Lamb, 1818

'Ah, humanity'

There would seem little need for proceeding further in this history. Imagination will readily supply the meager recital of poor Bartleby's interment. But, ere parting with the reader, let me say that if this little narrative has sufficiently interested him to awaken curiosity as to who Bartleby was, and what manner of life he led prior to the present narrator's making his acquaintance, I can only reply that in such curiosity I fully share, but am wholly unable to gratify it. Yet here I hardly know whether I should divulge one little item of rumor which came to my ear a few months after the scrivener's decease. Upon what basis it rested, I could never ascertain, and hence how true it is I cannot now tell. But, inasmuch as this vague report has not been without a certain suggestive interest to me, however sad, it may prove the same with some others, and so I will briefly mention it. The report was this: that Bartleby had been a subordinate clerk in the Dead Letter Office at Washington, from which he had been suddenly removed by a change in the administration. When I think over this rumor, hardly can I express the emotions which seize me. Dead letters! does it not sound like dead men? Conceive a man by nature and misfortune prone to a pallid hopelessness, can any business seem more fitted to heighten it than that of continually handling these dead letters, and assorting them for the flames? For by the cartload they are annually burned. Sometimes from out the folded paper the pale clerk takes a ring – the finger it was meant for, perhaps, molders in the grave; a bank note sent in swiftest charity – he whom it would relieve nor eats nor hungers any more; pardon for those who died despairing; hope for those who died unhoping; good tidings for those who died stifled by unrelieved calamities. On errands of life, these letters speed to death.

Ah, Bartleby! Ah, humanity!

From *Bartleby* by Herman Melville, 1853

Acknowledgements

The editor and publishers gratefully acknowledge permission to reprint copyright material as follows:

For 'September 1, 1939' from *The English Auden*, ed. by Edward Mandelson, and 'The Fall of Rome' from *Collected Poems* by W. H. Auden, ed. by Edward Mandelson: Faber & Faber Ltd and Random House, Inc., New York; for extracts from *The Mezzanine* by Nicholson Baker: Granta Publications Ltd and Random House, Inc.; for an extract from *Lost Upon the Roundabouts* by A. L. Barker: the author; for 'Peter Goole' from *Complete Verse* by Hilaire Belloc: the Peters, Fraser & Dunlop Group Ltd; for extracts from *The Underlings* by Barbara Benson: Constable Publishers; for 'The City', 'Business Girls', and 'Caprice' from *Collected Poems* by John Betjeman: John Murray (Publishers) Ltd; for extracts from *To the North* by Elizabeth Bowen: Jonathan Cape Ltd and Curtis Brown Ltd; for 'Office Party' from *Collected Poems* by Alan Brownjohn: the author; for an extract from *Mister Johnson* by Joyce Cary: Michael Joseph Ltd, 1947, copyright ©1939 by Joyce Cary; for an extract from *The High Window* by Raymond Chandler: Hamish Hamilton Ltd and Alfred A. Knopf, Inc.; for an extract from *Thy Hand, Great Anarch* by N. C. Chaudhuri: Chatto & Windus Ltd; for an extract from *Over the Bridge* by Richard Church: the Estate of Richard Church, William Heinemann Ltd and Laurence Pollinger Ltd; for an extract from *London Belongs to Me* by Norman Collins: HarperCollins and the Peters, Fraser & Dunlop Group Ltd; for an extract from 'The Square Peg' in *Lisa and Co* by Jilly Cooper: the author and Arlington Books Ltd; for extracts from *The Naked Civil Servant* by Quentin Crisp: HarperCollins Publishers Ltd; for extracts from *Without a Stitch in Time* and *Sauce for the Gander* by Peter de Vries: Victor Gollancz Ltd and Abner Stein; for 'Office' from *Explaining Magnetism* by Maura Dooley: Bloodaxe Books, Newcastle upon Tyne; for 'Takeover' from *Under the Circumstances* by D. J. Enright: Oxford University Press and Watson, Little Ltd; for 'Couples' from *The Deceptive Grin of the Gravel Porters*, 'The Boss is Thinking' and 'Sonnet: The Days and Nights to Come' from *The Gavin Ewart Show*, and 'Office Friendships' from *Pleasures of the Flesh*, all by Gavin Ewart: the author; for an extract from *Human Voices* by Penelope Fitzgerald: HarperCollins Publishers Ltd; extracts from *Towards the End of the Morning* by Michael Frayn: HarperCollins Publishers Ltd; for extracts from *The Father's Comedy* and *Image of a Society* by Roy Fuller: the Estate of Roy Fuller; for an extract from *Spanner and Pen* by Roy Fuller: Sinclair-Stevenson; for extracts from *Bad Behaviour* by Mary Gaitskill: the author and Tessa Sayle Agency, copyright © 1988 by Mary Gaitskill; for extracts from *The Office* by Jonathan Gathorne-Hardy: Curtis Brown Ltd, copyright © 1970 by Jonathan Gathorne-Hardy; for extracts from *Here Be Dragons* by Stella Gibbons: Curtis Brown Ltd on behalf of the Author's Estate; for extracts from *The Youngest Director* by Martyn Goff: the Bodley Head; for an extract from *The Transit of Venus* by Shirley Hazzard: Macmillan London Ltd; for extracts from *Something Happened* by Joseph Heller: Jonathan Cape Ltd and Alfred Knopf, Inc.; for extracts from *Letters from Constance* by Mary Hocking: the author; for an extract from *After Julius* by Elizabeth Jane Howard: Jonathan Cape Ltd; for an extract from *Coming from Behind* by Howard Jacobson: Chatto & Windus Ltd and A. M. Heath and Co. Ltd; for extracts from *The Philanderer* by Stanley Kauffmann: the author and John Johnson Ltd, copyright © 1952, 1980 by Stanley Kauffmann; for extracts from *A Boy at the Hogarth Press* by Richard Kennedy: the Estate of Richard Kennedy; for an extract from *Another Self* by James Lees-Milne: Faber & Faber and David Higham Associates; for an extract from *Thrown to the Woolfs* by John Lehmann: Weidenfeld & Nicolson Ltd and David Higham Associates; for extracts from *Out After Dark* by Hugh Leonard: André Deutsch Ltd; for extracts from *Babbitt* and *Dodsworth* by Sinclair Lewis: Jonathan Cape Ltd; for extracts from *The Job* and *Our Mr Wrenn* by Sinclair Lewis: the Estate of Sinclair Lewis; for an extract from *She Knew She Was Right* (Viking) by Ivy Litvinov: *The New Yorker Magazine* Inc., copyright © 1968; for extracts from *Nice Work* by David Lodge: Martin Secker & Warburg Ltd; for excerpts from *Bright Lights, Big City* by Jay McInerney: Jonathan Cape Ltd and Random House, Inc.; for an extract from *A Life to Remember* by William McQuilty: Quartet Books Ltd; for an extract from *Friends and Heroes* by Olivia Manning: William Heinemann Ltd; for extracts from *Memoirs of an Advertising Man* by John Mellors: the author and London Magazine Editions; for an extract from *Newspaper Days* by H. L. Mencken: Alfred A. Knopf, Inc.; for an extract from *Those Were The Days* by A. A. Milne: Curtis Brown Ltd., London, on behalf of the Author's Estate; for an extract from *A Morning at the Office* by Edgar Mittelholzer: Chatto & Windus Ltd; for an extract from *The Luck of Ginger Coffey* by Brian Moore: André Deutsch Ltd and McClelland & Stewart; for extracts from *Portrait of Elmbury* by John Moore: the John Moore Estate and The Peters, Fraser & Dunlop Group Ltd; for extracts from *Mr Stone and the Knights Companion* by V. S. Naipaul: André Deutsch Ltd and Aitken and Stone Ltd; for an extract from *Mr Sampath* by R. K. Narayan: William Heinemann Ltd; for extracts from *Something*

Wholesale by Eric Newby: the author; for extracts from *The Death of Reginald Perrin* by David Nobbs: Methuen London; for an extract from *Coming Up For Air* by George Orwell: the Estate of the late Sonia Brownell Orwell and Secker & Warburg; for extracts from *The Law and the Profits* by C. Northcote Parkinson: John Murray (Publishers) Ltd; for an extract from *What's Become of Waring* and *Messengers of Day* by Anthony Powell: William Heinemann Ltd and David Higham Associates; for extracts from *Angel Pavement* by J. B. Priestley: the Peters Fraser & Dunlop Group; for extracts from *A Cab at the Door* and from *It May Never Happen* in *Collected Stories* by V. S. Pritchett: Chatto & Windus Ltd and Random House, Inc.; for extracts from *Quartet in Autumn* by Barbara Pym: Macmillan London Ltd; for extracts from *The Last Hours of Sandra Lee* by William Sansom: the Hogarth Press and Elaine Greene Ltd., copyright © 1961 by William Sansom; for extracts from *Murder Must Advertise* by Dorothy L. Sayers: New English Library and David Higham Associates; for extracts from *The Fortnight in September* and *Greengates* by R. C. Sherriff: Victor Gollancz Ltd and Curtis Brown Ltd; for extracts from *The Holiday* and an extract from *Novel on Yellow Paper* by Stevie Smith: Virago Press; for 'Deeply Morbid' from *The Collected Poems of Stevie Smith*: Penguin Books and James MacGibbon; for extracts from *A Far Cry from Kensington* by Muriel Spark: Constable Publishers; for extracts from *The Puzzleheaded Girl* by Christina Stead: the Estate of Christina Stead, Secker & Warburg Ltd and the Joan Daves Literary Agency, New York; for an extract from *Forgetting's No Excuse* by Mary Stott: the author and Virago Press; for extracts from *Notes from Another Country* by Julian Symons: Curtis Brown Ltd, copyright © 1972 by Julian Symons; for an extract from *The Family Arsenal* by Paul Theroux: Hamish Hamilton Ltd and Aitken & Stone Ltd; for an extract from *The Years with Ross* by James Thurber: Atlantic-Little Brown, copyright © 1959 by James Thurber, copyright © 1987 by Rosemary A. Thurber; for an extract from 'Swivel' by James Thurlby: the author and London Magazine Editions; for extracts from *The Big Tomato* by Raleigh Trevelyan: the author, the Longman Group and A. M. Heath & Co. Ltd; for an extract from *Angels at the Ritz* by William Trevor: the Bodley Head; for extracts from *Office Life* by Keith Waterhouse: Michael Joseph Ltd and David Higham Associates; for an extract from *Scoop* by Evelyn Waugh: the Estate of Evelyn Waugh, and The Peters, Fraser & Dunlop Group Ltd; for an extract from *The Story of the Year of 1912 in the Village of Elza Darzins* by Thea Welsh: Simon & Schuster, East Roseville, N.S.W., Australia; for an extract from *The Dubious Codicil* by Michael Wharton: Chatto & Windus Ltd; for an extract from *Such Darling Dodos* and from *The Wrong Set* by Angus Wilson: Secker & Warburg; for extracts from *The Man in the Grey Flannel Suit* by Sloan Wilson: Simon and Schuster,

Inc., New York and Laurence Pollinger Ltd; for extracts from *Psmith in the City* by P. G. Wodehouse: Hutchinson & Co. (Publishers) Ltd and A. P. Watt Ltd; for extracts from *The Bonfire of the Vanities* by Tom Wolfe: Jonathan Cape and The Peters, Fraser & Dunlop Group Ltd.

Index of Authors

Auden, W. H.:
  Another Time 40
  Nones 117

Baker, Nicholson: *The Mezzanine*
  109–10, 325, 330–1, 332–4,
  335–7
Barker, A. L.: *Lost upon the*
  Roundabouts 363–5
Belloc, Hilaire: *Peter Goole* 9
Bennett, Arnold: *Lilian* 41–2,
  342–5
Benson, Barbara: *The Underlings*
  22–3, 379
Betjeman, John:
  A Few Late Chrysanthemums 131
  High and Low 349–50
  Mount Zion 127
Bowen, Elizabeth: *To the North* 87,
  143–5, 259
Brownjohn, Alan: *The Lions'*
  Mouths 293–4

Cary, Joyce: *Mister Johnson*
  176–7
Chandler, Raymond: *The High*
  Window 86
Chaudhuri, N.C.: *Thy Hand, Great*
  Anarch 227–8
Church, Richard: *Over the Bridge*
  73–4
Collins, Norman: *London Belongs to*
  Me 365–70
Cooper, Jilly: *Lisa and Co* 135–6
Crisp, Quentin: *The Naked Civil*
  Servant 184, 326

Davidson, John: *Ballads and Songs*
  119

Day, Clarence: *Life with Father* 262
de Vries, Peter:
  Sauce for the Gander 290
  Without a Stitch in Time 240–3,
  297–9
Dickens, Charles:
  Bleak House 223–4, 267
  David Copperfield 158–60, 225
  Dombey and Son 58–9, 195–8
  Great Expectations 39–40, 276,
  277–8
  Martin Chuzzlewit 81–3
  Nicholas Nickleby 124–6, 160–1
  The Old Curiosity Shop 76, 77,
  118, 229, 262
  The Pickwick Papers 119–20
  Sketches by Boz 115–16
  The Uncommercial Traveller 8
Dooley, Maura: *Explaining*
  Magnetism 233
Doyle, Sir Arthur Conan: *Memoirs*
  of Sherlock Holmes 118

Eliot, T. S. 271–2
Enright, D. J.: *Under the*
  Circumstances 362
Ewart, Gavin:
  The Deceptive Grin of the Gravel
  Porters 310
  The Gavin Ewart Show 136–7,
  290–1
  Pleasures of the Flesh 303

Fitzgerald, Penelope: *Human Voices*
  321–2
Frayn, Michael: *Towards the End of*
  the Morning 165, 179–81,
  352–4
Freeling, Sir Francis 49

Fuller, Roy 4
  The Father's Comedy 6, 10–11,
    319–20
  Image of a Society 9, 185,
    198–201, 205–6, 213–15,
    228–9, 281–2, 329, 331
  Spanner and Pen 228

Gaitskill, Mary: *Bad Behaviour*
  18–20, 133–5
Gathorne-Hardy, Jonathan: *The
  Office* 8, 48–9, 101–2, 106–9,
  216, 230, 308, 331
Gibbons, Stella: *Here Be Dragons*
  67–8, 347–8
Gissing, George:
  A Life's Morning 119
  The Odd Woman 117
Goff, Martyn: *The Youngest Director*
  109, 218
Grossmith, George and Weedon:
  The Diary of a Nobody 24–5,
  47–8, 165, 341–2, 355–9

Hazzard, Shirley: *The Transit of
  Venus* 132
Heller, Joseph: *Something Happened*
  103–4, 163–4, 209–11, 217,
  219, 306–7, 308–9, 348–9, 359
Hocking, Mary: *Letters from
  Constance* 304–6
Howard, Elizabeth Jane: *After Julius*
  55–6

Jacobson, Howard: *Coming from
  Behind* 262–3
Jerome, Jerome K.: *Three Men in a
  Boat* 189
Joyce, James: *Dubliners* 152–6

Kauffmann, Stanley: *The Philanderer*
  56–7, 229, 229–30, 342, 359
Kennedy, Richard: *A Boy at the
  Hogarth Press* 65–6, 175, 347

Lamb, Charles:
  Essays of Elia 272, 382–4

verse 11, 224
Lees-Milne, James: *Another Self*
  165–70
Lehmann, John: *Thrown to the
  Woolfs* 46
Leonard, Hugh: *Out After Dark*
  74–5, 307–8
Lewis, Jeremy: *Playing for Time*
  100–1, 256, 294–6, 326–7,
  354–5
Lewis, Sinclair 4
  Babbitt 10, 11–12, 37–9, 53–5,
    162–3, 164, 259–60, 269,
    271–2, 350–1
  Dodsworth 59–60
  The Job 52, 98–9, 137–9, 143,
    157, 193–5, 224, 258, 312
  Our Mr Wrenn 116, 247–8,
    250–1
Litvinov, Ivy: *She Knew She Was
  Right* 225
Lodge, David: *Nice Work* 52–3,
  282–3, 324–5, 338

McInerney, Jay: *Bright Lights, Big
  City* 49–51, 231, 261–2,
  345–6
McQuilty, William: *A Life to
  Remember* 76–7
Manning, Olivia: *Friends and Heroes*
  110–11
Mellors, John: *Memoirs of an
  Advertising Man*, 43, 296–7,
  325–6, 360
Melville, Herman: *Bartleby* 236–40,
  260–1, 385
Mencken, H. L.: *Newspaper Days*
  334–5
Milne, A. A.: *Those Were the Days*
  187–9
Mittelholzer, Edgar: *A Morning at
  the Office* 317–18
Moore, Brian: *The Luck of Ginger
  Coffey* 30–4
Moore, John: *Portrait of Elmbury* 74,
  84–5

Naipaul, V. S.: *Mr Stone and the Knights Companion* 102–3, 126, 211–13

Narayan, R. K.: *Mr Sampath* 218–19

Newby, Eric: *Something Wholesale* 83–4, 329

Nobbs, David: *The Death of Reginald Perrin* 43, 57–8, 150–2, 310–11

Oliphant, Mrs: *Hester* 365

Orwell, George: *Coming Up* 23–24

Pepys, Samuel: *Diary* 165, 174, 266–7

Powell, Anthony:
Messengers of Day 89–91
What's Become of Waring 86

Priestley, J. B.: *Angel Pavement* 117–18, 122–4, 131, 140–2, 178–9, 268–9

Pritchett, V. S.:
A Cab at the Door 20–2, 105, 225–6, 255, 267–8, 303–4, 309–10
It May Never Happen 223

Pym, Barbara: *Quartet in Autumn* 49, 273, 376–9

Sansom, William: *The Last Hours of Sandra Lee* 88, 270, 287–90

Sayers, Dorothy L.: *Murder Must Advertise* 44–6, 71–2, 106, 329–30

Sherriff, R. C.:
The Fortnight in September 270–1, 272–3
Greengates 370–6, 379–82

Smith, Stevie:
Harold's Leap 142–3
The Holiday 178, 185–6
Novel on Yellow Paper 139–40

Spark, Muriel: *A Far Cry from Kensington* 88–9, 324

Stead, Christina: *The Puzzleheaded Girl* 226–7, 318–9

Stott, Mary: *Forgetting's No Excuse* 91–2

Symons, Julian: *Notes from Another Country* 201–5, 283–4

Theroux, Paul: *The Family Arsenal* 40–1

Thurber, James: *The Years with Ross* 183

Thurlby, James: 'Swivel' 207–8

Trevelyan, Raleigh: *The Big Tomato* 184, 291–3, 351–2

Trevor, William: *Angels at the Ritz* 312–15

Trollope, Anthony 4
Autobiography 46–7, 120–1
John Caldigate 174–5
The Small House at Allington 150
The Three Clerks 27–9, 126–7, 256–8, 278–81

Usborne, Richard: verse 312

Waterhouse: Keith: *Office Life* 25–7, 68–71, 89, 99–100, 311, 316–17, 328, 337–8

Waugh, Evelyn: *Scoop* 156

Welsh, Thea: *The Story of the Year of 1912 in the Village of Elza Darzins* 327–8

Wharton, Michael: *The Dubious Codicil* 87–8

Wilson, Angus:
Such Darling Dodos 286–7
The Wrong Set 208–9

Wilson, Sloan: *The Man in the Gray Flannel Suit* 15–18, 66–7, 177, 186–7, 233

Wodehouse, P. G. 4, 38, 96
Psmith in the City 63–5, 95–7, 157–8, 173, 222–3, 243–6, 266

Wolfe, Tom: *The Bonfire of the Vanities* 181–3, 248–50

Woolf, Leonard 48, 68–9, 178, 353